Indian War Sites

To my children,
Jason *and* Kelly

INDIAN WAR SITES

*A Guidebook to Battlefields, Monuments,
and Memorials, State by State
with Canada and Mexico*

by
STEVE RAJTAR

McFarland & Company, Inc., Publishers
Jefferson, North Carolina, and London

ALSO BY STEVE RAJTAR

Hiking Trails, Western United States:
Address, Phone Number and Distances for
4300 Trails, with Indexing of Over 200 Guidebooks
(McFarland, 1995)

Hiking Trails, Eastern United States:
Address, Phone Number and Distances for
5000 Trails, with Indexing of Over 200 Guidebooks
(McFarland, 1996)

British Library Cataloguing-in-Publication data are available

Library of Congress Cataloguing-in-Publication Data

Rajtar, Steve, 1951–
    Indian war sites : a guidebook to battlefields, monuments, and
memorials, state by state with Canada and Mexico / by Steve Rajtar.
        p.   cm.
    Includes bibliographical references and indexes.
    ISBN 0-7864-0710-7 (case binding : 50# alkaline paper) ∞
    1. Indians of North America — Wars — Guidebooks.   2. Indians of North
America — History — Guidebooks.   3. Battlefields — North America —
Guidebooks.   4. War memorials — North America — Guidebooks.
5. Historic sites — North America — Guidebooks.   6. North America —
Description and travel — Guidebooks.   I. Title.
E81.R35   1999
970.004'97 — dc21   99-25893
                                                                            CIP

Manufactured in the United States of America

McFarland & Company, Inc., Publishers
  Box 611, Jefferson, North Carolina 28640

Table of Contents

Preface

The toughest part of writing this book was coming up with an appropriate title. The subject was clear — battles — but in today's society with attempts to use politically correct terminology, how can one best describe the people involved in those battles?

Nearly all of the written materials I used as sources for the information contained herein use the term "Indians." Of course, that word was based on Columbus' mistaken belief that he had reached India, but over the centuries that term has generally been the collective name of choice.

In recent years, the term "Native American" has gained in popularity, but that can be criticized on two fronts. If "native" is to mean a group that has always been here, there is no group of humans that qualifies, since the Indians' ancestors walked here recently, relatively speaking. An additional argument addresses the "native" status of any persons, not just Indians, who are born in "America." Further, "American" is usually said to have been derived from the name of an Italian, so we are again associating the people with a European.

After interviewing several individuals who are of Indian ancestry, I concluded that the older term is preferred more than is "Native Americans," which seems to be used more often by non–Indians. The American Indian Movement, which advocates the protection of rights for those of Indian ancestry, is just one example of a group for which the term "Indian" is acceptable for referring to those people.

Throughout the book, the nonwhite participants are described as "natives," "warriors," or by the band or tribe to which they belonged. In a few instances, the term "Indian" was the most appropriate and has therefore been used despite the possibility of objections from some critics.

The history of early America, as recounted in books, movies and television series, is full of tales of bloodshed involving mostly those of European descent and those who occupied North America before Columbus arrived. There are enough incidents that have become nearly legendary, or have been glorified, blown out of proportion, or merely exaggerated, that one would think that early America was in a constant state of warfare.

In reality, the numbers killed were low, especially when they are compared with the casualty figures of later wars. The numbers of aboriginal deaths in the five or six major "massacres" of the Old West, involving familiar names like Custer, Sand Creek, and Wounded Knee, are estimated to have been between 615 and 1,170. Those numbers are

1

relatively insignificant when compared to a single day's fighting in the Civil War or either World War. The importance of the conflicts lies more in their effect on the settlement of the lands by Europeans and their descendants, as well as some Africans and Asians, and the attempts at removal and extermination of the natives.

The material in this book is taken from hundreds of written sources located in public and university libraries, and numerous historical markers, monuments and tombstones that I have visited. Some of the sources are autobiographical, but most are accounts of events which happened long before the authors wrote them down, often before they were even born. Their sources were frequently accounts which were handed down, sometimes in oral rather than written form, and there are certainly variations in the descriptions resulting from varying points of view. Those that came from Indians present at the battle are decidedly different from those recounted by members of the U.S. Army.

This results in a quantitative range, especially when dealing with casualties or numbers of participants. For example, existing sources forming the basis for the entry for the 1835 Dade Massacre in Florida have a range of 180 to 400 for the number of Indians involved. One side may try to justify its loss by inflating the number of men on the other side, or might from its vantage point be unable to make an accurate count. The other side might want to give a lower number, to emphasize its superiority, needing fewer fighters to win a battle.

Rather than attempt to choose who is correct, where the existing literature has a range of claimed numbers, that range is what is included in this book. There are also some disputes as to dates or exact locations, and what appears here are the facts that appear to be a near consensus among the historians who have touched on the topic. Where there is a substantial minority opinion, such as the actual landing place of Ponce de Leon (Tampa Bay or Charlotte Harbor?), both are listed.

Each event has a name, one that has been used repeatedly in history books or a descriptive term that I have applied. Generally, if the historians have named it, it is the "Battle *of*..." or "Massacre *of*...." If it doesn't have a generally accepted name, in this book it is more likely referred to as the "Battle *at*..." or "Skirmish *at*...." Battles are bigger than skirmishes, and massacres are generally extremely one-sided attacks and killings. These are imprecise terms, and often reflect the prejudices and points of view of the authors of the existing literature. Such is history.

There were Indian wars throughout the country, some very local (as in Alaska), and some widespread (as the wars with the Sioux). In some instances, isolated battles did not assume sufficient importance in American history to justify their being named a "war," but did have significant local importance. Therefore, in the chronological section of this book, battles that could not be grouped into wars, or into related activities such as specific expeditions, are nevertheless listed.

This book includes not only encounters between Indians and whites (often accompanied by people of color), but also many battles of whites versus whites (such as the War of 1812 and the Civil War) in which Indians fought as allies of the whites. Often, the greater proportion of casualties in such encounters was suffered by the Indians, permitting the inference that white commanders sent them more frequently or more dangerously into battle.

The result of all of this was the extermination of many bands of Indians, and the relocation or assimilation of others, to make room for the settlement of those moving from abroad, chiefly from Europe. Despite most Europeans' fear and hatred of those who populated the continent before them, they had no qualms about utilizing their warring skills when they fought other Europeans and their descendants.

No attempt is made to characterize one "side" as "good" or another side as "bad." This traveler's and historian's guidebook to sites offers instead an attempt at objectivity in providing accounts of what happened. That these accounts may be read and interpreted differently by each reader is just another indication that history is quintessentially subjective.

There are many battles that do not appear herein. They are generally those which occurred solely between groups of Indians. Oral histories that do not relate well to the European calendar do not lend themselves well to this type of chronologically arranged reference work. Also not covered are tribal movements and treaty negotiations, signings and breakings. These are important for a full understanding of the course of conflict, and may be examined in detail in the works cited in the bibliography.

Each entry in this book concludes with a list of "Sources," which are keyed by serial number to the published works listed in the Bibliography.

Steve Rajtar
February 1999
Orlando, Florida

Chronology of Battles
and Events

Date	Larger Conflict	Book Entry	Battle or Event
6/3/1513	Spanish Exploration	FL1	Landing of Ponce de Leon
4/18/1517	Spanish Exploration	FL2	Landing of Cordova
7/1521	Spanish Exploration	FL3	Second Landing of Ponce de Leon
5/16/1528	Narvaez Expedition	FL4	Encounter at the Withlacoochee River
6/17/1528	Narvaez Expedition	FL5	Attacks at Apalachen
7/20/1528	Narvaez Expedition	FL6	Ambush South of Apalachen
8/2/1528	Narvaez Expedition	FL7	Attack at Aute
10/27/1528	Narvaez Expedition	FL8	Attack Near Pensacola
9/15/1539	DeSoto Expedition	FL9	Battle of the Two Lakes
6/2–4/1540	DeSoto Expedition	MS1	Attack on the Mississippi
7/7/1540	Mixton War	NM1	Battle of Hawikuh
10/18/1540	De Soto Expedition	AL1	Battle of Maubila
Late 1/1541	De Soto Expedition	MS2	Attack on Curace Camp
3/4/1541	De Soto Expedition	MS3	Battles in Chacaza
1547	Spanish Exploration	FL10	Massacre of Dominicans
1566	Spanish Exploration	FL11	Attack at Spanish Outpost
11/1566	Pardo Expedition	SC1	Battle at San Juan
4/13/1568	Spanish Exploration	FL12	Destruction of San Mateo
1569	Spanish Exploration	FL13	Attack on Landing Party
Spring 1572	Aviles Expedition	VA1	Attack on the Kiskiacks
1576	Spanish Exploration	SC2	Attack at Santa Elena
1577	Frobisher Expedition	CN1	Battle at Bloody Point
7/1585	Raleigh Expeditions	NC1	Attack on Aquascogoc
6/1/1586	Raleigh Expeditions	NC2	Attack on Dasemunkapeuc
1587–90	Raleigh Expeditions	NC3	Disappearance of Roanoke Settlement
1597	Mission Uprisings	GA1	Attacks on Spanish Missions
12/4/1598	Onate Expedition	NM2	Battle of Acoma
1/21/1599	Onate Expedition	NM3	Attack on Sky City
10/15/1606	Champlain Expedition	MA1	Attack at Almouchiquois

5

Date	Larger Conflict	Book Entry	Battle or Event
5/26/1607	First Anglo-Powhatan War	VA2	Attack on Jamestown
Fall 1607	First Anglo-Powhatan War	VA3	Skirmish at the James River
1608	-----	MD1	Attack on English Ship
7/30/1609	Champlain Expedition	NY1	Battle on Lake Champlain
Fall 1609	First Anglo-Powhatan War	VA4	Siege of James Fort
3/22/1622	Second Anglo-Powhatan War	VA5	Jamestown Massacre
Late 3/1623	-----	MA2	Attack at Wessagusett
7/1624	Second Anglo-Powhatan War	VA6	Raid on Powhatan Village
1631	Dutch Colonization	DE1	Massacre at Lewes
11/1632	Dutch Colonization	DE2	Swanendael Massacre
1634	Pequot War	CT1	Attack on the Connecticut River
5/20/1636	Pequot War	CT2	Attack at Block Island
Mid–1636	Pequot War	CT3	Attack at Long Island
10/1636	Pequot War	CT4	Attack at Butterfield's Meadow
2/22/1637	Pequot War	CT5	Attack Near Fort Saybrook
3/1637	Pequot War	CT6	Siege at Fort Saybrook
4/23/1637	Pequot War	CT7	Battle at Wethersfield
Early 5/1637	Pequot War	CT8	Battle at Saybrook
5/26/1637	Pequot War	CT9	Massacre at Fort Mystic
5/26/1637	Pequot War	CT10	Battle at New Haven
5/1637	Pequot War	CT11	Battle in Quinnipiac Swamp
7/28/1637	Pequot War	CT12	Attack at Fairfield
1640	Governor Kieft's War	NY2	Attack on Raritans
9/1/1641	Governor Kieft's War	NY3	Swanneken Massacre
2/25/1643	Governor Kieft's War	NY4	Massacre of Wappingers
4/18/1644	Powhatan Uprising	VA7	Attacks Against Settlements
2/19/1647–2/1648	Apalachee Rebellion	FL14	Skirmishes at Missions
1649	-----	NY5	Attack at Southhampton
3/16/1649	Beaver Wars	CN2	Huron Massacre
1653	Beaver Wars	WI1	Attack by Iroquois
9/15/1655	Peach War	NY6	Attack at New Amsterdam
1656	Timucua Rebellion	FL15	Destruction of Missions
1656	-----	VA8	Battle Along the James River
Early 5/1658	Esopus War	NY7	Skirmish at Esopus
9/20/1658	Esopus War	NY8	Attack at Esopus
1660	Beaver Wars	CN3	Assault on Montreal
6/1663	War at Wiltwyck	NY9	Attack at Wiltwyck
1/19/1675	King Philip's War	RI1	Raid on Pawtuxet
6/20–22/1675	King Philip's War	MA3	Looting in Swansea
6/24/1675	King Philip's War	MA4	Attack at Mattapoiset
6/24/1675	King Philip's War	MA5	Attack at Miles' Garrison
6/24/1675	King Philip's War	MA6	Attack at Swansea
6/28/1675	King Philip's War	MA7	Ambush Near Miles' Garrison
7/1675	King Philip's War	MA8	Attacks on Frontier Towns
7/1675	Susquehannock War	VA9	Raid on Mathews' Plantation
7/19/1675	King Philip's War	MA9	Skirmish Near Pocasset Swamp
Summer 1675	King Philip's War	NH1	Destruction of Native Villages

Date	Larger Conflict	Book Entry	Battle or Event
8/1/1675	King Philip's War	RI2	Attack at Nipsachuck
8/2–4/1675	King Philip's War	MA10	Ambush at Quabog
8/22/1675	King Philip's War	MA11	Attack at Lancaster
8/25/1675	King Philip's War	MA12	Battle of Sugarloaf Hill
8/24–25/1675	King Philip's War	MA13	Raids on Springfield
9/1675	King Philip's War	MA14	Connecticut Valley Campaign
9/18/1675	King Philip's War	MA15	Ambush at Bloody Brook
9–10/1675	King Philip's War	MA16	Attacks on Springfield
10/19/1675	King Philip's War	MA17	Ambush Near Hatfield
10/1675	King Philip's War	MA18	Attacks on Settlers
Late 1675	King Philip's War	NY10	Attack on King Philip's Camp
12/15/1675	King Philip's War	RI3	Attack at Wickford
12/16/1675	King Philip's War	RI4	Attack at Bull's Garrison
12/19/1675	King Philip's War	RI5	Great Swamp Fight
2/10/1676	King Philip's War	MA19	Attack on Lancaster
2/21/1676	King Philip's War	MA20	Attack at Medfield
3/12/1676	King Philip's War	MA21	Massacre at the Eel River
3/13/1676	King Philip's War	MA22	Attack at Groton
3/26/1676	King Philip's War	MA23	Attack at Longmeadow
3/26/1676	King Philip's War	RI6	Attack Along Pawtuxet River
3/29/1676	King Philip's War	RI7	Destruction of Providence
2–5/1676	King Philip's War	RI8	Attacks on Frontier Towns
4/21/1676	King Philip's War	MA24	Battle of Green Hill
2–5/1676	King Philip's War	MA25	Attacks on Frontier Towns
5/1676	Susquehannock War	VA10	Attack on Occoneechee Town
5/19/1676	King Philip's War	MA26	Battle of Turners Falls
6/2/1676	King Philip's War	CT13	Battle at Wabaquasset
6/7/1676	King Philip's War	MA27	Attack at Washaccum Pond
6/12/1676	King Philip's War	MA28	Raid on Hadley
7–9/1676	King Philip's War	RI9	Late Actions
7/20/1676	King Philip's War	RI10	Battle at Nipsachuck
7/27/1676	King Philip's War	MA29	Attack on Pomham
7–8/1676	King Philip's War	MA30	Late Actions
8/12/1676	King Philip's War	RI11	Death of Philip
8/14/1676	-----	ME1	Attack on Arrowsic
9/1677	-----	MA31	Attack at Hatfield
1679	-----	GA2	Attack on Santa Catalina
6/1679	-----	NH2	Attack on Cocheco
8/10/1680	Pueblo Revolt	NM4	Battle at Sky City
8/15–21/1680	Pueblo Revolt	NM5	Siege of Santa Fe
1686	-----	SC3	Attack on Port Royal
1687	-----	CN4	Destruction of LaChine
7/1688	-----	ME2	Attack on North Yarmouth
Early 1689	La Salle Expedition	TX1	Massacre at Fort St. Louis
6/1689	King William's War	NH3	Attack at Dover
8/5/1689	King William's War	CN5	Raid on LaChine
8/21/1689	King William's War	ME3	Attack at Fort Charles
2/1690	King William's War	ME4	Attack on Casco Bay
2/9/1690	King William's War	NY11	Destruction of Schenectady
3/18/1690	King William's War	ME5	Attack on Salmon Falls
1/25/1691	King William's War	ME6	Attack on York

Date	Larger Conflict	Book Entry	Battle or Event
2/1692	King William's War	ME7	Destruction of York
1692	-----	CN6	Attack Near Montreal
1694	King William's War	MA32	Raid on Groton
1694	Pueblo Uprisings	NM6	Conquest of Pueblos
7/18/1694	King William's War	NH4	Attack at Oyster River
1696	King William's War	NY12	Attack on Onandaga Village
6/4/1696	Pueblo Uprisings	NM7	Pima Uprising
3/1698	Mission Uprisings	AZ1	Attack at Santa Cruz de Quiburi
1699	-----	FL16	Attack on Hunting Party
3/20/1702	Queen Anne's War	FL17	Attack on Santa Fe
1702	Queen Anne's War	FL18	Ambush of Apalachee
Fall 1702	Queen Anne's War	FL19	Attack at St. Augustine
1703	Queen Anne's War	ME8	Raid on Casco
8/1703	Queen Anne's War	ME9	Attack on Wells
1–8/1704	Queen Anne's War	FL20	Attacks Against Apalachee
2/29/1704	Queen Anne's War	MA33	Massacre at Deerfield Missions
Late 1706	-----	LA1	Assassination of Priest
1707	-----	FL21	Attack at Pensacola
8/30/1708	-----	MA34	Destruction of Haverhill
5/1709	-----	AL2	Attack at Mobile
9/1711	Tuscarora War	NC4	Capture of von Graffenried
9/22/1711	Tuscarora War	NC5	Tuscarora Massacre
1712	Tuscarora War	SC4	Attacks by Tuscaroras
1/28/1712	Tuscarora War	NC6	Battle at Narhantes
3/6–7/1712	Tuscarora War	NC7	Battle at Hancock's Town
3/29/1712	Tuscarora War	NC8	Ruse at Hancock's Town
4/8/1712	Tuscarora War	NC9	Siege of Fort Hancock
Summer 1712	-----	MI1	Battle with Foxes
12/1712	Tuscarora War	SC5	Rout at the Tar River
3/20–23/1713	Tuscarora War	NC10	Attack at Fort Neoheroka
Spring 1714	-----	SC6	Attack at Chestowee
4/15/1715	Yamassee War	SC7	Pocotaligo Massacre
4/15/1715	Yamassee War	SC8	Attack at St. Bartholmew
Late 4/1715	Yamassee War	SC9	Battle Near Salkehatchie
Late 4/1715	Yamassee War	SC10	Capture of Pocotaligo
6/1715	Yamassee War	SC11	Massacre at Herne Plantation
6/1715	Yamassee War	SC12	Battle at Schenkingh Cowpen
7/19/1715	Yamassee War	SC13	Attack at Plantation
7/1715	Yamassee War	SC14	Attack at New London
Autumn 1715	Yamassee War	SC15	Battle at Dawfuskey Island
1716	Mission Uprisings	CO1	Attack at Cerro de San Antonio
1716	-----	NM8	Raid on Taos
8/1/1716	Yamassee War	SC16	Attack Near Port Royal
10/1719	Yamassee War	FL22	Attacks on Native Villages
6/1720	Yamassee War	SC17	Attacks on St. Helena
8/14/1720	-----	NE1	Battle on the Platte River
1722	Dummer's War	ME10	Attack at Brunswick
1723	-----	TX2	Defeat of Apaches
2/20/1725	Dummer's War	NH5	Battle at Wakefield
5/8/1725	Dummer's War	ME11	Battle of Pigwacket

Date	Larger Conflict	Book Entry	Battle or Event
8/1725	Dummer's War	ME12	Attack at Norridgewock
9/1726	Yamassee War	SC18	Attack on Edwards Home
1727	-----	VA11	Attack on Oneidas
6/1727	Yamassee War	SC19	Attack on English Settlements
7/23/1727	Yamassee War	SC20	Attack at Smallwood's Store
9/1727	Yamassee War	SC21	Attack on Dawson House
3/9/1728	Yamassee War	FL23	Attack on St. Augustine
1729	French-Natchez War	LA2	Destruction of Chaoucha Village
11/28/1729	French-Natchez War	MS4	Attack on Fort Rosalie
1730	-----	MO1	Battle Near Fort Orleans
1730	-----	TX3	Attack on San Antonio
9/9/1730	-----	IL1	Fox Massacre
1731	French-Natchez War	MS5	Natchez Massacre
3/1736	-----	MS6	Battle of Chocolissa
5/26/1736	-----	MS7	Battle of Ackia
1740	-----	GA3	Skirmish on the Flint River
5/1740	-----	FL24	Attack on St. Augustine
7/7/1742	-----	GA4	Battle of Bloody Marsh
Fall 1742	-----	GA5	Sack of Mount Venture
1744	-----	NM9	Attack on Pecos
Spring 1745	King George's War	ME13	Raids on Towns
10/2/1745	Red Shoe Rebellion	MS8	Attack on Convoy
11/28–29/1745	King George's War	NY13	Raid on Saratoga
1746-50	Choctaw Civil War	MS9	Destruction of Villages
6/1747	-----	CN7	Raid on Quebec
7/1748	-----	FL25	Attack on Sloop
10/1748	-----	NM10	Attack on Ute and Comanche Camp
1750	Cherokee-Creek War	GA6	Attacks on Lower Towns
11/1751	-----	NM11	Defeat of Comanches
11/20/1751	-----	NM12	Attacks on Missions
1752	-----	SC22	Attack Along the Savannah River
6/21/1752	-----	OH1	Attack on Pickawillany
1754	-----	SC23	Attack in York County
5/27–28/1754	French and Indian War	PA1	Skirmish at Jumonville Glen
7/3–4/1754	French and Indian War	PA2	Attack on Fort Necessity
8/27/1754	French and Indian War	NY14	Attack on Hoosick
1755	Cherokee-Creek War	GA8	Battle of the Taliwa
6/2/1755	French and Indian War	CN8	Attack on Fort Beausejour
7/8/1755	French and Indian War	WV1	Massacre at Draper's Meadows
7/8/1755	French and Indian War	WV2	Massacre at Muddy Creek
7/9/1755	French and Indian War	PA3	Rout of Braddock
9/8/1755	French and Indian War	NY15	Battle of Lake George
11/1755	French and Indian War	PA4	Attack on Moravian Village
3/27/1756	French and Indian War	NY16	Lery's Raid
7/3/1756	French and Indian War	NY17	Ambush Near Oswego
8/2/1756	French and Indian War	PA5	Capture of Fort Granville
8/14/1756	French and Indian War	NY18	Attack Against Oswego Forts
9/3/1756	-----	GA8	Ogeechee Incident
9/8/1756	French and Indian War	PA6	Raid on Kittanning
1/21/1757	French and Indian War	NY19	Attack at Fort Carillon

Date	Larger Conflict	Book Entry	Battle or Event
3/18/1757	French and Indian War	NY20	Attack on Fort William Henry
3/22/1757	French and Indian War	NY21	Attack on Vessels
7/21–24/1757	French and Indian War	NY22	Action on Lake George
7/1757	French and Indian War	NY23	Attack on Fort Edward
8/3–9/1757	French and Indian War	NY24	Siege of Fort William Henry
11/1757	French and Indian War	NY25	Raid on the Palatine
1/1758	French and Indian War	NY26	Attack on Fort Edward
3/13/1758	French and Indian War	NY27	Battle of the Snowshoes
3/16–20/1758	-----	TX4	Siege of San Saba Mission
Early 5/1758	First Cherokee War	VA12	Attacks in Halifax and Bedford Counties
7/6–8/1758	French and Indian War	NY28	Battle of Ticonderoga
8/26–27/1758	French and Indian War	CN9	Capture of Fort Frontenac
9/14/1758	French and Indian War	PA7	Defense of Fort Duquesne
10/12/1758	French and Indian War	PA8	Raid on Loyalhannon
Early 1759	French and Indian War	PA9	Massacre at Dunkard Creek
Early 1759	French and Indian War	WV3	Massacre at Decker's Creek
1759	French and Indian War	CN10	Attack on Odanak
7/13–25/1759	French and Indian War	NY29	Siege of Fort Niagara
7/31/1759	French and Indian War	CN11	Battle at Montmorency
8/1759	French and Indian War	CN12	Attacks Near Quebec
8/1759	-----	TX5	Attack on Tonkawa Village
9/13/1759	French and Indian War	CN13	First Battle of the Plains of Abraham
Early 10/1759	-----	OK1	Battle at Twin Villages
10/1759	-----	TX6	Battle at Red River
Late 1759	First Cherokee War	SC24	Attack on Fort Prince George
2/1/1760	First Cherokee War	SC25	Long Canes Massacre
2/16/1760	First Cherokee War	SC26	Attack on Fort Prince George
3/6/1760	First Cherokee War	SC27	Attack on Ninety Six
4/28/1760	French and Indian War	CN14	Second Battle of the Plains of Abraham
6/1/1760	First Cherokee War	SC28	Burning of Lower Towns
6/27/1760	First Cherokee War	NC11	Battle Near Franklin
8/1760	-----	NM13	Attack at Villapando Ranch House
8/1760	French and Indian War	TN1	Siege of and Attack on Fort Loudon
6/10/1761	First Cherokee War	NC12	Battle Near Franklin
12/27/1761	First Cherokee War	SC29	Attack at Long Canes
1763	-----	SC30	Ambush at Twelve Mile Creek
4/19/1763	French and Indian War	PA10	Assassination of Teedyuscung
5/7/1763	Pontiac's Rebellion	MI2	Ambush on Lake St. Claire
5/1763	French and Indian War	PA11	Attack on Clapham Settlement
5/9–12/1763	Pontiac's Rebellion	MI3	Siege of Detroit
5/16/1763	Pontiac's Rebellion	OH2	Capture of Fort Sandusky
5/25/1763	Pontiac's Rebellion	MI4	Capture of Fort St. Joseph
5/27/1763	Pontiac's Rebellion	IN1	Capture of Fort Miamis
5/27–8/1/1763	Pontiac's Rebellion	PA12	Siege of Fort Pitt
5/28/1763	Pontiac's Rebellion	MI5	Capture at Point Pelee
6/1/1763	Pontiac's Rebellion	IN2	Surrender of Fort Ouiatenon

Date	Larger Conflict	Book Entry	Battle or Event
6/2/1763	Pontiac's Rebellion	MI6	Capture of Fort Michilimackinac
6/1763	French and Indian War	PA13	Siege of Fort Ligonier
6/16/1763	Pontiac's Rebellion	PA14	Attack at Fort Venango
6/18/1763	Pontiac's Rebellion	PA15	Capture of Fort LeBoeuf
6/20–21/1763	Pontiac's Rebellion	PA16	Destruction of Fort Presqu' Isle
6/23/1763	Pontiac's Rebellion	MI7	Attack on the Sloop *Michigan*
7/31/1763	Pontiac's Rebellion	MI8	Battle of Bloody Bridge
8/5/1763	Pontiac's Rebellion	PA17	Battle of Bushy Run
9/2/1763	Pontiac's Rebellion	MI9	Attack on the Ship *Huron*
9/14/1763	Pontiac's Rebellion	NY30	Massacre at Devil's Hole
10/20/1763	Pontiac's Rebellion	NY31	Attack on Portage Road
12/14/1763	French and Indian War	PA18	Massacre of Christian Susquehannocks
5/1765	Pontiac's Rebellion	PA19	Attack Along the Ohio River
8/1765	-----	AL3	Attack at Mobile
1766	Russian Exploration	AK1	Attack on Aleuts
7/21/1766	First Cherokee War	NC13	Raid on Watauga
9/1768	-----	NM14	Skirmish at Ojo Caliente
1771	-----	TX7	Attack on Laredo
Spring 1772	-----	WV4	Stroud Massacre
4/25/1774	Lord Dunmore's War	WV5	Skirmish at Captina Creek
4/30/1774	Lord Dunmore's War	OH3	Yellow Creek Massacre
Early 7/1774	-----	NM15	Attacks in Chama Valley
Late 7/1774	-----	NM16	Attack at Albuquerque
8/1774	-----	NM17	Attack at Pecos
10/10/1774	Lord Dunmore's War	WV6	Battle of Point Pleasant
5/1775	-----	NM18	Attack at Pecos
1775	-----	NM19	Attack Along the Gila River
10/30/1775	Revolutionary War	CN15	Skirmish at Ile-Sainte-Helene
11/1775	Mission Uprisings	CA1	Uprising Against San Diego Mission
5/20/1776	Revolutionary War	CN16	Battle of the Cedars
6/28/1776	Revolutionary War	SC31	Battle of Fort Moultrie
7/15/1776	Revolutionary War	SC32	Attack at Ludley's Fort
7/20/1776	Second Cherokee War	TN2	Battle at Island Flats
7/20/1776	Second Cherokee War	TN3	Battle at Fort Caswell
7/20/1776	Second Cherokee War	TN4	Attack at Watauga Fort
7/20/1776	Revolutionary War	VA13	Raid on Eaton's Station
8/1/1776	Revolutionary War	SC33	Battle at Seneca Ford
8/1776	Revolutionary War	SC34	Attacks on Lower Towns
9/1776	Second Cherokee War	NC14	Destruction of Cherokee Towns
12/25/1776	Revolutionary War	KY1	Attack at Limestone Creek
5/17/1777	Revolutionary War	FL26	Battle of Thomas Creek
5/31/1777	Revolutionary War	KY2	Attack at McClelland's Station
6/25/1777	Revolutionary War	NY32	Attack at Fort Stanwix
7/27/1777	Revolutionary War	NY33	Attack at Fort Stanwix
8/3–22/1777	Revolutionary War	NY34	Battle of Oriskany
8/6/1777	Revolutionary War	NY35	Battle Near Oriskany
9/1–3/1777	Revolutionary War	WV7	First Siege of Wheeling
9/1777	Revolutionary War	KY3	Sieges of Boonesboro
9/22/1777	Revolutionary War	WV8	Ambush at The Narrows

Date	Larger Conflict	Book Entry	Battle or Event
9/25/1777	Revolutionary War	WV9	Attacks on Short Creek
5/30/1778	Revolutionary War	NY36	Burning of Cobleskill
6/18/1778	Revolutionary War	NY37	Attack at Springfield
7/3/1778	Revolutionary War	PA20	Attack at Forty Fort
7/18/1778	Revolutionary War	NY38	Attack at Andrustown
9/17/1778	Revolutionary War	NY39	Attack at German Flats
10/9/1778	Revolutionary War	NY40	Burning of Unadilla
11/11/1778	Revolutionary War	NY41	Cherry Valley Massacre
12/17/1778	Revolutionary War	IN3	Capture of Fort Vincennes
1/23–3/28/1779	Revolutionary War	OH4	Siege of Fort Laurens
4/20/1779	Revolutionary War	NY42	Burning of Onondaga Towns
4/26/1779	Revolutionary War	PA21	Attack on Fort Hand
4/26/1779	Revolutionary War	PA22	Attack on Sykes Cabin
Spring 1779	Revolutionary War	PA23	Attack on Sanford Cabin
7/30/1779	Revolutionary War	OH5	Attack on Chalahgawtha
8/25/1779	Revolutionary War	PA24	Ambush at Brady's Bend
8/29/1779	Revolutionary War	NY43	Battle of Newtown
Early 9/1779	Revolutionary War	PA25	Battle of Brokenstraw Creek
Fall 1779	De Anza Campaign	CO2	Battle of Greenhorn Peak
Fall 1779	-----	NM20	Raid on Taos
1780	Revolutionary War	AL6	Assault on Mobile
1780	Revolutionary War	IL2	Destruction of Saukenauk
3/14/1780	Revolutionary War	AL5	Attack at Muscle Shoals
5/26/1780	Revolutionary War	MO2	Attack on St. Louis
6/20/1780	Revolutionary War	KY4	Attack at Ruddle's Station
7/1780	Revolutionary War	WV10	Raids in the Kanawha Valley
Summer 1780	Revolutionary War	OH6	Burning of Chillicothe
8/8/1780	Revolutionary War	OH7	Battle at Piqua
9/18/1780	-----	TX8	Attack at Bexar
1780	-----	TX9	Massacre at Canon de Uvalde
1780s	Revolutionary War	OH8	Attacks on Settlers
12/1780	-----	TX10	Attack at the Medina River
12/8/1780	Revolutionary War	TN5	Battle of Boyd's Creek
2/12/1781	Revolutionary War	IL3	Attack at Fort St. Joseph
3–5/1781	Revolutionary War	FL27	Battle of Pensacola
3/15/1781	Revolutionary War	NC15	Battle of Guilford Courthouse
Spring 1781	Revolutionary War	OH9	Burning of Coshocton
4/1781	Revolutionary War	TN6	Attack at Nashborough
7/18/1781	Mission Uprisings	CA2	Yuma Massacre
8/24/1781	Revolutionary War	KY5	Ambush Along the Ohio River
9/1781	Revolutionary War	WV11	Second Siege of Wheeling
9/11–13/1782	Revolutionary War	WV12	Third Siege of Wheeling
10/12/1781	Revolutionary War	OH10	Brady's Ambush
1/1782	Revolutionary War	SC35	Attacks on Lower Towns
3/10/1782	Revolutionary War	OH11	Moravian Massacre
Spring 1782	Revolutionary War	KY6	Battle of Little Mountain
6/1782	Revolutionary War	SC36	Ambush Near Charleston
6/4–5/1782	Revolutionary War	OH12	Battle of Sandusky
6/6/1782	Revolutionary War	OH13	Battle of the Olentangy
7/13/1782	Revolutionary War	PA26	Destruction of Hannastown
8/14–15/1782	Revolutionary War	KY7	Attack at Bryan's Station

Date	Larger Conflict	Book Entry	Battle or Event
8/19/1782	Revolutionary War	KY8	Battle of Blue Licks
9/1782	Revolutionary War	TN7	Battle at Lookout Mountain
Fall 1782	Revolutionary War	GA9	Battle of Savannah
11/10/1782	Revolutionary War	OH14	Capture of Chillicothe
1783	-----	MN1	Attack on French Trading House
4/17/1783	Revolutionary War	AR1	Battle of Fort Carlos
Summer 1783	-----	TN8	Raid on Middle Towns
9/1783	-----	TN9	Massacre at Cavitt's Blockhouse
7/1784	-----	TX11	Battle Along the Guadalupe River
1785	Mission Uprisings	CA3	Uprising Against San Gabriel Mission
1786 and 1788	-----	TN10	Expeditions Against Valley Towns
10/1786	-----	IN4	Attacks on Shawnee Villages
3/1789	-----	PA27	Attacks at Dunkard Creek
3/1789	-----	WV13	Attack at Fort Vanmetre
3/1789	-----	WV14	Attacks on Monongahela River
1790	-----	TX13	Attack at Arroyo de Soledad
3/1790	Ohio Indian Wars	KY9	Attack at Lee's Creek
3/1790	Ohio Indian Wars	WV16	Attack Near Maysville
Early 4/1790	Ohio Indian Wars	OH15	Attack at Ludlow's Station
Late 4/1790	Ohio Indian Wars	WV17	Attack on King's Creek
Early 5/1790	Ohio Indian Wars	WV18	Attack at Purdy Cabin
Mid–5/1790	Ohio Indian Wars	WV19	Attack at Clendenin's Fort
5/29/1790	Ohio Indian Wars	WV20	Attack at Buffalo Creek
7/1790	Ohio Indian Wars	OH16	Attacks on Short Creek
7/1790	Ohio Indian Wars	WV21	Attack on Grave Creek
Summer 1790	Ohio Indian Wars	WV22	Attack at Tackett's Fort
9/27/1790	Ohio Indian Wars	WV23	Attack at Wheeling
10/19/1790	Ohio Indian Wars	IN5	Ambush Along the Eel River
10/22/1790	Ohio Indian Wars	IN6	Ambush Along the Maumee River
12/11/1790	Ohio Indian Wars	OH17	Attack at Stillwater Creek
1791	Ohio Indian Wars	IN7	Attack on Kickapoo Village
1/2/1791	Ohio Indian Wars	OH18	Big Bottom Massacre
1/1791	Ohio Indian Wars	OH19	Attack at Dunlap's Station
3/17/1791	Ohio Indian Wars	KY10	Attack in Mason County
4/16/1791	Ohio Indian Wars	KY11	Ambush at Snag Creek
5/1/1791	Ohio Indian Wars	PA28	Attack at Dunkard Creek
11/3–4/1791	Ohio Indian Wars	OH20	Attack Near Fort Hamilton
12/20/1791	Ohio Indian Wars	OH21	Attack at Big Bottom
3/10/1792	Ohio Indian Wars	OH22	Delaware Massacre
9/30/1792	Lower Cherokee War	TN11	Battle at Buchanan's Station
1793	Russian Exploration	AK2	Skirmish in Yschugat Bay
6/7/1793	-----	GA10	Attack on Echota
10/17/1793	Ohio Indian Wars	OH23	Attack on Supply Train
12/2/1793	Ohio Indian Wars	OH24	Attack at Holt's Creek
6/5/1794	-----	AL6	Attack at Muscle Shoals
6/25/1794	-----	TN12	Attack Along the Tennessee River
6/30/1794	Ohio Indian Wars	OH25	Attack on Fort Recovery
8/20/1794	Ohio Indian Wars	OH26	Battle of Fallen Timbers

Date	Larger Conflict	Book Entry	Battle or Event
9/6/1794	Ohio Indian Wars	WV24	Attack at Wheeling Creek
9/12/1794	-----	TN13	Destruction of Nickajack
10/1794	-----	GA11	Burning of Lower Towns
3/1795	-----	MO2	Attack on Canton Creek
4/1795	-----	IL4	Attack Near Fort Massac
6/15/1795	-----	PA29	Attack on Conneaut Outlet
1796	-----	MO4	Attack on Missouri River
1799	Russian Exploration	AK3	Attack on Russian Expedition
6/1802	Russian Exploration	AK4	Sitka Massacre
10/1/1804	Russian Exploration	AK5	Battle of Sitka
1805	-----	AZ2	Massacre at Canyon de Chelly
4/12/1810	-----	MT1	Attack at Three Forks
4/1811	-----	IL5	Attack at Fort Dearborn
11/7/1811	War of 1812	IN8	Battle of Tippecanoe
7/17/1812	War of 1812	MI10	Capture of Fort Michilimackinac
8/8/1812	War of 1812	CN18	Battle of Monguaga
8/14/1812	War of 1812	CN19	Attack on Detroit
8/15/1812	War of 1812	IL6	Fort Dearborn Massacre
8/16/1812	War of 1812	MI11	Defeat of Fort Detroit
9/3–16/1812	War of 1812	IN9	Siege of Fort Harrison
9/3/1812	War of 1812	IN10	Massacre at Pigeon Roost
9/27/1812	War of 1812	FL28	Battle of Newnans Lake
10/13/1812	War of 1812	CN20	Battle of Queenstown Heights
10/18/1812	War of 1812	IN11	Attack at Peoria Lake
11/11/1812	War of 1812	IN12	Attack at Prophetstown
12/18/1812	War of 1812	OH27	Attack Near Fort Greenville
1/18/1813	War of 1812	MI12	Battle of Frenchtown
1/22/1813	War of 1812	MI13	Raisin River Massacre
2/1813	-----	FL29	Border Incidents
4/25–5/9/1813	War of 1812	OH28	Sieges of Fort Meigs
6/24/1813	War of 1812	CN21	Battle of Beaver Dams
7/4/1813	War of 1812	NY44	Attack at Fort Schlosser
7/8/1813	War of 1812	NY45	Ambush of Eldridge
7/22/1813	Creek Indian War	AL7	Attack at Tuckabatchee
7/27/1813	Creek Indian War	AL8	Battle of Burnt Corn
8/2/1813	War of 1812	OH29	Attack on Fort Stephenson
8/30/1813	Creek Indian War	AL9	Battle of Fort Mims
10/5/1813	War of 1812	CN22	Battle of the Thames
11/3–4/1813	Creek Indian War	AL10	Battle of Tallusahatchee
11/9/1813	Creek Indian War	AL11	Battle of Talladaga
11/18/1813	Creek Indian War	AL12	Destruction of Hillabee Town
11/20/1813	Creek Indian War	AL13	Skirmish on the Alabama River
11/29/1813	Creek Indian War	AL14	Attack on Tallapoosa River
12/23/1813	Creek Indian War	AL15	Battle of Escanachaha
1/24/1814	Creek Indian War	AL16	Battle of Enotachopo Creek
1/27/1814	Creek Indian War	AL17	Battle at Calabee Creek
3/27/1814	Creek Indian War	AL18	Battle of Horseshoe Bend
5/30/1814	War of 1812	NY46	Battle of Sandy Creek
7/21/1814	War of 1812	WI2	Battle Near Prairie du Chien
7/25–26/1814	War of 1812	CN23	Battle of Lundy's Lane

Date	Larger Conflict	Book Entry	Battle or Event
7/26/1814	War of 1812	MI14	Attack at Sault Ste. Marie
Late 8/1814	War of 1812	IL7	Battle Near Rock Island
1/8/1815	War of 1812	LA3	Battle of New Orleans
7/26/1816	-----	FL30	Attack on Blount's Fort
10/1817	-----	OK2	Battle of Claremore Mound
11/1817	First Seminole War	FL31	Attack on Alachua Village
11/21/1817	First Seminole War	GA12	Attack on Neamathla's Village
4/7/1818	First Seminole War	FL32	Capture of St. Marks
4/13/1818	First Seminole War	FL33	Battle Along Ecofina Creek
4/22/1818	Creek War	GA13	Massacre of Chcraw
5/1823	Arikara War	MT2	Attacks in Montana
6/2/1823	Arikara War	ND1	Attack on Ashley Party
11/17/1823	-----	AR2	Attack at Blue River
2/1824	Mission Uprisings	CA4	Uprising Against Santa Ynez Mission
3/22/1824	-----	IN13	Massacre at Falls Creek
1827	-----	MN2	Attack at Fort Snelling
6/26/1827	Winnebago War	WI3	Attack at Prairie du Chien
7/1828	-----	WA1	Attack on Salish Village
7/14/1828	Smith Expedition	OR1	Umpqua Massacre
1829	-----	WY1	Siege of Mateo's Fort
6/26/1831	Black Hawk's War	IL8	Attack at Saukenuk
7/1831	-----	IL9	Attack on Menominees
4/1832	Black Hawk's War	IL10	Fight with Black Hawk
5/14/1832	Black Hawk's War	IL11	Battle of Stillman's Run
5/18/1832	Black Hawk's War	IL12	Attack on Mail Train
5/20/1832	Black Hawk's War	IL13	Massacre at Indian Creek
6/16/1832	Black Hawk's War	IL14	Battle of the Pecatonica
6/16/1832	Black Hawk's War	IL15	Battle of Waddam's Grove
6/24/1832	Black Hawk's War	IL16	Attack on Apple River Fort
6/25/1832	Black Hawk's War	IL17	Battles of Kellogg's Grove
7/18/1832	-----	WY2	Battle of Pierre's Hole
7/21/1832	Black Hawk's War	WI4	Battle of Wisconsin Heights
8/2–3/1832	Black Hawk's War	WI5	Battle of Bad Axe
6/1835	-----	FL34	Skirmish at Hickory Sink
9/1835	-----	FL35	Skirmish in Orlando
12/18/1835	Second Seminole War	FL36	Battle of Black Point
12/25–26/1835	Second Seminole War	FL37	Destruction of Halifax Plantations
12/28/1835	Second Seminole War	FL38	Dade Massacre
12/28/1835	Second Seminole War	FL39	Ambush at Fort King
12/31/1835	Second Seminole War	FL40	First Battle of the Withlacoochee
1/6/1836	Second Seminole War	FL41	Cooley Massacre
1/17/1836	Second Seminole War	FL42	Battle at Anderson's Plantation
2/27–3/6/1836	Second Seminole War	FL43	Second Battle of the Withlacoochee
3/22/1836	Second Seminole War	FL44	Skirmish at Volusia
3/26/1836	Second Seminole War	FL45	Battle Along Fort Brooke–Fort King Trail
3/29/1836	Second Seminole War	FL46	Battle at Camp Izard
4/5–17/1836	Second Seminole War	FL47	Siege of Cooper's Post
4/12–5/29/1836	Second Seminole War	FL48	Siege of Blockhouse
4/14/1836	Second Seminole War	FL49	Attack at Fort Barnwell

Date	Larger Conflict	Book Entry	Battle or Event
4/20/1836	Second Seminole War	FL50	Attack on Fort Drane
4/27/1836	Second Seminole War	FL51	Battle of Thonotosassa Creek
5/1836	Second Creek War	AL21	Attacks on White Settlements
5/19/1836	-----	TX13	Attack at Parker's Fort
6/9/1836	Second Seminole War	FL52	Skirmish at Fort Drane
6/9/1836	Second Seminole War	FL53	Attack on Fort Defiance
7/9/1836	Second Seminole War	FL54	Battle of Welika Pond
7/23/1836	Second Seminole War	FL55	Attack at Cape Florida
7/27/1836	Second Seminole War	FL56	Battle of Ridgely's Mill
7/28/1836	Second Seminole War	FL57	Attack on Travers Plantation
8/21/1836	Second Seminole War	FL58	Attack on Fort Drane
9/18/1836	Second Seminole War	FL59	Battle at San Felasco Hammock
9/30/1836	Second Seminole War	FL60	Border Skirmish
10/8/1836	Second Seminole War	FL61	Burning of the Schooner *Mary*
10/13–15/1836	Second Seminole War	FL62	Battle at Cove of the Withlacoochee
11/17/1836	Second Seminole War	FL63	Battle Along the Withlacoochee River
11/18/1836	Second Seminole War	FL64	Battle Near the Withlacoochee River
11/18–21/1836	Second Seminole War	FL65	Battle of Wahoo Swamp
1/23/1837	Second Seminole War	FL66	Battle Near Lake Apopka
1/27/1837	Second Seminole War	FL67	Battle of Hatcheelustee
2/8/1837	Second Seminole War	FL68	Battle of Fort Mellon
2/9/1837	Second Seminole War	FL69	Battle of Clear River
Summer 1837	-----	TX14	Raid on Kiowas
9/9/1837	Second Seminole War	FL70	Capture Near Dunlawton Plantation
Winter 1837	-----	MX1	Raid on Tamaulipas
12/25/1837	Second Seminole War	FL71	Battle of Okeechobee
1/15/1838	Second Seminole War	FL72	Battle of Jupiter Creek
1/24/1838	Second Seminole War	FL73	Battle of Loxahatchee
3/22/1838	Second Seminole War	FL74	Battle at the New River
4/24/1838	Second Seminole War	FL75	Skirmish with Sam Jones
5/27/1838	Second Seminole War	FL76	Battle at Okefenokee Swamp
6/4/1838	Second Seminole War	FL77	Battle at Fort Dade
6/17/1838	Second Seminole War	FL78	Battle Near Newnansville
7/13/1838	Second Seminole War	FL79	Attack at Singletary Home
Early 8/1838	Second Seminole War	FL80	Attack at Baker House
8/10/1838	-----	TX15	Attack by Comanches
10/16/1838	-----	TX16	Attack on Kickapoo Town
10/20/1838	-----	TX17	Attack Near San Antonio
7/15–16/1839	-----	TX18	Attack on Quapaws
7/23/1839	Second Seminole War	FL81	Harney Massacre
Summer 1839	-----	TX19	Attack at El Paso
7/1/1839	Second Seminole War	FL82	Attack at Chaires Cross Roads
8/7/1839	-----	TX20	Attack on Victoria
1840	Mission Uprisings	CA5	Raid on Mission San Luis Obispo
3/28/1840	Second Seminole War	FL83	Ambush at Fort King
5/19/1840	Second Seminole War	FL84	Battle of Levy's Prairie
6/2/1840	Second Seminole War	FL85	Attack at Chocachatti

Date	Larger Conflict	Book Entry	Battle or Event
8/7/1840	Second Seminole War	FL86	Indian Key Massacre
8/8/1840	-----	TX21	Great Linnville Raid
8/9/1840	-----	TX22	Skirmish Near Linnville
8/12/1840	-----	TX23	Battle of Plum Creek
9/6/1840	Second Seminole War	FL87	Battle at Wacahoota
Late 10/1840	-----	TX24	Attack on Comanche Camp
12/3–24/1840	Second Seminole War	FL88	Battle at Chekika's Island
12/28/1840	Second Seminole War	FL89	Attack on the Road to Wacahoota
1/1841	Second Seminole War	FL90	Attack at Fort Walker
3/2/1841	Second Seminole War	FL91	Battle Near Fort Brooks
8/30/1841	Santa Fe Expedition	TX25	Fight with Texan–Santa Fe Expedition
11/1841	Second Seminole War	FL92	Battle at Lake Worth
12/20/1841	Second Seminole War	FL93	Actions in Great Cypress Swamp
1/25/1842	Second Seminole War	FL94	Battle at Dunn's Lake
4/19/1842	Second Seminole War	FL95	Battle at Lake Ahapopka
5/17/1842	Second Seminole War	FL96	Battle at Blue Peter Springs
1844	-----	WA2	Attack on Fort Misqually
5/8–9/1846	Fremont Expedition	OR2	Raid on Fremont Party
1/19/1847	-----	NM21	Attack at Bent's House
5/21/1847	-----	NE2	Attack on Pawnee Village
Summer 1847	-----	OR3	Attacks on Wagon Trains
11/29/1847	Cayuse War	WA3	Whitman Massacre
1/8/1848	Cayuse War	OR4	Skirmish Near Fort Lee
1/29/1848	Cayuse War	OR5	Battle on the Deschutes River
2/24/1848	Cayuse War	OR6	Battle of Sand Hollow
Early 3/1848	Cayuse War	OR7	Battle of the Abiqua
3/15/1848	Cayuse War	WA4	Touchet Fight
7/13/1849	-----	FL97	Attack Along Indian River
7/17/1849	-----	FL98	Attack at Payne's Creek
10/1849	-----	NM22	White Massacre
5/1850	-----	CA6	Bloody Island Massacre
1/1851	-----	MX2	Attack on Raiding Party
1/19/1851	-----	MX3	Battle at Pozo Hediondo
3/5/1851	-----	MX4	Janos Massacre
1851	-----	MX5	Attack Near Arizpe
1851	-----	AK6	Attack on Nulato
6/1–2/1851	Rogue River War	OR8	Attacks in the Rogue Valley
6/2/1851	Rogue River War	OR9	Attack on McBride Party
6/10/1851	Rogue River War	OR10	Attack at Battle Rock
6/17/1851	Rogue River War	OR11	Attack on Wagon Train
6/17/1852	Rogue River War	OR12	Attack on Kearny Party
6/23–26/1851	Rogue River War	OR13	Skirmishes in the Rogue Valley
9/14/1851	Rogue River War	OR14	Attack on Coquille River
Late 1851	Rogue River War	CA7	Attack on Modoc Village
11/22/1851	Rogue River War	OR15	Attack on Coquille River
1852	-----	ID1	Massacre of Ward Party
8 or 9/1852	-----	CA8	Bloody Point Massacre
11/1852	-----	CA9	Ben Wright Massacre
8/17/1853	Rogue River War	OR16	Attacks in the Rogue Valley

Date	Larger Conflict	Book Entry	Battle or Event
8/24/1853	Rogue River War	OR17	Attack Near Evans Creek
9/1853	Rogue River War	OR18	Skirmishes on the Illinois River
1853–54	Klamath War	CA10	Smith River Massacres
1854	-----	KS1	Battle Near Fort Riley
1/29/1854	Rogue River War	OR19	Nasomah Massacre
2/15/1854	Rogue River War	OR20	Attack at the Chetco River
3/30/1854	-----	NM24	Battle of Cienequilla
8/19/1854	-----	WY3	Grattan Massacre
8/20/1854	-----	ID2	Massacre Near Fort Boise
10/6/1854	-----	WA5	Attack Along Toppenish Creek
12/24/1854	Ute War	CO3	Attack at Fort Pueblo
1/1855	Rogue River War	OR21	Attack Along the Illinois River
7/1855	-----	NE3	Attack on the Omahas
9/3/1855	-----	NE4	Battle of Ash Hollow
9/25/1855	Rogue River War	OR22	Attack on Wagon Train
10/3/1855	-----	WA6	Assassination of Bolon
10/5–6/1855	Cayuse War	WA7	Haller's Fight
10/9/1855	Rogue River War	OR23	Attacks in the Rogue Valley
10/17/1855	Rogue River War	OR24	Battle at Skull Creek
10/24/1855	Rogue River War	OR25	Attack on Supply Wagons
10/25/1855	Rogue River War	OR26	Attack at Looking Glass Prairie
10/31–11/1/1855	Rogue River War	OR27	Battle of Hungry Hill
11/1855	Cayuse War	WA8	Union Gap Fight
11/25/1855	Rogue River War	OR28	Attack at Whiskey Creek
12/4/1855	Cayuse War	OR29	Raid on Fort Henrietta
12/7–10/1855	Cayuse War	WA9	Touchet River Fight
12/20/1855	Third Seminole War	FL99	Battle of Big Cypress Swamp
1/6/1856	Third Seminole War	FL100	Attack at Johnson Home
1/18/1856	Third Seminole War	FL101	Attack at Fort Denaud
1/26/1856	Klamath War	CA11	Skirmish at Yreka Cave
1/26/1856	Yakima War	WA10	Attack on Seattle
2/22/1856	-----	OR30	Fort Miner Massacre
3/2/1856	Third Seminole War	FL102	Attack at Snell House
3/1856	Third Seminole War	FL103	Attack on Turner's River
Mid–3/1856	Cayuse War	WA11	Tucannon River Fight
3/18/1856	Rogue River War	OR31	Ambush at the Pistol River
3/22/1856	Rogue River War	OR32	Battle with Rogues
3/23/1856	Rogue River War	OR33	Attack on Pack Train
3/26/1856	Cayuse War	WA12	Attacks in Columbia Valley
3/31/1856	Third Seminole War	FL104	Attack on Braden Castle
4/3/1856	Third Seminole War	FL105	Attack at Big Charley Apopka Creek
4/7/1856	Third Seminole War	FL106	Battle in Big Cypress Swamp
4/12/1856	Third Seminole War	FL107	Attacks Near Addison's Fort
4/16/1856	Third Seminole War	FL108	Carney Massacre
4/20/1856	Cayuse War	OR34	Raid on Fort Henrietta
4/22/1856	Rogue River War	OR35	Ambush on Lobster Creek
4/29/1856	Rogue River War	OR36	Attack at the Chetco River
Early 1856	Second Cavalry Campaign	TX26	Skirmishes in Central Texas
5/2/1856	Third Seminole War	FL109	Skirmish in Big Cypress Swamp
5/14/1856	Third Seminole War	FL110	Bradley Massacre

Date	Larger Conflict	Book Entry	Battle or Event
5/17/1856	Third Seminole War	FL111	Ambush of Mule Train
5/27–28/1856	Rogue River War	OR37	Battle of Big Bend
5/27/1856	Rogue River War	OR38	Attack Near Big Meadows
6/5/1856	Rogue River War	OR39	Burning of Village
6/14/1856	Third Seminole War	FL112	Willoughby Tillis Battle
6/15–16/1856	Third Seminole War	FL113	Battle of Peace River Swamp
6/1856	Third Seminole War	FL114	Attack at Hooker Plantation
7/17/1856	Cayuse War	OR40	Battle of the Grande Ronde
8/2/1856	Third Seminole War	FL115	Attack at Punta Rassa
9/9/1856	Cayuse War	WA13	Attack on Steptoe Camp
Late 1856	2nd Cavalry Campaign	TX27	Skirmishes in Central Texas
12/17/1856	Third Seminole War	FL116	Attack at Shives House
2/12/1857	2nd Cavalry Campaign	TX28	Attack Near the North Concho River
3/8/1857	-----	IA1	Spirit Lake Massacre
5/1857	Third Seminole War	FL117	Ambush at Palm Hammock
5/1857	Third Seminole War	FL118	Skirmish at Bowlegs' Town
7/20/1857	2nd Cavalry Campaign	TX29	Battle at Devil's River
7/29/1857	Cheyenne Expedition	KS2	Battle of Solomon's Fork
9/7/1857	-----	UT1	Fancher Party Massacre
11/21/1857	Third Seminole War	FL119	Cone's First Raid
11/26/1857	Third Seminole War	FL120	Cone's Second Raid
12/1857	Third Seminole War	FL121	Ambushes in Big Cypress Swamp
1/1858	Third Seminole War	FL122	Attacks in Big Cypress Swamp
5/11/1858	-----	OK3	Battle Along the Canadian River
5/16–17/1858	Spokane War	WA14	Battle of Rosalia
Summer 1858	Apache War	MX6	Attack at Kaskiyeh
8/1858	-----	AZ3	Attack on Wagon Train
9/1/1858	Spokane War	WA15	Battle of Four Lakes
9/5/1858	Spokane War	WA16	Battle of Spokane Plains
1858	Spokane War	WA15	Execution of Natives
10/1/1858	-----	OK4	Battle of the Wichita Village
10/1858	Navajo War	AZ4	Attack Near Fort Defiance
6/17/1859	-----	KS3	Fight at Council Grove
Summer 1859	Apache War	MX7	Battle Near Arizpe
2/25/1860	-----	CA12	Humboldt Bay Massacre
4/30/1860	Navajo War	AZ5	Attack at Fort Defiance
5/9/1860	Paiute War	NV1	Pyramid Lake Massacre
6/2/1860	Paiute War	NV2	Rout of Paiutes
7/1860	-----	CO4	Attack at Bent's New Fort
Summer 1860	Apache War	MX8	Attack in Sierra de Sahuaripa Mountains
10/1860	Navajo War	AZ6	Attacks on Navajo Villages
2/4/1861	Cochise War	AZ7	Battle at Siphon Canyon
2/5/1861	Cochise War	AZ8	Battle at Stage Station
2/6/1861	Cochise War	AZ9	Capture of Wagon Train
2/8/1861	Cochise War	AZ10	Attack Near Stage Station
4/1861	Cochise War	AZ11	Ambush at Doubtful Canyon
Spring 1861	Apache War	MX9	Attack on Mule Train
6/20/1861	-----	WY4	Fight with Snakes
7/1861	Apache War	NM25	Ambushes Near Pinos Altos

Date	Larger Conflict	Book Entry	Battle or Event
11/19/1861	-----	OK5	Battle of Round Mountain
12/9/1861	Civil War	OK6	Battle of Caving Banks
12/26/1861	Civil War	OK7	Battle of Chustenahlah
1862	Hualapai Wars	AZ12	Raid on Havasupais
1862	-----	ID3	Wagon Train Massacre
3/7–8/1862	Civil War	AR3	Battle of Pea Ridge
3/28/1862	Apache War	NM26	Battle of La Glorieta
Spring 1862	Apache War	MX10	Attack in Sierra de Sahuaripa Mountains
4/1862	-----	WY5	Attacks on Stage Stations
5/31–6/1/1862	Civil War	VA14	Battle of Fair Oaks
6/25–7/1/1862	Civil War	VA15	Seven Days Battles
7/3/1862	Civil War	OK8	Battle at Locust Grove
7/15/1862	Cochise War	AZ13	Battle at Apache Pass
Summer 1862	Civil War	OK9	Battle of Bayou Menard
8/1862	Civil War	VA16	Second Battle of Bull Run
8/7/1862	Little Crow's War	MN3	Attack on Upper Sioux Agency
8/18/1862	Little Crow's War	MN4	Attack at Lower Sioux Agency
8/20/1862	Little Crow's War	MN5	Attack on Fort Ridgely
8/22/1862	Little Crow's War	MN6	Attack on Fort Ridgely
8/23/1862	Little Crow's War	MN7	Second Battle of New Ulm
Fall 1862	Apache War	NM27	Massacre of Mescaleros
9/1862	Little Crow's War	MN8	Battle Along the Minnesota River
9/5–6/1862	Little Crow's War	MN9	Battle at Birch Coulee
9/13–15/1862	Civil War	TN14	Battle of Baptist Gap
9/17/1862	Civil War	MD2	Battle of Antietam
9/20/1862	Civil War	MO5	Battle at Shirley's Ford
9/23/1862	Little Crow's War	MN10	Battle of Wood Lake
10/23–24/1862	Civil War	KS4	Sacking of Wichita Agency
12/24/1862	-----	ND2	Attack at Fort Berthold
1/29/1863	-----	ID4	Battle of Bear River
5/1863	-----	UT2	Attack on Stagecoach
5/1863	Civil War	KS5	Attack at the Verdigris River
6/1863	-----	SD1	Attacks on Sioux
7/5/1863	-----	WY6	Attack at Cooper's Creek Station
7/8/1863	-----	UT3	Ambush at Canyon Station
7/17/1863	Civil War	OK10	Battle of Honey Springs
9/1863	-----	ND3	Battle of Whitestone
10/29/1863	Civil War	OK11	Raid on Tahlequah
12/10/1863	Civil War	TN15	Skirmish at Gatlinburg
12/13/1863	Navajo War	AZ14	Attack Near Canyon de Chelly
1/6/1864	Navajo War	AZ15	Battle of Canyon de Chelly
1/24/1864	-----	AZ16	Woolsey Massacre
2/2/1864	Civil War	NC16	Attack at Deep Creek
4/18/1864	Civil War	AR4	Battle of Poison Springs
5/5/1864	Civil War	VA17	Battle of the Wilderness
5/11–12/1864	Civil War	VA18	Battle of Spotsylvania
5/16/1864	Cheyenne-Arapaho War	CO5	Battle at Ash Creek
5/1864	Cheyenne-Arapaho War	CO6	Fight at Fremont's Orchard
6/10/1864	Civil War	OK12	Capture of the Ferry *J.R. Williams*
6/14–18/1864	Civil War	VA19	Battle of Petersburg

Date	Larger Conflict	Book Entry	Battle or Event
Mid–7/1864	Cheyenne-Arapaho War	CO7	Attacks Along the South Platte River
7/30/1864	Civil War	VA20	Battle of the Crater
Early 8/1864	Cheyenne-Arapaho War	NE5	Attacks Along the Platte River
9/16/1864	Civil War	OK13	Attack Near Sand Town
9/19/1864	Civil War	OK14	Second Battle of Cabin Creek
10/13/1864	-----	TX30	Elm Creek Raid
11/25/1864	-----	TX31	Battle of Adobe Walls
11/29/1864	Cheyenne-Arapaho War	CO8	Sand Creek Massacre
Winter 1864	-----	MX11	Attack Near Pontoco
12/1864	Civil War	SC37	Sacking of Columbia
12/21/1864	Lowrie War	NC17	Murder of Barnes
1/1865	-----	ID5	Attack at Battle Creek
1/7/1865	Sioux War	WY7	Attack at Fort Laramie
1/8/1865	-----	TX32	Attack at Dove Creek
1/15/1865	Lowrie War	NC18	Assassination of Harris
1 and 2/1865	Cheyenne-Arapaho War	CO9	Attacks in Colorado
1 and 2/1865	Cheyenne-Arapaho War	NE6	Attacks in Nebraska
2/2/1865	Sioux War	WY8	Attack at Fort Laramie
2/27/1865	Lowrie War	NC19	Raid on Argyle Plantation
3/3/1865	Lowrie War	NC20	Execution of Lowries
6/14/1865	-----	NE7	Uprising at Horse Creek
7/24–26/1865	Cheyenne-Arapaho War	WY9	Battle at Platte Bridge Station
8/29/1865	Sioux War	WY10	Battle of Tongue River
8/1865	Sioux War	WY11	Action Along the Powder River
9/1–10/1865	Powder River Expedition	MT3	Attacks Along the Powder River
Autumn 1865	-----	MX12	Attack Near Arizpe
Late Autumn 1865	-----	MX13	Attack Near Gulf of California
1866	Apache War	AZ17	Massacre Near Prescott
Early Summer 1866	-----	MX14	Attack in Sierra de Sahuaripa Mountains
7/1866	Paiute War	ID6	Wagon Train Massacre
7/17/1866	Red Cloud's War	WY12	Fighting Along the Bozeman Trail
8/16/1866	Sioux War	WY13	Attack Near Fort Connor
9/1/1866	Sioux War	MT4	Battle of Tongue River
9/8/1866	Sioux War	MT5	Attack Along the Powder River
Early 9/1866	Sioux War	MT6	Attack on Wagon Train
9/1866	Sioux War	MT7	Roman Nose's Fight
12/6/1866	Red Cloud's War	WY14	Skirmish Near Fort Phil Kearny
12/20–21/1866	Red Cloud's War	WY15	Fetterman Massacre
1867	-----	MX15	Attack Near Arizpe
1867	-----	MX16	Attacks on Arizpe
6/1867	Hualapai Wars	AZ18	Attack on Havasupais
7/22/1867	-----	KS6	Kidder Massacre
8/1/1867	Red Cloud's War	MT8	Battle of Hayfield
8/2/1867	Red Cloud's War	WY16	Battle of Wagon Box
8/17/1867	-----	NE8	Battle of Plum Creek
1868	Outbreak of 1868	TX33	Raids in Panhandle
1868	-----	MX17	Raids in Sonora
4/16/1868	-----	NE9	Attack at Elm Creek Station

Date	Larger Conflict	Book Entry	Battle or Event
7/12/1868	Outbreak of 1868	TX34	Battle Near Seymour
9/1868	-----	NE10	Attack on Train
9/17/1868	-----	KS7	Battle of Beecher's Island
11/27/1868	-----	OK15	Battle of the Washita
Late 11/1868	War of 1868-69	OK16	Battle of Solider Spring
6/1869	-----	ND4	Attack at Fort Berthold
7/11/1869	-----	CO10	Battle of Summit Springs
10/1869	Apache War	AZ19	Attack on Stagecoach
Winter 1869	-----	MT9	Battle at Crow Rock
1/2/1870	-----	ND5	Attack on Fort Berthold
1/23/1870	Piegan War	MT10	Marias River Massacre
1/24/1871	-----	TX35	Attack on Wagon Train
4/30/1871	Apache War	AZ20	Camp Grant Massacre
5/5/1871	Apache War	AZ21	Battle Near Babocomari River
5/18/1871	-----	TX36	Salt Creek Wagon Train Massacre
8/1871	-----	KS8	Fight at Wichita Agency
9/4/1871	Apache War	AZ22	Raid on Fort Crittenden
Fall 1871	Apache War	AZ23	Attack on Wheeler Party
4/20/1872	-----	TX37	Attack on Wagon Train
5/18/1872	-----	MX18	Attack on Kickapoo Village
6/4 and 15/1872	-----	TX38	Raids on Fort Sill
6/9/1872	-----	TX39	Attack on Lee Home
8/14/1872	-----	MT11	Skirmish at Arrow Creek
9/25/1872	Apache War	AZ24	Attack at Muchoas Canyon
9/29/1872	-----	TX40	Attack at McClellan Creek
11/29/1872	Modoc War	OR41	Battle of Lost River
12/21/1872	Modoc War	CA13	Battle of Land's Ranch
12/28/1872	Tonto Basin Campaign	AZ25	Battle of Skeleton Cave
1873	-----	MX19	Battle of White Hill
1/16–17/1873	Modoc War	CA14	First Battle for the Stronghold
1/22/1873	Modoc War	CA15	First Battle of Scorpion Point
3/1873	Tonto Basin Campaign	AZ26	Attack on Wickenburg
4/15–17/1873	Modoc War	CA16	Second Battle for the Stronghold
4/26/1873	Modoc War	CA17	Thomas-Wright Massacre
5/2/1873	Modoc War	CA18	Second Battle of Scorpion Point
5/10/1873	Modoc War	CA19	Battle of Dry Lake
5/18/1873	-----	MX20	Attack Near Santa Rosa
5/22/1873	Modoc War	CA20	Battle of Willow Creek Ridge
8/4/1873	-----	MT12	Skirmish Along the Yellowstone River
8/5/1873	-----	NE11	Pawnee and Sioux Massacre
8/11/1873	-----	MT13	Attack on Stanley Expedition
Fall 1873	-----	MX21	Raid Near Eagle Pass
6/27/1874	Red River War	TX41	Battle of Adobe Walls
7/3/1874	-----	OK17	Attack on Wagon Train
7/16/1874	Red River War	TX42	Lost Valley Fight
Summer 1874	-----	KS9	Attack on Medicine Lodge Creek
9/28/1874	Red River War	TX43	Attack at Palo Duro Canyon
3/17/1876	Great Sioux War	MT14	Battle of Powder River
6/17/1876	Great Sioux War	MT15	Battle of the Rosebud
6/25/1876	Great Sioux War	MT16	Battle of the Little Bighorn

Date	Larger Conflict	Book Entry	Battle or Event
7/7/1876	Great Sioux War	MT17	Attack on Sibley's Scouts
7/17/1876	Great Sioux War	NE12	Skirmish at War Bonnet Creek
8/2/1876	Great Sioux War	MT18	Skirmish Near Wolf Rapids
9/9/1876	Great Sioux War	SD2	Attack on American Horse's Village
10/21/1876	Great Sioux War	MT19	Battle of Cedar Creek
11/25/1876	Great Sioux War	WY17	Attack on Dull Knife's Village
12/18/1876	Great Sioux War	MT20	Battle of Ash Creek
12/1876	Great Sioux War	MT21	Attack at Fort Keough
1/8/1877	Great Sioux War	MT22	Battle of Wolf Mountain
5/7/1877	Great Sioux War	MT23	Battle of Lame Deer
6/17/1877	Nez Perce War	ID7	Battle of White Bird Canyon
7/4–5/1877	Nez Perce War	ID8	Battle of Cottonwood Creek
7/11–12/1877	Nez Perce War	ID9	Battle of the Clearwater River
8/9–10/1877	Nez Perce War	MT24	Battle of the Big Hole
8/15/1877	Nez Perce War	ID10	Birch Creek Massacre
8/20/1877	Nez Perce War	ID11	Battle of Camas Meadows
8/22–31/1877	Nez Perce War	WY18	Attacks in Yellowstone
9/13/1877	Nez Perce War	MT25	Battle of Canyon Creek
9/13/1877	-----	OK18	Battle Near Cimarron River
Late 9/1877	Nez Perce War	MT26	Battles in Crow Country
9/30–10/5/1877	Nez Perce War	MT27	Battle of Bear Paw
Spring 1878	Bannock War	OR42	Battle of Big Camp Prairie
6/8/1878	Bannock War	ID12	Battle of Clark's Fork
7/8/1878	Bannock War	OR43	Battle of Pilot Rock
7/20/1878	Bannock War	OR44	Attack at John Day River
9/29/1878	-----	KS10	Dull Knife's Raid
12/25/1878	-----	OK19	Skirmish at Muskogee
1/9/1879	-----	NE13	Battle at Fort Robinson
1879	Sheepeater War	ID13	Attacks in Idaho
9/29/1879	Ute War	CO11	Meeker Massacre
1880	-----	MX22	Battle of Skolata
1880	-----	MX23	Attack at Nokode
1880	-----	MX24	Massacre at Casa Grande
4/1880	Victorio's Rebellion	AZ27	Battle in Hembrillo Canyon
5/1880	Victorio's Rebellion	AZ28	Battle on the Fresco River
7/26/1880	-----	OK20	Raid on Marshalltown
10/15–16/1880	Victorio's Rebellion	MX25	Battle at Tres Castillos
1881	-----	UT4	Ambush Near Moab
6–8/1881	Victorio's Rebellion	NM28	Nana's Raid
7/1881	Green Peach War	OK21	Killing of Lighthorsemen
8/30/1881	Apache War	AZ29	Battle at Cibecu Creek
9/1/1881	Apache War	AZ30	Attack at Fort Apache
7/17/1882	Apache War	AZ31	Battle of Big Dry Wash
11/1882	Geronimo's Rebellion	MX26	Ambush at Galeana
12/24/1882	-----	OK22	Battle Near Okmulgee
3/1883	Apache War	NM29	Chiricahua Raid
3/21–1/1/1883	Apache War	AZ32	Apache Raids
4/23/1883	-----	OK23	Encounter East of Wichita
5/1883	Apache War	MX27	Pursuit of Apaches
1885	Riel Rebellion	CN24	Encounter in Saskatchewan

Date	Larger Conflict	Book Entry	Battle or Event
6/8/1885	Geronimo's Rebellion	AZ33	Attack at Guadalupe Canyon
6/22/1885	Apache War	MX28	Attack at Bavispe Mountains
12/1885	Apache War	NM30	Attack by Apaches
1/10-11/1886	Apache War	MX29	Battle at Devil's Backbone
12/12/1890	Ghost Dance War	SD3	Clash at Daly's Ranch
12/15/1890	Ghost Dance War	SD4	Skirmish at Stronghold
Mid–12/1890	Ghost Dance War	SD5	Clash at Phinney's Ranch
12/15/1890	Ghost Dance War	SD6	Skirmish on the Grand River
12/29/1890	Ghost Dance War	SD7	Wounded Knee Massacre
12/30/1890	Ghost Dance War	SD8	Battle at Drexel Mission
1/1/1891	Ghost Dance War	SD9	Battle at White River
10/5/1898	-----	MN11	Battle of Leech Lake
1911	Mexican Revolution	MX30	Uprising at Villa de Ayala
6/17–23/1914	Mexican Revolution	MX31	Battle of Zacatecas
11/1–4/1915	Yaqui War	MX32	Capture of Agua Prieta

ALABAMA

AL1 *Battle of Maubila* • October 18, 1540
Location: Clarke County
War: De Soto Expedition
The 950 musket-bearing conquistadors led by Hernando de Soto headed south through Alabama toward the native town of Maubila (Mabila, Mabilia). On the way, he met Chief Tuscaloosa, from whom de Soto demanded 400 burden bearers. De Soto arrested Tuscaloosa and took him with his army on a three-day march. They entered the heavily walled town of Maubila, and Tuscaloosa escaped into one of the houses.

When a native refused de Soto's demands to bring out his chief, the native was killed. Warriors swarmed out to attack the Spaniards, most of whom got out of the fort. Fighting continued outside, and after three hours the natives retreated into the enclosure. The mounted Spaniards with their crossbows and swords were able to defeat the natives and their clubs and bows and arrows. The battle, which ended at dark, resulted in 18 to 23 Spanish deaths and 150 to 170 wounded. As many as 2,500 to 11,000 natives were killed.

A result of the battle was the collapse of the native chiefdom and the relocation of the villages.
Museum: A miniature diorama is on display in the Moundville Museum, Moundville, AL.
Sources: 8, 22, 85, 88, 89, 127, 135, 244, 284, 326, 412

AL2 *Atack at Mobile* • May, 1709
Location: Mobile
A party of 600 to 700 Alibamon warriors attacked Mobile and burned it down. Nearly 30 women and children were captured. The attackers were repulsed by French soldiers supported by Mobilians and Tahomes, who killed 34, captured five, and burned down the Alibamon village.
Sources: 111, 209

AL3 *Attack at Mobile* • August, 1765
Location: Mobile
A party of Creeks attacked the Choctaw camp at Mobile, killing ten. For the next

25

six years, these tribes carried on warfare, with the Chickasaws siding with the Choctaws.
Sources: 89

AL4   *Assault on Mobile* • 1780
Location: Mobile
War: Revolutionary War
An assault was made on the Spanish garrison at Mobile by British soldiers and Choctaws. They, the Creeks and the Chickasaws supported the British against the Americans. A major reason the assault failed was the cowardice of the British.
Sources: 20, 162, 199

AL5   *Attack at Muscle Shoals* • March 14, 1780
Location: Muscle Shoals
War: Revolutionary War
Capt. John Donelson led an expedition from Ft. Patrick Henry down the Holston and Tennessee Rivers, heading toward French Lick on the Cumberland River. Two days after they passed rough water at Muscle Shoals, two of the boats were fired at and five crewmen were wounded.
Sources: 412

AL6   *Attack at Muscle Shoals* • June 5, 1794
Location: Muscle Shoals
A band of Cherokees from the Chickamauga towns near the Tennessee River plundered a boat at Muscle Shoals and killed most of the people on board. They then fled west to Arkansas, where they were joined in the 1810s by other Cherokees who had been encouraged to leave their homes in the East.
Sources: 332

AL7   *Attack at Tuckabatchee* • July 22, 1813
Location: Tuckabatchee
War: Creek Indian War
Upper Creeks led by Opothle Micco had attended a conference with Tecumseh to the north, and on their way back killed seven white families near the mouth of the Ohio River. They may also have killed two or three others in Tennessee and Georgia. The state of Tennessee reacted by mobilizing a militia to wipe out the Creeks. To avoid warfare, Menawa and McIntosh had a party track down and kill about 11 of the warriors who had done the killing, during the period of April 16–26, 1813.

Others who had participated in the killings fought back and threatened the lives of Menawa and Tustennuggee Hopoie. The Red Sticks, named for the red painted sticks they carried into battle, fought with the rest of the Creeks in several locations in Alabama. Most of the Lower Creeks continued to be friendly with the United States, but some of the upper towns chose to remain neutral. This began the Red Stick Revolt.

The inhabitants of Kailuggee and Hatchechubba opposed the revolt and fled to Tuckabatchee, a town of 600 near the Coosa and Tallapoosa Rivers. The Red Sticks then attacked and destroyed Tuckabatchee. Its inhabitants fled to Coweta.
Sources: 112, 296, 340, 343, 355

AL8   *Battle of Burnt Corn* • July 27, 1813
Location: Burnt Corn Creek
War: Creek Indian War
A group of Red Sticks had traveled to Pensacola to trade for European goods and were on their way back home by pack train. They were attacked by 180 members of the militia of Washington County, Mississippi, at the village of Burnt Corn at the intersection of two trails about 40 miles northeast of the Bigbe settlements, 80 miles north of Pensacola. The rebels fled into the swamp, leaving their pack horses. The soldiers began to divide up the loot.

    The Red Sticks regrouped in the swamp and were joined by others who had heard the gunfire. They charged the militia, 100 of whom retreated. The remaining 80 fought the 100 Red Sticks for a while, then also retreated.
Sources: 18, 91, 319, 343, 347, 355, 400

AL9   *Battle of Fort Mims* or *Fort Mims Massacre* • August 30, 1813
Location: About 20 miles from Mobile, at the confluence of the Alabama and Tombigbee Rivers
War: Creek Indian War
The Upper Creeks from Alabama allied themselves with the British. After the Battle of Burnt Corn, several makeshift forts were constructed for protection of the white settlers. One such fort was a stockade built around the home of Samuel Mims. It housed about 400 people, including 120 militia, and was commanded by Maj. Daniel Beasley.

    Warriors numbering 750 to 1,000 from 13 towns, led by William Weatherford (Red Eagle), overwhelmed the Americans and their allies, the Lower Creeks from Georgia, at Fort Mims on Lake Tensa. The commander of the post was taken by surprise, and the attackers were able to rush in through open fort gates.

    They killed 107 soldiers, 160 white civilians, and 100 blacks. Only 36 escaped. About half of the attackers were killed or wounded. Federal troops and militia planned swift reprisals, including campaigns by forces led by Gens. Andrew Jackson and James White.

    Jackson later talked to the Creeks about peace, but refused any agreement until Weatherford was surrendered to him. A few days later, Weatherford walked into Jackson's tent, since he had no more warriors to continue the fighting.
Sources: 6, 8, 18, 20, 21, 22, 33, 34, 37, 38, 40, 41, 88, 90, 91, 92, 105, 112, 113, 133, 135, 147, 165, 189, 196, 198, 240, 295, 296, 340, 343, 347, 355, 380, 382, 396, 400

AL10   *Battle of Tallushatchee* • November 3–4, 1813
Location: East of Fort Strother
War: Creek Indian War
In response to the overwhelming defeat at Fort Mims, the Tennessee militia raised a 3,500-man army and placed Gen. Andrew Jackson in its command. Frontiersman Davy Crockett was a member of the army. They left for Alabama in October of 1813 and in early November, reached the Red Stick region between the Coosa and Tallapoosa Rivers.

    At Tallushatchee (Tallassiehatchee) on November 4, they and their allied Cherokees led by Maj. Ridge and Gen. John Coffee killed at least 200 Creeks and captured 80 to 84.
Sources: 33, 40, 41, 91, 113, 133, 144, 181, 240, 295, 340, 343, 347, 382, 396, 397, 400

AL11 *Battle of Talladaga* • November 9, 1813
Location: Talladaga
War: Creek Indian War
On November 9, Gen. Andrew Jackson and his Tennessee militia fought and won at Talladaga Town in 15 minutes of fierce fighting. About 300 Red Stick men were killed, and the soldiers had 15 to 17 killed and 83 to 85 wounded. The surviving 1,000 Creek warriors retreated south to Tohopeka, a fortified 100-acre area within a horseshoe-shaped bend in the Tallapoosa River.
Sources: 33, 40, 91, 113, 133, 144, 181, 240, 295, 340, 343, 347, 382, 396, 397, 400

AL12 *Destruction of Hillabee Town* • November 18, 1813
Location: Near Fort Strother
War: Creek Indian War
American soldiers led by Gen. James White destroyed a Hillabee town which had already surrendered to Gen. Andrew Jackson. The militia killed 60 Hillabees and captured 200 to 250 women and children. The Hillabees blamed Jackson for the unnecessary deaths.
Sources: 91, 295, 343, 355

AL13 *Skirmish on the Alabama River* • November 20, 1813
Location: Near Randon's Creek, Monroe County
War: Creek Indian War
A scouting party consisting of Sam Dale and three others noticed a large canoe traveling on the Alabama River. Launching onto the river, they discovered that the canoe contained 11 natives. They shot some with muskets and clubbed the others to death. Dale earned the nickname of "Big Sam."
Sources: 22

AL14 *Attack at Tallapoosa River* • November 29, 1813
Location: Tallapoosa River
War: Creek Indian War
The Georgia army led by Gen. John Floyd defeated a large group of Red Sticks at Autosee (Auttose), killing at least 200. Most of the survivors lived because they left their huts and hid in caves along the bluff at the river. The soldiers had 11 killed and 54 wounded.
Sources: 40, 91, 343, 397

AL15 *Battle of Escanachaha* • December 23, 1813
Location: On the Alabama River, near the Coosa and Tallapoosa Rivers
War: Creek Indian War
The Creek holy town of Escanachaha was supposedly protected by a barrier the white soldiers could not penetrate. William Weatherford (Red Eagle) gathered his warriors on a high bluff on the Alabama River, after he had been convinced by a medicine man that this was another sacred site and no white man could enter it.
    The town was attacked by Gen. Ferdinand L. Claiborne, commanding a force of 1,000 consisting of the 3rd Infantry and a Mississippi volunteer unit, plus 135 Choctaws. One soldier and 30 to 33 natives were killed, including a prophet and 12 black supporters. Red Eagle escaped by riding off a high bluff into deep water.
Sources: 18, 22, 88, 90, 133, 340, 343, 397

AL16 *Battle of Enotachopo Creek* • January 24, 1814
Location: Coffee (Enotachopo) Creek
War: Creek Indian War
The Creeks, retaliating for Gen. Andrew Jackson's burning of native towns, defeated his Tennessee soldiers. While his artillery was in the water, the soldiers panicked and broke. Two officers were court-martialed for their failure to control their men. In this and the Battle of Emuckfau, the soldiers had 19 to 24 killed and 71 to 76 wounded, while the natives lost 189 or 190.
Sources: 34, 40, 91, 133, 295, 397

AL17 *Battle at Calabee Creek* • January 27, 1814
Location: Artussee
War: Creek Indian War
The area near Artussee was believed by the Creeks to be an area where they were invulnerable. However, they were attacked by 1,500 Georgia militia led by Gen. John Floyd, accompanied by Tuckabatchees led by Tustennuggee Hopoie and Cowetas led by McIntosh. They fought with Lower Creeks from eight nearby towns, with 17 militia killed and 132 wounded. Of the friendly native forces, five were killed and 15 were wounded. Fifty opposing warriors were also killed.

Floyd then burned Artussee and Tallasi and left the Creek country after destroying about 400 native homes.
Sources: 91, 113, 133, 340, 343, 355, 397

AL18 *Battle of Horseshoe Bend* or *Battle of Tohopeka* • March 27, 1814
Location: 12 miles north of Dadeville
War: Creek Indian War
After the defeat at Fort Mims during the previous year, the Americans raised further support from the Lower Creeks led by McIntosh, Choctaws led by Pushmataha, and Cherokees. Two thousand foot soldiers, 700 cavalry, 600 Cherokees and some Lower Creeks, all led by Gen. Andrew Jackson, nearly wiped out the 1,000 Upper Creeks led by Menawa, who were trapped at a bend of the Tallapoosa River.

Jackson sent the cavalry and Cherokees across the Tallapoosa to surround the band, cutting off the Creeks' escape route. He then marched onto the peninsula toward a log barrier. Cannon fire proved ineffective in breaking through the barrier, and for an hour both sides exchanged rifle fire. At 12:30 p.m. he ordered a charge against the barricade. At the same time, Gen. John Coffee attacked from the rear with the cavalry and Cherokees.

For several hours, the peninsula was the scene of fierce hand-to-hand fighting. By nightfall, 800 to 1,000 Red Stick warriors had died fighting or while trying to escape, after refusing to surrender. Three hundred fifty Creek women and children had been taken prisoner. The force from Tennessee lost 49 and had 154 wounded.

At a treaty meeting months later, Jackson turned against the Lower Creeks and forced them to turn over to the U.S. almost eight million acres, or about two-thirds of the entire Creek territory. Many of the Red Sticks relocated with the Seminoles in Spanish Florida.

In 1836, Menawa joined forces with Opothle Yaholo of the Lower Creeks in the Second Seminole War and helped put down the revolting Upper Creeks. About 2,500 of those remaining fled south to join the Seminoles in Florida.

Monuments:(1) Horseshoe Bend National Military Park, SR 49, Dadeville, AL 36853, or Rt. 1, Box 103, Daviston, AL; (2) Bronze and stone monument at the grave of Chief Junaluska (Tsunu-la-hun-ski), who fought against the Creeks, near Robbinsville, NC.

Sources: 5, 6, 8, 13, 18, 19, 20, 21, 22, 33, 34, 37, 38, 39, 40, 41, 82, 88, 90, 112, 113, 133, 135, 143, 147, 169, 173, 181, 189, 198, 207, 240, 275, 288, 295, 296, 301, 319, 332, 340, 343, 347, 355, 380, 381, 382, 390, 396, 397, 418

AL19   *Attacks on White Settlements* • May, 1836
Location: Along the Chattahoochee River
War: Second Creek War
In response to the whites settling on native lands, Lower Creeks led by Eneah Emathla, Enea Micco and Jim Henry (a Yuchi) killed whites and destroyed their homes and crops. Many fled to the east side of the Chattahoochee River near Columbus, Georgia. The Creeks also burned a toll bridge, robbed a stagecoach and captured two steamboats on the river.

The Upper Creeks and whites organized a force to oppose the rebels led by Eneah Emathla, and by July the Lower Creek bands either surrendered or traveled to Florida to join the Seminoles.
Sources: 112, 354

ALASKA

AK1   *Attack on Aleuts* • 1766
Location: Aleutian Islands
War: Russian Exploration
In 1741, Vitus Bering, a Dane working for Czar Peter the Great, reported that sea mammals were plentiful in the area. As a result, sailing ships came in search of otters. They also took hostages and forced the natives to work for them.

On Atka, the Aleuts refused to deliver furs, but did not rebel. The traders killed some and destroyed a village to teach them a lesson.

At Unalaska in the Fox Islands group, a party of 14 traders and children was wiped out in January of 1762. Later that year, the natives destroyed four of a fleet of five Russian ships. In 1766, the Russians retaliated with an armada and bombarded and destroyed 18 Aleut villages with cannon.
Sources: 134, 190, 342

AK2   *Skirmish in Yschugat Bay* • 1793
Location: Yschugat Bay
War: Russian Exploration
Alexander Baranov and his party encountered a Tlingit raiding party which was in search of slaves. With muskets, they attacked the Russians, and were protected by

wooden armor and hats which deflected bullets. The Tlingits lost 12 in the battle, while the Russians lost two and their allied Aleuts lost nine.
Sources: 205

AK3   *Attack on Russian Expedition* • 1799
Location: Near Sitka
War: Russian Exploration
In 1799, Alexander Baranov led a small fleet of Russians with Aleuts in his crew to the southern part of Alaska. His contingent was made up of 100 Russians, 700 Aleuts and 300 mainlanders. At what is now Sitka, they built a fort called New Archangel. The area was the home of the Tlingits, and they allowed the Russians to remain on the basis of a promise to trade with them. However, few Russian supply ships came, and little trading occurred.

During that year, a band of Tlingits intercepted a Russian expedition as they slept on a mainland beach and killed or captured 26 men.
Sources: 20, 135, 205

AK4   *Sitka Massacre* • June, 1802
Location: Sitka
War: Russian Exploration
In 1802, a group of natives consisting mostly of Tlingits attacked the fort at a time that Baranov and most of its hunter inhabitants were away. The Tlingits massacred about a dozen of the Russian settlers who had remained, took otter skins, and captured three Russians, five Aleut hunters, and 18 women and children. This action provoked retaliation by the Russians two years later.

One source claims that the fort was burned in this action, and that 408 of its 450 defenders were killed.
Sources: 20, 24, 92, 135, 138, 190, 205, 268, 275, 288

AK5   *Battle of Sitka* • October 1, 1804
Location: Sitka
War: Russian Exploration
The fort which had been taken in 1802 was occupied by natives when the Russian warship "Neva" arrived in 1804. The Tlingits constructed their own stockade on the island, later known as Baranov Island. When Alexander Baranov sent a shore party to attack it, the Tlingits counterattacked and killed 14 Russians and wounded two, including Baranov.

The Tlingits temporarily put down their weapons and began talks. As that process occurred, it was discovered one morning that the Tlingits had fled during the night, killing their own children and dogs to prevent any noise which would awaken the Russians.

The Russians built a larger fort on Baranov Island and a colony on Yakutat Bay, located in Tlingit territory. The Tlingits burned down the Yakutat colony and killed or enslaved all but ten of its garrison in 1804, but the fort on Baranov Island remained.
Monument: Sitka National Historical Park, P.O. Box 738, 106 Metlakatla St., Sitka, AK 99835, is located one mile east of downtown Sitka near the end of Lincoln St.
Sources: 5, 19, 20, 92, 135, 138, 190, 205, 288

AK6   *Attack on Nulato* • 1851
Location: Lower Yukon River
An uprising of Koyukon warriors resulted in the destruction of the Russian settlement of Nulato.
Sources: 92

ARIZONA

AZ1   *Attack at Santa Cruz de Quiburi* • March, 1698
Location: 3 miles north of present Fairbank
A party of several hundred Apaches, Jocomes and Janos attacked the Sobaipuri mission known as Santa Cruz de Quiburi, terrorizing its inhabitants. Its chief sent a messenger five miles to Coro for help, which came in the form of 500 Pima warriors who had already been preparing for battle against the Apaches.
Apache El Capotcari proposed that each side choose ten warriors to fight and decide the outcome for all. The Pimas were victorious and the Apaches fled. They were pursued by the Sobaipuris, who killed more than 50 Apaches.
Sources: 46, 48

AZ2   *Massacre at Canyon de Chelly* • 1805
Location: Canyon de Chelly
In response to the Spaniards' stealing of Navajo children to become slaves, the Navajos stole Spanish children and assimilated them into their culture. In retaliation, the Spanish attacked bands of natives, including those who were not guilty of the abductions or other crimes. One retaliatory campaign took the Spaniards into the Y-shaped Canyon de Chelly. Navajos pursued by Spanish soldiers commanded by Antonio Narbona headed to the canyon.
The women and children hid in a cave, while the men attempted to lure the Spanish further into the canyon, but the soldiers found the women and children. They fired their guns into the cave, then entered and killed the rest with bayonets and blows from the butts of their guns. The site was thereafter known as Massacre Cave, and the arm of the canyon as the Canyon of the Dead. Over 100 died there.
Sources: 245, 277, 348

AZ3   *Attack on Wagon Train* • August, 1858
Location: Arizona
A band of Mojaves attacked a California-bound civilian wagon train along the road which had been roughed out by troops commanded by Naval Lt. Edward F. Beale. The surviving settlers retreated to New Mexico.
Sources: 174

AZ4   *Attack Near Fort Defiance* • October, 1858
         Location: Fort Defiance
         War: Navajo War
         In 1851, Fort Defiance was the first fort built in Navajo country, and was located
         in a grassy valley where the soldiers' horses grazed on pastureland used by
         Manuelito (Hasteen Chil Haadjiin, Man of Blackweeds) and his people. The
         officer in command, Maj. William T.H. Brooks, told the Navajos to keep their
         livestock off the land about 12 miles away from the fort, and when they did not,
         the animals were shot by a company of soldiers. In retaliation, the Navajos raided
         the soldiers' herds and supply trains, and the soldiers began attacking bands of
         Navajos.
                 In May of 1858 the army shot 60 head of Manuelito's livestock and drove off
         the rest. In October of that year, troops and 160 Zuni mercenaries burned
         Manuelito's village and fields.
         Sources: 70, 147, 245, 254

AZ5   *Attack at Fort Defiance* • April 30, 1860
         Location: Fort Defiance
         War: Navajo War
         Manuelito and Barboncito led 1,000 Navajos against Fort Defiance, attacking
         from three sides about two hours before dawn. They nearly overran it before
         they were driven off, deciding that the soldiers had been taught a lesson. One sol-
         dier had been killed with an arrow through his heart.
                 The army considered this to be an act of war, and Col. Edward Richard
         Sprigg Canby and six companies of cavalry plus nine of infantry spent most of
         the rest of the year searching the Chuska Mountains in search of the Navajos.
         There were small skirmishes but no direct attacks. When the Civil War broke out,
         the troops were shipped east and Fort Defiance was abandoned.
         Sources: 11, 66, 70, 91, 147, 245, 277, 348

AZ6   *Attacks on Navajo Villages* • October, 1860
         Location: Northeastern Arizona
         War: Navajo War
         In response to Navajo plundering and the April 30 attack on Fort Defiance, Col.
         Edward Canby attacked several Navajo villages beginning on October 11. His sol-
         diers killed a total of 34 natives and captured hundreds of horses and sheep.
         Sources: 66

AZ7   *Battle at Siphon Canyon* • February 4, 1861
         Location: Siphon Canyon
         War: Cochise War
         Lt. George Nicholas Bascom camped in Siphon Canyon in southern Arizona,
         and invited the Chiricahua chief Cochise to it as his "guest." After he entered
         Bascom's tent, it was surrounded by soldiers and he was accused of abducting
         Felix Ward, a 12-year-old white boy, which he claimed to know nothing about.
         Cochise sliced open the tent and escaped in a hail of bullets, but his six relatives
         who had accompanied him were captured.
                 Cochise returned an hour later demanding to see his brother, Coyuntara,

and was met with rifle fire. This began twelve years of fighting. The area where this occurred was then known as Apache Pass.
Sources: 48, 91, 298

AZ8   *Battle at Stage Station* • February 5, 1861
Location: A mile upstream from Siphon Canyon
War: Cochise War
Lt. George Bascom moved his troops to a camp at a stagecoach station, and met with Cochise regarding the release of his relatives. Bascom refused to release them until the abducted boy was returned, even though Cochise claimed he had no knowledge of the boy.

A group of Apaches hiding in a ravine seized James Wallace, a Butterfield stage driver. Other drivers escaped and ran toward the station, and in all of the excitement Cochise and the other three in his party fled for cover. Soldiers opened fire, and it was returned by the warriors. One stage employee was killed and another wounded.
Sources: 48, 298

AZ9   *Capture of Wagon Train* or *Bascom Affair* • February 6, 1861
Location: Near Butterfield Stage Station
War: Cochise War
Cochise offered Lt. George Bascom a trade of his hostage, James Wallace, for a return of his relatives, and Bascom refused unless the abducted boy was returned. That evening, the warriors ambushed a wagon train of flour heading toward New Mexico, and captured three Americans and nine Mexicans.

The Mexicans were tied to the wheels of the wagons, which were then burned, killing the prisoners. The Americans were further trading material, but Bascom still refused to release Cochise's relatives. The mutilated bodies of Wallace and the other three Americans were found on February 18.
Sources: 48, 166, 298

AZ10   *Attack Near Stage Station* • February 8, 1861
Location: Near Butterfield Stage Station
War: Cochise War
Two soldiers driving a mule herd about 600 yards from the station were attacked by a party of Apaches, resulting in the loss of all 56 mules.

At the same time, about 100 other Apaches began firing on the station. It was made of stone and withstood the gunfire, and Cochise decided that a charge on foot would bring too many losses. He withdrew and moved toward Mexico.

In response to the killing of the American hostages, Lt. George Bascom's superior officer ordered the execution of three of Cochise's relatives, freeing his wife and two children. Coyuntara, the two others, and three members of an unrelated band of Coyotero Apaches were hung and their skeletons were allowed to dangle in the air for months.
Sources: 48, 197, 298

AZ11   *Ambush at Doubtful Canyon* • Late April, 1861
Location: Near the New Mexico Border
War: Cochise War

In retaliation for the killing of his relatives, Cochise ambushed a Butterfield mail coach in Doubtful Canyon. Two captured whites were slowly burned to death. The other seven were also killed.

Through June, several more small parties of whites were attacked throughout southeastern Arizona. They killed everyone they found and vandalized property. By June, Cochise's band grew from about 30 to 100. It was their goal to drive the white settlers out of Arizona, and they killed any stragglers who did not leave fast enough.

Sources: 298

AZ12   *Raid on Havasupais* • 1862
Location: Grand Canyon
War: Hualapai Wars
The Yavapai who lived south of the Grand Canyon were enemies of the Havasupais. A small raid on the Havasupai home occurred in about 1840, and a larger one followed in 1855 when about 20 Yavapai were repulsed.

In 1862, about 200 Yavapai attacked by coming down the Apache Trail at night. The battle lasted a few days and then the Yavapai returned home.

Sources: 239

AZ13   *Battle at Apache Pass* • July 15, 1862
Location: Dos Cabezas Mountains
War: Cochise War
Cochise of the Chiricahuas (Chokonen) and Mangas Coloradas of the Chihenne enlisted the support of Geronimo (Goyahkla) of the Bedonkohe Apaches in a campaign against the whites. At the same time, a 45-man supply train supported by 68 soldiers, and leading 242 head of cattle, left camp near Tucson and headed for Apache Pass. They were allowed to march unimpeded over 40 miles of desert, reaching the abandoned stage station with a severe need for water. They were only 600 yards from a major spring.

Two hundred Apaches opened fire and were likely to win, except that the Americans had 12-pounder cannons with exploding shells. The battle lasted three hours, and two soldiers were killed. The artillery won the day for the soldiers. Apache loss estimates ran from zero to 63.

The soldiers built Fort Bowie on a hill overlooking the spring, and made it the headquarters of their campaign against the Chiricahuas.

Museum: Fort Bowie National Historic Site, Apache Pass Rd. off SR 186, Bowie, AZ.

Sources: 46, 197, 254, 297, 298, 348

AZ14   *Attack Near Canyon de Chelly* • December 13, 1863
Location: Near Canyon de Chelly
War: Navajo War
Gen. James Henry Carleton ordered Col. Christopher ("Kit") Carson to invade Canyon de Chelly with a force of 736 officers and men to destroy feed and livestock, plus kill or capture the Navajos in their stronghold. Carson assembled a pack herd to carry supplies for the campaign, and on December 13 warriors led by Barboncito swooped down upon it and ran the mules off for use by the Navajos as a winter meat supply. Carson sent soldiers in pursuit. Lt. Donanciano

Montoya and his cavalry came upon a small camp and captured 13 women and children, perhaps killing one warrior.
Sources: 70, 245

AZ15 *Battle of Canyon de Chelly* • January 6, 1864
Location: Chinle
War: Navajo War
Despite the lack of pack animals, the campaign in the canyon went on as planned. Col. Kit Carson entered at the west end with 1,000 men on January 6, and Capt. Albert Pfeiffer and a small force entered at the east end a week later. The 8,000 Navajos met the soldiers with stones and pieces of wood. On January 12, one of Carson's patrols killed 11 Navajos in the largest skirmish. By the middle of January, the remaining 60 Navajos surrendered and were taken to Fort Canby (formerly known as Fort Defiance). Carson's men destroyed the Navajo properties, including peach orchards consisting of over 5,000 trees.

Those who surrendered were marched (the "Long Walk") beginning on June 15 for more than 300 miles to the Bosque Redondo at Fort Sumner in New Mexico, where they were imprisoned for four years.
Monument: Canyon de Chelly National Monument, P.O. Box 588, SRs 191 and 7, Chinle, AZ 86503.
Sources: 5, 11, 31, 70, 92, 197, 202, 230, 245, 254, 276, 277, 281, 348

AZ16 *Woolsey Massacre* • January 24, 1864
Location: Near the Verde River
War: Apache War
King Woolsey, a rancher, hated all Apaches. He led three punitive expeditions against Pinalenos, Tontos and Yavapais. He poisoned some of the more peaceful ones with strychnine and led a group of 28 volunteers and Pima and Maricopa natives in a hunt for stolen cattle.

They came upon an Apache camp, but it was not proven whether its inhabitants were the ones responsible for the theft. He pretended to come in peace, and when they were within range his party opened fire, killing about 24 Apaches. In the action, only one of Woolsey's men was killed.

Woolsey was called a hero by some. In 1879, a historian lauded him as "the most notable, the most enterprising and the most courageous of all the great host of trailblazers who first penetrated Arizona."
Sources: 46, 48, 298

AZ17 *Massacre Near Prescott* • 1866
Location: Near Prescott
War: Apache War
The Apaches were pursued through Arizona by an army led by Gen. James Henry Carleton, but many settlers in the area wanted a quicker end to the natives. One company of mercenaries and volunteers which formed was the Yavapai Rangers, which followed a peaceful party of Apaches to their camp and attacked them. They killed 23 Apaches, allowing the sole survivor to escape.
Sources: 298

AZ18 *Attack on Havasupais* • June, 1867
Location: Grand Canyon
War: Hualapai Wars
Two hundred fifty Havasupais battled troops from Fort Mohave for nine hours during 1867. They finally surrendered in 1869. In 1871, they were concentrated into a compound at Camp Beale Springs north of Kingman.
Sources: 239

AZ19 *Attack on Stagecoach* • October, 1869
Location: Dragoon Springs
War: Apache War
A stagecoach was attacked by a war party of Apaches, who killed the passengers and their military escort.
Sources: 48

AZ20 *Camp Grant Massacre* • April 30, 1871
Location: Camp Grant
War: Apache War
The Apaches, consisting of six allied tribes, resisted the removal efforts of the army and the settlers in the southwest, infuriating the whites. Eskiminzin was the leader of a band of Aravaipa Apaches who settled in an unarmed village near Camp Grant. They lived under the supervision of Lt. Royal E. Whitman, the military commander, and were employed by him to cut hay for the post's horses. Some of the natives also worked as laborers on nearby ranches. The settlement appeared to be working out well and other Apaches joined them.

Unfortunately, another band of Apaches raided San Xavier del Bac south of Tucson on April 10, and on April 13, killed four whites in a raid near San Pedro, about 30 miles to the east. The settlers near Camp Grant formed a Committee of Public Safety to protect the whites from Apaches. In the latter half of April, experienced Indian fighter William S. Oury organized an expedition to attack the Aravaipa village, located 55 miles away.

The contingent consisted of six Americans, 48 Mexicans, and 92 Papagos who had previously been converted to Christianity by Spanish priests. They left for the village on April 28, and Lt. Whitman learned of the expedition on the morning of April 30. He sent a messenger to the village to warn the Apaches and invite them to come into the fort for protection, but the messenger returned with the news that there were no survivors in the village. The contingent from Tucson had murdered, raped and mutilated from 85 to 144 natives, mostly women and children. Twenty-seven children were captured by the Papagos to be sold into slavery in Mexico. Although they were later tried, the jury found none of the attackers guilty of a crime.

Eskiminzin and others who had escaped returned and rebuilt the village and lived peacefully until Camp Grant was relocated 60 miles to the southeast. The government then moved the Aravaipas to San Carlos on the Gila River.
Memorial: Tucson's Oury Park honors William S. Oury, the organizer of the massacre.
Sources: 46, 47, 48, 66, 70, 147, 166, 254, 298, 348, 357, 380

AZ21   *Battle Near Babocomari River* • May 5, 1871
Location: Whetstone Mountains, 2 miles north of the Babocomari River
War: Apache War
The patrol of Lt. Howard Cushing, while pursuing the Apaches found the grass recently burned, offering his horses little to eat. North of the Babocomari River, they came upon a track of a single native woman and a pony heading toward Bear Springs in the Whetstone Mountains. Sgt. John Mott and two soldiers formed an advance party to follow the trail, while the rest of the men came up behind. As they approached a canyon, Mott suspected a trap and instead of going into the canyon went up its left wall.

Fifteen Apaches appeared behind him and a larger band up ahead cut off his escape. They opened fire, killing a private and a horse. Although the Apaches could have killed the other two quickly, they toyed with them, likely trying to lure Cushing into attempting a rescue.

Cushing charged, followed by an Apache charge. Cushing and others were killed, and the soldiers retreated. The Apaches pursued them in a running battle for about a mile through the canyon. They then broke off the fight, and the surviving soldiers staggered to Fort Crittenden (formerly Fort Buchanan).
Sources: 46, 91, 298

AZ22   *Raid on Fort Crittenden* • September 4, 1871
Location: Fort Crittenden
War: Apache War
Cochise led a party of warriors in a raid on Fort Crittenden, driving off and capturing the army's herd of 54 horses and seven mules. The soldiers who were supposed to be guarding the animals panicked and did not even wound a single Apache.
Sources: 298

AZ23   *Attack on Wheeler Party* • Fall, 1871
Location: Between Wickenburg and Ehrenburg
War: Apache War
Lt. Wheeler's exploring expedition en route from Nevada was to terminate at Whipple Barracks, a mile northeast of Prescott. Between Wickenburg and Ehrenburg, a stagecoach carrying his party was attacked by Yuma Apaches and several were killed.

On September 8, 1872, Gen. George Crook attempted to arrest the guilty natives at Date Creek, and a fight broke out. Several natives were killed by rifle fire.
Sources: 47

AZ24   *Attack at Muchoas Canyon* • September 25, 1872
Location: Muchoas Canyon
War: Apache War
Col. J.W. Mason, leading a portion of the 5th Cavalry, rode out from Camp Hualapi and attacked a band of natives at Muchoas Canyon near the Santa Maria Mountains. They killed several and the defeat demoralized the rest.
Sources: 47, 91

AZ25 *Battle of Skeleton Cave* or *Battle of the Caves* • December 28, 1872
Location: Mazatzal Mountains near the Salt River
War: Tonto Basin Campaign
Gen. George Crook, during a successful Tonto Basin Campaign in which he claimed that he and his men killed over 500 Apaches over a span of 142 days, sought to kill Delche, an Apache chief. Crook was told by one native that Delche's stronghold was in a cave north of the Salt River, and Nantaje (an Apache scout hired by Crook) offered to take him there.

When Crook's force arrived in the area, his 220 soldiers camped near the cave. Before dawn on December 28, a party of 12 to 15 sharpshooters sneaked near the cave and discovered warriors dancing around a fire. The soldiers fired, killing six. At the sound of gunfire, the rest of the army came and surrounded the cave.

The soldiers ordered the natives to surrender, and did so in a language they believed the Apaches would understand. However, they were mistaken as to the identity of the natives, who turned out to be Yavapais, who spoke a totally different language. When the natives did not surrender, the soldiers dropped rocks on them, forcing them further into the cave. Shots fired into the cave ricocheted off the ceiling and walls and killed several. A charge by 20 warriors armed with bows and arrows resulted in the deaths of six or seven of them.

When the battle ended, 76 of the Yavapais were dead, with 20 women and children taken prisoner. The attackers lost only one, a Pima scout.
Sources: 47, 48, 91, 298

AZ26 *Attack on Wickenburg* • March, 1873
Location: Wickenburg
War: Tonto Basin Campaign
While Gen. George Crook and his soldiers were patrolling the mountains, a war party attacked Wickenburg and killed several. They ran off herds of horses and cattle, then headed toward the edge of Bradshaw Mountain and the Tonto Basin. Maj. George M. Randall, Lt. Bourke, and scouts and cavalry pursued them, but were unsuccessful because they waited to begin until the following day.
Sources: 48

AZ27 *Battle in Hembrillo Canyon* • April, 1880
Location: Hembrillo Canyon
War: Victorio's Rebellion
Col. Edward Hatch had three battalions converging on Mescalero in an attempt to devastate the Apaches, while Col. Benjamin H. Grierson marched a column west from Fort Concho in Texas to fight any Mescaleros heading east. Capt. Henry Carroll led another unit, which became ill from drinking from a spring which contained gypsum.

Carroll's men came into Hembrillo Canyon in search of good water and found springs, but they also found Victorio and his Mescaleros. The warriors surrounded the soldiers and the battle commenced, lasting into the night. The arrival of a portion of Col. Edward Hatch's battalion saved Carroll from total annihilation.
Sources: 48

AZ28 *Battle on the Fresco River* • May, 1880
Location: Fresco River
War: Victorio's Rebellion
Col. Edward Hatch and his men camped along the Fresco River and requested additional troops and scouts to continue his pursuit of the Mescaleros. Henry K. Parker and Apache scouts also set out in pursuit, and found Victorio and his band in an isolated canyon at the headwaters of the Palomas River. He sent word to Hatch to join him in the attack.

Parker had 30 scouts positioned so that at daybreak they opened fire. The Mescaleros ran, but into a line of 20 more scouts. The Mescaleros then established defensive positions and began to fight back. By the end of the day, at least 30 of Victorio's men had been killed, but Parker's group was nearly out of ammunition. They withdrew with a victory, but it is believed that if Hatch had responded with troops, the war could have been ended with this battle.
Sources: 48

AZ29 *Battle at Cibecu Creek* or *Cibecu Massacre* • August 30, 1881
Location: White Mountains
War: Apache War
Medicine man Nochedelklinne was preaching a new religion to the Apaches and teaching that dead warriors would return to drive out the whites. According to the white eyewitnesses, he was arrested by Col. Eugene A. Carr of the 6th Cavalry, then taken toward Fort Apache along Cibecu Creek. They set up camp for the night, and Nochedelklinne's supporters crowded close to the camp. During a gun battle which broke out, Carr ordered the medicine man killed, but he was only shot in the thighs and crawled away. Another soldier shot him after thrusting the barrel of his gun into Nochedelklinne's mouth, and then a civilian guide smashed his head with an axe. Six soldiers and one officer were killed during the battle, which lasted until dark.

The White Mountain Apache version of the encounter tells of Nochedelklinne being shot before any shots were fired by natives. The Apaches who had served as army scouts deserted their post and fought on the side of Nochedelklinne's supporters. The army estimated that they killed 18 Apaches.
Sources: 47, 48, 66, 91, 134, 167, 298, 385

AZ30 *Attack at Fort Apache* • September 1, 1881
Location: Fort Apache
War: Apache War
After the death of Nochedelklinne, Col. Eugene A. Carr headed back with his troops toward Fort Apache. They reached it on September 2, dispelling rumors that they had been massacred.

While they were on the way, the natives conducted several attacks near the fort and killed six whites. On September 1, they attacked the fort from two sides, unusual for a people who generally engaged in guerrilla warfare. They wounded an officer, shot Carr's horse out from under him, and burned several buildings in fighting that ended at dark.
Sources: 47, 48, 91, 167, 298

AZ31   *Battle of Big Dry Wash* • July 17, 1882
Location: Canyon Diablo, Tonto Basin
War: Apache War
Two companies of cavalry led by Majs. A.W. Evans and A.R. Chaffee left from Fort Thomas and another left from Fort McDowell, all to chase the Apaches who were reported to be heading toward the Tonto Basin. On July 16, they found evidence of the presence of the natives. The next morning, they began climbing toward the Tonto Basin and sighted warriors at about 11:00 a.m.

At a branch of Canyon Diablo, the Apaches opened fire, believing the army to be much smaller than it actually was. The soldiers recaptured 70 horses and killed and wounded some warriors, with the rest retreating to the Sierra Madre in Mexico.
Sources: 46, 47, 385

AZ32   *Apache Raids* • March 21–April 1, 1883
Location: Southwest of Fort Huachuca
War: Apache War
Chatto, Chihuahua and Bonito, Chiricahua minor chiefs, led a band of 25 warriors out of Mexico and into Arizona, where they carried on raids. They were sought, but never sighted, by several army units. Over a route of over 400 miles, they killed 26 while losing only one.
Sources: 20, 45, 46, 70, 91, 168

AZ33   *Attack at Guadalupe Canyon* • June 8, 1885
Location: Guadalupe Canyon
War: Geronimo's Rebellion
A band of Apaches led by Chihuahua attacked the 4th Cavalry led by Capt. Henry W. Lawton. It happened at noon, while Lawton and his officers were out scouting. The warriors killed five and took two horses and five mules.
Sources: 91

ARKANSAS

AR1   *Battle of Fort Carlos* • April 17, 1783
Location: Arkansas River
War: Revolutionary War
British sympathizer James Colbert, who had married a Chickasaw woman and become one of their leaders, led 100 whites and 14 natives by canoe to attack Spanish Fort Carlos, commanded by Capt. Jacob Dubreuil. They overran the nearby white settlement and captured Lt. de Villiers and his family.

Dubreuil asked for help from the nearby Kappa village, but those natives did not want to get involved. Colbert attacked the fort, which was defended by cannon. A counterattack was mounted by Sgt. Pastor, some Spanish soldiers and four

Quapaws, who caused the attackers to flee back to their boats and in the confusion several of their captives escaped.
Sources: 330, 355

AR2   *Attack at Blue River* • November 17, 1823
Location: Blue River
In response to increasing white intrusion into their territory, 200 Osages led by Mad Buffalo attacked a hunting party of whites and mixed-blood Quapaws. They killed and decapitated five. A demand from Col. Matthew Arbuckle of Fort Smith that Osage chief Clermont give up the guilty warriors was ignored.
Sources: 304

AR3   *Battle of Pea Ridge* or *Battle of Elkhorn Tavern* • March 7–8, 1862
Location: Pea Ridge
War: Civil War
Natives often fought with armies in minor skirmishes during the Civil War, some for each side, and usually in the western theater. At Pea Ridge, the only major battle in Arkansas in which natives participated, the Union utilized about 3,000 natives. Of the 135 Oneidas who fought, only 55 returned. On the Confederate side were about 1,000 Cherokees led by Albert Pike.

Gen. Earl Van Dorn split his force of 16,000 Confederate soldiers, and personally led half on a night march around Pea Ridge into the rear of the 10,500-man Union army. The other half of the Confederates were taken by Gen. Ben McCulloch and Pike to the west end of Pea Ridge. They intended to catch the Union army commanded by Gen. Samuel Ryan Curtis between them and destroy it.

The Confederates attacked the Union soldiers, pushing them back. Three surges over six hours gained ground for the Confederates, and each time the Union soldiers formed a new defensive line. The other prong of the Confederate attack was met by artillery fire which caused the 1,000 Cherokees to desert the fight.

The next morning, the tired graycoats spread out in a defensive line, which Curtis attacked. Weakening the defenders with artillery and charging with infantry, the Union army was able to break the Confederates, who fled to the north, east and west. The Confederate dead included McCulloch and Gen. James McQueen. The Union victory ended the Confederate threat to Missouri.
Monument: Pea Ridge National Military Park, US 62E, Pea Ridge, AR 72751.
Sources: 5, 19, 20, 51, 58, 60, 93, 105, 133, 173, 197, 294

AR4   *Battle of Poison Springs* • April 18, 1864
Location: Near Camden
War: Civil War
Choctaw Col. Tandy Walker led the 1st Regiment of Choctaw and Chickasaw Mounted Rifles for the Confederacy. At the Battle of Poison Springs, they inflicted a major defeat on Union forces and were commended for noble, gallant and glorious service.
Sources: 60

CALIFORNIA

CA1 *Uprising Against San Diego Mission* • November, 1775
Location: San Diego
War: Mission Uprisings
Natives were rounded up to live at Spanish missions and were forced to use Spanish names and wear clothing very different from their native dress. When they were punished for even slight infractions, they were whipped, mutilated, branded, executed, or placed in solitary confinement without water. Within the missions, men and women were forced to live separately, and they were fed inadequate food.
   Several uprisings against the missions were attempted, but were generally unsuccessful. In 1775, 800 Ipai and Tipai natives from nine villages united to burn down the San Diego mission. In the year it took to put down the uprising, Father Luis Juame and two other Spaniards were killed.
Sources: 90, 147

CA2 *Yuma Massacre* • July 18, 1781
Location: Lompoc
War: Mission Uprisings
The missions of Purisima Conception and San Pedro y San Pablo were attacked by a band of Yuma warriors. Shot or clubbed to death were all of the missions' friars and all of the male settlers in the area. Also killed were Capt. Rivera and the men in his command, plus Father Garces, the trails priest.
   Gov. Neve and military commander Pedro Fages began a campaign against the natives, who took refuge in an inaccessible rocky area safe from the Spaniards.
Museum: The Fort Yuma Quechan Museum is located directly across the bridge from downtown Yuma.
Sources: 72, 73, 74, 75, 76, 288

CA3 *Uprising Against San Gabriel Mission* • 1785
Location: San Gabriel
War: Mission Uprisings
Toypurina, a native medicine woman, lead an unsuccessful attempt to destroy the mission located east of Los Angeles.
Sources: 147

CA4 *Uprising Against Santa Ynez Mission* • February, 1824
Location: Santa Ynez
War: Mission Uprisings
A group of Chumash natives destroyed a portion of the mission at Santa Ynez, then with other natives from San Fernando captured La Purisima in Baja California. They then fought and drove off troops at the mission at Santa Barbara, sacked it, and fled to the hills. Casualties included seven natives and four Spaniards. Later, a truce was reached and several who had led the uprisings were executed or sentenced to years of hard labor.
Sources: 74, 147

CA5 *Raid on Mission San Luis Obispo* • 1840
Location: San Luis Obispo
War: Mission Uprisings
Working with white traders, horses were supplied for the white settlers by Utes, Navajos, Nez Perce, Yakimas, Shawnees and Delawares. To get them, they often raided the Spanish missions. In one raid on Mission San Luis Obispo by a force led by Walkara of the Utes and mountain man Pegleg Smith, 1,200 horses were captured and sold to the white settlers.

Later, Walkara continued to raid and sell the captured horses to the Mormons, who needed them for their new settlement in Utah.
Sources: 20

CA6 *Bloody Island Massacre* • May, 1850
Location: Clear Lake, east of Ukiah
Two Americans, Andrew Kelsey and Charles Stone, captured hundreds of Pomo natives and forced them to work on a cattle ranch they had taken over from the Mexicans. Some died from starvation, some from whipping, and another was shot. When two of the Pomos lost one of Kelsey's horses, they knew the punishment would be severe. Before the lost horse was discovered, the Pomos decided to strike.

Five men found Kelsey and Stone and killed them both. The tribe fled into the hills. They were found by soldiers led by Capt. Nathanial Lyon who unsuccessfully searched for the five who had killed the white men. They instead killed 130 warriors, women and children on what came to be known as Bloody Island, then killed every group of natives they encountered on their way out of the valley.
Sources: 69, 124, 147, 275

CA7 *Attack on Modoc Village* • Late 1851
Location: Near Yreka
War: Rogue River War
During the summer of 1851, natives attacked a pack train bound for gold fields along the Shasta River and stole 46 mules and horses. They may have been Snakes or Paiutes, but the animals wound up in the hands of the Modocs, likely by trade.

Three packers were attacked on Bear Creek near the Rogue River in Oregon, and the two survivors traveled to Yreka. About 20 settlers in Yreka assembled a party led by Ben Wright to recover the stolen animals and punish the offenders. They rode into the Rogue Valley and shot two natives, taking four hostages.

The volunteers also attacked the Shasta village near Yreka, then carried on pre-dawn attacks in the Scott Valley. They attacked a Tolowa village and killed four in an hour-long battle.

In the later part of 1851, they attacked a Modoc village at dawn, killing several and recovering the horses which had been taken during the summer.
Sources: 262, 337

CA8 *Bloody Point Massacre* • August or September, 1852
Location: Eastern shore of Tule Lake
It is believed by many that a massacre of settlers by Modocs occurred at Bloody

Point on the eastern shore of Tule Lake. Some descriptions of the event, however, indicate that it was a composite of a series of events. Ben White and Col. John E. Ross found from 22 to 36 bodies, which they buried. Other reports place the number in the area killed by the Modocs that summer as high as 70.

The draining of Tule Lake decades later exposed several charred wagons and portions of human skeletons.
Sources: 72, 75, 138, 254, 263, 337

CA9 *Ben Wright Massacre* • November, 1852
Location: Black Bluff
Ben Wright led a party of settlers to a supposed parley with a band of Modocs. Instead, the whites attacked the native village in retaliation for attacks on supply wagons. Only five of the 46 warriors present at the time of the attack escaped.
Sources: 74, 75, 124, 138, 262

CA10 *Smith River Massacres* • 1853–54
Location: Smith River
War: Klamath War
During 1853, the Tolowa village of Hawunkwutwas was burned and about 70 natives were killed in an attack by white settlers. In January of 1854, another seven natives were killed by the whites.
Sources: 337

CA11 *Skirmish at Yreka Cave* • January 26, 1856
Location: Near Yreka
War: Klamath War
Lt. George Crook, Henry Judah, John Bonnycastle and 20 volunteers from Fort Jones rode to Yreka, and the Shastas took refuge in a cave by the Klamath River. The troops shot a few howitzer charges into the cave, and when a volunteer poked his head over the cliff to survey the damage, he was shot dead. By dark, both sides agreed to a peace and about 50 Shastas emerged from the cave.
Sources: 124, 337

CA12 *Humboldt Bay Massacre* • February 25, 1860
Location: Near Arcata
Fifteen to 20 men, constituting a portion of the army company led by Capt. Thomas F. Wright, took the boats of Capt. Buhner and sneaked across Humboldt Bay to Gunther's Island, and killed nine native men and 47 women and children. The following day, they rode to Indian Island near Eureka and killed three more men. All but two of the rest of the native men ran away, and the whites then killed the remaining two men and the 51 women and children, using hatchets.

When the action was criticized in the *Northern Californian* newspaper, the anti-native whites in Union (now Arcata) forced the youthful editor, Bret Harte, to leave town.
Sources: 75, 76, 124, 147

CA13 *Battle of Land's Ranch* • December 21, 1872
Location: East of Tule Lake
War: Modoc War

After the Modocs left southern Oregon for the Lava Beds in California, the army sent out parties to station various areas. This included Capt. R.F. Bernard, who was positioned at the ranch of Louis Land. On December 21, an ammunition train from Fort Bidwell arrived, and the Modocs attacked it before it was unloaded.

The first volley killed two of the five white escorts and five of the horses. Lt. J.G. Kyle saved the ammunition by ordering his men to march from the ranch to the battle scene, before getting their horses ready, and arriving before the wagons could be unloaded.

Sources: 69, 91, 263

CA14 *First Battle for the Stronghold* • January 16–17, 1873
Location: South shore of Tule Lake
War: Modoc War

At the time of the November 29 attack at Captain Jack's village on the Lost River in Oregon, white settlers attacked another Modoc Village on the same river. Two of the attackers were killed and one was wounded. Hooker Jim and his warriors escaped, and on the way to Tule Lake killed 12 to 14 white homesteaders. The two bands of Modocs, totalling 160, found shelter in a natural fortress in the lava beds along the north shore in an area known as Captain Jack's Stronghold.

In December, 225 regular soldiers and 104 volunteers from Oregon and California arrived and camped nearby. On January 13, they were driven away by a few shots fired at a great distance.

They attacked on January 16 with a pincers movement designed to trap the Modocs. However, they had trouble with the terrain and the accurate native rifle fire, which pinned down the soldiers. At nightfall, the soldiers retreated and returned the next day only to recover their dead. They had nine killed and 28 wounded, while the 50 to 100 Modoc warriors suffered no casualties. They were so well hidden, they were not even seen.

Monument: Lava Beds National Monument, SR 139, P.O. Box 867, Tulelake, CA 96134.

Sources: 33, 66, 69, 70, 72, 74, 75, 91, 135, 138, 236, 262, 263, 380

CA15 *First Battle of Scorpion Point* • January 22, 1873
Location: Southeast corner of Tule Lake
War: Modoc War

Capt. R.F. Bernard was ordered to leave Land's ranch with his men and proceed to Applegate's ranch on Clear Lake. The following morning, he sent a party back to Land's to retrieve three tons of grain. As they passed Scorpion Point on the way back to Applegate's, the Modocs opened fire on the two wagons and 22 escorts. The escorts abandoned the wagons and later returned to get them. Although the grain and wagons had been destroyed, the horses were retrieved. The natives suffered no casualties.

Sources: 69, 91, 263

CA16 *Second Battle for the Stronghold* • April 15–17, 1873
Location: South shore of Tule Lake
War: Modoc War

On April 11, a council was held to attempt to establish peace. Captain Jack repeated his demand for a separate reservation for his people, but he was again denied. He then pulled out a pistol and killed Gen. Edward R.S. Canby; two other whites were shot and stabbed, and a fourth escaped.

In retaliation, Col. Alvin Gillem led troops and 72 Tenino mercenary scouts onto the lava beds, supported by mortars and mountain howitzers. Two companies took positions a mile west at Hovey Point, ready to come out of concealment if the Modocs were to flee the Stronghold. On the morning of April 15, troops led by Capt. M.P. Miller and others advanced.

The first shot of the battle happened accidentally, when a soldier stumbled on the rough ground. The Modocs returned fire, and eight natives moved into position to slow down the oncoming army of 400, and were successful for six hours. On the first day, three soldiers were killed and six were injured.

The army attempted to bombard the Stronghold with artillery fire, but they had mistakenly set up too far away, so few shells made it to their target. The next day, the companies of Majs. John Green and E.C. Mason coordinated their efforts and built six-man rock forts close to the headquarters of Captain Jack. They eroded the prestige of shaman Curley Headed Doctor by crossing a "magic" red tule rope and killing a warrior, two events that the shaman said could not happen.

During the second night, Jack ordered an evacuation since the camp was running out of water. On April 17, the Modocs left the Stronghold to establish a new position to the south in another natural lava fortress. The army did not notice the evacuation until after it was complete at about 11:00 a.m. on April 17. Reports stated that eleven Modocs had been killed in the fighting.

Sources: 5, 33, 66, 69, 70, 72, 74, 75, 91, 132, 138, 254, 262, 263, 380, 408

CA17   *Thomas-Wright Massacre* • April 26, 1873
Location: South of Tule Lake
War: Modoc War

Col. Alvin Gillem sent Capt. Evan Thomas of the 4th Artillery and Capt. Thomas F. Wright of the 12th Infantry plus 62 others, to the new position of the Modocs in the lava plateau south of Tule Lake. They marched into an area where the Modocs were concealed in ambush.

As the warriors were about to open fire, the soldiers broke ranks and rested for lunch in the shade of Hardin Butte (named after an army private) near the edge of the Schonchin Lava Flow (then called the Black Ledge). No sentries were positioned, and the men were bunched together in a small area. When Modoc marksmen opened fire, the soldiers ran out of the cul de sac. An attempt was made by the infantry to charge the main Modoc position, but heavy fire caused them to break and run.

The Modocs shot and killed Thomas, Wright and 20 others and wounded 16 more. The Modocs lost none. About 3:00 p.m., Scarfaced Charley announced that the battle was over, allowing the survivors to retreat back to their headquarters. The Modocs allowed a rescue party the following day to retrieve the few wounded survivors.

Sources: 33, 66, 69, 91, 254, 262, 263

CA18   *Second Battle of Scorpion Point* • May 2, 1873
Location: Southeast corner of Tule Lake
War: Modoc War

From 15 to 20 Modocs attacked a train of three or four wagons which were carrying supplies to the camp on Scorpion Point. During the fighting, two infantrymen and one cavalryman from the escort were wounded, but were able to escape with the rest.
Sources: 254, 263

CA19   *Battle of Dry Lake* • May 10, 1873
Location: 10 miles southeast of Tule Lake
War: Modoc War
Capt. H.C. Hasbrouck took a portion of the 4th Artillery and camped at Dry Lake in an expedition to find and fight the Modocs. They found the water in the nearby Sorass Lake to be undrinkable, and had no success in digging wells. They decided to spend the night there and leave in the morning. Before they could, Captain Jack attempted to drive the soldiers out of the region with an attack on their camp. Initially, the soldiers attempted to run away, but the officers brought them under control.

They surprised the Modocs by charging, and fatally wounded one of the warriors. Then, Donald McKay and his Warm Springs native scouts began firing on the Modocs at their rear. The Modocs became discouraged. Hooker Jim broke away from the rest with 13 warriors and their families and headed toward Dorris. Captain Jack left with about 30 warriors toward Clear Lake.
Sources: 33, 66, 69, 70, 132, 254, 262, 263

CA20   *Battle of Willow Creek Ridge* • May 22, 1873
Location: West of Tule Lake
War: Modoc War
On May 14, the army began pursuit of Hooker Jim and his band. He had a safe camp on Sheep Mountain which might have remained unfound for weeks, but when he and his band moved out to Willow Creek to see what was going on, the army located their trail. The cavalry pursued them for eight miles along a ridge and captured five women, five children and a few horses. With the help of the captured women, the warriors surrendered on May 22 and offered to help the army track down Captain Jack in exchange for clemency. They reached Jack's camp on May 28 and attacked the next day.

The Modocs scattered, and over the next four days the army hunted them down and killed them. Captain Jack himself surrendered on June 3. He and four others were hanged on October 3 at Fort Klamath, and Jack's remains were placed on display in Washington, D.C. The remaining 155 Modocs were shipped to Oklahoma, where many died of disease.
Sources: 33, 69, 70, 91, 135, 138, 254, 262, 263

COLORADO

CO1 *Attack at Cerro de San Antonio* • 1716
Location: South of Antonito
War: Mission Uprisings
Comanches and Ute allies had attacked Taos, Tewa pueblos, and Spanish settlements. In response, interim governor Don Felix Martinez sent Capt. Cristobal de la Serna to attack a large Ute camp south of the mountain of Cerro de San Antonio. He included within his force 50 natives, likely Jicarilla Apaches.

The Utes believed that the Spanish were coming to their camp to discuss peace terms, and were surprised when de la Serna attacked. Several Utes were killed and many others fled. Many prisoners were taken by de la Serna back to Santa Fe, and from there they went to Mexico where they were sold into slavery.
Sources: 246

CO2 *Battle of Greenhorn Peak* • Fall, 1779
Location: Southeast Colorado
War: De Anza Campaign
Don Juan Bautista de Anza was assigned a post in New Mexico in 1779, and assembled a force of 600 men including 259 native allies. They and allied Pueblos proceeded north into Comanche country in eastern Colorado and found the camp of Cuerno Verde (Kuhtsoo-ehkuh, or Green Horn).

The chief and most of the warriors were away from the camp, raiding Taos, when de Anza attacked. He destroyed the lodges and killed the women and children. Knowing that Cuerno Verde and the warriors would be returning soon, he laid an ambush for them near Greenhorn Peak. Cuerno Verde was killed and only a few survived, and de Anza returned to Santa Fe in triumph.
Sources: 29, 103, 284

CO3 *Attack at Fort Pueblo* • December 24, 1854
Location: Pueblo
War: Ute War
A party of Utes led by Chief Tierra Blanca attacked Fort Pueblo on the Arkansas River and killed all of its inhabitants except Romaldo, a herder. He was shot through the jaw, had his tongue cut off, and reached the Baca ranch two miles away before he died. The Utes then attacked settlements in the San Luis Valley and threatened Fort Massachusetts.
Sources: 29, 229, 356

CO4 *Attack at Bent's New Fort* • July, 1860
Location: Near Fowler
Lt. J.E.B. Stuart leading 20 soldiers followed a small party of Kiowas to an area not far from Bent's new fort. Combining with a force led by Capt. William Steele, they killed two warriors and captured 16 women and children.
Sources: 227

CO5   *Battle at Ash Creek* • May 16, 1864
Location: Near the South Platte River
War: Cheyenne-Arapaho War
Lean Bear of the Cheyennes had been presented a medal by president Lincoln and a large American flag by Col. A.B. Greenwood, and believed that he would be treated well by soldiers when he returned to his homeland from a trip to Washington, D.C. After he returned, he heard that soldiers had attacked some Cheyennes along the South Platte River, and moved his camp one day's march north to find out what was going on.

Early on the morning after they established camp, hunters returned with the news that soldiers were approaching with cannon. Lean Bear and an escort of warriors rode out to meet with soldiers and talk with them. The warriors remained at a distance while Lean Bear approached alone, wearing his medal and carrying papers he had been given in Washington certifying that he was a friend of the United States.

When he got within 20 or 30 yards of the soldiers, they opened fire on him and his escort party. The warriors fought back with guns and bows and arrows while the soldiers used grapeshot in the cannons. Black Kettle, another chief who had been honored in Washington, rode up and ordered his braves to stop the fighting. When they did, the soldiers ran off. The Cheyennes had three dead, including Lean Bear and Star, and several were wounded. Some of the warriors chased the soldiers to Fort Larned in a running battle.

The soldiers were members of the Colorado Volunteers commanded by Col. John M. Chivington, who had no authority to operate in Kansas. According to the officer in the patrol, Lt. George S. Eayre, they were ordered by Chivington to kill Cheyennes "whenever and wherever found."
Sources: 70

CO6   *Fight at Fremont's Orchard* • May, 1864
Location: North of Denver
War: Cheyenne-Arapaho War
The Hotamitaneos of the Southern Cheyenne were known as Dog Soldiers. A band of them was attacked at Fremont's Orchard by a patrol of Colorado Volunteers, led by Col. John M. Chivington, who had been looking for stolen horses. The Cheyennes were herding a mule and horse picked up as strays, and Chivington's men opened fire without giving them a chance to explain where they got them.
Sources: 70

CO7   *Attacks Along the South Platte River* • Mid-July, 1864
Location: Northeastern Colorado
War: Cheyenne-Arapaho War
A band of natives killed two settlers at Bijou Ranch and stole 17 horses. They then went to the Junction stage station and took five horses, then took 60 more from Murray's Ranch. They conducted a raid near Valley Station (now Sterling) on July 18, killing cattle and causing the women and children of the area to seek safety in Denver.
Sources: 362

CO8 *Sand Creek Massacre* or *Chivington Massacre* • November 29, 1864
Location: Sand Creek
War: Cheyenne-Arapaho War
After meeting in Denver with Territorial Governor John Evans and the Colorado military commander, Col. John M. Chivington, Black Kettle and his Cheyennes believed that they had received assurances that they could safely camp near Fort Lyon. They headed to the fort in southeastern Colorado and set up camp.

Chivington arrived at the fort and told the officers of his plan to attack the camp. Several protested, considering it to be a breach of the pledge of safety that had been given by Majs. Edward W. Wynkoop and Scott J. Anthony. Chivington explained that his men were trained to kill Indians and that was what they were going to do. Many had avoided the draft into the armies fighting in the Civil War going on in the east, choosing instead to serve against poorly equipped natives closer to their homes in Colorado. Court martial threats convinced the officers to go with Chivington.

At dawn on November 29, Chivington and a force of over 700 volunteers attacked the sleeping Cheyenne village while many of the warriors were away on a hunting expedition. Estimates of the dead ranged from 69 to over 600, many being cut down as they ran from the village toward the creek bed for protection. Food stores were plundered and dead men, women and children were mutilated by the soldiers. Those who survived the attack faced freezing or starvation.

The remaining Cheyennes crossed the plains to another Cheyenne camp of Dog Soldiers, those who preferred fighting with the white man rather than peace.
Memorial: There is a marker at the site of the massacre, on a dirt road leading from SR 96 about 8 miles north of Chivington, CO.
Sources: 7, 8, 20, 28, 29, 57, 59, 60, 62, 66, 70, 92, 101, 102, 103, 109, 110, 114, 135, 142, 147, 159, 182, 189, 197, 213, 218, 220, 224, 227, 253, 254, 267, 275, 278, 288, 315, 325, 362, 380, 392, 405, 407

CO9 *Attacks in Colorado* • January and February, 1865
Location: Platte River
War: Cheyenne-Arapaho War
War parties composed of Sioux, Cheyenne and Arapahos conducted raids along the Platte River and both of its branches. They burned ranches and stage stations, tore down telegraph wires, and halted the mails, supply trains and stagecoaches. They effectively cut off Denver, Salt Lake City and San Francisco from communication with the eastern portion of the country.

A thousand Cheyennes and Lakotas attacked and burned the town of Julesburg on January 7. To Fort Sedgwick (formerly called Fort Rankin) were brought the bodies of 13 soldiers and five civilians. Fifty-five warriors were killed during the raid.

The war parties left Colorado in mid-February and headed toward the White River in South Dakota.
Museum: Fort Sedgwick Depot Museum, 200 W. 1st St., Julesburg, CO 80737, has exhibits relating to local history.
Sources: 66, 70, 110, 147, 267, 350, 362

CO10 *Battle of Summit Springs* • July 11, 1869
Location: Atwood
Tall Bull and his Dog Soldiers had come west after their battle with the soldiers

along the Republican River in Nebraska in May. As they were preparing to cross the Platte River, Pawnee scouts working for Maj. Frank North found their trail. They followed the trail for over 160 miles until they came upon the Sioux and Cheyenne camp of 85 lodges, housing about 500.

The soldiers and the 150 Pawnee moved to within a mile and a half of the camp, undetected until one cavalry company unnecessarily allowed itself to be seen. At about 3:00 p.m., the soldiers led by Gen. Eugene A. Carr attacked the camp from east and west, so the only escape was to the south. Twenty, including Tall Bull, took cover in a ravine. The only survivor from that party was a wounded German immigrant that Tall Bull had captured in May.

A total of 52 Cheyenne were killed, including Tall Bull. A band of warriors sacrificed themselves to allow the retreat of the women and children.

The natives scattered into small groups and avoided Carr's pursuit parties, meeting back together a few days later. As revenge, they tore up railroad tracks, attacked small settlements, and killed many. They captured German immigrants Maria Weichel and Susannah Allerdice (Alderdice) at a ranch house.
Sources: 13, 29, 70, 91, 114, 201, 275, 328, 350, 380, 410

CO11 *Meeker Massacre* or *Thornburgh Ambush* or
       White River Massacre • September 29, 1879
Location: Meeker
War: Ute War
Indian Agent Nathan Meeker was facing an uprising at the White River Agency as a result of native protests over white plowing of grazing land, so he sent for help. Maj. Thomas Thornburgh led a party from Fort Fred Steele, near Rawlins, WY, and was ambushed by the Utes. Thornburgh and nine of his men were killed and 43 were captured.

After the massacre, 25 Northern Ute rebels led by Douglas attacked the agency and took white captives including Josephine, the daughter of Nathan Meeker. Meeker and seven or eight young men working for him were killed, and three to five captives were held for 23 days. Southern Ute Chief Ouray intervened and assisted in their release.
Museums: (1) The Ute Indian Museum is located at 17253 Chipeta Dr., Montrose, CO 81401, on the site of the farm that was Ouray's last residence; (2) The Meeker Home Museum is located at 1324 9th Ave., Meeker, CO 81641; (3) The White River Museum at 265 Park Ave., Meeker, CO, also has some relevant exhibits.
Sources: 13, 19, 25, 29, 66, 91, 101, 133, 203, 254, 331, 350, 356, 421

CONNECTICUT

CT1 *Attack on the Connecticut River* • 1634
       Location: About 6 miles north of the mouth of the Connecticut River

War: Pequot War

The Pequots began a campaign to eliminate the British from Connecticut. In 1634, Capt. Stone and his seven men were killed on and near his boat as it sat in the Connecticut River. The natives were not Pequots, but had dealings with them including trading some of the goods plundered from Capt. Stone's bark. They turned out to be Niantics, allies of the Pequots.

The Council of Massachusetts spoke with the Pequots and entered into treaties with them, but were not completely satisfied.

Also during the same year, the Pequots attacked the Hope, a Dutch trading post near present Hartford.

Sources: 1, 199, 275

CT2   *Attack at Block Island* • May 20, 1636
        Location: Block Island
        War: Pequot War
        John Gallop was sailing by Block Island with his sons and a servant when he spotted the pinnace of fellow trader Capt. John Oldham. Its deck was full of natives, so he rammed it and they jumped overboard. He captured and bound four, then threw them into the water.

He found Oldham's body, still warm, with his head bashed in. The hands and feet appeared to be cut as if the natives were in the process of removing them. Oldham had been a friend and frequent trader with the Narragansetts.

The English retaliated in August with an expedition of 90 volunteers, but the natives were alerted to it early and they were only able to kill a few strays and loot the Narragansett village.

Sources: 1, 53, 95, 133, 199, 212, 279, 320, 334, 412

CT3   *Attack at Long Island* • Mid-1636
        Location: Long Island
        War: Pequot War
        Two white settlers were killed at Long Island. In retaliation, a force of 120 led by Capts. Turner, John Underhill and John Endicott, met with the Pequots, killed one and burned some of their homes.

The Pequots became enraged against the British. In early 1636, five more were killed and seven were taken prisoner by the Pequots. It was reported that those taken alive were later tortured to death.

Sources: 1, 133, 199, 334, 412

CT4   *Attack at Butterfield's Meadow* • October, 1636
        Location: Calve's Island
        War: Pequot War
        Lt. Lion Gardiner sent five men to gather hay on an island near the Lyme shore, when they were attacked by Pequots. They caught one named Butterfield, killed him, and then ate him. The place was then referred to as Butterfield's Meadow.
        Sources: 412

CT5   *Attack Near Fort Saybrook* • February 22, 1637
        Location: Fort Saybrook
        War: Pequot War

Lt. Lion Gardiner, ten men and three dogs traveled about half a mile from Fort Saybrook to burn weeds and reeds in which the Pequots might conceal themselves. Four natives were hiding in the burning reeds and ran off. Others attacked, wounding John Spencer and Lt. Gardiner and killing two others. Several arrows made Gardiner look a pincushion, but his buffcoat saved him from death.
Sources: 412

CT6 *Siege at Fort Saybrook* • March, 1637
Location: Fort Saybrook
War: Pequot War
John Endicott and a force of 90 volunteers carried on a brief expedition against the Pequots, and in one action along the Pequot River a warrior was killed and scalped.

 In retaliation for this action, the Pequots besieged Fort Saybrook, named after two landowners, Viscount Say and Lord Brooke. The Pequots concealed themselves in whatever cover was available. When a settler or trader would venture out to collect hay, they would kill him. Occasionally, skirmishes would break out and several settlers were killed. The siege was broken by small forces of private citizens who arrived from Boston and Hartford.
Sources: 53, 95, 275, 334, 412

CT7 *Battle at Wethersfield* • April 23, 1637
Location: Wethersfield
War: Pequot War
About 100 Pequots set an ambush here for the British, and during the battle which ensued killed six men, three women, 20 cows and a horse, and captured two young women. They butchered the animals and burned the haystacks and storehouses. Within two days, the Pequots canoed past the fort with the two girls and the victims' shirts billowing like sails, to taunt the soldiers. The girls were later rescued by the Dutch.

 The Pequots attempted to enlist the help of the Narragansetts and the Mohegans, but those groups chose not to take up arms against the British.
Sources: 1, 212, 279, 320, 334, 412

CT8 *Battle at Fort Saybrook* • Early May, 1637
Location: Fort at Saybrook
War: Pequot War
Capt. John Mason and 90 Connecticut men, plus a band of 100 to 200 friendly Mohegans led by Uncas, had difficulty traveling down the shallow waters of the Connecticut River toward Saybrook, and at the Mohegans' request the warriors were put ashore to make better time on their journey. Along the way, they encountered the Pequots near the fort at Saybrook and killed seven.
Sources: 1, 334

CT9 *Massacre at Fort Mystic* • May 26, 1637
Location: Stonington
War: Pequot War
John Underhill, Lt. Lion Gardiner and Capt. John Mason, leading 77 Englishmen and a band of Mohegans led by Uncas, sailed east from Fort Saybrook and

arrived at Point Judith on May 20. They put ashore and marched west to the Mystic River, reaching it on May 24. They were accompanied by Miantonomo's 200 Narragansetts, many of whom were intimidated by the size of the Pequot force, and drifted away.

They attacked the Pequots just before dawn on May 25. The English force entered the fort through the barricaded entrances, and the waking Pequots fought back fiercely. When they saw they could not subdue the natives, Mason and Underhill had their men set fire to the wigwams, and the flames soon engulfed the entire fort. Hundreds of Pequots burned to death, and those that attempted to escape were shot down as they exited the fort. Between 300 and 700 Pequots were killed (only seven survived), while the English lost only two and had 20 wounded.

The battle site was finally determined in 1987 to be a two-acre plot atop a circular embankment known as Pequot Hill.

Sources: 1, 34, 53, 60, 92, 106, 126, 135, 189, 199, 272, 275, 279, 284, 320, 334, 380, 412

CT10   *Battle at New Haven* • May 26, 1637
Location: Near New Haven
War: Pequot War
The soldiers commanded by Capt. John Mason and John Underhill sailed into Quinnypiag, later known as New Haven. Ensign Davenport and Sgt. Jeffries met a party of Pequots in a swamp and killed few, but reinforcements arrived and surrounded the natives within the swamp. The British considered cutting down the swamp or building a structure to enclose it.

Instead of taking further aggressive action against the Pequots, they sent in Thomas Stanton to talk with them, resulting in the surrender of 200 old men, women and children. The following day, the soldiers engaged the Pequots in fighting. The soldiers held them off, killing few, and 50 to 70 Pequots escaped.

Sources: 1, 133, 279

CT11   *Battle in Quinnipiac Swamp* • May, 1637
Location: Connecticut Coast near New Haven
War: Pequot War
Following the massacre at Fort Mystic, several of the Pequots went to live with the Montauks or the Narragansetts. Sassacus, on the other hand, persuaded some to follow him toward the Mohawk country to the west. Along the way to the Connecticut River, they killed several English settlers.

At Quinnipiac Swamp near New Haven, a force led by Capt. John Mason attacked a group of Pequot women and children, and annihilated them.

Sources: 90, 334, 381

CT12   *Attack at Fairfield* • July 28, 1637
Location: Fairfield
War: Pequot War
At Fairfield, 200 of the band led by Sassacus surrendered to the English, and the remaining 80 warriors fought until they broke through the English encirclement and escaped.

When the Pequots reached the Mohawks, they were rebuffed. Sassacus had

planned on an alliance with the Mohawks, but they were more interested in trading with the Europeans, so they killed him, ending the Pequot War. The few remaining Pequots joined other tribes.
Sources: 53, 90, 133, 334, 381

CT13   *Battle at Wabaquasset* • June 2, 1676
Location: Wabaquasset
War: King Philip's War
Maj. John Talcott led a force of 440 English soldiers and natives north from Norwich in an expedition against the enemy. They located a native fort at Wabaquasset and a growing corn crop, but no natives. They continued on and found them, killing or capturing 52 of them. Talcott, having lost none of his own men, then continued north to Quabaug.
Sources: 152, 226

DELAWARE

DE1   *Massacre at Lewes* • 1631
Location: Lewes
War: Dutch Colonization
Dutch settlers established the settlement of Lewes, just inside Cape Henlopen. For two years during the mid-1620s, they had maintained a trading post at the mouth of Timber Creek, Pennsylvania, near the Schuylkill River.

    In 1631, a massacre by natives wiped out Lewes, and the Dutch shifted their emphasis from settlement to the fur trade.
Sources: 290

DE2   *Swanendael Massacre* • November, 1632
Location: Cape Henlopen
War: Dutch Colonization
Three natives pretended to arrive for a trade at the farm of Gillis van Hoossett. In revenge for the death of their chief (actually killed by the natives themselves, after being accused by the settlers of theft), they killed van Hoossett and another man. They also put 25 arrows into the bulldog chained to the house.

    Other natives attacked 32 colonists in the fields, killing them all.
Sources: 16, 179

FLORIDA

FL1   *Landing of Ponce de Leon* • June 3, 1513
Location: Southwest Coast
War: Spanish Exploration
In 1513, Juan Ponce de Leon left from Puerto Rico with three ships, the "Santiago," "San Cristobal," and the "Santa Maria de la Consolacion." He began his search for the Fountain of Youth, which he had heard about from a native of Puerto Rico. He also searched for gold and men with tails. What he did find was the Gulf Stream and what he believed to be an immense island which turned out to be Florida.

> After initially landing on the east coast, perhaps north of New Smyrna Beach, he sailed south, west and north around the cape to the area near Apalachicola, then southeast to Charlotte Harbor before sailing to Hispanola. He and his men were repulsed by 20 Calusa or Ais in 20 war canoes. Several natives and one Spaniard were killed, and eight natives were captured. The next day, 80 war canoes appeared and fired arrows at the Spanish ships, but did no damage.
Sources: 88, 92, 127, 327, 347, 360, 368

FL2   *Landing of Cordova* • April 18, 1517
Location: Charlotte Harbor
War: Spanish Exploration
Francisco Hernandez de Cordova's expedition to Mexico stopped at the prior landing place of Ponce de Leon, in search of water. Twenty-one men led by Diaz del Castillo went ashore, dug wells, and filled water casks for the remainder of their voyage. As they prepared to return to their ship a band of Calusas or Ais attacked and wounded about six Spaniards. One was carried off alive, and presumably was sacrificed. Estimates of the number of natives killed in the battle ranged from 23 to 32.
Sources: 327, 360, 368

FL3   *Second Landing of Ponce de Leon* • July, 1521
Location: Charlotte Harbor
War: Spanish Exploration
When Ponce de Leon and 200 to 250 men landed (some believe the landing place to be at Tampa Bay) to establish settlements, they were attacked by the natives. They recalled an incident which caused the Spaniards to leave quickly on their previous voyage. It may have been related to de Leon's reputation as a slave catcher. He was seriously wounded in the thigh by an infected arrow, retired to Cuba, and died a few days later. At least 80 Spaniards died during the battle or later of their wounds.

> The Calusas and their king, Carlos, enhanced their power and prestige through the capture and enslavement or sacrifice of the survivors of Spanish shipwrecks, along with the salvage of gold, silver, and other cargo.
Monument: A historic marker to commemorate the landing is located at 98 Tamiami Tr., Punta Gorda, FL.
Sources: 17, 108, 127, 137, 145, 147, 153, 275, 327, 347, 360, 368

FL4   *Encounter at the Withlacoochee River* • May 16, 1528
       Location: Withlacoochee River
       War: Narvaez Expedition
       Gov. Pamfilo de Narvaez sailed in 1527 from Spain to conquer and govern
       provinces in the New World. On his way northward through Florida, he encoun-
       tered several groups of natives. Leaving 100 with his three ships in Tampa Bay,
       Narvaez took 260 men on foot with 40 mounted soldiers and headed north
       through the Florida peninsula.
             As they completed a northbound crossing of the Withlacoochee by raft, they
       were met by 200 Timucuans who were felt to be gesturing menacingly, so the
       Spanish soldiers seized six of them. They were forced to show the soldiers their
       homes, from which the soldiers took corn.
       Sources: 71, 127, 137, 360, 412

FL5   *Attacks at Apalachen* • June 17, 1528
       Location: West bank of the Apalachicola River
       War: Narvaez Expedition
       Gov. Pamfilo de Narvaez ordered Cabeza de Vaca to attack the native village of
       Apalachen (Apalache), and he led nine cavalrymen and fifty foot solders on the
       invasion. When they arrived, they found only women and children, but the men
       soon returned and fired on the soldiers with arrows. Inspector Solis' horse was
       the only casualty, and the warriors fled. Two hours later, they returned to ask for
       the release of the women and children, which was granted by the Spanish.
             On June 18, the warriors attacked because of agitation over the soldiers'
       holding of one of their chiefs. One native was killed before they withdrew. On
       June 19, a similar attack and withdrawal resulted in the death of another native.
       Sources: 71, 354, 360, 412

FL6   *Ambush South of Apalachen* • July 20, 1528
       Location: South of Apalachen
       War: Narvaez Expedition
       The Spanish army left Apalachen in search of Aute on the Gulf of Mexico, a nine
       days' walk away. Two days out of Apalachen, they were crossing a lake when they
       were attacked by natives who wounded several and captured the soldiers' guide.
       The soldiers returned the fire and the natives withdrew. Dismounted cavalry
       chased the warriors back to the lake.
             On the following day, another ambush chased the Spanish onto an open
       plain, and then they worked their way back into the woods. The counterattack
       resulted in the deaths of two warriors, with three or four soldiers sustaining
       wounds.
       Sources: 71, 145, 412

FL7   *Attack at Aute* • August 2, 1528
       Location: Mouth of the Apalachicola River
       War: Narvaez Expedition
       Natives attacked the camp of Gov. Pamfilo de Narvaez, finding many of the sol-
       diers ill with malaria. The attack resulted in the death of one Spanish horse.
       Sources: 71, 145, 360, 412

FL8   *Attack Near Pensacola* • October 27, 1528
Location: Near Pensacola
War: Narvaez Expedition
During the daytime, the 242 Spaniards were met by unarmed natives who canoed to them and spoke with them. They were offered food and water, and Gov. Pamfilo de Narvaez presented them with presents. Narvaez and a small party were lodged in the chief's residence and the rest slept along the beach.

During the night, the Panzacola natives attacked the soldiers and killed three. Narvaez was hit in the face with a rock. About 150 natives battled with the soldiers, who forced them to flee when Capts. Dorantes, Penalosa and Tellez attacked their rear with 15 men.
Sources: 71, 360, 412

FL9   *Battle of the Two Lakes* • September 15, 1539
Location: Napituca (near present Luraville)
War: De Soto Expedition
Hernando de Soto, on his way north to Apalache, had his men spend the night at the village of Napituca, near the Suwannee River. While they were there, a party of about 15 Utinas, from one of the Timucua tribes, approached de Soto to ask for the release of their leader, the cacique of Caliquen. De Soto said that he was not held captive, but resisted giving him up.

Between 300 and 400 Utinas came within sight of the camp and emissaries again asked for the release of the cacique. The Spanish attacked, killing 30 to 40 with lances. The rest retreated to two large shallow lakes. During the night, fighting went on in the shallow water, so neither side had any rest.

The following day, Juan Ortiz convinced them that it would be better to surrender, and all but 12 did. When those resisting were pulled out of the lake, a brief skirmish ensued, resulting in the deaths of several more of the natives. De Soto and his expedition continued north.
Monument: De Soto National Memorial, 75th St. NW, P.O. Box 14871, Bradenton, FL 34280.
Sources: 5, 121, 122, 177, 186, 244, 327, 360, 368

FL10   *Massacre of Dominicans* • 1547
Location: Tampa Bay
War: Spanish Exploration
A party of Dominicans was martyred on the beach as they disembarked in Tampa Bay.
Sources: 326

FL11   *Attack at Spanish Outpost* • 1566
Location: Mound Key, southwest of Fort Myers
War: Spanish Exploration
Don Juan Menendez led the expedition in this part of Florida, near the Calusa capital at Mound Key. Under the command of Capt. Francisco de Reinoso, an outpost was established nearby. While it was being constructed, a boat party was attacked by the Calusa, resulting in the deaths of three Spanish soldiers. Menendez was hit in the chest with a spear, but was saved from injury by his breastplate.

Later, the Calusas attempted to capture Father Juan de Rogel and make him a human sacrifice. The Spanish were frequently harassed by the Calusas and other natives.
Sources: 327, 368

FL12 *Destruction of San Mateo* • April 13, 1568
Location: Jacksonville
War: Spanish Exploration
Fort Caroline was established in 1564 near the mouth of the St. Johns River by French Hugenots led by Rene Goulaine de Laudonniere. On September 20, 1565, the colony was destroyed by Pedro Menendez de Aviles and reestablished as the colony of San Mateo.
In 1568, it was attacked and destroyed by French soldier Dominique de Gourgues and a party of 180, assisted by a band of Timucuans.
Museum: A reconstructed fort and museum are located near the intersection of Monument and Fort Caroline Rds., Jacksonville.
Sources: 19, 162, 232, 381

FL13 *Attack on Landing Party* • 1569
Location: Mound Key
War: Spanish Exploration
Pedro Menendez Marquez, a nephew of Don Juan Menendez, sent out a landing party in 1569. It was attacked on Mound Key by a band of Calusas. To retaliate, Menendez Marquez killed Don Felipe, the native leader whom the Spanish had put in charge of the natives.
Sources: 327

FL14 *Skirmishes at Missions* • February 19, 1647–February, 1648
Location: Near Tallahassee
War: Apalachee Rebellion
The Apalachinos rebelled as a result of demands made by the military garrison at Apalache. The revolt began at the frontier mission of San Antonio de Bacuqua where people had gathered to celebrate the feast day of the mission's patron saint. Thirty-one Spanish soldiers were sent from St. Augustine, and were accompanied by 500 Timicuans.
Spanish losses included the deaths of three missionaries and the burning of seven churches. Some friendly Apalachees helped end the violence, and the rebellion's leaders were sentenced to death or forced labor. The revolution was believed to have been brought about by the influence of the Yuchi (Chisca) tribe.
A party of soldiers led by Capt. Don Martin de Cuera fought the natives in a lengthy engagement, but failed to subdue it. Later, Franciso Menendez Marquez obtained the help of the Christian chiefs and was able to round up the ringleaders and execute 12 of them with a garrote. Another 26 were sentenced to labor, and the rebellion ended.
Sources: 49, 104, 332, 333, 359, 366, 368

FL15 *Destruction of Missions* • 1656
Location: Near St. Augustine
War: Timucua Rebellion

In April, Spanish governor Diego de Rebolledo heard that the English were planning to invade Florida. He wanted to recruit 500 Timucuans to serve at San Agustin, but the natives rebelled, apparently beginning with the western Apalachee and the Yustega mission natives. Included in those killed was Francisco Menendez Marquez, who had put down the hostilities in 1647.

Rebolledo was blamed for the rebellion, was imprisoned, and died shortly thereafter. The hostilities were put down eight months after they began by Adrian de Canicares.

Sources: 49, 92, 137, 241, 359, 360, 368

FL16 *Attack on Hunting Party* • 1699
Location: Northern Florida
Francisco de Florencia was accompanying 40 Chacatos on a buffalo hunt when they came upon a party of 24 natives traveling from Taisquique to Apalache to trade skins, shirts and other goods. Florencia and his party attacked and killed 16 and took the goods they had carried for trade. They took them to Ayubale to be the first targets in 1704 in the major assault on Apalache.
Sources: 49

FL17 *Attack on Santa Fe* • March 20, 1702
Location: Santa Fe, Alachua County
War: Queen Anne's War
Encouraged by the British, bands of Lower Creeks, Yuchis and Cherokees attacked tribes across the border in Florida. On this date, the natives attacked the Timucuan town and burned the church before being driven off. Other similar raids in the northern part of the state effectively eliminated the north Florida aborigines, creating a void which later was filled by the Lower Creeks.
Sources: 49, 111, 241, 368

FL18 *Ambush of Apalachee* • 1702
Location: Apalachicola River
War: Queen Anne's War
In retaliation of the attack on Santa Fe and the murder of three Apalachee traders, 800 Apalachee and a few Spanish soldiers attacked towns along the Apalachicola River. On the way there, they were ambushed, reducing their numbers to 300.
Sources: 49

FL19 *Attack at St. Augustine* • Fall, 1702
Location: St. Augustine
War: Queen Anne's War
Creek warriors accompanied and encouraged by several hundred British militiamen sailed from Port Royal, South Carolina, and attacked Spanish St. Augustine. Led by Gov. James Moore, the force destroyed native settlements around the town but, lacking sufficient artillery, could not conduct a siege of the fort. When two hostile Spanish frigates arrived, the South Carolina force returned home.
Museum: Castillo de San Marcos National Monument is located on Avenida Menendez, SR A1A and US 1, St. Augustine.
Sources: 137, 326, 328, 353, 354, 359

FL20   *Attacks Against Apalachee Missions* • January–August, 1704
Location: Northern Florida
War: Queen Anne's War
South Carolina Gov. James Moore, 50 British soldiers and 1,000 to 1,300 Creeks, Yamassees, Muskogees and Apalachicolas left Ocmulgee in December of 1703 on an expedition to attack and destroy all of the Apalachee towns in north Florida. The first attack was January 14, 1704, at the Ayubale mission, resulting in a burned building and the death of 25 Apalachees. The 84 who survived were captured and taken to Charleston, South Carolina. On the following day, Spanish troops led by Capt. Ruiz Mexia arrived from Fort San Luis. They were able to kill seven English and about 100 natives before all of the Spanish were killed or taken prisoner.

The second major attack took place in June, with the capture of the towns of Patale and Aspalaga and the destruction of Escambe. The populations of San Luis and Ivitachuco abandoned their homes.

The chief of Ibitachka surrendered his church and ten horses with provisions. Five other towns unconditionally surrendered. A few of the Apalachee who were not killed or taken prisoner resettled in the area near present-day Mobile, Alabama. Some also settled near Pensacola, and after the British took over in 1763, moved again to Vera Cruz in Mexico.

With the destruction of 14 towns and the elimination of the Apalachee from the region, a mixed group of Hitchiti, Oconee and other Muskhogean-speaking tribes moved in. They were later known as Seminoles.
Monument: A historic marker was erected on private property at the site of the Mission of San Pedro in Tallahassee.
Sources: 49, 89, 92, 111, 137, 143, 153, 275, 284, 326, 328, 332, 333, 343, 354, 355, 368, 388

FL21   *Attack at Pensacola* • 1707
Location: Pensacola
A band of Tallapooses stormed into Pensacola and burned the town, laying siege to the Spanish fort. They could not capture the fort, but returned in October of 1708 and killed many Spaniards and natives. They were still unable to take the fort.
Sources: 111

FL22   *Attacks on Native Villages* • October, 1719
Location: Near St. Augustine
War: Yamassee War
To avenge an attack on English settlements in South Carolina, including the capture of the wife and child of Capt. Burroughs, Col. John Barnwell organized an expedition to attack the Spaniards and Yamassees living near St. Augustine. They left Port Royal, South Carolina, on September 28 with a band of Coosa led by King Gilbert, plus a few Tuscaroras. On October 10, they landed at San Juan and traveled the rest of the way to St. Augustine on foot.

On October 12, they reached the native towns. The residents of Pocotaligo Town were alerted by one of the expedition's native scouts, whose family lived there. Nevertheless, several natives were killed and the homes were burned. At the town of Tuloomata, within a mile of Castile de San Marcos, the Spanish church was burned but Friar Pedro de la Lastras escaped. An Apalachee village was found deserted, and the invaders burned its granary and town house.

A company of Spanish soldiers came upon the scene, and the invaders explained that they had no quarrel with them, only with the Yamassees who had taken the Burroughs as captives. The Spanish engaged them in battle anyway, had 14 of their soldiers killed, and had about ten taken prisoner as they retreated.

The expedition returned to South Carolina, reaching Col. Barnwell's home on October 28.

Sources: 332

FL23 *Attack on St. Augustine* • March 9, 1728
Location: St. Augustine
War: Yamassee War
Gov. Middleton had the South Carolina Assembly raise an army in mid-1727, consisting of 110 white men and about the same number of natives, likely Lower Chickasaws. It also included a few Cusabos, Tuscaroras and Cape Fears. The force was led by Capt. John Hunt, Capt. William Peter and Col. John Palmer. Their goal was to fight the Yamassee and subdue them without conflict with the Spaniards, with whom they were, at least officially, at peace.

On March 9, they attacked a native town near Castillo de San Marcos and killed at least 30 of the Yamassees. Fourteen were taken captive, and the town was set on fire. The church was plundered and the Spaniards in the fort began a three-day ineffective artillery bombardment. After four days, the English left for South Carolina.

The expedition was successful in showing the Yamassees that the English were more powerful than previously thought, and lifted the fear of the native attacks in South Carolina.

Sources: 92, 111, 332, 359

FL24 *Attack on St. Augustine* • May, 1740
Location: St. Augustine
Cowkeeper assisted Gen. James Oglethorpe in his unsuccessful attack on Spanish St. Augustine, with a force including several hundred Cherokees plus Yamacraws, Creeks and other natives. Fort St. Francis de Pupa, about five miles southeast of present Green Cove Springs, FL, was captured by Oglethorpe and then destroyed when he and his men withdrew during the summer. This period marked the beginning of the Alachua Seminoles' settlement in the area.

Sources: 111, 153, 241, 381

FL25 *Attack on Sloop* • July, 1748
Location: Near Cape Florida
An English sloop carrying a cargo of logs from Honduras to New England ran aground about five leagues off Cape Florida. It was attacked by about 60 natives in 20 canoes, and 11 men aboard the vessel were killed. The incident was reported by Briton Hammon, a black who was taken prisoner.

Sources: 368

FL26 *Battle of Thomas Creek* • May 17, 1777
Location: Thomas Creek, on the Duval/Nassau county line
War: Revolutionary War
An American expedition to capture St. Augustine led by Lt. Col. Samuel Elbert

was attacked by British soldiers, mounted East Florida Rangers, and natives. Led by Maj. J.M. Prevost and Col. Thomas Brown, they repelled the Americans, who retreated from Florida.

Monument: A historic marker was erected in the median of US 1 south of Callahan, FL, in 1975.

Sources: 153

FL27 *Battle of Pensacola* • March–May, 1781
Location: Pensacola
War: Revolutionary War

An army of 4,000 Spanish grenadiers, French chasseurs, seamen, Louisiana creoles, blacks, Belgians, Irish, Walloonians, Hatians and natives led by Bernardo de Galvez sailed to Pensacola. They were defeated by 1,500 British soldiers supported by 500 to 2,000 Choctaws and Creeks led by Alexander McGillivray and William McIntosh. The Choctaws fought well, but received little help from the British regulars. After the Spanish army was increased to 7,000 by reinforcements, Gen. John Campbell surrendered the town to the Spanish.

Sources: 162, 199, 209, 319, 355, 380

FL28 *Battle of Newnans Lake* • September 27, 1812
Location: East of Gainesville
War: War of 1812

Settlers in Georgia, with the help of a regiment of soldiers from Tennessee, sought to take Florida from Spain. Border incidents occurred without the support of the federal government. Spanish Gov. Kindelan encouraged the Florida Seminoles to attack the Georgians, beginning in July. In response, Col. Daniel Newnan led 117 Georgians about 100 miles into Spanish Florida to destroy the natives. He attacked, or was attacked by, 75 to 150 Seminoles and blacks led by King Payne and Billy Bowlegs. From September 27 to October 11, a running fight ensued.

At least three of Newnan's men were killed and seven were wounded on September 27, as was King Payne. The soldiers erected breastworks and after about a week, they became sick and returned to New Hope on the St. Johns River. The fighting hardened feelings between the Georgians and Creeks on one side, and the Seminoles on the other.

Memorial: A bronze marker dedicated by the Gainesville Chapter of the D.A.R. was placed at the site of the battle. It has been stolen and replaced several times, and might still be found northeast of Rochelle on the northwest side of CR 234, between SR 20 and SE 16th Ave.

Sources: 23, 92, 143, 153, 155, 187, 335, 368, 397

FL29 *Border Incidents* • February, 1813
Location: North Central Florida

Col. John Williams, the adjutant general of the Tennessee militia, and 250 mounted Tennessee volunteers crossed south from Georgia with a detachment of U.S. regular soldiers. Included was Maj. Gen. Thomas Pinckney, the former governor of South Carolina. For three weeks beginning on February 7, they burned 386 Seminole homes in two towns, destroyed 1,500–2,000 bushels of corn, and drove away several hundred head of cattle and horses.

The Seminoles in this part of Florida faced starvation and lacked their former military strength.

Sources: 187, 368

FL30   *Attack on Blount's Fort* • July 26, 1816
Location: West bank of Apalachicola River, about 60 miles south of Georgia
At the end of the War of 1812, the British turned over Fort Apalachicola, also known as Blount's Fort, to the natives and blacks who had assisted them in the war. Gen. Edmund P. Gaines, the commander of Fort Scott further up the river, contacted the U.S. Secretary of War and inquired about what he should do about it. His reply from Gen. Andrew Jackson was to blow it up, as it was believed to "have been established by some villains for the purpose of rapine and plunder." Gaines assigned the task to Lt. Col. Duncan L. Clinch.

Clinch, his army of regulars and 500 Creeks led by half-breed William McIntosh traveled to the fort. Two navy gunboats were sent up the Apalachicola for transport of slaves back to their owners. Firing began at dawn, and Capt. Jairus Loomis realized that the heavy earth walls could not be damaged. Instead, he had the cannonballs heated and fired at the fort's powder magazine, which exploded and burned the fort.

The explosion instantly killed 270 of the fort's 334 inhabitants. Only three of the survivors escaped without injury, and the rest were taken to Georgia for their return to slave owners. The Creek allies were given over $200,000 of property to compensate them for their support.

Sources: 34, 54, 113, 133, 240, 296, 333, 335, 340, 354, 402

FL31   *Attack on Alachua Village* • November, 1817
Location: Old Town
War: First Seminole War
After his successes in the Creek War, Gen. Andrew Jackson was placed in charge of the army's campaign to rid Florida of Seminoles. The U.S. raid on a tribal village here marked the first encounter of the First Seminole War.

The natives were led by Billy Bowlegs and initially did well in the battle, but Jackson's training and numbers proved to be the decisive factors. In the face of a general charge by the army, the Seminoles pulled back to the swamp. Jackson reported the killing of several, plus the capture of 300 women and children and several thousand cattle and horses.

Sources: 151, 402

FL32   *Capture of St. Marks* • April 7, 1818
Location: Panhandle
War: First Seminole War
Gen. Andrew Jackson led an army of nearly 3,500 American soldiers and 2,000 Lower Creeks, marching into Florida to attack the Upper Creeks (Red Sticks) and Seminoles. They burned villages along the Suwannee River and captured St. Marks and, on May 24, Pensacola, each of which had been held by the Spanish.

Sources: 34, 37, 38, 39, 41, 90, 133, 147, 151, 157, 240, 296, 315, 333, 335

FL33   *Battle Along Ecofina Creek* • April 13, 1818
Location: Ecofina Creek

War: First Seminole War

In the morning, William McIntosh led his Creek warriors with the army of Gen. Andrew Jackson against the Red Stick band of 200 led by Peter McQueen and the Ockmulgee chief Oponay. During the running battle, the Red Sticks had 36 or 37 killed, while Jackson's force lost only three. The black allies of the natives fought while the Seminoles and Red Sticks escaped.

The war soon ended and the Spanish ceded Florida to the U.S. on February 22, 1819.

Sources: 39, 157, 333

FL34   *Skirmish at Hickory Sink* • June, 1835

Location: 3½ miles northeast of Archer

Two or three members of the Spring Grove Guard were helping settlers search for lost cattle that they thought may have been stolen, when they came across a Seminole hunting party roasting beef near Hickory Sink. They overpowered the natives and took their packs and rifles. As they were beating them with whips to teach them a lesson, other members of the hunting party arrived and fired at the settlers.

Two or three settlers were wounded, and they returned the fire and killed one Seminole. Everyone quickly retreated. Area whites became more incensed against the natives, and future senator David Yulee urged the government to do whatever it would take to move the Seminoles out of Florida.

Sources: 61

FL35   *Skirmish in Orlando* • September, 1835

Location: Downtown Orlando

While troops were sleeping, Orlando Reeves kept watch for hostile Indians. He saw what he thought was a log in the lake, but as he realized it was an Indian and gave an alarm, he was killed with an arrow. The exact location of the battle is not known, but is believed to have been at Lake Cherokee about a mile to the southeast, as the area around Lake Eola was a swamp in 1835 and an unlikely camp.

It is generally accepted that Reeves' grave and the settlement that grew up near it was called "Orlando's Grave," and then simply "Orlando." Early Orlando historian E.H. Gore believed that the grave was located beneath the large oak tree near the present sidewalk in front of 16 Lake Ave., a few blocks to the southeast of Lake Eola.

Monument: An engraved stone tablet was placed in Lake Eola Park, Orlando, in 1939 by students from Cherokee Junior High School.

Sources: 151, 184, 185, 302, 303

FL36   *Battle of Black Point* or *Battle of Kanapaha Prairie* • December 18, 1835

Location: Along the rim of the Alachua Savannah, 5 miles east of Archer

War: Second Seminole War

Maj. Gen. Richard K. Call and 500 horsemen constituted a militia force near the camps of the natives in Alachua County, with the intention of preventing attacks which had been made against isolated homes, such as those which had occurred in the Wacahoota area. The baggage train of Col. John Warren was detached at Kanapaha, so that it could be taken through Micanopy to Wetumpka, when it was attacked by about 80 warriors led by Osceola.

Capt. Richards and his men left at the beginning of the attack. The rest continued shooting until a soldier was shot through the body. They loaded him onto a cart and began to retreat. Three Seminoles attacking the cart were shot dead by rifle fire. Other natives looted the abandoned wagons.

Dr. McLemore arrived with 30 horsemen, but did not charge as a united group despite his orders to do so, resulting in the deaths of six and the wounding of eight. The survivors left for Fort Crum to get reinforcements.

Days later, the band of warriors was located and engaged by six companies, with some of the fighting taking place in waist-deep water in a pond. The warriors fled, leaving the papers and some of the belongings which had been taken previously.

Sources: 157, 187, 287, 335, 402

FL37 *Destruction of Halifax Plantations* • December 25–26, 1835
Location: In and near Bulowville
War: Second Seminole War

John von Bulow and other plantation owners felt that the presence of the army might antagonize the natives in the area, with whom they generally had good relations. The settlers resisted the efforts of Brig. Gen. Joseph M. Hernandez who tried to protect them.

The sugar plantations, including the Cruger-DePeyster Plantation, were destroyed by Philip and his Mikasuki warriors. Destruction of the successful plantations destroyed the local sugar industry and caused a significant portion of Florida to be deserted by the white settlers.

Sources: 151, 187

FL38 *Dade Massacre* • December 28, 1835
Location: Southwest of Bushnell
War: Second Seminole War

In late December, Maj. Francis L. Dade was leading 107 men from Fort Brooke (Tampa) to reinforce the garrison northeast at Fort King (Ocala). At 8 a.m. on December 28, Chief Alligator and a party of from 180 to 400 Seminoles attacked and caught the soldiers off guard. The weather was cold and the men had their overcoats buttoned over their ammunition boxes.

The Seminoles and blacks were anxious to avenge the army's 1816 attack on Blount's Fort. The first volley from the Seminoles led by chiefs Micanopy and Jumper killed about half of the soldiers, and by 2 p.m. all but five were dead. Four made it back to Tampa. The Seminoles had three killed and five wounded. Seven weeks later, other troops discovered the 103 vulture-picked bodies lying where they fell, and buried them. They were reburied on August 15, 1842, in the National Cemetery in St. Augustine.

The army's slave guide, Louis Pacheco, may have notified the Seminoles of the planned march, allowing them to prepare for the ambush. During the battle, Pacheco escaped and fled to the Seminoles for protection. He became a good friend of Coachoochee (Wildcat).

This marked the essential beginning of the war, starting just days before the Indians' removal to Oklahoma was to commence on January 1, 1836. After Maj. Dade were named Dade City in Pasco County, and Dade County which includes Miami.

Memorials: (1) Dade Battlefield State Historic Site, P.O. Box 938, (intersection of CRs 603 and 605), Bushnell, FL 33513, has a visitor center, lodge (built 1955), log breastwork, nature trail, and remnants of the Fort King Military Road built in 1828; (2) The National Cemetery in St. Augustine has large pyramidal grave markers, under which the remains of the soldiers are buried.

Sources: 13, 17, 19, 91, 92, 113, 117, 118, 143, 151, 153, 156, 157, 180, 187, 196, 207, 252, 275, 291, 315, 333, 335, 367, 402

FL39   *Ambush at Fort King* • December 28, 1835
Location: Ocala
War: Second Seminole War

On a knoll was located Fort King, first occupied in 1827 and named after Col. William King. Adjacent to it was a Seminole agency established in 1825. Chief Osceola (also known as Billy Powell, a Red Stick Creek) in 1833 refused to go along with other Seminoles who had agreed to their relocation. The soldiers did not understand the importance of his refusal to "touch the pen" at the parley at Payne's Landing. In November of 1835, Osceola killed petty chieftain Charley Emathla, who had spoken in favor of relocation.

   On the afternoon of December 28, 1835, while most of the soldiers were about 20 miles to the northwest at Gen. Clinch's plantation, Indian agent Gen. Wiley Thompson and Lt. Constantine Smith were ambushed and killed about 300 yards from the fort by Osceola and his warriors. Osceola had previously been placed in irons and (he believed) had been insulted by Thompson. The warriors then went to the fort's store a short distance away and killed its three occupants. They were buried at the site of the present monument, then later reburied in the National Cemetery in St. Augustine.

   This was another battle marking the substantial beginning of the war, taking place on the same day as the Dade Massacre. The settlement which was established near the fort became Ocala, the county seat of Marion County.
Monument: There is an engraved stone marker at the Fort King site at the northwest corner of Ft. King St. and 43rd Ave. in Ocala.
Sources: 13, 17, 34, 153, 154, 157, 173, 187, 241, 291, 315, 335, 402

FL40   *First Battle of the Withlacoochee* • December 31, 1835
Location: Cove of the Withlacoochee
War: Second Seminole War

After a three-day march from Fort Drane, the army reached the north bank of the Withlacoochee River where the north-flowing water forms a big bend. The army had not yet heard of the Dade Massacre of three days before.

   Fortunately, they did not arrive at the most likely fording spot, where the Seminoles were waiting in ambush. They only way to cross was an old native canoe on the far bank, across 50 yards of swift, deep water. The regular soldiers crossed the river in the canoe in shifts, and continued about 400 yards into a horseshoe-shaped clearing surrounded by a thick hammock. The volunteers remained on the north bank.

   The 200 regulars and 30 volunteers were attacked by about 150 to 250 Seminoles and 30 blacks led by Osceola and Alligator. At the suggestion of Lt. Col. Fanning, Lt. Col. Duncan L. Clinch ordered three bayonet charges. A third of the soldiers died. The volunteers crossed the river to help, and that turned out to be essential. They formed two lines and the regulars fell back to form a defensible position until the volunteers constructed a log bridge, which the regulars used to cross to safety.

The army had four killed and 59 wounded, while the natives lost three and had five wounded. The army left to return to Fort Drane. The Seminoles were confident in the leadership of Osceola.

Sources: 13, 91, 113, 143, 157, 187, 196, 241, 291, 315, 333, 335, 367

FL41 *Cooley Massacre* • January 6, 1836
Location: Tarpon Bend of New River, Fort Lauderdale
War: Second Seminole War
While the regular lighthouse keeper was away on vacation, William Cooley was in charge of the lighthouse on Key Biscayne. While Cooley was away from his home on the New River, his family was attacked by a band of Seminole warriors who murdered Mrs. Cooley, their three children and Joseph Flinton, their tutor.
Sources: 153, 367

FL42 *Battle at Anderson's Plantation* • January 17, 1836
Location: Dunlawton
War: Second Seminole War
Brig. Gen. Joseph M. Hernandez established a strong point at the Bulow Plantation, and led citizen soldiers who were involved in several skirmishes in the area. The most severe was at the Anderson Plantation, where Maj. Benjamin A. Putnam of the Florida Volunteers led the St. Augustine Guards.

The 120 Seminoles led by Coacoochee killed four and wounded 13. This constituted half of his men, and Putnam ordered a retreat.
Sources: 94, 187, 335

FL43 *Second Battle of the Withlacoochee* or
     Battle of Camp Izard • February 27–March 6, 1836
Location: Withlacoochee River
War: Second Seminole War
Maj. Gen. Edmund P. Gaines left Fort King on February 26 for Fort Brooke, along the route taken by Maj. Francis L. Dade. The following day, when he and his 980 men reached the area in which Gen. Duncan L. Clinch had fought two months before, there were shots fired at them by a force of 700 to 1,100 Seminoles from the south bank across the Withlacoochee River. After an hour, they withdrew into the woods north of the river bank for the night.

On the morning of February 28, the army moved down the river for two to three miles to the ford. The Seminoles on the south bank shot Lt. James F. Izard as he was making preparations to cross with an advance party. He died five days later. During the natives' fire, lasting from 9 a.m. to 4 p.m., the army erected a log breastwork enclosing about 250 yards square, called Camp Izard.

On February 29, shots were fired from three sides into Camp Izard, and the Seminoles set fire to the brush and grass. A wind shift saved the camp. Gaines sent for reinforcements, but a lack of food necessitated the butchering of the horses and mules. Gen. Clinch, who could have left from Fort Drane to rescue Gaines, was ordered by Gen. Winfield Scott on March 1 not to take his men to help at Camp Izard.

However, Clinch was also obligated to obey Gaines, who had ordered him to help, and he prepared to disobey Scott. On March 4, Scott changed his mind and allowed Clinch to rescue Gaines, but by the time this message reached Clinch, he had already begun his march toward Camp Izard.

On the evening of March 5, Gaines and Osceola agreed to a council to be held the following day. Jumper, Alligator and Osceola attended and agreed to lift the siege if Gaines would allow them to remain in the area. Before a definitive answer could be given, Clinch arrived with his column. A volley chased the natives away and the men in the camp mobilized, reaching Fort Drane on March 8.

This battle resulted in the deaths of 44 soldiers and the wounding of many others.

Sources: 91, 157, 187, 241, 291, 315, 335, 402

FL44   *Skirmish at Volusia* • March 22, 1836
Location: Volusia/Astor
War: Second Seminole War
Brevet Brig. Gen. Abraham Eustis reached St. Augustine on February 15 to lead South Carolina volunteers in establishing small posts along the east coast. On March 15, he took his column to the St. Johns River near present Astor. After two companies crossed, they were shot at by Seminoles. Three of the volunteers were killed and six were wounded. It took four more days to complete the crossing for the 1,400 men.

Eustis continued on to the native village of Peliklakaha, which he found abandoned. After burning it, he led his men on the road to Fort Brooke, where he met up with wings commanded by Col. William Lindsay and Gen. Duncan L. Clinch.

Sources: 187

FL45   *Battle Along Fort Brooke–Fort King Trail* • March 26, 1836
Location: Near Fort Alabama
War: Second Seminole War
Col. William Lindsay led the center section of troops and built a fort where the Fort Brooke–Fort King Trail crossed the Hillsborough River. Calling it Fort Alabama, it functioned as a supply base. When completed on March 20, a small garrison remained to defend it, while the rest returned to Fort Brooke. On March 21, Lindsay received orders to move his men to Chocachatti on March 25.

On March 26, on the way to Chocachatti, Seminole fire struck the column from a thick hammock. Lindsay ordered a bayonet charge, and in it two soldiers were killed and two were wounded. The column continued on and reached Chocachatti on March 28 to meet up with the other two wings of the army. On March 31, they headed toward Fort Brooke, frightened the Seminoles out of Fort Alabama, and re-stationed a garrison there.

Sources: 143, 187

FL46   *Battle at Camp Izard* • March 29, 1836
Location: Camp Izard
War: Second Seminole War
Commanded by Gen. Duncan L. Clinch and consisting of 1,968 men, a wing of the army left Fort Drane on March 26 and arrived on March 28 at Camp Izard,

now commanded by Gen. Winfield Scott. During the evening, the enemy came into camp and killed two.

At 4 a.m. on March 29, the army began crossing the Withlacoochee River to the south shore on large flatboats constructed at Fort Drane. Rifle fire came from the south bank and a midstream island. Scott ordered bayonet charges, and the Seminoles were dislodged from the bank. On March 31, there was additional shooting which resulted in two dead and 13 wounded soldiers.
Sources: 187, 241

FL47 *Siege of Cooper's Post* • April 5–17, 1836
Location: Near Inverness
War: Second Seminole War
Fort Cooper, a picket fort in the heart of the area known as the Cove of the Withlacoochee, was closely surrounded by about 250 Seminoles from April 5 to 17. Inside was a battalion of Georgia volunteers and a few regulars, commanded by Maj. A. Cooper.
Memorial: An interpretive center at the fort site is in Fort Cooper State Park, 3100 S. Old Floral City Rd., Inverness.
Sources: 187, 335

FL48 *Siege of Blockhouse* • April 12–May 29, 1836
Location: 12 miles from the mouth of the Withlacoochee River
War: Second Seminole War
On April 4, a blockhouse was established by Maj. John McLemore, who left a garrison of 50 Florida militia commanded by Capt. Holleman. On April 12, Seminoles surrounded it and kept it under siege for 48 days. They burned off the roof and the provisions dwindled to parched corn. Nevertheless, the soldiers held off the 500 natives. Holleman died and was replaced by Lt. L.B. Walker.

After a man left the fort and sneaked through the enemy line, Gen. Winfield Scott was apprised of the situation. On May 1, he ordered Gen. Duncan L. Clinch to help. After consulting with his officers, Clinch concluded that he had an insufficient force, and called to citizens in nearby counties for volunteers.

For nearly a month, volunteers did not appear. Then a detachment led by Leigh Read arrived and saved the soldiers, who accused Gen. Scott of having abandoned them.
Sources: 187

FL49 *Attack at Fort Barnwell* • April 14, 1836
Location: Volusia
War: Second Seminole War
A burial party sent out from Fort Barnwell was attacked by a band of Seminoles, killing one soldier and wounding two. As the burial party was chased into the fort, they left two bodies outside. Because they remained there for 24 hours, Maj. William Gates was court-martialled. Largely on the testimony of Gen. Winfield Scott, Gates was removed from the army on June 11. He was reinstated on January 7, 1837, when the high command was persuaded that it would have been imprudent to risk lives to fetch dead bodies.
Sources: 187, 241

FL50   *Attack on Fort Drane* • April 20, 1836
Location: 1½ miles south of Irvine
War: Second Seminole War
In an unusual night attack, Seminoles rushed the pickets at Fort Drane, located at Gen. Duncan L. Clinch's plantation eight miles from Micanopy, from 1 to 3 a.m. The fort, built under the direction of Capt. Gustavus S. Drane, served as a major supply headquarters for the northern part of Florida. The natives were unable to overpower the garrison, and four days later Gen. Clinch led his right wing back to the fort. He found no natives.
Sources: 187, 291, 315, 335, 367

FL51   *Battle of Thonotosassa Creek* • April 27, 1836
Location: Fort Alabama
War: Second Seminole War
A month after Col. William Lindsay had established Fort Alabama, the campaign for which it was designed was winding down. Lindsay decided to dismantle it, and sent 600 men with Col. Chisolm and Lt. Col. William S. Foster to take care of it. At 3 p.m. on April 27 as they approached the fort, Seminole guns opened on them. They responded with artillery fire and a bayonet charge. The regulars and volunteers crossed Thonotosassa Creek and dispersed the natives, who killed five and wounded 24.

Chisolm departed the fort, which he left intact but booby-trapped. Only 21 minutes after they left the fort, they heard it explode, throwing its logs far into the woods. It was not known how many native casualties resulted.

This was essentially the last action of the campaign led by Gen. Winfield Scott, which generally was an army failure.
Sources: 91, 143, 187, 291

FL52   *Skirmish at Fort Drane* • June 9, 1836
Location: Fort Drane, Micanopy
War: Second Seminole War
On May 29, Capt. Lemuel Gates arrived and took command of Fort Drane. For days, he was pressed by Seminoles, requiring constant defensive action. To end the pressure, he had a howitzer hauled in front of the fort and fired, causing the natives to yell. He sent a bayonet charge to the location of the yell, which scattered some but also disclosed the site of the main group. At this, he fired the howitzer several times until the Seminoles went away.
Sources: 91, 187

FL53   *Attack on Fort Defiance* • June 9, 1836
Location: Near Micanopy
War: Second Seminole War
Maj. Julius F. Heilman commanded the post at Fort Defiance and concluded that Osceola was trying to draw him out of the fortification. When he came out, one foot artillery company went around the Seminole right flank, dragoons went to the left, and a third element advanced in the center. The dragoons on horseback charged on the order of Lt. Thompson B. Wheelock, while the artillery charged the enemy's rear. Heilman advanced with a six-pound howitzer.

The 70 soldiers held off the 250 Seminoles, who disappeared into the Cuscawilla Hammock, where the first Seminole village had been founded by Cowkeeper about 100 years before. Two days later, Heilman moved his headquarters to Fort Drane.
Sources: 187, 335

FL54 *Battle of Welika Pond* • July 9, 1836
Location: 1/4 mile from Micanopy
War: Second Seminole War
Capt. William S. Maitland left Fort Drane before dawn with 62 men and 22 wagons of supplies, heading toward Fort Defiance. Nearly at Micanopy, about 200 Seminoles led by Osceola opened fire. The soldiers were outnumbered, and waited to take action until 31 men joined them from Fort Defiance. When they did, they charged and pushed the Seminoles back to cannon range. Cannon fire allowed the men to reach the fort. The army had five killed and six wounded. No record was made of the Seminole casualties.
Sources: 91, 187, 335

FL55 *Attack at Cape Florida* • July 23, 1836
Location: Southern tip of Key Biscayne
War: Second Seminole War
White John W.B. Thompson and a black helper, Mr. Carter, tenders of the lighthouse at Cape Florida, were attacked by a band of natives. They defended the ground floor until two kegs of oil ignited, causing the two to climb 90 feet to the top of the lighthouse. The fire followed them, and they had only a narrow plank to use as a platform. They were wounded by the Seminole gunfire and practically roasted alive, and half hoped to kill themselves by dropping a keg of powder down the shaft. The explosion merely resulted in a loud noise and little else.

The black assistant was shot and killed, and the natives believed that they had killed both. They left the area, and Thompson remained on the plank all night, having been wounded in both feet. The next day, sailors from the *Motto* rescued him by lowering him on a rope.
Monument: A historic monument was erected at the site of the attack.
Sources: 13, 153, 187, 215

FL56 *Battle of Ridgely's Mill* • July 27, 1836
Location: Ridgely's Mill
War: Second Seminole War
Detachments of Batteries A and D of the 1st Artillery clashed with Seminole warriors.
Sources: 91, 335

FL57 *Attack on Travers Plantation* • July 28, 1836
Location: East of the St. Johns River
War: Second Seminole War
Lt. Alfred Herbert attacked the Travers Plantation ruins from his boat. His men loaded their weapons with buckshot and waited. When the natives approached to 40 paces, the soldiers opened fire. Several warriors were killed, but after 80 minutes Herbert's ammunition was running low. While the Seminoles continued to fire, Herbert led his men back to their boat.
Sources: 187

FL58   *Attack on Fort Drane* • August 21, 1836
Location: Fort Drane, Micanopy
War: Second Seminole War
Fort Drane had been abandoned by the army and taken over by Osceola and his Seminoles. On August 15, Maj. B.K. Pierce left St. Augustine with 125 men and 27 wagons to close out Fort Defiance and retrieve the supplies located there. He reached Micanopy on August 20, and at 2 a.m. on the following day, sent 110 men to attack Fort Drane ten miles away.

They caught the Seminoles in the open and they moved into the edge of a hammock, returning heavy fire. The army cannon fired back with canister fire into the palmettos. After an hour, Pierce decided that he did not have enough force to charge into the hammock, and returned to Micanopy. The army suffered one dead and 16 wounded, with Seminole losses being unknown.
Sources: 91, 143, 187, 335

FL59   *Battle at San Felasco Hammock* • September 18, 1836
Location: West of Gainesville
War: Second Seminole War
Col. John Warren was leading 100 men of the Florida militia and one cannon on a reconnaissance mission in San Felasco Hammock, when they were attacked by Seminoles. They surrounded the soldiers and tried to turn one flank and then the other, but were repulsed by mounted charges. The artillery piece saved the whites, especially when the Seminoles charged it twice. After 90 minutes, the battle ended. Numbers of casualties were not recorded.
Sources: 91, 187, 335

FL60   *Border Skirmish* • September 30, 1836
Location: Florida/Georgia border
War: Second Seminole War
Col. Lane led a regiment of Creeks across the border into Florida and engaged a group of Seminoles.
Sources: 187

FL61   *Burning of the Schooner* Mary • October 8, 1836
Location: Tavernier Key
War: Second Seminole War
A band of warriors captured the schooner *Mary* and burned it. A marine pursuit party from the *Vandalia* attempted to retaliate, but the natives escaped first.
Sources: 187

FL62   *Battle at Cove of the Withlacoochee* • October 13–15, 1836
Location: Near Powell's Town
War: Second Seminole War
An advance guard from Gen. Richard K. Call's force occupying the area in and around the ruins of Fort Drane came upon 40 to 50 natives and killed 14 of them. This guard included Creek volunteers and was commanded by Capt. J.F. Lane.
Sources: 187, 241

FL63 *Battle Along the Withlacoochee River* • November 17, 1836
Location: East side of the Withlacoochee River
War: Second Seminole War
Gen. Thomas S. Jesup divided his forces into three wings, himself taking a Tennessee volunteer brigade, the Florida militia, and some regulars to the east bank of the river. They came across a large native camp, which the mounted Tennesseans charged. The natives broke ranks and were again charged by the mounted volunteers.

    The fighting continued in waist-deep mud and water. The soldiers had one killed and 10 wounded, while the warriors had 20 dead, and they lost their horses and possessions.
Location: 143, 187

FL64 *Battle Near the Withlacoochee River* • November 18, 1836
Location: Near the Withlacoochee River
War: Second Seminole War
Gen. Richard K. Call led a wing of Gen. Thomas S. Jesup's army southward from the Withlacoochee River, and came upon 600 to 700 Seminole warriors near the edge of a hammock. Facing a cleared area, the warriors were ready for a battle. Call sent mounted soldiers to the Seminoles' flanks, then charged the line. When the warriors threatened to surround the soldiers, the flankers dismounted and charged, foiling the Seminoles' tactic.

    The battle ended within 30 minutes. The soldiers lost three and had 12 wounded, while the natives lost 25.
Sources: 143, 187

FL65 *Battle of Wahoo Swamp* • November 18–21, 1836
Location: 5 miles from Dade Battleground
War: Second Seminole War
Divisions led by Gen. Richard K. Call and Lt. Col. B.K. Pierce combined at the Dade battleground, and their scouts determined that the Seminoles intended to make a stand on the edge of dense woods next to an open field. On November 18, Call arranged his 800 men in a mile-long line with the Tennessee brigade on the right, the Florida militia and regulars in the center, and the Creeks on the left. They marched toward the Seminoles.

    When they reached a distance of 50 yards, they shot and charged. The Seminoles pulled back and the soldiers and Creeks searched for them in the dense swamp. After a mile and half of wading, the Creeks reached a black-water stream and the Seminoles on the opposite bank opened fire. At about 3:30 p.m., the hostile fire appeared to decrease.

    On November 21, 420 Seminoles and 200 blacks attacked the soldiers, who fought for four hours. Fifteen soldiers were killed and 30 were wounded, while 25 of the attackers were killed. Rather than attempt to cross the stream, the soldiers withdrew from the area.

    The commanders were criticized for failing to attack across the stream. They had thought it was too deep because of its dark color, but the cypress leaching masked the fact that it was only three feet deep. The only man who had tried to ford the stream was shot down in the water and the army withdrew, as did the Seminoles. Call was replaced by Gen. Thomas S. Jesup as the head of the war effort.

Monument: There is a stone and bronze marker at the site of the battle on the north side of CR 48, east of Bushnell.
Sources: 14, 113, 143, 153, 187, 335, 402

FL66 *Battle Near Lake Apopka* • January 23, 1837
Location: Near Lake Apopka
War: Second Seminole War
In December of 1836, an army commanded by Gen. Thomas Sidney Jesup built a new fort in the vicinity of the Dade battlefield and named it for Robert Armstrong, the commander of the brigade from Tennessee. From that point on January 22, he led his army east and the next day surprised Seminole chief Osuchee (Cooper). He and four others were killed, and the army captured eight blacks and eight Seminoles.
Sources: 187

FL67 *Battle of Hatcheelustee* • January 27, 1837
Location: Near Lake Tohopekaliga
War: Second Seminole War
Gen. Thomas S. Jesup assembled a force of about 1,000 soldiers at the site of the present Kissimmee airport. He intended to pursue a Seminole band.

A scouting patrol of the 2nd Brigade commanded by Col. Archibald Henderson encountered a band of natives including Micanopy, Jumper and Alligator. A great deal of rifle fire occurred. In a charge led by Lt. Chambers of the Alabama volunteers, a Seminole camp was overrun. They captured 100 ponies and packs, and chased the natives into the nearby 15-square-mile Big Cypress Swamp. Fighting continued across a 75-yard wide stream. The soldiers killed 28 and captured 25, but the rest of the warriors and blacks escaped.
Sources: 13, 91, 151, 187, 315, 335

FL68 *Battle of Fort Mellon* • February 8, 1837
Location: East of downtown Sanford (formerly Mellonville)
War: Second Seminole War
A fort was established here by Col. William Selby Harney in December of 1836 to protect settlers from the natives. It was first known as Camp Monroe because it was on the shore of Lake Monroe, and then Camp Fanning for its first commander, Col. A.C.W. Fanning. Just before dawn on February 8, it was attacked by Chiefs Coacoochee (Wildcat) and King Philip and from 200 to 500 Seminoles and blacks, catching soldiers sleeping behind a low log breastwork.

The fighting lasted for three hours, resulting in the deaths of three attackers and one soldier, Capt. Charles Mellon. Fifteen other soldiers were injured, as were two attackers. The white losses would have been worse, but six-pound rounds from the steamer *Santee* in Lake Monroe caused the Seminoles to retreat.

The fort was renamed after Mellon, as was the later settlement. The fort was dismantled in June of 1837 and the troops were moved to St. Augustine. The fort was re-established in November and lasted for a short time.
Monument: There is a bronze plaque on a large stone, placed in May of 1925 by the D.A.R. at the northeast corner of Mellonville Ave. and 2nd St., Sanford.
Sources: 34, 91, 94, 151, 153, 160, 180, 196, 335, 344, 367, 402

FL69 *Battle of Clear River* • February 9, 1837
Location: Clear River
War: Second Seminole War
Capt. George W. Allen led a force from Company K of the 4th U.S. Infantry against a band of Seminoles. One officer was killed.
Sources: 91, 335

FL70 *Capture Near Dunlawton Plantation* • September 9, 1837
Location: Port Orange
War: Second Seminole War
Brig. Gen. Joseph M. Hernandez led 170 men to the ruined Dunlawton Plantation near a native camp. During the night of September 8, members of the Florida militia enclosed three sides of the camp, while the regular soldiers readied for a charge. They attacked at dawn. All but one of the natives were captured, and there were no deaths or injuries.

The Seminole prisoners included King Philip and his son, Coacoochee, the most important capture since the beginning of the war. Another was Tomoka John, who led the soldiers to capture the inhabitants of a camp of Yuchis about six miles away, using the same surrounding tactic with 100 men. Lt. John Winfield Scott McNeil was the only white casualty, and the natives also lost only one. The captured included Yuchi Billy and his brother Jack, which further cut into the Seminole leadership.
Museum: Sugar Mill Gardens, including the ruins of the mill, is located on Sugar Mill Rd., one mile west of US 1, Port Orange.
Sources: 91, 187, 215, 315, 335, 402

FL71 *Battle of Okeechobee* • December 25, 1837
Location: Near Lake Okeechobee
War: Second Seminole War
On December 19, Col. Zachary Taylor headed southward from Fort Gardner on the Kissimmee River with 1,032 men. The contingent included 180 Missouri volunteers, 47 in a company called "Morgan's Spies," and 70 Shawnee and Delaware warriors, with the rest being regular soldiers. On the way toward Lake Okeechobee, several Seminoles along the way surrendered, including Jumper. On December 21, they built Fort Bassinger and then headed south again. More surrendered, and one warrior showed them where the rest had prepared to fight.

The battleground was a hammock by a swamp not far from Lake Okeechobee. Sam Jones commanded most of the force of from 380 to 480 natives, Alligator had 120, and Coacoochee had 80. Taylor planned to charge at their front through the swamp. At 12:30 p.m. on December 25, the soldiers attacked. Rifle fire cut down Cols. Richard Gentry and Ramsey Thompson.

Taylor then ordered an attack on the right flank, the one led by Sam Jones. After they got into position, the natives fired one volley and retreated toward the lake. The fighting ended by 3:00 p.m. White losses were 26 dead and 112 wounded, while the Seminoles lost 11 and had 14 wounded. The next day was spent caring for the wounded and getting ready to travel back to Fort Bassinger, which happened on December 27. They reached it on December 28, and continued on to Fort Gardner where they arrived on December 31.

In a separate action on December 26, a wandering band of Seminoles, perhaps still retreating from the battle, were engaged in light combat by a group of Georgia volunteers led by Maj. Gen. Charles H. Nelson along the Wacasassa River.

Col. Zachary Taylor was later promoted to brigadier general and on May 15, 1838, replaced Gen. Thomas S. Jesup as the head of the Florida forces. His military successes helped him later to be elected president of the U.S.

Monument: There are historical markers on US 441/98, 6.4 miles from the intersection with SR 70, Okeechobee, and in front of the Okeechobee courthouse.

Sources: 34, 54, 90, 91, 94, 113, 155, 156, 157, 187, 207, 275, 335, 381, 402, 423

FL72 *Battle of Jupiter Creek* • January 15, 1838
Location: Mouth of the Loxahatchee River
War: Second Seminole War
A detachment of 80 sailors led by navy Lt. Levi Powell had skirmished with natives in the Everglades several times, then emerged to the east. They captured a squaw who led them to a swamp, into which they charged. At the mouth of the river at about 4:00 p.m., they came upon a band of about 80 Seminoles which they attacked immediately, but they met fierce gunfire. The sailors were not trained to stand and fight in this manner, so they retreated to their boats by sundown. The Seminole guns had wounded all four officers and Dr. Leiter.
Sources: 54, 91, 94, 187, 215, 335, 367

FL73 *Battle of Loxahatchee* • January 24, 1838
Location: Near Jonathan Dickinson State Park
War: Second Seminole War
After leaving the Everglades and taking more than two days to march from Fort Pierce through the Al-pa-ti-o-kee Swamp, Maj. Gen. Thomas S. Jesup's army of 1,200 halted its slow progress through the wilderness at the report of natives located nearby. Jesup ordered an attack, beginning with the crossing of a cypress swamp. A charge was led by dismounted dragoons, since the water was too deep for a horse charge, supported by five-pound artillery fire. The 150 to 300 warriors fell back to a position across a stream 30 yards wide.

The Tennessee volunteers appeared to lose their momentum while under fire, until Gen. Jesup rode up and, dismounted, went to the edge of the creek. He was wounded in the face by a bullet that shattered his glasses, but was able to wave the soldiers on to attack the natives. They retreated and the hammock was taken over by the whites, who counted seven soldiers killed and 31 wounded. Only one dead Seminole was found.

The next day, the army constructed Fort Jupiter, in which they waited for over a week until shoes arrived for the nearly 400 who had marched barefoot through the sawgrass.

Museum: The Loxahatchee Historical Museum is located at 805 N. US 1, Jupiter, FL 33477.
Sources: 54, 91, 94, 187, 215, 335

FL74 *Battle at the New River* • March 22, 1838
Location: Fort Lauderdale
War: Second Seminole War
Lt. Col. James Bankhead and his 4th Artillery located a band of natives in a

defensive position along the edge of a hammock. He ordered two companies to stay in the front as a holding force, while four were placed in two-foot deep water to the left. To the right went soldiers and sailors in boats in deeper water, and began shooting from the right a four-pounder piece. This caused the natives to retreat.

Sources: 94, 187

FL75 *Skirmish with Sam Jones* • April 24, 1838
Location: South of Fort Lauderdale
War: Second Seminole War
Lt. Col. William S. Harney, leading 50 dragoons with Colt rifles and 50 artillery-men with muskets, set off in search of Sam Jones, the Seminole warrior. They started out on horseback, transferred to canoes, and ended up on foot. When on April 24 they found a native encampment, Harney divided his force into three sections and approached the camp.

They were met by Seminole fire, which they returned. After a while, the warriors pulled back and the soldiers gave chase. After a total of two and a half hours, the battle ended with one Seminole killed and one captured.

Sources: 187, 196

FL76 *Battle at Okefenokee Swamp* • May 27, 1838
Location: Georgia-Florida Border
War: Second Seminole War
For about 30 minutes, 40 Florida militiamen led by Capt. Sandelung fought with about 20 natives about one mile from the Okefenokee Swamp. Two soldiers were wounded.

Sources: 187

FL77 *Battle at Fort Dade* • June 4, 1838
Location: Fort Dade
War: Second Seminole War
Near the former battleground where Maj. Gen. Edmund P. Gaines and Gen. Duncan L. Clinch had met the Seminoles in major battles, dragoons and Seminoles exchanged heavy gunfire until rains brought an end to the battle. There was no clear winner, and although the warriors were unsuccessful in burning down the log bridge across the Withlacoochee, they were able to burn Fort Dade.

Sources: 187

FL78 *Battle Near Newnansville* • June 17, 1838
Location: Newnansville
War: Second Seminole War
Thirty soldiers from Companies C and F of the 2nd Dragoons, led by Capt. L.J. Beall, were attacked by a band of Seminoles. Six soldiers were wounded.

Sources: 91, 445

FL79 *Attack at Singletary Home* • July 13, 1838
Location: Jefferson County
War: Second Seminole War
The home of Mr. and Mrs. Singletary was attacked by four natives and one black.

Both adults and two of the children were killed with three-foot-long arrows, a departure from the previous use of only guns and knives. The only survivor was a five-year-old girl.
Sources: 333

FL80   *Attack at Baker House* • Early August, 1838
Location: 15 miles east of Monticello
War: Second Seminole War
While the Bakers were eating supper, they were attacked by natives who shot and killed Mr. and Mrs. Baker and one of their grandchildren. Another grandchild was the only survivor.
Sources: 333

FL81   *Harney Massacre* • July 23, 1839
Location: 15 to 20 miles from the mouth of the Caloosahatchee River
War: Second Seminole War
A party of soldiers and civilians was charged with the task of opening a trading post within the Seminole reservation along the Caloosahatchee River. It was led by James B. Dallam, and the eight soldiers armed with Colt rifles were led by Lt. Col. William S. Harney. They erected a store building with the soldiers camping nearby, and were attacked by 160 to 250 natives led by Chekika and Hospetarke.

Harney, who had come in late from hunting the night before, had camped apart from his men. When he was awakened by gunfire, he ran in his underwear to the river and, with two others, escaped by boat. The warriors searching for him assumed that he had drowned in the river. Sixteen whites were killed and the other ten escaped.
Sources: 61, 91, 143, 155, 187, 196, 335, 367, 402

FL82   *Attack at Chaires Cross Roads* • July, 1839
Location: 10 miles from Tallahassee
War: Second Seminole War
At a community on the St. Augustine Road on the north side of Lake Lafayette, a party of Seminoles attacked the home of Green H. Chaires. He and his wife and one of their two children were killed. The area was supposed to be protected by the "Minute Men," a home guard organization. One of them was killed when a gun accidently discharged into another's back.
Sources: 333

FL83   *Ambush at Fort King* • March 28, 1840
Location: Fort King
War: Second Seminole War
Capt. Gabriel J. Rains led 16 men from the 7th Infantry out of Fort King on a scouting mission, and they were fired on by 93 warriors who had set an ambush. Two soldiers were killed and one was wounded by the first volley. They then took cover behind trees and began to return the fire.

Rains led 12 men in a charge back to the fort, and he went down with severe wounds. Three men carried him back to the fort and it took him two months to recover to the point that he could make a report of the action. Rains was lauded for his gallant action and was promoted to major.
Sources: 91, 187, 335

FL84 *Battle of Levy's Prairie* • May 19, 1840
Location: 8 miles from Micanopy
War: Second Seminole War
From 80 to 100 warriors led by Coacoochee attacked a detachment led by Lt. James S. Sanderson, killing him and five soldiers.
Sources: 91, 187, 335

FL85 *Attack at Chocachatti* • June 2, 1840
Location: Chocachatti
War: Second Seminole War
Gen. Walker Keith Armistead gave permission to Lt. Col. Bennett Riley, who was skillful at guerilla warfare, to attack an important Seminole stronghold. He was able to destroy it, and for his action received a brevet colonelcy.
Sources: 187

FL86 *Indian Key Massacre* • August 7, 1840
Location: Halfway between Cape Florida and Key West
War: Second Seminole War
Horticulturalist Dr. Henry Perrine moved in December of 1838 to Indian Key, east of Lower Matacumbe Key. The war had prevented his moving into a mainland township which the government granted him for plant experiments. He was awakened on August 7 by a band of Seminoles (known as Spanish Indians) led by Chekika (Chikika), paddling the 30 miles from the mainland in 17 canoes.

While they pillaged the seven-acre island, Dr. Perrine tried to reason with them, so they killed him. They set his house on fire and the rest of the Perrine family escaped by hiding in its cellar while it burned. They then made it to Tea Table Key, where a navy surgeon and 12 patients were located. Midshipman Murray and five other patients boarded a boat and sailed to Indian Key with a small cannon.

In response to bullets from the warriors, they fired the cannon, the recoil of which sent it into the water. The Seminoles fired a six-pounder which they had found, requiring the sailors to retreat. Thirteen of the 70 Indian Key residents were killed in the action. The survivors' homes were destroyed.
Sources: 143, 187, 335, 367

FL87 *Battle at Wacahoota* • September 6, 1840
Location: Levy County
War: Second Seminole War
One soldier was killed and three were wounded when members of Companies B and H of the 7th Infantry battled with Seminoles.
Sources: 91, 335

FL88 *Battle at Chekika's Island* • December 3–24, 1840
Location: Everglades
War: Second Seminole War
On December 4, Lt. Col. William S. Harney led 90 men in 16 canoes from Fort Dallas, now the site of Miami, to satisfy Harney's desire for revenge for the attack on his camp in July of 1839. One of the men was John, a black guide who had been captured by the Seminoles in 1835, and who knew where they were hiding.

Along the way, they encountered Seminoles in canoes, and Harney had them hanged on the spot.

They surprised Chekika by arriving at his island an hour or two after sunrise. Seeing that he could not escape, Chekika offered his hand to the white soldiers, one of which shot him dead. A battle ensued, resulting in four warriors being killed and 36 taken prisoner. After the battle, Harney had two captured warriors hanged. A third was kept for use as a guide. Twelve days after the expedition began, it returned to Fort Dallas.

Sources: 91, 157, 187, 196, 335

FL89 *Attack on the Road to Wacahoota* • December 28, 1840
Location: Martin's Point Hammock
War: Second Seminole War
Fort Wacahoota was built after 1835 near the Levy County line on present SR 121. It was the destination of a party of 13, consisting of Lt. Walter Sherwood, Mrs. Montgomery (the wife of Lt. Alexander Montgomery), and 11 soldiers. Four miles from the fort, they were attacked by 30 Miccasukis.

Hand to hand combat resulted in the deaths of Lt. Sherwood, Mrs. Montgomery and four soldiers, plus one native.

Sources: 91, 187, 287, 335

FL90 *Attack at Fort Walker* • January, 1841
Location: Kanapaha Prairie, near Archer
War: Second Seminole War
Fort Walker was built as a citizen's fort with only a small military attachment. It was erected at the site of the 1835 Battle of Kanapaha Prairie, and was named after the Spring Grove Guard captain who was killed in that fighting.

In this encounter, slaves working outside the fort were attacked by Seminoles. Six were killed and one woman inside the fort was wounded.

Sources: 287

FL91 *Battle Near Fort Brooks* • March 2, 1841
Location: Junction of Oklawaha River and Orange Creek, Putnam County
War: Second Seminole War
Lt. William Alburtis led a party of soldiers in two engagements with the Seminoles. In one, 22 soldiers fought 70 warriors, and in the other 17 fought about 100. Army losses totalled three killed and six wounded.

Sources: 91, 335

FL92 *Battle at Lake Worth* • November, 1841
Location: Lake Worth
War: Second Seminole War
A company of 60 men led by Capt. R.D.A. Wade surprised two Seminole camps near Lake Worth. In the encounters, eight Seminoles were killed and 48 were captured. The army also destroyed 20 canoes and a cache of provisions.

Sources: 335

FL93 *Actions in Great Cypress Swamp* • December 20, 1841
Location: Everglades

War: Second Seminole War

Maj. William G. Belknap sent parties of soldiers out to engage the Seminoles who remained in the area. One encounter involved bands led by Billy Bowlegs and Otulkethlocko (the Prophet). The natives were surrounded by water two to three feet deep, studded with cypress knees.

The soldiers attacked at their front and took some prisoners, suffered a few casualties, and had little effect on the Seminoles. Belknap's action earned him a promotion to lieutenant colonel.

Sources: 13, 91, 187

FL94   *Battle at Dunn's Lake* • January 25, 1842
Location: Haw Creek, east of the St. Johns River
War: Second Seminole War

On December 20, Halleck Tustenuggee and a band of 15 Mikasuki warriors attacked the settlement at Mandarin, 35 miles northwest of St. Augustine. They murdered four and burned two buildings. A militia force was organized by Col. William Jenkins Worth.

Under Worth's supervision, 102 men of the 2nd Infantry headed toward Dunn's Lake under the command of Maj. Joseph Plympton. They found Halleck and his band in a hammock and charged the camp in a single line. Reaching the camp, Plympton discovered that the Mikasukis had left the camp and were positioned to his rear. They battled for an hour and a quarter, but no prisoners were captured.

Sources: 91, 187, 335

FL95   *Battle at Lake Ahapopka* • April 19, 1842
Location: Southeast of Peliklakaha, near the Great Wahoo Swamp
War: Second Seminole War

In a hammock surrounded by water, Halleck Tustenuggee made a stand with a band of 40 Seminoles. With fire, they had cleared a field and built a log barricade across the front. A force of 400 led by Col. William Jenkins Worth fired on the position and approached in two lines through heavy mud and thick, smelly vegetation. A group was sent to the Seminoles' rear.

When the rear group engaged the warriors, the defenders retreated. Two Seminoles were killed, three were wounded and one was taken prisoner. With only one soldier killed and three wounded, the army captured the main camp and the warriors' gear.

Sources: 91, 143, 187, 335

FL96   *Battle at Blue Peter Springs* • May 17, 1842
Location: Fort Wacahoota, near Archer
War: Second Seminole War

A Creek war party led by Halpatter Tustenuggee headed south and crossed the Suwannee River, killing several in one family and burning their home near Newnansville. Further south, the Creeks ambushed a patrol from Fort Wacahoota from tall grass on either side of the military trail near Blue Peter Springs. Pvts. Daniels McNeil and Christopher Duff were killed, and the rest returned to Fort Wacahoota. When reinforcements arrived on the scene, they found that the attackers had already departed.

Sources: 91, 287

FL97   *Attack Along Indian River* • July 13, 1849
Location: 4 miles north of Fort Pierce
A young warrior who may have been branded as an outlaw by his own people attempted to avoid Seminole justice by attacking the whites. He recruited four others, and they set up camp near the Kissimmee River.

Four of the five attacked a small settlement after stalking James Barker and William Russell, who were working in a field. Wounded, they ran to avoid escape. Barker was caught and stabbed to death, but Russell made it to the settlement and the settlers responded with musket fire. They retreated to a large boat in the river.

When the settlers returned the next day, they found one home burned down and two others sacked and vandalized. Assinwah, an assistant to Billy Bowlegs, was sent to apprehend the party of five, since the Seminoles wanted to remain in Florida in peace.
Sources: 61, 335

FL98   *Attack at Payne's Creek* • July 17, 1849
Location: Charlo-Popka-Hatchee-Chee (Little Trout Eating Creek, later known as Payne's Creek)
The band of five Seminole outlaws crossed the state to the west coast and struck an isolated outpost on the Gulf of Mexico near Charlotte Harbor at Payne's Creek. A trading post had been established there by Kennedy and Darling, and its storekeeper was approached by the natives who requested permission to use a canoe to bring skins across the water for trading.

After crossing the creek, the party opened fire and killed Capt. George S. Payne and Dempsey Whidden, and wounded store clerk William McCulloch. McCulloch and his wife and child were able to escape to Tampa, but the store was looted and burned.

This and the earlier attack on the east coast frightened the settlers, who believed that another Seminole war had begun. Many packed up and moved to fortified towns such as Palatka, St. Augustine, Tampa and Garey's Ferry. Three of the outlaws were captured by the Seminoles and turned over to the army. Another was killed trying to escape, and the fifth got away.
Sources: 61, 157, 335

FL99   *Battle of Big Cypress Swamp* • December 20, 1855
Location: Big Cypress Swamp
War: Third Seminole War
Billy Bowlegs (Bolech, Holatamico or Holatter Micco) resisted the government's resettlement of the Seminoles. Although he turned over to the soldiers native outlaws who killed settlers, he would not cooperate with their efforts to remove him from the Everglades.

In response, the army cut off trade and harassed the Seminoles. Bowlegs could still not be found, until an army engineer surveying party of 11 led by Lt. George L. Hartsuff located his garden about two miles from Bonnet Pond. They trampled his bananas, smashed his pumpkins and uprooted his potatoes. When Bowlegs discovered the damage, he demanded an apology and restitution. The soldiers laughed at him.

Bowlegs' response was a pre-dawn attack by 30 warriors on the engineers' camp, killing two and wounding four. It began two years of skirmishes and raids on forts and pioneer settlements, known as the Billy Bowlegs (or Third Seminole) War. Eventually, the government gave up on their pursuit and instead offered cash to the Seminoles who would relocate. Bowlegs headed to Arkansas in May of 1858. **Monuments:** (1) A historical marker at the site of Fort Hartsuff was erected by the Peace River Historical Society in 1978; (2) The Billy Bowlegs Memorial Stadium is located on SR 80 between Fort Myers and Tice, FL. **Sources:** 61, 91, 151, 153, 156, 157, 196, 335

FL100 *Attack at Johnson Home* • January 6, 1856
Location: 6 miles south of Miami
War: Third Seminole War
The Third Seminole War was different from the first two, in that the natives did not attempt to drive the white man away or even win the war. Instead, they focused their attacks on relatively unprotected locations. One was the home of Peter Johnson, located about six miles south of Fort Dallas. In addition to Johnson, the party of Seminoles also killed Edward Farrell, who had been digging arrowroot in the woods.
Sources: 61

FL101 *Attack at Fort Denaud* • January 18, 1856
Location: Caloosahatchee River
War: Third Seminole War
Maj. Lewis Arnold, the commander of the 150 men stationed at the Fort Denaud outpost, angered the Seminoles when he burned their village. Wood-cutting parties were required to venture out of the fort frequently to keep burning the seven fires which were constantly lit to repel mosquitos.

A party of six soldiers returning to the fort with a load of cypress logs was attacked by at least 20 Seminoles led by Oscen Tustenuggee. Only one soldier made it all the way to the fort. The Seminoles stripped the five bodies of their victims of their weapons and ammunition.
Sources: 61, 91, 335

FL102 *Attack at Snell House* • March 2, 1856
Location: Sarasota Bayou
War: Third Seminole War
Approximately 12 Seminoles attacked the home of Col. Hamlin Snell, burning it and torturing and killing Owen Cunningham. A black resident was found by a Seminole who recognized him as having saved his life previously, and helped the black escape. After burning the home of Joseph Woodruff, they returned to their villages.

For safety, some residents crowded into Fort Hamer at Manateee (Bradenton) or boarded the schooner *Ann Elizabeth* on the Manatee River or the mail steamer *Florida*.
Sources: 61

FL103 *Attack on Turner's River* • March, 1856
Location: 40 miles south of Punta Rassa
War: Third Seminole War

A band of Seminoles attacked a party of 11 soldiers in two small skiffs on the Fa-Ke-Hatchee (Turner's) River. The natives fired on them from a protected position, killing two and wounding one. No effective fire was returned.
Sources: 61

FL104 *Attack on Braden Castle* • March 31, 1856
Location: Bradenton
War: Third Seminole War
At the request of Billy Bowlegs for more black people in his village, a war party led by Oscen Tustenuggee traveled to the 1,000-acre plantation of Hector and Dr. Joseph W. Braden to recruit some of their 100 slaves. After supper, Joseph heard some of the natives calling to him and when he would not answer, they cursed him and fired one shot.

Braden, his family, and his two guests went to the second floor of the home and began returning the gunfire. The Seminoles tried to burn down the house, but found it to be effectively fireproof. When the Seminoles departed, they took with them seven blacks, food, blankets, and several mules.
Sources: 61, 157

FL105 *Attack at Big Charley Apopka Creek* • April 3, 1856
Location: 8 miles east of the Peace River
War: Third Seminole War
Members of the militia followed the tracks of the mules stolen by the Seminole war party days before at the Braden home, and found their camp on the south bank of the creek. Twenty-two men on horseback surprised the natives during lunch and killed two of them. The rest jumped into the 20-foot wide deep creek and hid under heavy vegetation. The militia fired into it for 30 minutes, and may have killed some.
Sources: 61, 157

FL106 *Battle in Big Cypress Swamp* • April 7, 1856
Location: Eastern edge of Big Cypress Swamp
War: Third Seminole War
About 100 members of the 1st and 2nd Artillery commanded by Maj. Lewis Arnold entered the Big Cypress Swamp and erected a blockhouse for a garrison of 22 men. They then moved toward the town of Billy Bowlegs, and while traveling through two-foot deep water, were attacked by about 50 Seminoles. Four soldiers were killed and three were wounded, and after about six hours the natives withdrew into a dense hammock.
Sources: 61, 91, 335

FL107 *Attacks Near Addison's Fort* • April 12, 1856
Location: Upper Manatee River
War: Third Seminole War
Within two miles of the outpost known as Addison's Fort, a band of Seminoles burned Asa Goodard's abandoned house and burglarized the deserted home of John Craig.
Sources: 61

FL108 *Carney Massacre* • April 16, 1856
Location: Near Bloomingdale
War: Third Seminole War
John Carney sent his wife and children to Tampa for their protection, but remained to prepare his field for spring planting. He spent the night at the home of John Vickers, who in the morning looked for Carney in the field after he heard gunfire. Not finding Carney, Vickers went five miles to Alafia to tell the militia. On April 17, they found Carney's body with five bullet holes, lying in the field. They unsuccessfully searched for the attackers.
Monument: A simple stone marker was placed at the grave of Carney on the farm of D.H. Sewell located on Stearns Rd., Bloomingdale.
Sources: 61

FL109 *Skirmish in Big Cypress Swamp* • May 2, 1856
Location: Big Cypress Swamp
War: Third Seminole War
Capt. Abner D. Johnston of the Florida Mounted Volunteers commanded a force made up of 38 from his own company, 20 from Capt. Edward T. Kendrick's company, and 26 from Capt. Francis Durrance's company. On May 2, two soldiers hunting in the area were shot at by a few warriors, and most of the soldiers came to their rescue. They pursued the natives into the woods and, finding no more natives, the soldiers merely burned several deserted villages and then left the area.
Sources: 61

FL110 *Bradley Massacre* • May 14, 1856
Location: Darby, Pasco County
War: Third Seminole War
A band of about 15 natives opened fire on the children of Florida Foot Volunteers member Capt. Robert Duke Bradley as they played in the breezeway of their log cabin. The two youngest were killed before the militia, summoned by a neighbor, arrived and caused the natives to retreat.
The news of the attack resulted in several settlers from the area relocating to the protection of forts.
Monument: A metal historical marker was erected by the Pioneer Florida Museum Association at the intersection of SRs 578 and 581, Darby.
Sources: 61, 153

FL111 *Ambush of Mule Train* • May 17, 1856
Location: Near Moore's Lake, Dover
War: Third Seminole War
Three wagons carrying grain to Fort Fraser were stopped at a small creek for water. James Starling, his son, and Albert Hinson were killed when a party of Seminoles opened fire, and three others escaped to alert settlers at a nearby campground.
Eight men from the campground came to the site, but the natives had already disappeared from the area with captured provisions.
Monument: A metal historic marker was erected along US 92, west of McIntosh Rd. in Plant City.
Sources: 61, 153

FL112 *Willoughby Tillis Battle* • June 14, 1856
Location: Fort Meade
War: Third Seminole War
While their homes were being built, a ramshackle building was the home of Willoughby Tillis, his wife and three children, and Thomas Underwood. While Mrs. Tillis was milking their cow on the morning of June 14, she saw a native watching her through the rails of the cowpen. She screamed a warning to her children and servant, and all raced into the house. The warriors circled the house and fired at the openings between the logs, and their fire was returned by Tillis and Underwood, who killed one. The black servant was the only one wounded inside the house. The natives killed about ten of the horses.
     The gunfire was heard by two boys who lived nearby, who went to Fort Meade for help. Lt. Alderman Carlton and six soldiers rode to the Tillis house, causing the natives to retreat into the nearby hammock. The outnumbered soldiers attacked the warriors, resulting in the deaths of Lt. Carlton, Lott Whidden and William Parker. Three others were wounded.
Monument: See FL113 below.
Sources: 61, 153, 157

FL113 *Battle of Peace River Swamp* • June 15–16, 1856
Location: East of Fort Meade
War: Third Seminole War
On June 15, Lt. Streaty Parker left Fort Meade with a party of 18 soldiers against Seminoles concealed in swampland along the river. A wild charge on horseback on June 16 surprised the natives and several were killed by the gunfire. Others, including Oscen Tustenuggee, were shot as they attempted to escape by swimming across the river. When the Seminoles returned the fire effectively, killing Robert F. Prine and George Howell and wounding three others, Parker and his men retreated to the home of William Brooker.
     A party of cavalry led by Capt. William B. Hooker pursued the retreating Seminoles, but did not find them.
Monument: There is a tall stone marker at the center of a park in Fort Meade, marking the common grave of Prine, Howell, Carlton, Parker and Whidden.
Sources: 61, 157

FL114 *Attack at Hooker Plantation* • June, 1856
Location: Along the Manatee River
War: Third Seminole War
A band of natives attacked the Hooker Plantation along the river, forcing the pioneers to flee. They left their cattle and hogs behind, and the natives burned the plantation.
Sources: 61

FL115 *Attack at Punta Rassa* • August 2, 1856
Location: Punta Rassa
War: Third Seminole War
One hundred yards from the blockhouse commanded by Lt. H. Benson, two soldiers were attacked by a party of Seminoles. One was killed by gunfire and one was wounded.
Sources: 61, 91

FL116 *Attack at Shives House* • December 17, 1856
Location: 8 miles south of New Smyrna Beach
War: Third Seminole War
A band of warriors attacked the home of Peter Shives and killed all four of its occupants. This alerted nearby settlers to abandon their homes, and the natives burned some of the deserted Dunlawton houses. Regular troops and militia eventually reached the site, but found no natives.
Sources: 61

FL117 *Ambush at Palm Hammock* • May, 1857
Location: Near Pavilion Key
War: Third Seminole War
A patrol of regular soldiers was traveling through dense vegetation when a party of natives opened fire. Two soldiers were killed, two were wounded, and three threw down their guns and ran back to camp. The remaining three kept firing and drove the natives away.
Sources: 61

FL118 *Skirmish at Bowlegs' Town* • May, 1857
Location: Near Fort Myers
War: Third Seminole War
A patrol from Company G of the 5th Infantry entered Bowlegs' town and were surprised by a band of Mikasukis who killed one and wounded three. A contingent of soldiers arrived to rescue them and drove the natives from a hammock, and in the encounter lost two more, with four wounded.
Sources: 61

FL119 *Cone's First Raid* • November 21, 1857
Location: West of Okaloacoochee River and south of Fort Doane, near Lake Istokpoga
War: Third Seminole War
Capt. William H. Cone led a force of Florida Militia chiefly from Alachua and Columbia Counties against the band of Billy Bowlegs. On November 20, they destroyed a native field of corn, rice and pumpkins. Using a native trail and following experienced woodmen the next day, the soldiers came upon a cluster of dwellings and surprised a band of Seminoles.

Two natives were killed and the remaining 19 were captured. One of those captured was Tigertail, who in captivity at Punta Rassa swallowed broken glass and died. The soldiers also destroyed several nearby villages consisting of about 40 dwellings.
Sources: 61, 335

FL120 *Cone's Second Raid* • November 26, 1857
Location: Big Cypress Swamp
War: Third Seminole War
On November 17, Col. S. St. George Rogers led a party from Capt. William H. Cone's militia from Fort Myers into Big Cypress Swamp, reaching Chokoloskee Island on November 22. Capt. John Parkhill left with one detachment of 75 to paddle upstream in Turner's River. On November 26, they destroyed a 40-acre

field of corn, pumpkins, potatoes and peas near the Royal Palm Hammock. On November 27, they vandalized other fields, but on November 28, Parkhill and about five soldiers were ambushed by Seminoles who killed Parkhill and wounded the others.
Sources: 61, 44

FL121 *Ambushes in Big Cypress Swamp* • December, 1857
Location: Big Cypress Swamp
War: Third Seminole War
Capt. C.L. Stephens of the 5th Infantry led a contingent into the Big Cypress Swamp in retaliation for the Seminoles' earlier killing of horses belonging to his unit. Ninety-one regulars and militiamen followed a trail to a deserted Seminole village, fanning out into smaller groups.

One group was ambushed and one soldier was killed. The patrol then retreated and laid its own ambush for the natives. That resulted in three Seminoles being shot, and three hours later three more were killed when they attempted to remove the bodies of the first three.
Sources: 61, 335

FL122 *Attacks in Big Cypress Swamp* • January, 1858
Location: Big Cypress Swamp
War: Third Seminole War
Col. S. St. George Rogers formed a large contingent of soldiers, dividing it into three detachments led by Maj. J.L. Dozier, Capt. Leroy Lesley and Capt. Simeon Sparkman. They destroyed several villages and cultivated fields within the swamp, traveling on foot and by rowboat. They located the hiding places of many of Billy Bowlegs' people, and were finally having consistent successes.

Before they could complete their mission of destroying the Seminoles, a new peace initiative was under way. It resulted in a negotiated peace and the removal of many of the remaining Seminoles to reservations. The Third Seminole War was declared ended by Col. Gustavus Loomis on May 8, 1858.
Sources: 61

GEORGIA

GA1 *Attacks on Spanish Missions* • 1597
Location: Georgia Coast
War: Mission Uprisings
Yupaha (Guale), the Spanish coastal region inhabited by the Yamassees, had Jesuit priests settle there as early as 1569. After a time, they abandoned it. In about 1590, the Franciscans began establishing missions.

A native revolt beginning in 1597 was led by Don Juanillo, who felt he was the one entitled to be recognized as the head of the Guale Confederacy. Instead, the Spanish recognized Don Francisco as the chief.

Juanillo and his band killed the deputy of the Guale mission, Father Pedro de Corpa, and then went to the town of Tupique and killed Father Blas Rodriguez. They traveled to Assopo and killed Fathers Aunon and Badajoz, and then to Asao where they killed Father Francisco de Velascola. Father Davila was tortured, then exchanged for a native held prisoner in St. Augustine.

After an unsuccessful expedition to the island of San Pedro, the Spanish retaliated and burned the native towns. A second such retaliatory campaign was waged in 1601. Juanillo, Francisco, and others were killed in the town of Yfusinique and the uprising ended.
Sources: 332, 359

GA2 *Attack on Santa Catalina* • 1679
Location: Saint Catherines Island
At the time the English settled the Georgia coast, there still existed the Spanish mission of Santa Catalina on Saint Catherines Island. Working there were 100 semi-civilized Catholic natives. That mission and another at Guadalquini were invaded by Chichumechus (Westos), Chiluques (Cherokees) and Uchizes (Creeks). According to the Spanish, the attack was encouraged by the English.

As a result, the Catholicized natives abandoned the island.
Sources: 332

GA3 *Skirmish on the Flint River* • 1740
Location: Flint River
A Spanish army supported by 900 Apalachee warriors conducted a campaign against the British and their Creek allies. The Creeks encouraged the British traders to form a defense force of 500 and with them, defeated the Spanish along the banks of the Flint River.
Sources: 368

GA4 *Battle of Bloody Marsh* • July 7, 1742
Location: St. Simons Island
In May, 30 Spanish ships with 1,300 men sailed from Havana, obtained additional men in St. Augustine, and captured Fort Frederica on St. Simons Island. Gen. James E. Oglethorpe with his soldiers and several hundred Creek allies ambushed the Spaniards at Bloody Marsh and pushed them back in a state of disorder. Oglethorpe then returned to England.
Sources: 310

GA5 *Sack of Mount Venture* • Fall, 1742
Location: Mount Venture
The trading post at Mount Venture was the victim of a surprise attack by Spanish Yamassees. They looted and burned it, killing several Creeks.
Sources: 111

GA6 *Attacks on Lower Towns* • 1750
Location: Georgia
War: Cherokee-Creek War

Following minor clashes between bands of Cherokees and Creeks, Malatchi led 500 Lower Creek warriors against the Lower Cherokee towns of Echoi and Estatoe. At the latter location, they pulled down the English trader's store which had supplied the Cherokees with ammunition.
Sources: 111

GA7   *Battle of the Taliwa* • 1755
Location: Northern Georgia
War: Cherokee-Creek War
Nancy Ward, wife of war chief Kingfisher, was known for her fierce fighting in this battle, in which the Cherokees defeated the Creeks.
Sources: 3, 135

GA8   *Ogeechee Incident* • September 3, 1756
Location: Ogeechee
Tuckabatchee warriors near the town of Ogeechee stole horses and were pursued by white settlers. In a gunfight, three Creeks and no whites were killed. Instead of a major Creek reprisal, the matter was calmly handled through diplomatic channels.
Sources: 111

GA9   *Battle of Savannah* • Fall, 1782
Location: Savannah
War: Revolutionary War
Emistesigo led a band of Creeks to relieve the British forces at Savannah. In cutting their way through the besieging force of Gen. Anthony Wayne, Emistesigo was a casualty. The Creeks then accepted a peace offered by Wayne.
Sources: 355

GA10   *Attack on Echota* • June 7, 1793
Location: Echota
In retaliation for the death of Mr. Gilliam and his son, Capt. John Beard raised a force of 56 men and marched to the Cherokee town of Echota. There, they attacked and wounded Chief Hanging Maw and killed his wife, town chief Fool Charlie, and others named Scantee, Betty, Roseberry, and others.
Sources: 332

GA11   *Burning of Lower Towns* • October, 1794
Location: Northern Georgia
In violation of the orders he had been given, Brig. Gen. John Sevier invaded the lands of the Cherokees and burned several Lower Towns in Georgia, including Oostanaula.
Sources: 355

GA12   *Attack on Neamathla's Village* • November 21, 1817
Location: Fowltown, north of Tallahassee
War: First Seminole War
The border between the United States and Florida, which was then owned by Spain, was set by the 1814 Treaty of Fort Jackson. Creek chief Neamathla warned

the army not to cross the Clinch River or cut one stick of his timber. Considering this to be a declaration of war, Gen. Edmund Pendleton Gaines sent Maj. David E. Twiggs and 250 soldiers to attack his village at Fowltown.

They were fired on by Seminoles as they approached the village, and returned fire caused the natives to retreat into the swamps. The soldiers killed and wounded several warriors, and looted and burned down Fowltown.

In retaliation, the Creeks ambushed Lt. R.W. Scott and a boatload of soldiers and their families on their way up the Apalachicola River to Fort Scott, capturing or killing 45 of the 51 people aboard.

The attack on Scott's detachment resulted in Washington's appointing Gen. Andrew Jackson to take command in an effort to bring the Seminoles under control. The deserted Fowltown was burned by the whites on January 4, 1818.
Sources: 20, 34, 37, 39, 42, 54, 91, 113, 143, 187, 296, 333, 354, 402

GA13   *Massacre of Cheraw* • April 22, 1818
Location: Cheraw
War: Creek War
Capt. Obed Wright led a force of 270 Chatham County men, heading west from Hartford to attack Hopaunee and Felemma's towns. Stopping at Fort Early, he acquired additional men and headed toward the Flint River.

Instead of his original targets, he attacked Cheraw. They burned the homes and butchered the inhabitants, approximately seven men, an old woman, a young woman, and a young girl.
Sources: 296

IDAHO

ID1   *Massacre of Ward Party* • 1852
Location: Boise River
Two wagons carrying the Ward party of 15 camped along the Boise River on their way to the Willamette Valley. The Shoshoni believed that they intended to settle in their area along the Boise and attacked them, killing 13 and wounding the other two.
Sources: 203

ID2   *Massacre Near Fort Boise* • August 20, 1854
Location: Boise
A party of Bannock Shoshonis massacred a group of immigrants near Fort Boise. Maj. Granville O. Haller led an expedition from The Dalles in pursuit of them.
Sources: 81

ID3 *Wagon Train Massacre* • 1862
Location: 10 miles southwest of American Falls
The first two of a group of three wagon trains heading west on the Oregon Trail were attacked by 200 warriors. Nine whites were killed and six were scalped, and their livestock and clothing were taken.
Monument: A monument is located in Massacre Rocks State Park, I-86/US 30, American Falls.
Sources: 203, 350

ID4 *Battle of Bear River* • January 29, 1863
Location: 3 miles northwest of Preston
Gen. Patrick Edward Connor was in the region to protect the Overland Express mail route and to prevent the Mormons from seceding from the Union. He led a force of 225 California volunteers on a 120-mile trek against the Shoshoni, killing unarmed natives along the way. The Shoshoni and some Paiutes set up a battle line along the Bear River, threatening to kill any white man on the north bank. The army arrived at the mouth of Beaver Creek and crushed the natives in a three-hour encounter.

Connor's losses included 23 killed, 44 wounded and 79 treated for frozen toes and feet. Estimates of natives killed ranged from 224 to 400, two-thirds of them women and children. The action earned Connor the reputation as a brave defender of the frontier from the "red foe."
Monuments: The graves of Connor and the 23 men who died in the action are in the Post Cemetery of Fort Douglas, Potter St., Salt Lake City, UT 84113. There is also a monument on the east side of US 91, northwest of Preston, ID.
Sources: 66, 70, 192, 203, 348, 350, 362

ID5 *Attack at Battle Creek* • January, 1865
Location: Battle Creek
Army troops attacked a camp of Bannocks in retaliation for raids on settlements and wagon trains. Native deaths totalled 224.
Sources: 426

ID6 *Wagon Train Massacre* • July, 1866
Location: Western Idaho
War: Paiute War
W.C. McKay recruited Warm Springs warriors to serve as army scouts in the campaign against the Paiutes. With enthusiasm, the scouts killed 14 prisoners that had been taken by the army. In retaliation, the Paiutes captured a wagon train along the Oregon Trail and killed all of its people. Well publicized was the fact that several of the women and children had not been killed immediately, but had been tortured before their murders.
Sources: 263

ID7 *Battle of White Bird Canyon* • June 17, 1877
Location: 14 miles south of Grangeville
War: Nez Perce War
On June 13–14, 1877, shortly before the Nez Perce were to be relocated from the Wallowa Valley to the Lapwai Reservation, three of their warriors attacked and

killed four white settlers (August Bacon, Mrs. Manuel, William Osburn and Harry Mason) and wounded a fifth. Those warriors killed as revenge for the whites' taking of their livestock and their impending removal from their homeland.

Even though the tribe led by five chiefs including Chief Joseph (Heinmot Tooyalaket) had promised Gen. Oliver O. Howard that they would move onto the reservation with 30 days, they believed that the killings would result in violent retribution. Rather than head for the reservation, they sought shelter in White Bird Canyon.

On June 17, they were attacked in the canyon by a detachment of 110 tired soldiers commanded by Capt. David Perry, who were repulsed by the natives on fresh horses after suffering heavy casualties. Killed were one officer and 33 enlisted men, with four wounded. Two Nez Perce were wounded and none were killed. Howard returned on June 26 to fight again, but the Nez Perce retreated into the mountains so the 227 troops and 20 militia merely buried the dead.

Monument: The site of a fort built in 1877 by Capt. Charles Rawn to protect the area from the Nez Perce is denoted by a marker on SR 12, 6 miles west of Lolo.

Sources: 9, 18, 66, 70, 86, 91, 175, 191, 197, 203, 213, 236, 254, 265, 285, 286, 315, 350, 366, 378, 405

ID8 *Battle of Cottonwood Creek* • July 4–5, 1877
Location: 2 miles south of Cottonwood
War: Nez Perce War

At the southeastern tip of the Nez Perce reservation, Cottonwood Creek ran into the South Fork of the Clearwater River. The band of Nez Perce led by Looking Glass camped there, and until the army attacked them they were opposed to the hostilities which were supported by Joseph's band.

Twelve white soldiers from Gen. Oliver O. Howard's camp and a scout, all led by Lt. S.M. Rains, were killed by a party of Nez Perce near the Cottonwood ranch. While the rest of the tribe attempted to leave the area, the rest of the soldiers were occupied by several warriors who attacked the ranch with long-range rifle fire.

The following day a five to six hour battle between the warriors and a party of civilian volunteers ensued about a mile and half from the ranch.

Sources: 86, 91, 175, 191, 203, 236, 285, 286, 315, 350, 405

ID9 *Battle of the Clearwater River* • July 11–12, 1877
Location: Clearwater River near Sapachesap
War: Nez Perce War

The army and the natives met in a hilly area along the Clearwater River. Some of the warriors' leaders were Ollokot, Rainbow, Five Wounds and Toohoolhoolzote, who jockeyed their men into position while the soldiers sought to do the same. As a pack train came into the area, the warriors attacked it and killed two of the packers, but had insufficient force to capture it.

About 100 warriors kept 400 soldiers and 100 civilians essentially besieged at a distance of up to 600 yards. After a night of light gunfire, the soldiers were able to capture a vital spring through the use of howitzers. At about 2 p.m., reinforcements from Fort Klamath arrived and charged, and the Nez Perce retreated. The soldiers plundered and destroyed the abandoned tipis. Thirteen soldiers were

killed and 27 were wounded. Two died later from their wounds. Six Nez Perce were killed and the same number were wounded.
Monument: Nez Perce National Historical Park, P.O. Box 93, US 95, Spalding, ID 83551.
Sources: 5, 9, 19, 33, 66, 86, 91, 114, 175, 191, 197, 203, 236, 265, 285, 286, 315, 366, 378, 380, 405

ID10   *Birch Creek Massacre* • August 15, 1877
Location: Birch Creek Canyon
War: Nez Perce War
An advance party of Nez Perce came upon a train of eight wagons manned by five whites and two Chinese. The natives demanded guns and supplies, then broke open barrels of the drivers' whiskey. They got drunk and harassed the others, then killed the five white men and burned the wagons. A sixth white man, a horse herder who had joined the train just before the attack, escaped and was later rescued by cowboys.
Sources: 191, 366

ID11   *Battle of Camas Meadows* • August 20, 1877
Location: East of Kilgore, 4 miles west of Grangeville
War: Nez Perce War
The Nez Perce made several raids to acquire horses, and to keep them away from Gen. Oliver O. Howard. On August 13, they killed three men at the Montague-Winters ranch and stole its horses. They killed two others about five miles further up the valley.
Between Camas and Spring Creeks was a shallow valley a mile wide, and the Nez Perce camped there to take care of the wounded from the Battle of Big Hole a week before. On August 19, they moved out, knowing that they were being pursued. That day, they discovered hundreds of soldiers following their trail. They were led by Gen. Howard, who had arrived late at the Battle of Big Hole. Watching the army, they saw that it was going to camp at Camas Meadows, and a plan was laid to stampede the horses and mules and attack the camp, hopefully taking it by surprise.
Before dawn, the soldiers were awakened by screeches and war whoops. Many horses and nearly all of the 150 mules were stampeded. Soldiers chased the Nez Perce about eight miles, which was about halfway back to their camp. They caught up with the warriors in an area where they could hide among lava and bushes and shoot at the soldiers from long distance. Capt. Randolph Norwood and his men were pinned down for hours until Gen. Howard arrived with reserves. At that time, the Nez Perce withdrew through Targhee Pass essentially without injury, while the whites had one killed and eight wounded.
Monument: A historic marker for Camas Prairie and White Bird Battlefield is on US 95 south of Grangeville, ID.
Sources: 86, 91, 175, 191, 203, 236, 254, 265, 288, 350, 366, 378

ID12   *Battle of Clark's Fork* • June 8, 1878
Location: Clark's Fork
War: Bannock War
Two white men reported to the army that they had been wounded by a Bannock

warrior. At about the same time, about 200 Bannock and Northern Paiute warriors united under the leadership of Buffalo Horn, a Bannock chief. In June, they clashed at Clark's Fork near South Mountain with a volunteer patrol of 60 from Silver City and Buffalo Horn was killed.

The natives regrouped at Steens Mountain in Oregon with Paiutes from the Malheur Reservation. Their new leaders were Egan and Oytes.

Gen. Nelson A. Miles captured several natives while on a pleasure trip, and in the fighting Capt. Andrew S. Bennett was killed.

Sources: 9, 114, 134, 192, 350, 380

ID13 *Attacks in Idaho* • 1879
Location: Salmon River Mountains
War: Sheepeater War

In February, five Chinese miners were killed at Oro Grande by the Tukuarika of the Shoshonis, known as the "Sheepeaters." In May, they killed two ranchers.

About 50 Bannocks and Shoshonis began raiding settlers who were crowding them in their homeland. The were chased by army patrols, one of which was routed and the other was eluded. The army did not give up on their tracking and wore them down, so the Sheepeaters gave up in October after negotiating with a company of Umatilla scouts led by Lts. Edward S. Farrow and W.C. Brown. They were resettled with other Bannocks and Shoshonis on the Fort Hall Reservation.

Sources: 9, 66, 134

ILLINOIS

IL1 *Fox Massacre* • September 9, 1730
Location: Southwestern Illinois

The Foxes, having been defeated by several tribes, left their homeland in Wisconsin to seek refuge with the Iroquois. When they crossed the Illinois River in July of 1730, they were attacked by warriors from the Illinois tribe, which was soon joined by a party of Kickapoos, Potawatomis and Mascoutens. On August 17, they were joined by 500 French soldiers and more Illinois warriors.

The Foxes asked the French for leniency, which was denied. After a while, the Foxes ran out of food and water. On September 8, they attempted to retreat during a rainstorm, but they were pursued by the French. Between 200 and 300 Fox warriors were killed, plus many more women and children. Only about 60 Fox warriors escaped to live with the Sacs at Green Bay in Wisconsin.

Sources: 324

IL2 *Destruction of Saukenuk* • 1780
Location: Rock Island
War: Revolutionary War

The Sauk and Mesquakie (Fox) occupied a large site, including the town of Saukenuk which served as the capital of the Sauk nation. Because of the Sauk alliance with the British, the Americans destroyed the town, one of the largest native villages in North America. Most of its inhabitants relocated on the other side of the Mississippi River.

Museum: Hauberg Indian Museum, Black Hawk State Historic Site, 1510 46th Ave., Rock Island, IL 61201.

Sources: 349

IL3   *Attack at Fort St. Joseph* • February 12, 1781
Location: Saint Joseph River
War: Revolutionary War
Capt. Eugene Poure and 65 Spanish soldiers traveled north from St. Louis, along the way being joined by Siggenauk and Naakewoin and a force of 60 Ottawas, Potawatomis and Chippewas. They warned the St. Joseph natives not to interfere, and on the morning of February 12 they crossed the frozen river and surprised a party of British traders.

Two traders were killed and the remaining eight surrendered and their goods were divided among the warriors. Poure claimed the area for Spain, remained in the fort for 24 hours, then took his force back to St. Louis.

Sources: 324

IL4   *Attack Near Fort Massac* • April, 1795
Location: Near Fort Massac
Samuel Chew and a party of five were attacked by Potawatomis and Kickapoos. He was scalped and mutilated, and another was scalped, dismembered and disemboweled. Chew's slaves were also killed. Some of the responsible warriors were apprehended and taken to Kaskaskia, where they were killed by an angry mob.

In retaliation, Potawatomis from Lake Peoria banded with Kickapoos to conduct a series of attacks in southern Illinois. The final one in May involved the killing of a white family and 13 blacks near the mouth of the Ohio River.

Sources: 374

IL5   *Attack at Fort Dearborn* • April, 1811
Location: Near Fort Dearborn
A band of Winnebagos arrived at a farm on the south branch of the Illinois River. Two farmers were killed and mutilated, and the attackers got away.

Sources: 176

IL6   *Fort Dearborn Massacre* • August 15, 1812
Location: Chicago
War: War of 1812
Approximately 60 soldiers and militiamen were defeated by a force of Potawatomi. The traders and their families evacuated the fort and were attacked by warriors along a trail which later became Indiana Ave. Only one trader and two women survived, and the fort was razed.

Sources: 14, 91, 92, 133, 144, 169, 275, 349

IL7 *Battle Near Rock Island* • Late August, 1814
Location: Rock Island
War: War of 1812
Maj. Zachary Taylor was sent to the Sauk and Fox area to destroy native villages on the Rock River. As they approached, a force of 1,000 Winnebagos, Sioux, and Sauk and Fox organized at the native town of Saukenuk. Thirty British also arrived with a three-pounder gun to help Black Hawk.

The Americans spent the night on a willow-covered island across from the mouth of the Rock River, and were attacked by warriors in canoes before dawn. At daylight, the British opened fire on the American boats, splintering them. Taylor quickly retreated south to the mouth of the Des Moines River, where he attempted to rebuild Fort Madison.
Sources: 315, 386

IL8 *Attack at Saukenuk* • June 26, 1831
Location: Rock Island
War: Black Hawk's War
Gen. Edmund P. Gaines and 1,500 militia attacked the Sauk village of Saukenuk, first with artillery bombardment and then with a charge into the village. However, they found it deserted, since Black Hawk and his people had crossed to the west bank of the Mississippi River the night before. The soldiers burned down the village.
Sources: 315

IL9 *Attack on Menominees* • July, 1831
Location: Western Illinois
During 1830, a band of Sioux and Menominees killed some Fox chiefs, and for retribution the Foxes nearly wiped out one of the Menominee camps. Although Black Hawk had signed an agreement with Gen. Edmund P. Gaines to end the Sauk and Fox fighting with the whites, the intertribal warfare caused the settlers to be concerned about the tribe, anyway.

Black Hawk complemented the Foxes for their action, and told them the Americans had no right to interfere in matters between tribes. This resulted in the Foxes aligning with the Sauks against the whites.
Sources: 315

IL10 *Fight with Black Hawk* • April, 1832
Location: Prophetstown
War: Black Hawk's War
Black Hawk (Makataimeshekiakiak) and the Sauk and Fox tribe, by treaty, had left their homeland for Iowa. Later, he had a dream that his ancestors returned and encouraged the tribe to return to Illinois. Based on the dream, they packed up and headed east across the Mississippi River. The party consisted of 1,000 Sauk and Fox, plus 200 mounted British soldiers.

On April 5, the Sauks led by Black Hawk crossed back to the eastern bank of the Mississippi River at the mouth of the Iowa River, south of Saukenuk. They headed north to their old village and began planting corn in their former fields. Settlers killed two natives who had sought a parley under a flag of truce. Black Hawk began retaliation by killing settlers.

Monuments: (1) Black Hawk Statue at Black Hawk State Park, SR 2, Rock Island, IL; (2) Black Hawk Statue at Lowden State Park, SR 29, Oregon, IL.
Sources: 19, 20, 88, 133, 189, 193, 195, 211, 288, 384

IL11   *Battle of Stillman's Run* • May 14, 1832
Location: Dixon's Ferry, 15 miles south of Rockford
War: Black Hawk's War
Black Hawk and his people traveled up the Rock River past the Kishwaukee River, when they discovered 272 militia led by Maj. Isaiah Stillman. Black Hawk's first three emissaries sent under a white flag were taken prisoner by the soldiers, and later one was killed. Five more emissaries were attacked and two were killed, three making it back to report to Black Hawk. Stillman then attacked Black Hawk's warriors, who were camped on the Sycamore River.

Black Hawk was ready, and the 40 warriors hid until the 270 militia passed by, then attacked their rear. The soldiers panicked and were chased by about 25 warriors back to their camp, and then downriver to Gen. Whiteside's camp at Dixon's Ferry. Although the soldiers had only 11 missing, the battle was a humiliating defeat for Stillman and the army.

When Black Hawk and his people retreated from the area, they killed settlers along the way. Black Hawk asked for help from the Ottawas, Chippewas and Potawatomis, but they declined. He was, however, joined by 120 Kickapoos led by Mecina.

The shock among the whites which was generated by this battle ended any hope that Black Hawk may have had that they could return to Iowa in peace.
Memorial: Battleground Memorial Park, SR 72, Stillman Valley, IL 61084, has a 50-foot granite marker and 12 tombstones of men killed in the battle.
Sources: 20, 88, 195, 196, 223, 292, 293, 315, 324, 349, 375, 384, 395, 423

IL12   *Attack on Mail Train* • May 18, 1832
Location: Buffalo Grove
War: Black Hawk's War
Four privates under the command of Sgt. Stahl, all from Capt. James Stephenson's company in Galena, were an escort of mail contractor John D. Winters. They themselves were also carrying dispatches from Galena to Gen. Henry Atkinson and Gov. Reynolds at Dixon's Ferry.

As they reached the northwestern edge of Buffalo Grove, six Winnebago warriors rose out of the buffalo grass and fired on the soldiers. Pvt. William Durley was shot and killed, and as the others rode off without fighting back, Durley was scalped.
Sources: 292

IL13   *Massacre at Indian Creek* • May 20, 1832
Location: LaSalle County
War: Black Hawk's War
William Davis established a small farm on Indian Creek with a blacksmith shop and grist mill. Damming the creek provided power for the mill, but angered the natives by preventing fish in the Fox River from reaching the Potawatomi village upstream. Davis was warned by Shabbona that the dam might result in violence to him and the other 22 people living at the location.

On the afternoon of May 20, about 40 Potawatomis led by Toquamee and Comee and a few Sacs entered the Davis cabin. They killed 15 settlers and took two young women as prisoners. They were taken to Black Hawk's camp near the Turtle River, ransomed by White Crow, and turned over to the Americans unharmed.

Sources: 195, 292, 324, 375

IL14 *Battle of the Pecatonica* • June 16, 1832
Location: Pecatonica River
War: Black Hawk's War
A party led by Col. Henry Dodge sought natives in the area, and came upon 11 Sacs, following them to a small tributary stream of the Pecatonica River. In an area known as Horseshoe Bend, the 20 soldiers formed two lines and prepared for battle. When the Sacs opened fire, they killed Samuel Wells and F. Montaville Morris. Others were seriously wounded, but all 11 Sacs died in the fighting.

The soldiers returned to Fort Hamilton, where there was a party of Sioux and Menominees. When they heard of the fighting, they went to the battle site and cut the 11 Sac bodies into pieces and held a war dance around them.

Sources: 292, 375

IL15 *Battle of Waddam's Grove* • June 16, 1832
Location: North Crossroads Rd., northwest of Lena
War: Black Hawk's War
Capt. James Stephenson and his men chased Black Hawk and the warriors who had stolen ten horses from Apple River fort, 20 miles to the west. The warriors took refuge in a thicket, into which the soldiers charged three times. Both sides then departed. The natives had one killed, and the soldiers had three.

Sources: 292, 384

IL16 *Attack on Apple River Fort* • June 24, 1832
Location: Apple River
War: Black Hawk's War
The Apple River Fort was guarded by 20 men commanded by Capt. Clack Stone. Four men were traveling from the fort, and when they had gone about 300 yards they were attacked by about 24 Sacs. The gunfire alerted the people in and around the fort. About 200 warriors attacked the fort and after about an hour, most of the attackers went into the adjacent settlement to burn cabins and drive away the cattle and horses.

No natives were hurt in the action and three whites were killed or wounded.

Sources: 292

IL17 *Battles of Kellogg's Grove* • June 25, 1832
Location: Kent
War: Black Hawk's War
One hundred warriors led by Black Hawk ambushed a party of untrained farm boys in an effort to obtain horses and supplies from the inn at Kellogg's Grove. Two battles resulted in the deaths of 23 whites and nine natives. An army of 1,000 volunteers including 23-year-old Abraham Lincoln arrived too late to do anything more than bury the dead.

Monument: A historic marker was erected in 1886 by Stephenson County.
Sources: 195, 375, 384, 386

INDIANA

IN1 *Capture of Fort Miamis* • May 27, 1763
Location: Fort Wayne
War: Pontiac's Rebellion
Ensign Holmes was told by his native concubine that there was a sick squaw three hundred yards from the fort in a cabin. He left the fort to help her and was ambushed. A war party from Detroit combined with some local Miami warriors to force the surrender of Fort Miamis.
Sources: 315, 324, 412

IN2 *Surrender of Fort Ouiatenon* • June 1, 1763
Location: Lafayette
War: Pontiac's Rebellion
The Miami warriors who had participated in the capture of Fort Miamis were joined by Weas, Kickapoos and Mascoutens. The united force traveled to the Wabash River and forced the surrender of Fort Ouiatenon.
Sources: 315, 324

IN3 *Capture of Fort Vincennes* • December 17, 1778
Location: Vincennes
War: Revolutionary War
British Lt. Gov. Henry Hamilton recruited Kickapoos to fight against the Virginians. A small war party traveled with Hamilton and captured Fort Vincennes, the American Capt. Leonard Helm surrendering the fort and the village. When Brig. Gen. George Rogers Clark returned to the fort in February of 1779, the Kickapoos declined to participate in its defense.
Sources: 3, 176, 223, 238, 324

IN4 *Attacks on Shawnee Villages* • October, 1786
Location: Wabash River
Brig. Gen. George Rogers Clark led 1,800 mounted Kentuckians into Indiana to fight the Miamis, and the Shawnees formed a war party to assist the natives. At the same time, Clark sent Col. Benjamin Logan to attack the Shawnee villages along the Wabash River.
    When Clark and the Miamis arrived at the Wabash, they had successful peace talks and had dispersed, with Clark heading to Vincennes. When the Shawnees returned to their villages, they found that Col. Logan had killed 10 warriors and 12 others, including Chief Moluntha. Thirty-three were captured.

Only three whites were killed and three wounded. Included in the 13 villages which were destroyed were Mackachack, Wapatomica, Puckshanoses, Waccachalla, Kispoko Town, Solomon's Town, Blue Jacket's Town, Mingo Town, Mamacomink, Pecowick, Kekeko, Peckuwe and Wapakoneta.
Sources: 374

IN5 *Ambush Along the Eel River* • October 19, 1790
Location: Northwest of Kekionga
War: Ohio Indian Wars
Settlers in the Northwest Territory who chose to live in the areas reserved for natives often found themselves under attack, and many were killed. By 1789, the United States was at war with the tribes in the area.

Brig. Gen. Josiah Harmar set up his headquarters near Cincinnati and in late September burned five Miami towns, including Kekionga in present-day Indiana. Blue Jacket and Michikiniqua were surprised by Harmar's splitting of his force and sending out of 200 led by Col. John Hardin, with Capt. John Armstrong in charge of 30 regular soldiers. Little Turtle retaliated for Harmar's actions with an ambush at the Eel River.

Armstrong and only eight of his men survived from his group, and a total of 70 were killed. Those who survived returned to the main army and, to their surprise, Harmar did not pursue the warriors. Instead, he ordered a retreat.
Sources: 34, 91, 135, 176, 292, 323, 324, 374

IN6 *Ambush Along the Maumee River* • October 22, 1790
Location: Maumee River
War: Ohio Indian Wars
The government sent a punitive expedition from Fort Washington (Cincinnati) 120 miles north to the Maumee River area. The army of 1,133 militia and 320 regular soldiers commanded by Brig Gen. Josiah Harmar blundered into an ambush. Little Turtle and Blue Jacket, leading the Miamis and Shawnees, killed 183 Americans, sending the rest fleeing in panic. The militiamen had panicked and broken ranks and were slaughtered by the Miamis.

The natives were bolstered by their victories and believed they could force the Americans from their lands. They reoccupied their villages and replenished their food supplies. Blue Jacket and 200 warriors in January commenced a new series of raids against settlers and Ohio River traffic.
Sources: 20, 34, 56, 91, 123, 135, 147, 172, 200, 257, 293, 339, 383, 393, 412

IN7 *Attack on Kickapoo Village* • 1791
Location: Tippecanoe River
War: Ohio Indian Wars
Gen. Charles Scott led mounted Kentucky militia against a Kickapoo village on the Tippecanoe River. It was essentially undefended, since the Kickapoo warriors had left to aid their Miami allies in defending their villages against the Americans. Scott's attack resulted in the capture of 58 women and children and the destruction of the village and its corn.

Later in the year, Gen. James Wilkinson attacked while the warriors were hunting to the west. That resulted in the dispersal of most of the Wabash group of Kickapoos, who headed to Missouri and Illinois.
Sources: 223

IN8   *Battle of Tippecanoe* • November 7, 1811
        Location: Prophetstown
        War: War of 1812
        In October, Gen. William Henry Harrison invaded the lands of the Shawnees with
        800 to 1,000 men. They reached Prophetstown on the Tippecanoe River on
        November 6. Tecumseh had warned his brother, Tenskwatawa (formerly known
        as Lalawethika, The Open Door, also known as The Prophet) not to begin hos-
        tilities before he formed a coalition with the Chickasaws, Choctaws, Creeks and
        others. Nevertheless, Tenskwatawa attacked Harrison's camp before dawn with
        450 to 600 Winnebagos, Potawatomis and Kickapoos. They fought furiously to
        a standstill with the whites, then withdrew to the trees and kept up some fire
        throughout the day, then left for their homes the next day. The whites had 61 killed
        and 127 wounded, while the native dead were estimated to be from 25 to 40,
        including nine Kickapoos.
             The warriors blamed Tenskwatawa for what they considered to be a defeat,
        and he lost his influence over the Shawnees. Harrison led his men into the
        deserted Prophetstown and burned all of the wigwams and log buildings, destroy-
        ing the food and supplies. Later, some of the bands of warriors carried on their
        own raids against the Americans. Others sought an all-out war under the lead-
        ership of Tecumseh.
             Although the battle was not really very decisive, that the natives considered
        the battle to have been won by the army enhanced the prestige of Harrison. In
        1840, he was elected president.
             When Congress heard that Harrison's men had found British weapons on
        the Tippecanoe battlefield, they concluded that England was attempting to impede
        American expansion westward. The sentiment was in favor of war against Eng-
        land, including the capture of Canada and/or Florida.
        Monument: Tippecanoe Battlefield, Railroad St., Battle Ground, IN 47920, is
        located at the SR 43 exit of Interstate 65.
        Sources: 14, 18, 19, 20, 26, 27, 30, 34, 90, 91, 92, 126, 133, 144, 147, 170, 172, 176,
        178, 181, 189, 196, 199, 200, 223, 256, 257, 275, 288, 289, 299, 301, 311, 315, 324,
        349, 364, 380, 381, 389, 397, 398, 412, 422, 423

IN9   *Siege of Fort Harrison* • September 3–16, 1812
        Location: Vincennes
        War: War of 1812
        The British and their Kickapoo allies planned several attacks on posts in the
        northwest, including Fort Harrison on the Wabash River. On September 3,
        Pakoisheecan led a party against the fort and attempted to burn it down while
        warriors attacked the opposite side as a diversion. Two soldiers were killed out-
        side the fort, and the following day the lower blockhouse was set on fire, burn-
        ing whiskey that was stored there. Fort commander Zachary Taylor was able to
        save the fort with the help of a column of 1,200 soldiers led by William Russell,
        which reached the fort on September 16.
        Sources: 19, 91, 181, 200, 223, 397, 399

IN10   *Massacre at Pigeon Roost* • September 3, 1812
        Location: Pigeon Roost
        War: War of 1812

The frustrated Kickapoo warriors attacked civilians at Pigeon Roost, scalping 21 of them. In response, Brig. Gen. Samuel Hopkins led an army against them and destroyed 160 homes at their village along the Tippecanoe River.
Monument: Pigeon Roost State Historic Site, US 31, Underwood, IN, has a 44-foot monument marking the site of the early settlement.
Sources: 181, 223, 397, 399

IN11 *Attack at Peoria Lake* • October 18, 1812
Location: Salt Fork of the Sagamon River
War: War of 1812
Illinois governor Ninian Edwards marched 362 militiamen from Edwardsville to Peoria Lake and attacked the villages of Kickapoo Chief Pawatomo, White Hair and Black Partridge. The village was burned, 1,000 bushels of corn were destroyed, and 24 Kickapoos were killed.
Sources: 223, 324

IN12 *Attack at Prophetstown* • November 11, 1812
Location: Prophetstown
War: War of 1812
Brig. Gen. Samuel Hopkins led three regiments of Kentucky infantry and others, totalling 1,200, and destroyed 40 huts at Prophetstown and 160 huts at a Kickapoo village. They also cut down all the growing corn.
Sources: 397

IN13 *Massacre at Falls Creek* • March 22, 1824
Location: Pendleton
A band of white men supposedly looking for stray horses came upon some friendly Miamis and Senecas and killed nine of them. The victims' families were given $300 and a promise of prosecution of the guilty parties. Most of the white individuals involved were convicted and hanged.
Monument: Falls Park and monument are on Pendleton Ave., just outside downtown Pendleton.
Sources: 199, 288

IOWA

IA1 *Spirit Lake Massacre* • March 8, 1857
Location: Extreme northwest corner of Iowa
On February 13, Inkpaduta and his band of Sioux came to Clay County, about 50 miles from Spirit Lake and demanded food at the Bicknell farm. They took flour and cornmeal and vandalized the home. The Sioux headed north and found that other whites had settled on what had been their land. On March 8, they went from cabin to cabin on a killing spree.

Thirty-four settlers living in cabins on the shores of Lakes Okoboji and Spirit were killed. When their bodies were discovered by another settler returning from a trip for supplies, the whites in the area became very afraid. Two of the women taken to Minnesota as captives were recovered, but the other two were killed.

Sources: 211, 259

KANSAS

KS1　*Battle Near Fort Riley* • 1854
Location: Near Fort Riley
Nearly 1,000 warriors from the Comanche, Kiowa, Cheyenne and Osage tribes surprised 100 Sac and Fox buffalo hunters on the Kansas plains. The Sac and Fox had newer, more reliable rifles and were able to repel the larger force, which attempted several massed charges. The attackers lost 26 warriors and dozens of horses, then withdrew.
Sources: 20, 217

KS2　*Battle of Solomon's Fork* • July 29, 1857
Location: Solomon River
War: Cheyenne Expedition
Col. Edwin Vose Sumner led six cavalry companies from Fort Leavenworth into battle against 300 Cheyenne warriors. He ordered his men to draw their sabers and charge, without waiting for support from infantry or artillery. The natives fled and were chased seven miles. Along the way, nine warriors and two soldiers were killed.
Sources: 66, 91, 110

KS3　*Fight at Council Grove* • June 17, 1859
Location: Council Grove
A Kansa raiding party stole two horses from the Mexican freighting firm of R. Otise. A citizens' committee demanded that they be brought back, so 100 Kansa warriors accompanied them the Council Grove. They were confronted by merchant Seth M. Hays, who fired two pistol shots into the air. A fight broke out, wounding Charles Gilky and William Park.

The Kansas then retreated to an area four miles from town. They sent a peace delegation back to town, but they were driven back by the residents. At the demand of the citizens' committee, the Kansas turned over the two natives who had wounded the settlers, and they were hanged.
Sources: 217

KS4 *Sacking of Wichita Agency* • October 23–24, 1862
Location: Wichita
War: Civil War
A Union cavalry party consisting of 100 Southern Kickapoos, 70 Delawares and 26 Shawnees traveled 500 miles from Fort Leavenworth to the Wichita Agency to attack Confederate officials and allied natives. Delaware native Capt. Ben Simon was the overall leader of the party.

On October 23, they attacked the agency and killed Agent Leeper and four other agency personnel, while one Delaware was killed and one Shawnee was wounded. They took 100 ponies and other loot and burned the agency building.

On October 24, they attacked the Tonkawas, trapping them in a blackjack thicket along the Washita River. They killed chief Placido, 23 warriors and 113 women and children. The Union force had 27 casualties.
Sources: 60

KS5 *Attack at the Verdigris River* • May, 1863
Location: Upper Verdigris River
War: Civil War
A party of 22 Confederate soldiers was attacked by a band of Little Osages. The soldiers made a defensive stand along the Verdigris River, and then were annihilated by the warriors.
Sources: 304

KS6 *Kidder Massacre* • July 22, 1867
Location: Fort Riley
A party of 11 men led by Lt. Lyman S. Kidder was completely wiped out by Sioux warriors. Their remains were later found by a contingent led by Gen. George Armstrong Custer.
Sources: 91, 115

KS7 *Battle of Beecher's Island* or *Battle of Aricaree Fork* • September 17, 1868
Location: Aricaree Fork of the Republican River
The Cheyenne believed that Roman Nose had special medicine to protect him, and urged him to lead an attack against the soldiers who were led by George A. Forsyth. That occurred the morning following Roman Nose's purification ceremony, necessitated by his discovery that his food had been prepared with an impermissible iron fork.

Between 500 and 600 Cheyenne and Sioux rode to the soldiers' camp and waited for the order to attack as one, so that no small parties would engage the enemy on their own. Despite the plan, two Cheyenne and six Sioux left on their own and attempted to capture the soldiers' horse herd. They captured a few, but the soldiers were then alerted to the presence of the warriors, and the element of surprise was lost. The soldiers had time to move to an island and take cover in the high grass and willows.

The warriors swarmed around the island, circling it for most of the morning. The soldiers' Spencer repeating rifles repulsed all direct attacks. When Roman Nose arrived, most of the warriors stopped fighting to see what order he would give. After painting himself for battle, he led a charge directly at the island. He was cut down with a bullet in the spine and died later that night. Others in the front line of the charge were also killed.

The Cheyenne and Sioux withdrew to a position that kept the soldiers on the island for eight days, eating their horses and digging in the sand for water. A relief column then arrived and the natives departed. The battle was named by the whites after Lt. Frederick H. Beecher, a nephew of Henry Ward Beecher, who was killed during the battle. The natives called it the Fight When Roman Nose Was Killed.

Sources: 29, 66, 70, 92, 197, 218, 220, 380, 392, 407

KS8 *Fight at Wichita Agency* • August, 1871
Location: Anadarko
After a brief fight at the Wichita Agency, a party of Comanches traveled to the Staked Plain. The Kiowas went to the head of the Red River, pursued by soldiers. After the Kiowas were captured on their return from a horse-stealing raid into New Mexico, they were sent into captivity at Fort Marion, Florida.
Sources: 227

KS9 *Attack on Medicine Lodge Creek* • Summer, 1874
Location: Medicine Lodge Creek
A group of 29 Osages were planning to leave their hunting camp on their old Kansas reservation lands and return to Oklahoma. Shortly before they were about to leave, they were attacked by a party of whites who killed four Osages and took the party's horses, meat, robes and kettles.

To make the attack seem less like murder and more like official business, the Kansas governor mustered the killers into the militia and backdated their paperwork. The attack then appeared to be one by the militia itself, rather than by individuals.
Sources: 304

KS10 *Dull Knife's Raid* • September 29, 1878
Location: Oberlin
A band of Northern Cheyenne were taken to Oklahoma in 1877 and nearly 1,000 of them were relocated to the Cheyenne reservation near Darlington Agency. Under the leadership of Dull Knife, a band of 89 men and 246 women and children left the reservation and headed north toward home. Along the way, they killed settlers and cowboys.

In southern Kansas, they became surrounded by a force of cowboys and soldiers. They fought one day from a distance, then slipped away during the night.

When they reached the northern plains, they were captured and returned to the reservation in Oklahoma.
Museum: The Last Indian Raid Museum is located on S. Penn Ave. in Oberlin.
Sources: 19, 91

KENTUCKY

KY1 *Attack at Limestone Creek* • December 25, 1776
Location: Maysville
War: Revolutionary War
At the mouth of Limestone Creek where it empties into the Ohio River, the expedition led by Brig. Gen. George Rogers Clark left attorney John Gabriel Jones and five of his exhausted men, while Clark continued inland to Harrodsburg. Not long after that, a party of eight surveyors also arrived in the Maysville area. When Clark returned, he found that on Christmas Day, natives led by Pluggy had overwhelmed the group, killing Jones and William Graden, and taking four as prisoners.
Sources: 3

KY2 *Attack at McClelland's Station* • May 31, 1777
Location: Maysville
War: Revolutionary War
Brig. Gen. George Rogers Clark remained in the area near Limestone Creek to defend nearby McClelland's Station. The natives soon attacked, and in the battle their leader, Pluggy (Plukkemehnotee), was killed along with George McClelland. The natives left the battle without taking the fort, but the whites abandoned the fort and went inland to help protect Harrodsburg.
Sources: 3, 120, 222, 374

KY3 *Sieges of Boonesborough* • September, 1777
Location: Boonesborough
War: Revolutionary War
Chiungalla, a lifelong friend of Plukkemehnotee, was angered over the death of his friend at McClelland's Station, and organized a war party for a winter attack. His force included some British from Detroit and members of other tribes. They attacked some villages, causing settlers to seek refuge in Harrodsburg, Boonesborough and Col. Benjamin Logan's St. Asaph's Station.

These settlements were repeatedly the targets of Chiungalla. Boonesborough, for example, was besieged three separate times over a period of months including one on February 7, 1778, which included the Shawnee capture of Daniel Boone and 26 companions. After some severe weather, Chiungalla gave up the campaign and took many of his warriors across the Ohio River.
Museum: Fort Boonesborough, located 6 miles north of Interstate 75 on SR 627 in Fort Boonesborough State Park, is a recreation of the fort built in 1775 by Daniel Boone.
Sources: 3, 19, 119, 120, 221, 238, 242, 374, 380

KY4 *Attack at Ruddle's Station* • June 20, 1780
Location: Licking River
War: Revolutionary War
In April, the British command in Detroit sent Capt. Henry Bird (Byrd) on an

expedition to Kentucky with over 1,000 natives. Initially, they intended to strike first at Louisville, but the natives' enthusiasm for battle caused them to instead head to the more populated central part of the territory.

They attacked Ruddle's (Ruddell's or Hinkston's) Station and two cannon shots at the entrance to the stockade convinced the 300 settlers to surrender. They were promised safe passage out of the stockade, but as soon as the gate was opened the warriors rushed in and butchered most of the settlers.

The British and natives then went to the smaller Martin's Station, which surrendered and 50 captives were taken. The natives and soldiers were then frightened away by the news of the approach of Brig. Gen. George Rogers Clark.

Sources: 3, 14, 120, 222, 395

KY5   *Ambush Along the Ohio River* • August 24, 1781
Location: Near Aurora
War: Revolutionary War
Brig. Gen. George Rogers Clark assembled an army of 400 from Pittsburgh with a goal of attacking Detroit. They followed the Ohio River to Fort Nelson, followed by Pennsylvania soldiers under the command of Col. Archibald Lochry. At their camp near the present site of Aurora, they were ambushed by natives and British militia from Detroit. Forty-one were killed and the 55 survivors were captured.
Sources: 374, 395

KY6   *Battle of Little Mountain* • Spring, 1782
Location: Mount Sterling
War: Revolutionary War
Although British Gen. Cornwallis surrendered at Yorktown in 1781, the British kept up the war effort by trying to hang onto Canada and the Great Lakes region. Capt. James Estill led 34 men into battle with a party of Wyandots. Both sides lost several men, and the news of the conflict caused concern among the area's stations and forts.
Sources: 221

KY7   *Attack at Bryan's Station* • August 14–15, 1782
Location: North of Lexington
War: Revolutionary War
British militia from Detroit and native allies, comprising a force of about 500, attacked the settlement of Bryan's (Bryant's) Station, which had a population of 90. The settlers defended their fort for three days, then approaching reinforcements scared off the attackers. The settlers, however, lost their crops, hogs, cattle and horses.
Sources: 3, 120, 169, 221, 222, 238, 395

KY8   *Battle of Blue Licks* • August 19, 1782
Location: Along present US 68, between the Licking River and Maysville in Mason County
War: Revolutionary War
The 50 militia led by Capt. William Caldwell and 550 natives led by Simon Girty who had attacked Bryan's Station were pursued to Blue Licks on the Licking River

by 182 Kentuckians led by Col. Richard Todd. The contingent including Daniel Boone was ambushed in a ravine. Within a few minutes the smaller force of Kentuckians was driven back in panic across the Licking River. Their losses were 72 killed, including Todd and Boone's son, 12 wounded, and seven taken captive. The natives had three killed and four wounded.

Monument: Blue Licks Battlefield State Park on US 68 between Paris and Maysville includes a granite obelisk, burial grounds and museum.

Sources: 3, 14, 19, 119, 120, 169, 221, 222, 238, 324, 374, 380, 395, 413

KY9 *Attack at Lee's Creek* • March, 1790
Location: Near the mouth of Lee's Creek at the Ohio River
War: Ohio Indian Wars
Ignatius Ross, an experienced Indian fighter, was wounded in a short fight with a band of Shawnees. They then fled across to the north side of the Ohio River, at the time a safe area for natives.
Sources: 374

KY10 *Attack in Mason County* • March 17, 1791
Location: Near Maysville
War: Ohio Indian Wars
A detachment of soldiers traveling south from Pittsburgh with several families picked up other settlers and a second boat near Marietta, some heading for Cincinnati and others for Louisville. While they were on the Ohio River, three large Shawnee canoes headed for them. When they were at a range of 40 yards, the soldiers opened fire and killed three natives. The remaining warriors returned the gunfire, pulled out of range, then struck again. A shot killed Capt. Kirkpatrick and several others were wounded. After five warriors and six whites were killed, the canoes pulled out of range for a final time and the settlers' boats drifted to Maysville.

Twenty-one others in the party who declined to sail with this contingent, and who remained on the Kentucky shore, were found the following month by a force of 200 led by Cols. Orr and Rankin. They had been shot or tomahawked and then scalped. Nearby was a burned ruin of a flatboat on which 13 men and two women had been killed, including John May.
Sources: 374

KY11 *Ambush at Snag Creek* • April 16, 1791
Location: Just below Bradford
War: Ohio Indian Wars
Ben Whiteman and Neil Washburn patrolled the Ohio River shore about 30 miles below Maysville, and found four large canoes at the mouth of Snag Creek. They had been covered with old driftwood and brush. Whiteman and Washburn reported their find to Simon Kenton, who sent word to 30 scouts to meet in Maysville. The party included Jacob Wetzel, and set off in an old keelboat and a 40-foot canoe.

They waited near the hidden canoes in ambush, and after two days three Shawnees showed up. They killed and scalped all three and took the six horses which they had. The scene was repeated the following day, except that one of the new victims' heads was placed on a pole to warn others. Two additional war-

riors were killed in a separate skirmish, and a total of 32 stolen horses were recovered.
Sources: 374

LOUISIANA

LA1   *Assassination of Priest* • Late 1706
Location: Louisiana
A group of Chitimachas killed a priest in the foreign missions named Jean Francois de Saint-Cosme. The killing touched off more than a decade of fighting. Many Chitimachas were sold into slavery in Louisiana and in the Caribbean by the French and allied tribes.
Sources: 326

LA2   *Destruction of Chaoucha Village* • 1729
Location: Just below New Orleans
War: French-Natchez War
Fearing the nearby Chaouchas and a potential black-native coalition, the governor sent a small army of slaves to the village closest to New Orleans. What resulted was the destruction of the village.
Sources: 326

LA3   *Battle of New Orleans* • January 8, 1815
Location: 6 miles south of New Orleans
War: War of 1812
Several Choctaws joined about 1,800 regular American soldiers, a black regiment, and recruits from New Orleans to fight under Gen. Andrew Jackson against the British. A treaty ending the war had been signed 15 days earlier, but the news had not yet reached the front.

Jackson reached New Orleans on December 2 to fight the 2,000 British troops led by Gen. Sir Edward Pakenham and camped on the levee below Chalmette. On December 23, they made an unsuccessful assault on the British position, then fell back to a defensive posture at Chalmette Plantation. The British increased their size to 8,900 men, including Hitchitis led by Kinache, and attacked on January 8.

The American force had also grown in size, to about 5,400. They fought on open ground and the British suffered 2,036 casualties, while the Americans had only 13. Jackson's political career was greatly helped by this military victory.
Monument: Chalmette National Historical Park, 8606 W. St. Bernard Hwy., Chalmette, LA 70043, has a 100-foot marble obelisk monument and visitor center within the 141-acre park.
Sources: 19, 36, 41, 42, 113, 133, 181, 240, 295, 347, 396, 398, 400

MAINE

ME1 *Attack on Arrowsic* • August 14, 1676
Location: Arrowsic
An Abenaki woman arrived at the Arrowsic community, seeking shelter for the night within the stockade. During the night, she opened the gates and in rushed a band of warriors, who killed many of the inhabitants. The survivors, including Capt. Thomas Lake, fled to nearby Georgetown Island, and alerted the settlers in Sagahadoc.
Sources: 334, 363

ME2 *Attack on North Yarmouth* • July, 1688
Location: North Yarmouth
Increasing tension in the area led the Justice of the Peace, Capt. Benjamin Blackman, to have some of the local Abenakis ("Eastern Indians") brought in for questioning. This was accomplished by Capt. Peter Sargent, and the natives responded by taking several English prisoners. While a company led by Capt. Walter Gendell was building a fort in the area of present-day North Yarmouth, 70 to 80 natives approached where they were working.

To reach safety, the soldiers crossed the river but accidentally ran right into the natives, who had several white captives. The soldiers attempted to free the captives, and the struggle erupted into gunfire. Some were killed on each side before the natives were chased across the river.

In the evening, believing the fighting was over, Capt. Gendell and a servant canoed across the river, where they were killed by concealed warriors. Some time later (Cotton Mather stated that the date was September 5), a band of natives attacked the town of Sheepscot and burned all except two or three homes. The settlers were saved by congregating in the fort. A smaller attack also occurred at Kennebunk before the winter set in.
Sources: 274, 328

ME3 *Attack at Fort Charles* • August 21, 1689
Location: Pemaquid Point, Lincoln County
War: King William's War
The local natives were encouraged to attack the British settlement at Pemaquid Point by the French, who had settled at nearby Penobscot Bay. On August 21, while fighting was going on at Fort Charles, a band of about 30 natives attacked Thomas Gyles and three of his sons who were harvesting wheat at his farm about three miles above the fort. The father was killed and the boys were taken prisoner, being held for six years.
Sources: 412

ME4 *Attack on Casco Bay* • February, 1690
Location: Portland
War: King William's War
French governor Count Frontenac sent out an expedition consisting of Canadian

soldiers and natives led by French officers. They attacked and destroyed the fort and village of Casco Bay on the coast.
Sources: 128, 328, 381

ME5   *Attack on Salmon Falls* • March 18, 1690
Location: Salmon Falls
War: King William's War
Sent by French governor Count Frontenac, about an equal number of French led by Francois Hertel and natives led by Hopehood (Wohawa) attacked the settlement of Salmon Falls. They killed about 30 settlers and captured about 50. Several buildings were burned.
Sources: 92, 274, 290, 328

ME6   *Attack on York* • January 25, 1691
Location: York
War: King William's War
A band of Popish warriors, estimated in the hundreds, attacked the town of York, killing 48 to 75, including Shubael Dummer, the Minister of York. Some of the homes were well defended by the settlers, and the natives retreated with from 73 to more than 100 captives. The captives were taken to Sagadahoc and several were recovered at a later date.
Sources: 128, 274

ME7   *Destruction of York* • February, 1692
Location: York
War: King William's War
The Abenakis were encouraged by the Jesuits to again become active along the Maine frontier. They attacked and destroyed York, then made an unsuccessful attack against Wells. There was also a series of small raids in central Massachusetts.
Sources: 128, 328

ME8   *Raid on Casco* • 1703
Location: Portland
War: Queen Anne's War
Two months after signing a treaty with Joseph Dudley, governor of Massachusetts and New Hampshire, the Abenakis were influenced by the French Jesuits to attack. They nearly wiped out the settlement of Casco.
Sources: 328

ME9   *Attack on Wells* • August, 1703
Location: Wells
War: Queen Anne's War
Bands of Abenakis led by French attacked the village of Wells on the coast, plus other nearby towns. The attacks generally consisted of stealthy approach, a sudden assault, indiscriminate slaughter, burning of structures, and a hasty retreat with goods and prisoners.
Sources: 290

ME10 *Attack at Brunswick* • 1722
Location: Brunswick
War: Dummer's War
Father Sebastian Rale, an agent of the French regime headquartered at Quebec, convinced the local natives that their support of the French could bring about the defeat of the English. In response, the English attempted to seize Rale, and the natives responded with attacks on settlements, including Brunswick. Several residents were carried off.
Sources: 290

ME11 *Battle of Pigwacket* • May 8, 1725
Location: Fryeburg
War: Dummer's War
Capt. John Lovewell of Dunstable organized a group of hardy frontiersmen for the express purpose of hunting down natives. At Pigwacket, they fought against a band of warriors that he initially underestimated. About a third of Lovewell's men survived, but he himself did not.
    After this battle, enthusiasm lessened for hunting and scalping the natives.
Sources: 290

ME12 *Attack at Norridgewock* • August, 1725
Location: Norridgewock
War: Dummer's War
Father Sebastian Rale lived with the Abenakis at Norridgewock for almost 30 years, converting them to Christianity. The English believed he incited the natives to attack English settlements, and in retaliation they attacked his fortified mission. Killed were several native leaders and Father Rale himself, who was mutilated by the English.
    The village was burned and about 100 natives were killed. This event weakened the scattered warriors, who could then offer only sporadic resistance.
    Dummer's (Lovewell's) War ended with an agreement with the natives on December 15, 1725.
Sources: 92, 135, 249, 284, 290

ME13 *Raids on Towns* • Spring, 1745
Location: Kennebec
War: King George's War
French soldiers and natives raided Maine towns, including Kennebec. Waldoboro was destroyed.
Sources: 290, 381

MARYLAND

MD1 *Attack on English Ship* • 1608
Location: Nanticoke

Capt. John Smith led a party exploring Chesapeake Bay by water. After visiting with some small tribes on the lower Eastern Shore, they sailed into the Kuskarawaok (now, Nanticoke) River. The natives, now called Nanticokes, climbed trees and shot arrows at the boat, but they fell short. The boat stayed anchored in the middle of the river.

The next morning, the Nanticokes brought baskets of food and appeared to have ceased the hostilities. The soldiers shot their muskets over the natives' heads, causing them to drop their baskets and flee. The English then noticed warriors hiding among the reeds, ready to attack if they had come ashore to receive the "gifts."

Smith soon convinced four men that they meant no harm, and they brought additional natives with food and water in exchange for gifts. The Nanticokes agreed to serve as guides for the expedition along the river.
Sources: 271

MD2 *Battle of Antietam* • September 17, 1862
Location: Sharpsburg
War: Civil War

The 12th South Carolina Volunteer Infantry, including some Catawbas, fought in the Battle of Antietam. They were a part of the brigade led by Gen. Maxcy Gregg, who attacked the Union soldiers by surprise in the early evening, killing over 300 Connecticut troops at a range of about ten feet in a matter of minutes.
Sources: 60

MASSACHUSETTS

MA1 *Attack at Almouchiquois* • October 15, 1606
Location: Chatham
War: Champlain Expedition

Samuel de Champlain and 50 men sailed southward along the New England coast, and put in at the native village of Almouchiquois on Cape Cod. They presented gifts to the natives, who nevertheless ordered them back onto their ship. Five Frenchmen disobeyed and got drunk on shore. The next morning, they were attacked by a party who killed four of them with bows and arrows. The fifth survived with an arrow in his chest.
Sources: 412

MA2 *Attack at Wessagusett* • Late March, 1623
Location: Wessagusett, south of Plymouth
Settlers at Wessagusett, near the southern shore of Massachusetts Bay, reportedly stole corn and committed other abuses against the local natives. Massasoit of the Wampanoags was friendly and encouraged the settlers to kill the offenders.

The Pilgrims dispatched Miles Standish and eight others to seize the native ringleaders of a conspiracy to eliminate Wessagusett. To placate the natives, some English were whipped or stocked and one was hanged for stealing. By that time, the settlement's organization was disintegrating.

Standish and his men attacked the natives and shot and killed eight, then hanged one. Three more warriors were killed later in the day.
Sources: 279, 380

MA3 *Looting in Swansea* • June 20–22, 1675
Location: In and near Swansea
War: King Philip's War
Beginning in the 1660s, chief Massasoit's grandson, Metacom or Metacomet (called King Philip by the British colonists), and other members of his Wampanoag tribe felt that they were being unfairly treated by the white settlers. In 1674, a Harvard-educated Wampanoag named John Sansamon was murdered by other natives, who were then executed by the English. Wampanoags retaliated with violence, and the English strove to drive them off what they considered to be English land.

Beginning in 1675, while they camped on the Mount Hope Peninsula in Rhode Island, just over the border from Swansea, they unsuccessfully attempted to goad the settlers into drawing first blood. They had believed that whoever attacked first would lose, and the area would be rid of the unwelcome Europeans.

A group of young Wampanoags looted the house of Job Winslow in Swansea on June 18 or 19. On June 20, they began three days of burning and looting of empty homes on the southern fringes of Swansea. On June 23, a Wampanoag (Pokanoket) looter was shot by an English boy.
Sources: 90, 125, 133, 135, 147, 150, 152, 199, 225, 226, 251, 268, 270, 274, 290, 310, 315, 334

MA4 *Attack at Mattapoiset* • June 24, 1675
Location: Gardner's Neck (Mattapoiset)
War: King Philip's War
A Wampanoag party came upon a party of settlers who were in the process of retrieving corn from a deserted farm, a distance away from the garrison house. The natives killed six to eight, including the boy who had shot the Wampanoag looter the day before.

The heads of the dead were later displayed by the Wampanoags on poles at Kickamuit.
Sources: 150, 152, 334

MA5 *Attack at Miles' Garrison* • June 24, 1675
Location: Swansea
War: King Philip's War

At a supposedly well-defended garrison, a party of Wampanoags sneaked close and killed a sentry, mortally wounding two others. They were found later, beheaded and missing their hands and feet. A messenger was sent to Rehoboth to fetch a doctor for the wounded in the garrison. On June 25, their mutilated bodies were found along the trail by Capts. Thomas Savage, James Oliver and Thomas Brattle.
Sources: 150, 152

MA6 *Attack on Swansea* • June 24, 1675
Location: Swansea
War: King Philip's War
A Wampanoag war party decided not to wait any longer to see if the settlers would draw first blood, or perhaps they acted upon the previous day's shooting of one of their own as a looter. They ambushed a congregation returning home from church, killing one and wounding several. By the time soldiers from Plymouth and Boston arrived in the New Hope area on June 26, King Philip and his braves had fled across Narragansett Bay into Pocasset territory. The British force failed to follow.

The soldiers' movement west, away from the Wampanoags to make peace with the Narragansetts, was taken by the Pocassets as a cowardly or stupid move, and they allied with the Wampanoags against the settlers. The soldiers antagonized the previously neutral Narragansetts, then searched for King Philip who by this time had gone to and enlisted the Nipmucks in his campaign.
Sources: 34, 125, 147, 152, 188, 212, 225, 226, 233, 251, 270, 274, 310, 315, 334

MA7 *Ambush Near Miles' Garrison* • June 28, 1675
Location: Swansea
War: King Philip's War
Troops from Massachusetts came to Miles' Garrison and joined the Plymouth troops who were already there, making it the army's main advance base. To demonstrate their capability, Benjamin Church and 12 men intended to ride into Wampanoag territory. They were guided by William Hammond of Rehoboth.

Just as they crossed the bridge into native land, shots rang out from concealed warriors. Hammond and Quartermaster Joseph Belcher were wounded. The soldiers quickly returned to the garrison house, but Corp. Gill and Church returned to bring Hammond back to safety, where he later died.

On the following day, soldiers were again sent across the bridge to seek out the natives. The only action was a brief exchange of shots between two groups of soldiers who mistook each other for Wampanoags, with only one minor casualty resulting.
Sources: 34, 152, 188, 334

MA8 *Attacks on Frontier Towns* • July, 1675
Location: Massachusetts
War: King Philip's War
Both Rehoboth and Taunton had been attacked, and on July 9, most of the homes in Middleborough were burned, causing it to be abandoned. Several settlers were killed and their 36 homes were burned in Dartmouth, and then Russell's garrison in Poneganset was attacked. Narragansetts attacked a portion of Providence, and on July 14, Nipmucks led by Matoonas killed six in Mendon.
Sources: 150, 152, 315, 334

MA9 *Skirmish Near Pocasset Swamp* • July 19, 1675
Location: Near Taunton
War: King Philip's War
The governors of the colonies were feeling pressure to demobilize some of their armies, cutting costs and letting the men get back to their farming duties. Those that remained from the Massachusetts army returned from the Narragansett area to combine with the Plymouth army to fight the Wampanoags. They moved toward the Pocasset swamp area and ran into a party of natives who killed two of their advance guard.

The army pressed on through the swamp but never could engage the warriors in battle. They were only able to capture one old man.
Sources: 34, 53, 150, 152, 188, 233, 315

MA10 *Ambush at Quaboag* • August 2–4, 1675
Location: Within 3 miles of Brookfield
War: King Philip's War
A company of men led by Capt. Edward Hutchinson was to meet with the Nipmucks at a town known as Quaboag (also called Quabaog and Wickabaug). Upon their arrival on August 1, they found that the natives had not arrived, so they headed to where they thought they were. They were ambushed by supposedly neutral Nipmucks on a narrow trail which passed between a thick swamp and a steep hillside.

Without an obvious escape route, confusion reigned. Some charged up the hill toward the enemy, while others were killed by rifle fire on the trail. The survivors, including the wounded Hutchinson, made it back to Brookfield and, with the townspeople, crowded into a single house on a hill. They sent Ephraim Curtis and Henry Young for help, but they came upon natives and were forced back to Brookfield.

The warriors converged on the house and the sides exchanged fierce fire. Some Nipmucks took over the barn, where they would be protected as they shot at the house. They shot flaming arrows onto the roof of the house, but its defenders cut holes in the roof so they could extinguish the flames. Other attempts at burning down the house were unsuccessful.

The siege continued until August 4, when help arrived from Lancaster. Maj. Simon Willard and his troops made it to the house and the warriors withdrew. Hutchinson was moved to Marlborough and died from his wounds on August 14.
Sources: 133, 135, 152, 188, 268, 274, 315, 334

MA11 *Attack at Lancaster* • August 22, 1675
Location: Lancaster
War: King Philip's War
A house was burned and seven residents of the town were killed by a small group of initially unidentified natives. They were first believed to be local natives from Marlborough, but were later determined to be Nashaways led by their sachem, One-eyed John (Monoco).
Sources: 152, 270, 310, 334

MA12 *Battle of Sugarloaf Hill* • August 25, 1675
Location: Halfway between Hatfield and Deerfield
War: King Philip's War

Mohegan sachem Uncas, to cause trouble for his Indian enemies, reported to the British that the Norwottock natives living near Hatfield were behaving in a suspicious manner. Settlers demanded that they hand over their weapons, but the Norwottocks left during the night and headed for New Hampshire. Capts. Thomas Lathrop and Richard Beers and 100 solders pursued them and initially lost four or five men in a skirmish on the way to Deerfield, and an equal number were wounded.

Although the English did well against the first band of 160 warriors, more arrived and inflicted many more casualties. Capt. Samuel Moseley and 60 men arrived while the battle was raging, and continued it for about three hours. They claimed to have killed nearly 40 of the Norwottocks.

Loyalty of local Indians was destroyed. Nearby towns prepared for trouble.
Sources: 125, 152, 225, 274, 334

MA13 *Raids on Springfield* • August 24–25, 1675
Location: Springfield
War: King Philip's War
Raids on the settlement of Springfield were carried out by bands of roving Nipmucks.
Sources: 334

MA14 *Connecticut Valley Campaign* • September, 1675
Location: Deerfield
War: King Philip's War
Half of the buildings in Deerfield were burned by attacking natives who killed one man there on September 1. On September 2, eight men near Northfield (Squkeag) were attacked and killed in the woods.

On September 3, Capt. Richard Beers led a company of 36 to evacuate Northfield. They were ambushed on September 4 and over half the soldiers were killed, with the survivors going to Hadley. Maj. Robert Treat accomplished the evacuation of Northfield on September 6. Settlers returning from worship in Deerfield were attacked on September 12 by a group of Pocumtucks, with one settler taken prisoner.

The town of Deerfield was evacuated, with the settlers being taken to Northampton under armed escort.
Sources: 125, 133, 135, 150, 152, 188, 225, 233, 290, 315, 334, 393

MA15 *Ambush at Bloody Brook* • September 18, 1675
Location: Between Deerfield and Hatfield
War: King Philip's War
When the settlers were evacuated from Deerfield because of increasing tension with the natives, they left about 3,000 bushels of corn growing in the fields. Capt. Thomas Lathrop returned with 80 soldiers to harvest it, and returned south with tired men with their guns piled on the grain wagons. As they passed through a swampy, narrow gully, Lathrop and 60 to 70 others were killed. The final nine were saved only when Capt. Samuel Moseley arrived with 60 more to join the battle, followed by more led by Maj. Robert Treat from the garrison at Hadley. The name of the watercourse was changed from Muddy Brook to Bloody Brook.

The Indians, who had previously considered Moseley to be superhuman

(because he could scalp himself at will — remove his wig), no longer held him in awe. The Commissioners of the United Colonies decided to raise an army of over 1,000 and eliminate the hostile Indians from the Connecticut Valley.
Sources: 34, 125, 152, 225, 270, 315, 334

MA16   *Attacks on Springfield* • September–October, 1675
Location: Springfield
War: King Philip's War
The Commissioners of the United Colonies had met in Boston to develop a strategy for protection of the white settlers. Because it had not been seriously attacked, Springfield was guarded only by a small force. In October, its constable Thomas Miller, Lt. Thomas Cooper, and a small party heading toward the native fort to investigate were attacked, resulting in the deaths of Miller and Cooper.

On October 5, a force of Nipmucks and Agawams burned 30 houses in Springfield. Maj. Robert Treat and his men arrived too late to stop the attack, and needed help from Hadley to get his company out from the surrounding warriors.

On October 12, the natives circled and attacked, but most of the inhabitants had sufficient warning to congregate in fortified homes. The other homes were burned and livestock was killed or driven away.

Springfield was saved from total destruction by Majs. Treat and John Pynchon and their forces, who arrived in the town after receiving news of the attack. The British formally declared war on the Narragansetts in November.
Sources: 152, 188, 225, 226, 268, 270, 274, 315, 334

MA17   *Ambush Near Hatfield* • October 19, 1675
Location: Near Hatfield
War: King Philip's War
Seeing smoke rising from the nearby woods, a scouting party of ten from the command of Capt. Samuel Moseley was sent to investigate. The fires had been set by the natives to attract the soldiers, and the ploy was successful. Only one or two of the party survived the ambush to alert the settlers at Hatfield.

Later that day, the warriors led by Muttawmp arrived at Hatfield, which had prepared for a defense with additional troops from Hadley and Northampton. Both sides suffered casualties and the natives withdrew. The settlers' victory told both sides that the strength of the natives was not as great as had previously been assumed.
Sources: 152, 188, 270, 315, 334

MA18   *Attacks on Settlers* • October, 1675
Location: Connecticut Valley
War: King Philip's War
On October 25, a group of residents of Northampton were surprised by a band of natives, but all made it back to the village without injury. On October 26, a group of Springfield men who were in Westfield to grind grain were attacked, and three were killed. The natives then burned several houses in Westfield. On October 29, several settlers were killed by natives in a meadow at Northampton.
Sources: 152

MA19 *Attack on Lancaster* • February 10, 1676
Location: Lancaster
War: King Philip's War
Job Kattenanit, a native spy, informed Capt. Daniel Gookin on February 9 of an attack planned by 400 Nipmucks on the village of Lancaster. Gookin sent word to Concord, Lancaster and Marlborough for troops to converge at the expected attack point. On the following morning, Capt. Samuel Wadsworth led his 40 men from Marlborough to Lancaster. They forced their way across the partially destroyed bridge leading into town, as the natives were still shooting and burning the structures.

The attackers, some 400 strong, were led by One-eyed John, who had led the smaller raid on Lancaster the previous August. Most of the village's residents had taken shelter in six garrison houses only one of which, that of Rev. Joseph Rowlandson, was defeated by the natives. From that house, one escaped, 12 were killed, and the remaining 24 were captured, including Mary Rowlandson and her child. The town suffered about 50 casualties, and within six weeks was abandoned.
Sources: 125, 133, 135, 150, 152, 226, 268, 270, 273, 274, 290, 369

MA20 *Attack at Medfield* • February 21, 1676
Location: Medfield
War: King Philip's War
About 100 local soldiers and an equal number of colony soldiers led by Lt. Edward Oakes were quartered in Medfield, so the residents felt relatively secure. During the night, 300 Nipmucks and Narragansetts quietly came into town and, at first light, shot farmers and soldiers as they emerged from their homes. From 40 to 50 homes were burned.

The attackers withdrew when they discovered how many soldiers there were in Medfield, and when they shot off their large cannon to alert the town of Dedham of the attack. As they left, they burned the bridge heading toward Sherborn, which prevented the English from following.
Sources: 65, 125, 150, 152, 188, 226, 233, 251, 270, 274, 290, 315, 334, 369

MA21 *Massacre at the Eel River* • March 12, 1676
Location: Eel River, 3 miles south of Plymouth
War: King Philip's War
William Clark's isolated garrison house at Eel River was attacked by a band of warriors led by Totoson. They killed 11 defenseless settlers. They took the garrison's provisions, guns, and ammunition, and then burned the house.
Sources: 150, 152

MA22 *Attack at Groton* • March 13, 1676
Location: Groton
War: King Philip's War
One-eyed John led a force of Nipmucks and Narragansetts against the village of Groton, located north of Lancaster. They killed one settler and burned 65 homes. John claimed to have 500 warriors. On the order of Maj. Simon Willard, the inhabitants of Groton were soon evacuated to Boston. Along the way, they were ambushed and two more were killed.
Sources: 150, 152, 270, 274, 290, 315, 334

MA23 *Attack at Longmeadow* • March 26, 1676
Location: Longmeadow
War: King Philip's War
Settlers arriving in Longmeadow to attend worship services were attacked by a band of natives who killed a man and a girl, and captured two women and two small children. A rescue party overtook the natives, who then killed the children and wounded the women before escaping.
Sources: 150, 152, 270

MA24 *Battle of Green Hill* • April 21, 1676
Location: Sudbury
War: King Philip's War
With the abandonment of several towns, Sudbury became the most exposed frontier outpost. About 500 Algonquians living near Mount Wachusett traveled to the town on April 20, and attacked the following morning. Initially, the residents were safe in fortified homes while the natives burned the unoccupied ones.

A dozen armed men from Concord rode to Sudbury to join in the battle. The few that were not killed on the spot were captured, tortured and killed later. A group from Watertown was more successful, driving the warriors to the western side of the Sudbury River.

A group of 60 from Marlborough led by Capts. Samuel Wadsworth and Samuel Brocklebank encountered a small band of natives and chased them for quite a distance, until they found themselves in a trap set by several hundred. They fought bravely to the top of Green Hill. The Watertown men tried to help, but could not get that far and retreated to the Goodnow garrison. Other groups came from Charlestown, Brookfield and Marlborough.

The natives set fire to the grass on Green Hill, and when the soldiers became confused and tried to escape, the warriors attacked. At least 30 soldiers were killed, including Wadsworth and Brocklebank. Only about 13 managed to escape to a fortified mill, from which they were later rescued.
Sources: 150, 152, 270, 334

MA25 *Attacks on Frontier Towns* • February to May, 1676
Location: Near Boston to the Connecticut River
War: King Philip's War
Nipmuck warriors raided the towns of Sudbury (February 1 and April 12), Weymouth (February 25), Northampton (March 14), Marlborough (March 14), and Wrenthan. Wampanoags and Narragansetts attacked Rehoboth (March 28), Bridgewater and other settlements. In early April, a force led by Capt. George Denison skirmished with a band that had participated in some of these raids and captured Canonchet, an important chief.

On May 5, Capt. Daniel Henchman led a force of colonists and about 40 of the Praying Indians (natives who lived peacefully beside the colonists, often adopting Christianity) against the Wampanoags at Hassanamassett and killed 11, without suffering any casualties themselves. On May 11, 16 homes were burned in Plymouth.

On May 12, a band of warriors drove off 70 head of cattle from Hatfield. On May 24, Capt. Thomas Brattle and his troops encountered a party of the enemy fishing near Rehoboth, killing 12 while losing only one.
Sources: 65, 125, 150, 152, 226, 233, 274, 334

MA26 *Battle of Turners Falls* • May 19, 1676
Location: Turners Falls
War: King Philip's War
Capts. Holyoke and William Turner were in charge of forces from Massachusetts and Connecticut for the purpose of recovering the Connecticut Valley. They led a force of 150 men and boys from Hatfield, Hadley and Northampton to the falls about five miles north of Deerfield, where natives were catching and curing fish for the future. Several who attempted to escape by canoe were killed when they crashed over the falls. The natives had 26 killed and 50 captured, while the British lost only one.

Those who escaped were joined by others from nearby villages to set an ambush along the road back to Hadley, and killed Turner and 38 of his men. The native losses at the falls permanently crippled their strength, and by mid-June the area was again considered safe for settlers.
Sources: 53, 150, 152, 212, 225, 226, 274, 334

MA27 *Attack at Washaccum Pond* • June 7, 1676
Location: 5 miles west of Lancaster
War: King Philip's War
A force led by Capt. Daniel Henchman, heading from Concord toward Mount Wachusett with tracker Tom Dublet, came upon a party of natives fishing at Washaccum Pond. They killed seven natives, captured 29, and rescued an English boy who had previously been taken prisoner by the natives. Henchman then marched to Marlborough to replenish his ammunition supply.
Sources: 152, 270

MA28 *Raid on Hadley* • June 12, 1676
Location: Hadley
War: King Philip's War
A large force of natives attacked the town of Hadley and were repulsed by Connecticut soldiers and townsmen. While the attack was going on, a band of Mohawks went to the native camp and killed many of the Wampanoag and Narragansett women and children.
Sources: 152, 188, 270

MA29 *Attack on Pomham* • July 27, 1676
Location: Near Dedham
War: King Philip's War
Capt. Samuel Harding led a force of English and friendly natives against an encampment of Narragansetts, including the sachem, Pomham. He was mortally wounded in the action. Fifteen other Narragansetts were killed and 34 were captured.
Sources: 150

MA30 *Late Actions* • July to August, 1676
Location: Southern Massachusetts
War: King Philip's War
Maj. Bradford organized a force to patrol the area in and around Swansea, Rehoboth and Taunton. Capt. Benjamin Church came out of retirement and was

commissioned to organize a force composed of British settlers and natives. Some bands of natives surrendered.

On July 3, Connecticut troops killed or captured 67 Narragansetts near Warwick. Seven natives were killed in action near Mendham. On July 11, Church's men captured a party of natives near Middleborough, then hurried to Monponsett Pond and captured another group. Narragansett sachem Pomham was killed with 20 warriors at Mendon on July 25. Nipmuck sachem Matoonas was captured July 27 and was executed on the Boston Common.

King Philip's uncle Unkompoin was killed in a skirmish near the Taunton River on August 1, the same day Philip's wife and young son were captured in a battle in which 173 natives were killed. His sister-in-law Weetamoo drowned August 6 after escaping capture. Her husband Quinnapin was executed August 25, as was Philip's captain Annawon on September 11.
Sources: 53, 125, 147, 150, 152, 225, 226, 233, 315, 381

MA31 *Attack at Hatfield* • September, 1677
Location: Hatfield
A band of Mohawks attacked the town of Hatfield for no apparent reason, shooting down several of its residents. About 20 English were taken captive, and most were later redeemed.
Sources: 290

MA32 *Raid on Groton* • 1694
Location: Groton
War: King William's War
Despite a 1693 treaty, the Abenakis were encouraged by the French to attack English settlements in New England. In 1694, one of their victims was the village of Groton, about 30 miles from Boston.
Sources: 328

MA33 *Massacre at Deerfield* • February 29, 1704
Location: Deerfield
War: Queen Anne's War
Before dawn, a force of 300 French Canadians, Caughnawagas and Abenakis led by Hertel de Rouville attacked Deerfield, which was then a town of 290 settlers. Seventeen homes were burned. They butchered 48 men, women and children and took about 111 prisoners to Canada, including pastor Rev. John Williams. Several prisoners died on the way to Canada, including Rev. Williams' wife. She had recently given birth and could not keep up, so she was tomahawked. Rev. Williams was freed after two and a half years.
Memorial: Twelve buildings in Old Deerfield have been preserved along The Street (off US 5 and SR 10), including a gravestone for the 48 who died in the massacre.
Sources: 19, 32, 90, 133, 210, 284, 290, 299, 328, 380, 381, 388, 393

MA34 *Destruction of Haverhill* • August 30, 1708
Location: Haverhill
A force of French and natives destroyed the English colony at Haverhill.
Sources: 261, 381

MICHIGAN

MI1   *Battle with Foxes* • Summer, 1712
Location: Site of the present Penobscot Building near Savoyard Creek, Detroit
The Foxes and the French fought. The Missourias sent warriors north to help the French, led by Sieur Dubuisson, wipe out a party of Foxes and Mascoutens. The Potawatomis were also opposed to the Mascoutens, who had established a village on the Upper Saint Joseph River in the middle of the Potawatomi hunting lands. The Potawatomis assisted in the attack, which resulted in the deaths of about 50 Mascoutens.
Sources: 261, 306, 324, 415

MI2   *Ambush on Lake Ste. Claire* • May 7, 1763
Location: East of Detroit
War: Pontiac's Rebellion
Fort Detroit, occupied by two companies of colonial troops and one of British regular soldiers, had a total of about 125 men within a wall 1,200 yards in circumference. Camped nearby were chief Pontiac and 800 to 900 Ottawa warriors, still angry at the British since the French and Indian War. On May 7, Lt. Charles Robertson and 12 men traveled by boat across Lake Ste. Claire to take depth soundings. Pontiac informed a group of Chippewas from Saginaw Bay of the party's whereabouts, and the Chippewas ambushed and killed four soldiers, taking the rest as prisoners.
Sources: 257, 315, 322

MI3   *Siege of Detroit* • May 9–12, 1763
Location: Fort Detroit
War: Pontiac's Rebellion
After the French surrendered in 1760, Fort Detroit was occupied by the British and commanded by Maj. Henry Gladwin. In 1763, he became aware of a plot by Pontiac and his Ottawa and Chippewa warriors to enter the fort with concealed weapons and fight the British. Gladwin armed and prepared his troops, and kept the Ottawas in small groups when they visited for trading or other purposes.

Because of the preparations of the soldiers, the attack on the fort was aborted, and the Ottawas instead went against those settlers who had not moved into the fort. One war party killed Mrs. Turnbull and her two sons, who lived across the river from the fort. On Isle au Cochon (now known as Belle Isle), six were killed and five were taken prisoner. The Ottawas then came within 100 feet of the fort and opened fire on it and the schooner "Huron" in the Detroit River, but the attack and the returned fire had little effect.

This battle ended with Pontiac remaining outside the fort in a state of siege, which lasted from May until late October. Involved were Ottawas, Chippewas, Ojibways, Hurons, Mississaugas, Potwatomis, and others.

Pontiac threatened a band of Christianized Hurons living across the Detroit River, who then joined him to avoid being destroyed.
Sources: 20, 79, 131, 135, 256, 299, 315, 322, 324, 336, 349, 374, 412

MI4   *Capture of Fort St. Joseph* • May 25, 1763
Location: Niles
War: Pontiac's Rebellion
Fort St. Joseph, built by the French in 1691, was taken over by the British in 1761 and was occupied by Ensign Francis Schlosser and 14 others. In 1763, a party of Potawatomis attacked, killing eleven. Schlosser and three others were captured and taken to Detroit and the natives kept the fort for two years.

This was part of a simultaneous attack engineered by Pontiac which also included Forts Sandusky, Miamis, Ouiatenon, Michilimackinac, Presque Isle, Machault, Le Boeuf and Edward Augustus.
Marker: The fort site is at the corner of Fort and Bond Streets, Niles.
Sources: 315, 324, 336, 349, 374

MI5   *Capture at Point Pelee* • May 28, 1763
Location: About 25 miles east of Detroit
War: Pontiac's Rebellion
Lt. Abraham Cuyler left Fort Niagara on May 13 in ten flat-bottomed boats with 96 men and supplies, bound for Fort Detroit. When they put ashore on the evening of May 28, they discovered that they were surrounded by natives, whose first rush caused the soldiers to break and run for their boats. A wounded Lt. Cuyler and 40 men returned to Fort Niagara.

The prisoners were taken by the natives up the Detroit River, where they found that Capt. Newman had already left on the sloop *Michigan* for Fort Niagara. On May 30, the soldiers in the fort at first thought their supplies and reinforcements had arrived, but as the boats came closer they saw that there were natives in each, guarding their prisoners. Some of the captured soldiers were able to escape and make it to a British schooner near the fort with seven barrels of supplies. Over the next three days, all of the remaining prisoners were killed.

Over the next two years, the British broke the sieges of Forts Detroit and Pitt, and made peace with most of the area tribes. In April of 1769, Pontiac was murdered by a Peoria warrior.
Sources: 147, 315, 322, 324

MI6   *Capture of Fort Michilimackinac* • June 2, 1763
Location: Mackinaw City
War: Pontiac's Rebellion
Fort Michilimackinac was located on an island of the same name, meaning "green turtle." The fort was defended by 35 soldiers led by Capt. George Etherington. Groups of Sauk and Chippewa, pretending to play a lacrosse-like ball game known as baug-ah-ud-o-way, threw the ball inside the fort. Etherington and Lt. Lessley brought the ball out to the natives, who captured them and took them to the woods. Others ran into the fort, killed 17, and took 15 prisoners to be used as slaves.
Museum: A 27-acre living history attraction is on the grounds of the old fort in Mackinaw City.
Sources: 92, 133, 183, 256, 315, 324, 336, 380, 412, 415

MI7   *Attack on the Sloop* Michigan • June 23, 1763
Location: Detroit River
War: Pontiac's Rebellion

To protect British supply ships expected at Fort Detroit, Maj. Henry Gladwin sent the sloop *Michigan* to the mouth of the river. On June 23, Pontiac and his warriors lay in ambush on Turkey Island (now called Fighting Island), and at nightfall staged a canoe attack against what appeared to be a helpless ship. However, its commander, Capt. Newman, was ready and 54 hidden soldiers came on deck. They and the ship's cannon killed 14 and wounded 14 more. The warriors quickly retreated.

The presence of the ship since May told Pontiac that the British expected supplies and/or reinforcements by river. He sent a band of warriors eastward along the northern shore of Lake Erie to attack any British force coming from Fort Niagara.

The *Michigan* on June 30 sailed to Detroit, and along the way fired a volley of grapeshot into a native village, wounding several.

Sources: 322, 324

MI8 *Battle of Bloody Bridge* or *Battle of Bloody Run* • July 31, 1763
Location: Near Fort Detroit
War: Pontiac's Rebellion
Capt. James Dalyell and 247 men left Fort Detroit quietly before dawn on July 31, intending to march five miles north to Pontiac's camp and defeat him. Two flat-bottomed boats were sailed up the river next to the road to facilitate the return of the dead and wounded.

About two miles from the fort, they approached a narrow wooden bridge crossing Parent's Creek. As the first men reached the middle of the bridge, they were met by musket fire which dropped Lt. Archibald Brown and about 12 of the advance guard. Other soldiers charged the bridge and cleared the natives from a ridge on the opposite side of the creek, and then the soldiers experienced fire from the side and rear.

Dalyell ordered a retreat, which required a charge at a house to their rear, in which a party of warriors was holed up. Dalyell led the charge and was quickly killed. Capt. James Grant replaced him and was successful in dislodging the natives. He was able to free other portions of the army which had been trapped, and the survivors reached the fort. The soldiers lost four officers and 19 enlisted men, and had 39 wounded. Of the 400 natives, approximately seven were killed and 12 were wounded.

The creek turned red with blood, and it was then known as Bloody Run, with the bridge called Bloody Bridge.

Location: 14, 256, 315, 322, 324

MI9 *Attack on the Ship* Huron • September 2, 1763
Location: Detroit River
War: Pontiac's Rebellion
The ship *Huron* successfully ran a native gauntlet along the river on August 5 to bring 60 soldiers to Fort Detroit.

The ship arrived at Fort Detroit on September 2 with six Mohawk chiefs who were to try to persuade the besieging tribes to end the fighting. That evening, Pontiac had 340 Chippewas and Ottawas attack the ship in their canoes. They were discovered when they were 100 yards away, and the bow gun was able to get off one blast. The natives reached the ship and climbed up its sides, meeting a crew of 22 who fought with muskets, swivel guns, pistols and spears. The fight resulted in the deaths of Capt. Horsey and four of his men.

Some of the warriors cut the anchor cable, causing the ship to swing around in the current. The canoes scattered and the swivel guns were again brought into play. The six remaining crewmen said they would fight to the death and threatened to blow up the ship, and the warriors departed. A total of 15 of the whites died.

On October 29, Pontiac received news that the French and British had made peace, so there would be no more French army to help him. He then made his peace with the British.

Sources: 315, 322

MI10   *Capture of Fort Michilimackinac* • July 17, 1812
Location: Near Mackinaw City
War: War of 1812
British Governor General Sir Isaac Brock captured Fort Michilimackinac with a force of British regulars, fur traders and natives. After the British victory, most of the local natives sided with them.
Museum: The reconstructed fort is located at Interstate 75 beneath the south approach of the Mackinac Bridge in Mackinaw City.
Sources: 26, 91, 144, 178, 324, 349, 422, 423

MI11   *Defeat of Fort Detroit* • August 16, 1812
Location: Detroit
War: War of 1812
Tecumseh assembled a coalition of Potawatomis, Kickapoos, Delawares and his own Shawnees, and went to Fort Malden across the Detroit River in Canada to offer their services to the British. Soon, he was also joined by bands of Wyandots, Chippewas, Sioux, Winnebagos and Sauk and Fox, to fight against the Americans. They fought as allies of Sir Isaac Brock, the British governor general.

They laid siege to Fort Detroit, which was defended by a larger force commanded by Gen. William Hull. However, Hull's forces were less disciplined, and with fears that food supplies would be depleted, they surrendered to the British. Hull was later court-martialled for cowardice and sentenced to be shot, but was allowed to live through the intervention of President James Madison.
Sources: 18, 26, 91, 147, 178, 293, 324, 398, 400

MI12   *Battle of Frenchtown* • January 18, 1813
Location: Near Detroit
War: War of 1812
American Brig. Gen. James Winchester prepared for an assault on Detroit and camped along the Maumee River. When he heard that the British defensive force was small, he sent 650 men out of his force of 850 to 1,000 to Frenchtown and defeated the British and natives. Thirteen Americans were killed and 54 were wounded. On January 20, Winchester's forces were bolstered by an additional 300 troops.
Sources: 14, 91, 169, 257, 324, 397

MI13   *Raisin River Massacre* • January 22, 1813
Location: Monroe

War: War of 1812

British Maj. Gen. Henry Procter led 600 British regulars and militia and about 800 hundred natives, including Kickapoos and Potawatomis, against Brig. Gen. James Winchester's army camped on the Raisin River. As had been the case the year before, the British were far more disciplined and prepared for battle. The Americans failed to send out patrols, post pickets or issue ammunition to their soldiers.

The Americans were trapped by the British force. The Kentuckians fought fiercely after learning that they were surrounded, but still had 100 to 400 killed and several hundred taken prisoner. The Americans surrendered after being promised by Procter that they would receive British protection. The healthy prisoners were taken to the British camp on Stony Creek.

That night, a band of Potawatomis, Ottawas, Chippewas, Wyandots and Delawares came upon the battlefield, where the wounded prisoners remained with interpreters. The natives came upon a cache of whiskey, became drunk, and killed some of the prisoners, taking other captives back to their villages.

Museum: The River Raisin Battlefield Visitor Center is located at 1403 E. Elm St., Monroe, MI, and includes a diorama, maps and mannequins.

Sources: 19, 26, 90, 91, 144, 181, 223, 257, 315, 324, 396, 397, 398, 400

MI14 *Attack at Sault Ste. Marie* • July 26, 1814

Location: Sault Ste. Marie

War: War of 1812

Lt. D. Turner landed the U.S. Navy ship *Scorpion* at Sault Ste. Marie and a detachment of infantry led by Maj. Holmes went ashore and burned the homes of members of the British Northwest Company. Its agent had previously taken up arms against the Americans, as had some of the traders. Holmes was killed in an attack against the British at Mackinaw on August 4.

Sources: 149, 183

MINNESOTA

MN1 *Attack on French Trading House* • 1783

Location: Confluence of Partridge and Crow Wing Rivers

A party of about 200 Dakotas attacked a trading house built by a French man called Blacksmith by the natives. Nearby were the homes and families of ten Ojibway hunters, who had left for a beaver-trapping expedition. The Dakotas fired arrows into the enclosure until they ran out of ammunition, and then retreated. Before they left, they took their dead and threw them into holes in the ice over the frozen river, so the Ojibways and French could not scalp them.

Sources: 183

MN2 *Attack at Fort Snelling* • 1827

Location: Minneapolis

A party of Ojibways came to Fort Snelling in 1826 to visit the agent and camped across the Mississippi River on the eastern shore. They were soon attacked by the Sioux.

Seven Ojibway warriors and about 16 women and children returned on May 28, 1827, and this time camped closer to its walls. They had been promised by Col. Snelling and agent Taliaferro that they would be secure. One evening, a party of Sioux attacked, killing two and wounding six. Capt. Clark and a party of soldiers pursued the Sioux the next morning.

They brought back 32 prisoners and the Ojibways identified them as the ones that had attacked the night before. The soldiers told the Sioux to run for their lives, but the Ojibway rifles were too quick to allow them to escape. Later, a party of Sioux arrived at the fort to apologize for the actions of those who were executed, and delivered two more for punishment.

Memorial: Historic Fort Snelling, a restored limestone fort, is located near the junction of SRs 5 and 55.

Sources: 19, 183, 259

MN3 *Attack on Upper Sioux Agency* • August 17, 1862
Location: 9 miles south of Granite Falls
War: Little Crow's War
Prior to the Civil War, about 150,000 white settlers moved onto the lands of the Santee Sioux. The Mdewkanton division of the Santees was led by Little Crow (Ta-oya-te-duta), who attempted in July and August to get provisions which the soldiers had promised them by treaty. On August 4, they obtained the pork and flour only because 500 warriors surrounded the soldiers while the provisions were removed from the storeroom. On August 17, a band of four young Santees killed five settlers at their homes, and the Mdewkantons expected a strong reprisal from the soldiers at the agency.

Monument: The Upper Sioux Agency State Park is located on SR 67 in Granite Falls.

Sources: 19, 34, 70, 147, 197, 259, 288, 309, 349

MN4 *Attack at Lower Sioux Agency* • August 18, 1862
Location: Redwood Agency, along the Minnesota River
War: Little Crow's War
Instead of waiting to be attacked, Little Crow was goaded into attacking first, and he encouraged the Wahpeton and Sisseton Santees to join in the war. On August 18, the warriors attacked the agency, killing 20 men and capturing 10 women and children. The agency buildings were burned and the remaining 47 fled to Fort Ridgely. On the way, they met a company of 45 commanded by Capt. John Marsh, who rushed to the agency and lost 24 in a Santee ambush. Little Crow's early successes encouraged him, so he decided to attack Fort Ridgely.

Museum: The Lower Sioux Agency Interpretive Center is located 6 miles east of Redwood Falls off US 71 on CR 2.

Sources: 19, 34, 70, 147, 197, 259, 288, 309, 349

MN5 *Attack on Fort Ridgely* • August 20, 1862
Location: Fort Ridgely
War: Little Crow's War

Little Crow and his band of 400 Mdewkanton Santee Sioux, supported by bands led by Wabasha and Mankato, assembled west of the fort in the Minnesota Valley on August 19. When they saw the well-defended stone buildings, some were reluctant to attack and the action was postponed until the next day. Plans were drawn up for an organized attack, but when it actually occurred on the morning of August 20, the plans were ignored and the attack proceeded haphazardly.

Four Sioux were killed and little damage was done to the fort. The 400 warriors involved in the battle returned to Little Crow's village.

Museum: The stone powder magazine, restored stone commissary, and several of the fort's building foundations are located in Fort Ridgely State Park off SR 4, 6 miles south of Fairfax.

Sources: 19, 34, 70, 88, 259, 309, 349

MN6 *Attack on Fort Ridgely* • August 22, 1862
Location: Fort Ridgely
War: Little Crow's War
Little Crow, Wabasha and Mankato and their 400 warriors were joined by 400 more from the Wahpeton and Sisseton divisions of the Santee. They attacked the fort in the middle of the day, camouflaging themselves with flowers and prairie grass until they could get within firing range. Flaming arrows set the roofs on fire and the soldiers countered with artillery. The 150 soldiers and 25 civilians successfully defended the fort, and late in the afternoon the Sioux retreated to Little Crow's village.

Museum: See MN5.

Sources: 34, 70, 88, 259, 309

MN7 *Battles of New Ulm* • August 23, 1862
Location: Village of New Ulm, on the Cottonwood River
War: Little Crow's War
On August 19, 100 Santee had attacked New Ulm but were held at bay by a band of citizens. They then left to attack Fort Ridgely.

Unable to overtake the fort, the Santee chose to return to nearby New Ulm, which they still thought was a target they could overpower, if they could get there before Col. Henry H. Sibley and his 1,400 to 1,500 soldiers of the 6th Minnesota Regiment who were on their way from St. Paul. On the morning of August 23, the Santee came out of the woods and formed an arc, sweeping toward the town. They were met by well-armed settlers behind barricades, ready for the attack.

The Santee, led by Mankato because Little Crow had been wounded in the previous day's attack on Fort Ridgely, killed 34 settlers, wounded 60 and set fire to 190 buildings, but left at nightfall without taking the town. Sibley's forces arrived on August 26 but he was inept and timid and accomplished little. Despite that, the Santee and their 200 prisoners withdrew up the Minnesota Valley. The surviving settlers moved to Mankato.

Museum: Displays relating to the Sioux uprising are in the Brown County Historical Museum at the intersection of Center St. and Broadway in New Ulm.

Sources: 34, 70, 88, 259, 267, 309, 349, 392

MN8 *Battle Along the Minnesota River* • September, 1862
Location: North side of the Minnesota River

War: Little Crow's War

After avoiding the soldiers of Col. Henry H. Sibley for a time, beginning on September 1, Little Crow led a party of 110 warriors along the north side of the Minnesota River to test the strength of the army. At the same time, Big Eagle and Mankato led a larger force along the south bank. On September 2, the force split, with 75 warriors following a subchief to plunder small villages in the area. Little Crow and the 35 remaining warriors encountered 75 soldiers on September 3, killing six and wounding 15.

Sources: 70, 309

MN9 *Battle at Birch Coulee* • September 5–6, 1862

Location: 2 miles north of Morton

War: Little Crow's War

On the evening of September 4, the Santee force proceeding along the south side of the Minnesota River quietly surrounded the forces of Col. Henry H. Sibley. The battle commenced on the morning of September 5, and the soldiers were supported by cavalry from Fort Ridgely. On the morning of September 6, Sibley's forces repulsed the Santee, who crossed the river and rejoined Little Crow.

After the fighting stopped, Sibley opened a line of communication with Little Crow, who explained that the fighting was the result of the soldiers, agents and the government not living up to the provisions of their treaty. Sibley considered the Santees' actions murders without sufficient cause.

Monument: There is a historic marker at Birch Coulee Park, at the junction of SRs 71 and 2 near Morton.

Sources: 70, 309, 349

MN10 *Battle of Wood Lake* • September 23, 1862

Location: Between Wood Lake and Yellow Medicine

War: Little Crow's War

Col. Henry H. Sibley's 1,600 soldiers and volunteers headed from their camp at Wood Lake (Lone Tree Lake) to the old Yellow Medicine Agency, about five miles away, to dig potatoes. The 700 Santee laid in ambush in the grass, and as the wagons approached the warriors opened fire. Only those close to the wagons were actively involved, and most of the warriors were too far away. At least 15 Santee were killed, including chief Mankato.

After the Santee retreated toward their camp 12 miles above Yellow Medicine, the soldiers mutilated the bodies of the dead. Later, Sibley ordered a stop to such action. Sibley entered the Santee camp under a flag of truce on September 26 with Wabasha's help, demanded the return of the prisoners, and declared the Santee to be prisoners of war.

They were surrounded by artillery, and the suspected guilty warriors were tried by five officers, with no defense counsel. The trials continued until November 5, resulting in 303 death sentences and 16 long prison sentences. Little Crow was killed by two settlers for a $25 dollar bounty and $500 bonus on July 3, 1863, while he and his son were picking raspberries near the settlement of Hutchinson.

Monument: A marker at the corner of Front and Main Sts. in Mankato commemorates the hangings of 38 Santee on December 26, 1862, after the sentences of 265 others were commuted by Pres. Lincoln.

Sources: 70, 88, 92, 197, 309, 349

MN11 *Battle of Leech Lake* • October 5, 1898
Location: Leech Lake
Chippewa natives fought with soldiers led by Brevet Maj. Melville C. Wilkinson, who was killed along with five members of his 3rd Infantry. This was the last battle in which soldiers were killed.
Sources: 66

MISSISSIPPI

MS1 *Attack on the Mississippi* • June 2–4, 1540
Location: Near Vicksburg
War: De Soto Expedition
Hernando De Soto's party, after wintering at Aminoya, built seven boats and headed south on the Mississippi River. Over the next two days, they were attacked by a fleet of large canoes from the chiefdom of Quigualtam. When they passed out of that area, the attack was taken up by canoes from the next chiefdom for the next two days.
Sources: 145

MS2 *Attack on Curaca Camp* • Late January, 1541
Location: Mississippi
War: De Soto Expedition
After leaving Alabama and the Choctaws, Hernando De Soto and his Spanish army headed west toward the Mississippi through Chickasaw country. Rather than all-out battles, they engaged in short and quick attacks on the army camp.

On one January night, war chief Curaca called the warriors to arms, making much noise with shouts, drums, fifes and shells. They attacked the town with torches and lighted arrows, which ignited the straw roofs in the strong wind. The Spanish found it difficult to defend themselves in the heavy smoke, and the Chickasaws killed many.
Sources: 88

MS3 *Battles in Chicaza* • March 4, 1541
Location: West bank of the Tombigbee River
War: De Soto Expedition
When De Soto announced that he was ready to continue his travels, the Chickasaws were angered that he demanded 200 warriors to carry his baggage. During one night, they sneaked into the Spanish camp and set the barracks on fire. As the Spaniards fled to a nearby village, 12 were killed with bows, as were 57 horses.

Before the soldiers could leave the area, the natives attacked again, but the Spaniards were able to repel them. They left the area by April 26.
Sources: 85, 92, 244, 412

MS4   *Attack on Fort Rosalie* • November 28, 1729
   Location: Natchez
   War: French-Natchez War
   Relations between the Natchez and the French were not good, and the natives suffered from contagious diseases which they had not known prior to the coming of the white settlers. Roused by the Chickasaws and perhaps the English, the Natchez in 1729 attacked Fort Rosalie, a French outpost, and killed 237. They also took 300 women and children captive. This followed their having been told by an officer that they would have to move their villages.
   One of the men killed by the Natchez was Father du Poisson, a friend of the Quapaws. As a result of his death, the Quapaws stated that they were enemies of the Natchez and the Yazoo, and the following spring attacked a party of Yazoos and Koras, taking four scalps.
   The French also responded to the attack over the next two years with brutal retaliation. They nearly exterminated the Natchez tribe. The French believed that the Natchez raid had been encouraged by the English.
   Memorial: Fort Rosalie is part of the Natchez National Historical Park, 1 Melrose-Montabello Pkwy., Natchez.
   Sources: 18, 31, 85, 89, 92, 111, 135, 209, 260, 275, 324, 326, 330, 334, 347, 380, 383

MS5   *Natchez Massacre* • 1731
   Location: Near Natchez
   War: French-Natchez War
   The French established their Louisiana colony during the eighteenth century, and the small Natchez tribe managed to live at peace with the white soldiers and farmers in their villages. They were provoked and abused, and then rebelled against the whites. In retaliation, the French and the Choctaws attacked and nearly wiped out the Natchez tribe by 1731. Some were sold as slaves, and a few survivors escaped to join the Creeks and Cherokees. By 1836, their numbers had dwindled to 300.
   Monument: The Grand Village of the Natchez Indians is located at US 61 at 400 Jefferson Davis Blvd., Natchez, MS 39120.
   Sources: 18, 19, 31, 92, 135, 288, 324, 326, 347, 418

MS6   *Battle of Chocolissa* • March 25, 1736
   Location: South of Memphis, TN
   Louisiana governor Jean Baptiste Le Moyne de Bienville decided to exterminate the Chickasaws and eliminate the British advantage in the area. He organized a 600-man army and built Fort Tombeckbe as a base. He notified Maj. Pierre d'Artaquette to bring forces with him from Illinois, so he assembled a force of 140 regular soldiers and militia at Fort Charters. They headed south along the Mississippi River to fight the Chickasaws. He was joined by 28 Quapaws and was supposed to meet the other French army led by Bienville, who did not arrive.
   Without Bienville, d'Artaquette attacked the Chickasaw town of Chocolissa, which was defended by 500 to 600 Chickasaws and 20 Englishmen. The French were badly defeated, having 100 killed and 20 taken captive, 13 of whom were burned alive.
   Sources: 85, 92, 330

MS7 *Battle of Ackia* • May 26, 1736
Location: Tupelo
Gov. Jean Baptiste Le Moyne de Bienville was ignorant of what had happened to
Maj. Pierre d'Artaquette's army at Chocolissa, and headed north to fight the
Chickasaws at the town of Ackia. Chevalier de Noyan led 180 men in a storming
of the town and was caught in a deadly crossfire. Twenty-four French soldiers
were killed and 53 others were wounded. When Bienville arrived with rein-
forcements, they were driven back. After three hours, the French retreated.
Monument: Ackia Battleground National Monument is located between US 78
and SR 6 on Natchez Trace, Tupelo.
Sources: 85, 330, 418

MS8 *Attack on Convoy* • October 2, 1745
Location: Blue Wood
War: Red Shoe Rebellion
The Choctaw village of Blue Wood assembled a party of warriors which attacked
an English convoy on its way to the Chickasaws. Two English traders were killed.
Sources: 2

MS9 *Destruction of Villages* • 1746–50
Location: Mississippi
War: Choctaw Civil War
In a series of conflicts, over 800 natives lost their lives and the villages of West
Abeka, Couechitto and Nushkobo were destroyed.
Sources: 89

MISSOURI

MO1 *Battle Near Fort Orleans* • 1730
Location: Fort Orleans, near Brunswick
In 1729, the French abandoned Fort Orleans, located on the Missouri River a few
miles above the mouth of the Grand River. Without French support, the Missourias were vulnerable and were attacked by the Sacs. The Missouria village
near the abandoned Fort Orleans was overwhelmed by the Sacs, who killed nearly
300.
Sources: 306

MO2 *Attack on St. Louis* • May 26, 1780
Location: St. Louis
War: Revolutionary War
St. Louis was the principal town on the upper part of its region, and was attacked
by 300 English soldiers and 900 natives. They were mostly Iroquois from Canada,

and included some French and Algonkians. Led by Emanuel Hesse, they traveled south along the Illinois River.

    The attack was a mad dash, the English finding that they could not control the warriors. Fernando de Leyba, the Spanish governor of the area, had received prior news of the coming attack and had a tower built on the west corner of St. Louis. Its cannon was sufficient to repulse the attackers and send them back up the Mississippi River. Settlers living outside of the area protected by the cannon were killed and mutilated by the Iroquois before they departed.
Sources: 305

MO3   *Attack on Canteen Creek* • March, 1795
Location: 12 miles above St. Louis
A party of Osages crossed the Mississippi River and attacked a white settlement at Canteen Creek. This was one of many skirmishes the Osages had with the Spanish in the region.
Sources: 305

MO4   *Attack on Missouri River* • 1796
Location: Missouri River
The Missourias, who survived an eighteenth century which saw their numbers decline were traveling down the Missouri River in canoes. They were attacked by Sacs and Foxes who had concealed themselves in the willows along the river bank. Warriors were killed by deadly fire from the bank, then the attackers rushed into the water and capsized the canoes, drowning the women and children. Survivors took refuge with the Little Osages and Otoes.
Sources: 306

MO5   *Battle at Shirley's Ford* • September 20, 1862
Location: Spring River
War: Civil War
The 2nd Indian Home Guard, affiliated with the Department of Kansas, fought against Confederate forces along the Spring River. Union losses were between 12 and 20, with nine wounded. Inexplicably, the Union-allied warriors began fighting against other Union troops in the brigade led by Col. Benjamin Weer.
Sources: 60

MONTANA

MT1   *Attack at Three Forks* • April 12, 1810
Location: Near Three Forks, at the confluence of the Jefferson and Madison Rivers
A trading expedition headed by Andrew Henry, Manuel Lisa and Pierre Menard left St. Louis in June of 1809 to reach the Yellowstone River. They visited Mandan

villages in central North Dakota and then headed west, Henry overland to Fort Raymond at the mouth of the Big Horn River, and Menard by river. After a while, both Henry and Menard and their parties headed through the Bozeman Pass to Three Forks, where they built a crude headquarters post.

On April 12, a party of Blackfeet attacked the 18 trappers, killing two of the expedition. Three other whites disappeared, and were presumably captured by the natives for torture and death.

Later, the Blackfeet struck again, beheading hunter George Drouillard and killing two Delaware native trappers.
Sources: 10, 265, 410

MT2   *Attacks in Montana* • May, 1823
Location: Central Montana
War: Arikara War
In October of 1822, the Missouri Fur Company occupied Fort Benton, located at the mouth of the Big Horn River, where Fort Raymond used to be. Thirteen of the company deserted during the winter, and as they headed north along the Missouri River, four were killed by a party of Blackfeet.

When spring arrived, the company packed their pelts and headed south, and on May 31 they were ambushed by Blackfeet in a narrow Yellowstone River gorge near the mouth of Pryor's Fork. Leaders Michael Immel and Robert Jones, plus five of their men, were killed, and four were wounded.

Previously, on May 4, a group of Andrew Henry's men had been attacked a few miles above Great Falls, and four were butchered. The remainder headed back to their Yellowstone stockade.
Sources: 10, 59, 66, 144, 182, 229, 265, 410

MT3   *Attacks Along the Powder River* • September 1, 4, 5, 8 and 10, 1865
Location: Powder River
War: Powder River Expedition
Col. Nelson Cole led 2,000 soldiers up the Powder River in search of warriors to fight, and small parties rode out to meet them. Crazy Horse went out with Cheyennes led by Roman Nose and took a herd of 80 of the soldiers' horses which were unprotected. The warriors skirmished with soldiers from Cole's column on September 1, 4, and 5, and fleeing soldiers on September 8 and 10.
Sources: 64, 110, 325, 346

MT4   *Battle of Tongue River* • September 1, 1866
Location: Tongue River
War: Sioux War
Little Horse, a Cheyenne, was traveling with his wife, an Arapaho, to visit her relatives at Black Bear's camp along the river. On the way there, she spotted cavalry and informed the camp upon their arrival, but the leaders there did not believe that soldiers could be in the area. A few of the people moved several miles away, but most were still there the next morning when the force commanded by Gen. Patrick E. Connor attacked.

Eighty Pawnee scouts and 250 cavalrymen charged from two sides while the Arapahos unsuccessfully tried to form a line of defense. Those who could get to ponies retreated ten miles up the Wolf River, pursued by the army. They then turned around and pushed the army back to the village, where artillerymen had mounted two howitzers.

While the Arapahos watched from a distance, the soldiers destroyed the village and all of the Arapahos' possessions. The Pawnees took 1,000 ponies, a third of the herd. Little Horse, after the soldiers left, came back to the village and found over 50 dead, including his brother-in-law, Panther.

Sources: 64, 70, 91

MT5 *Attack Along the Powder River* • September 8, 1866
Location: Powder River
War: Sioux War

Two thousand soldiers in columns commanded by Cols. Samuel Walker and Nelson Cole arrived in Montana to rendezvous with the third column led by Gen. Patrick E. Connor. However, he was nowhere to be found, as he was preparing to attack an Arapaho village on the Tongue River to the south. Cole and Walker decided to move south in the hope that the dwindling food supplies and low morale among their troops might be alleviated.

At the same time, bands of Minneconjou and Hunkpapas led by Tatanka Yotanka (Sitting Bull) were following a trail out of the Black Hills. The 400 warriors found the soldiers camped along the Powder River, and despite some warriors wanting to trade with the soldiers in a peaceful manner, Sitting Bull did not trust them. He did, however, let others send a truce party toward the army camp.

When they came within easy rifle range, the soldiers fired and killed several. The survivors stole some of the soldiers' horses as they escaped. A look at the starving horses convinced the chiefs, Sitting Bull, Swift Bear, Black Moon, Stands-Looking-Back, and Red Leaf, that the 400 prepared warriors could defeat 2,000 starving soldiers.

The Sioux circled and picked off several soldiers guarding the horse herd, then retreated when a company of cavalry charged. They turned around and fought with the pursuers, then dashed away. The soldiers attacked, and the Sioux were able to keep out of range. When the soldiers' horses tired, they stopped and the Sioux attacked from all sides. Rather than killing the soldiers, they knocked them off their horses.

Cole and Walker marched their troops south along the Powder River, with Sioux harassing them along the way. A major sleet storm struck, and the Sioux took shelter for two days. When they resumed their pursuit, they found hundreds of dead horses that the soldiers had shot because they could not make them go any further. The soldiers continued south on foot.

Sources: 70, 346

MT6 *Attack on Wagon Train* • Early September, 1866
Location: Near the Tongue River
War: Sioux War

The day after the Battle of Tongue River, Arapaho warriors set out to follow Gen. Patrick E. Connor and his soldiers, and on the way encountered the wagon train of James A. Sawyers, heading toward Montana. The Arapahos ambushed the advance party of soldier escorts, stampeded the trailing herd of cattle, and shot some of the wagon drivers. A lack of sufficient ammunition, most of which was

used in the previous day's battle, prevented a strong attack. They did continue to harass the settlers until they reached Montana.
Sources: 70

MT7 *Roman Nose's Fight* • September, 1866
Location: Powder River
War: Sioux War
Roman Nose, leader of the Cheyennes, heard about the soldiers fleeing on foot from the battle they had with the Sioux downriver to the north. Believing that he had special medicine that would protect him from harm, Roman Nose wanted the privilege of leading a charge against the army, which camped at a bend in the river between high bluffs and thick timber.

Several hundred warriors were positioned around the camp, and they unsuccessfully attempted to lure the soldiers out of their position. Roman Nose had his warriors form a line facing the soldiers, rather than fighting singly as they usually did. He told them to wait while he emptied the soldiers' guns, and rode quickly back and forth in front of the soldiers while they shot at him. He was not hit, but when his pony fell, the rest of the warriors attacked.

The Cheyennes were able to do little damage, because their bows, clubs, lances and few firearms were no match for the howitzers and modern rifles of the army. For days afterward, warriors continued to harass the barefoot soldiers who killed their remaining horses for food. They were finally rescued when the column commanded by Gen. Connor arrived, and they traveled to Fort Connor. During the winter, half died of disease, and many others deserted.
Sources: 70

MT8 *Battle of Hayfield* • August 1, 1867
Location: Fort C.F. Smith
War: Red Cloud's War
Fort C.F. Smith was the northernmost of the three forts established by Col. Henry B. Carrington to protect the Bozeman Trail in 1866. While Red Cloud's Sioux went after Fort Phil Kearny to the south in Wyoming, about 500 to 1,000 Cheyennes headed toward Fort C.F. Smith. They came upon and attacked a haying detail led by Lt. Sigismund Sternberg and its escort about two miles from the fort.

Although the white men numbered only 30, they had repeating rifles which were sufficient to repel the Cheyennes. The natives set fire to the high dry grass, which gave them a smoke screen to enable them to carry off their 20 dead and several wounded. They headed back south to see if Red Cloud had done better with his attack on Fort Phil Kearny.

Eventually, the government decided that the opening of the Bozeman Trail was not worth the expense and fighting. The army abandoned the forts in 1868 and they were then burned by the natives. On July 29, Fort C.F. Smith was emptied of soldiers and was burned down by Red Cloud and his warriors.
Sources: 64, 66, 70, 91, 110, 114, 147, 159, 220, 265, 325

MT9 *Battle at Crow Rock* • Winter, 1869
Location: Near Terry
The Hunkpapas led by Sitting Bull were hunting along the Yellowstone River

near the mouth of the Powder River. Two Hunkpapa boys out hunting buffalo were chased by 30 Crow warriors, only one of whom had a horse. He carried warriors, one by one, to catch up with the running boys. They killed one of the boys, but the other outran them. The Crows gave up and headed for Big Dry Creek.

When the survivor told his story to his village, 100 mounted Hunkpapas rode off after the Crows. They caught them at sunrise the next day on a knoll now known as Crow Rock, near Spoon Horn (Mountain Sheep) Butte. The Sioux charge was met by strong gunfire, and Turning Hawk was injured.

Jumping Bull charged the knoll and drew the Crows' fire. When their guns were empty, the Sioux charged. Many Sioux were shot, but eventually they killed most of the defenders. The Sioux then charged on foot over barriers and engaged the Crows in hand-to-hand combat. Within a half hour all the Crows were dead. Fourteen Hunkpapas had also died and 18 were wounded.

Sources: 346

MT10 *Marias River Massacre* or *Baker Massacre* • January 23, 1870
Location: Marias River
War: Piegan War
A camp of Piegan Blackfeet was surrounded and massacred, "like rabbits trapped in a hole" in a temperature of 20 degrees below zero. The army attempted to keep this action a secret, but news of it leaked out to other natives. The official story was that Maj. Eugene M. Baker had led a company of cavalry from Fort Ellis to punish a group of Blackfeet horse thieves.

The real story, as told by Lt. William B. Pease to the Commission of Indian Affairs, was that Baker had marched out on the pretext of a theft of a few mules from a wagon freighter. He attacked the first Piegan village he came to, killing 33 men, 90 women and 50 children.

Although the Blackfeet were enemies of the Plains tribes, any government action against any tribe caused concern among them all. Shortly thereafter, there were uprisings at several agencies.

Sources: 63, 70, 91, 92, 224, 265, 266

MT11 *Skirmish at Arrow Creek* • August 14, 1872
Location: Near Priors Fork
Crazy Horse led a war party in a fight with Maj. Eugene M. Baker, who escorted a survey party for the Northern Pacific Railroad. He taunted the soldiers by riding in front of them while they consistently missed with their rifles.
Monument: The Crazy Horse memorial, a gigantic carved mountain, was begun in 1948, and is located on US 16 north of Custer.
Sources: 109, 110, 114, 265, 288

MT12 *Skirmish Along the Yellowstone River* • August 4, 1873
Location: Mouth of the Tongue River, at the Yellowstone River
Gen. George Armstrong Custer and a small advance party encountered 300 Sioux, who were unsuccessful in luring them into an ambush. The soldiers attacked and drove the Sioux off, and they attacked the soldiers again seven days later while Custer was following their trail.
Sources: 66, 91, 114, 115, 159, 220

MT13 *Attack on Stanley Expedition* • August 11, 1873
Location: Near the mouth of the Rosebud River, at the Yellowstone River
Crazy Horse fought against Col. Stanley's troops, with Gen. George ("Long Hair")
Custer along. The troops were accompanying a survey party sent out in advance
of the construction of a railroad through Lakota hunting grounds. Some of the
Cheyennes who had been with Black Kettle at the Sand Creek Massacre recognized Custer and rushed to fight him before the planned ambush could be sprung.
The fighting was minor and spread out over time, with a few soldiers and horses
being lost. The official report claimed 40 warriors were killed.
Sources: 66, 91, 110, 114, 115, 220, 315

MT14 *Battle of Powder River* • March 17, 1876
Location: Near Broadus
War: Great Sioux War
Before dawn, the advance column of Gen. George Crook, under the command
of Col. Joseph J. Reynolds, attacked Two Moons' camp of Northern Cheyennes
and Oglala Sioux. They had left the reservations and joined some nonagency
natives to hunt for buffalo and antelope in the Powder River country.

   One cavalry troop swept into the village on the right, a second on the left,
and a third separated the horse herd. The women and children ran to a rugged
mountain slope to head toward safety, and the warriors took defensive positions
behind rocks and on ledges. The village of Two Moons and He Dog was burned
by the soldiers and the 1,200 to 1,500 horses were taken. However, during the
night the natives took back the horses. For his failure, Reynolds was court-martialled.
Sources: 4, 62, 70, 91, 110, 114, 159, 224, 265, 346, 380

MT15 *Battle of the Rosebud* or *Battle of Rosebud Creek* • June 17, 1876
Location: Rosebud River
War: Great Sioux War
Early in 1876, Gen. Philip Sheridan planned a three-pronged campaign for the
spring to force the remaining native bands to come into the agencies for relocation to reservations. At the Rosebud River, Gen. George Crook and 1,300 soldiers,
accompanied by Shoshoni and Crow scouts, were stopped by a force of 1,000
Cheyenne and Sioux warriors led by Crazy Horse, Two Moons and Sitting Bull.
The battle lasted about six hours.

   Instead of the former native tactic of rushing into cavalry charges, Crazy
Horse had his warriors fade off to the side and strike weak places in the attackers' lines. The warriors remained on horseback and constantly kept moving. The
soldiers were confused when they could not merely form stationary skirmish
lines. "Three Stars" Crook and his men withdrew to the south.

   The Cheyennes called this the Battle Where the Girl Saved Her Brother,
because Chief-Comes-in-Sight was saved by his sister, Calf-Road-Woman, after
his horse was shot out from under him after a charge.
Monument: The Sitting Bull Memorial is located across the Mission Bridge from
Mobridge, MT, on US 12, then south on SR 1806.
Sources: 4, 62, 66, 70, 91, 109, 110, 114, 147, 159, 182, 197, 213, 220, 224, 235, 265,
278, 315, 325, 346, 351, 380, 406

MT16 *Battle of the Little Bighorn* or *Custer's Last Stand* or
        Battle of Greasy Grass • June 25, 1876
Location: Little Bighorn River
War: Great Sioux War
After a successful encounter with American soldiers at the Rosebud River, Crazy
Horse led his Sioux warriors east to the Little Bighorn River valley. They joined
a large village already consisting of 7,000 to 10,000 Lakotas, Yanktonais, North-
ern Arapahos, Northern Cheyennes, and Santees. The army had a prong led by
Col. John Gibbon coming from Fort Ellis, Montana, in the west, one led by Gen.
Alfred Terry coming from Fort Abraham Lincoln near Bismarck in the east, and
a third led by Gen. George Crook coming north from Fort Fetterman in
Wyoming, and hoped to trap the natives.

The fastest portion of Terry's column was the 7th Cavalry, commanded by
Gen. George Armstrong Custer. He took 215 men along the north bank of a small
creek approaching the river, Maj. Marcus Reno took 140 along the south bank,
and Capt. Frederick Benteen took 125 more to the southwest. After 2:00 p.m.,
Reno and Custer approached the village. The army had estimated that there were
no more than 800 warriors in that area, but it turned out that there were between
2,000 and 4,000.

Reno had his men cross the river and gallop toward the supposedly undefended Hunkpapa village, where they were met by a mass of warriors led by Gall.
Reno ordered his men to dismount and form a skirmish line, which quickly
crumbled and they retreated into a stand of timber. As they attempted to make
a run for it on horseback, many were cut down. Some survivors made it to some
bluffs, and then the natives left the battle.

Custer's force headed north, then tried to cross the river near the Cheyenne
camp. The soldiers' bullets were met by thousands of arrows coming from the
warriors led by Gall. Other warriors, including Cheyennes led by Two Moons,
crossed the river to join the battle from the west. Crazy Horse led his Oglala Sioux
to tighten the circle around the soldiers on the north and east. In less than 30
minutes, all 215 were dead.

Reno and Benteen combined their forces at about 4:30 p.m. on bluffs overlooking the river, to the southeast of Custer's last stand. They were surrounded
by the Sioux and Cheyenne, and the soldiers dug pits to protect themselves. At
sunset, most of the natives returned to the village for a victory dance.

On the following day, the armies of Terry and Gibbon approached up the
valley. The warriors set fire to the grass to provide a smoke screen and headed to
the Big Horn Mountains. Their losses were estimated at less than 100.

News of the battle reached the government on July 4, 1876, spoiling the cen-
tennial celebration. The attack by the soldiers was reported as a massacre by the
natives, and the American public cried out for punishment. The victory at the Little
Bighorn, with the strong reaction, probably quickened the natives' eventual demise.
Museums: (1) Custer Battlefield National Monument, P.O. Box 39, Crow Agency,
MT 59022; (2) Monroe County Historical Museum, 126 S. Monroe St., Monroe,
MI 48161 has exhibits on the life and death of Custer.
Sources: 4, 5, 13, 19, 20, 29, 30, 31, 32, 33, 34, 50, 62, 66, 68, 70, 84, 90, 91, 92,
109, 110, 114, 115, 116, 126, 133, 135, 147, 158, 197, 201, 203, 213, 220, 224, 235, 243,
254, 258, 264, 265, 266, 278, 288, 299, 308, 315, 325, 341, 346, 350, 351, 366, 380,
381, 392, 393, 401, 405, 406, 416, 417

MT17 *Attack on Sibley's Scouts* • July 7, 1876
Location: Head of Tongue River
War: Great Sioux War
A band of Cheyennes and Oglalas located some soldiers and scouts in the Big Horn Mountains and attempted to make friendly conversation. Instead, they opened fire and the warriors were chased into a patch of trees. White Antelope, a Cheyenne, was killed and the scouts ran back to Gen. George Crook's headquarters.
Sources: 91, 110

MT18 *Skirmish Near Wolf Rapids* • August 2, 1876
Location: Powder River, near the mouth of the Rosebud River
War: Great Sioux War
Maj. Orlando H. Moore led a party of infantry, plus a 12-pound Napoleon gun and a Gatling gun to the mouth of the Powder River. He had the steamboat put them ashore upstream at the abandoned depot. The troops were deployed to a nearby ridge, and warriors soon appeared.

Moore had Lt. Charles A. Woodruff shell them, causing them to flee. When other warriors arrived near the rapids, they were also dispersed by the Napoleon gun. Later in the day, other shells dispersed warriors who had approached the steamboat. One soldier and one native were killed, and the Sioux left the area.
Sources: 91, 420

MT19 *Battle of Cedar Creek* • October 21, 1876
Location: Near Miles City
War: Great Sioux War
Col. Nelson A. Miles led the 5th Infantry and other soldiers, comprising a force of 500. They met with the Sioux leadership and demanded a surrender, but received no response. Miles considered this to be an act of hostility. Early action involved soldier and warrior positioning, without shots being fired.

When the soldiers' ordnance rifle was finally used, it supported an advance of the troops which forced a Sioux withdrawal. Sitting Bull and his people headed north toward Canada.
Sources: 91, 265, 346, 350

MT20 *Battle of Ash Creek* • December 18, 1876
Location: Ash Creek
War: Great Sioux War
Lt. Frank D. Baldwin heard at the Wolf Point Agency that Sitting Bull planned to merge his forces with those of Crazy Horse on the Yellowstone River. Baldwin moved his troops to a camp on the valley of the Red Water, arriving on December 17.

At 7:00 a.m. the following morning, he moved his men east and south. Seven hours later, they were within four miles of the natives' camp of 190 lodges, while most of the warriors were out hunting. Scattering the remaining warriors with howitzer fire, the infantry shot at the tipis, forcing the natives out. The entire camp was captured. No people were killed, but the Sioux lost 60 horses and mules. The soldiers prevented the natives from returning to the United States to hunt buffalo, and in 1881 the Sioux surrendered.

Monument: A stone pyramid with a bronze marker is located at the site of the battle.

Sources: 4, 224, 265, 346, 350, 420

MT21 *Attack at Fort Keough* • December, 1876
Location: Fort Keough
War: Great Sioux War
A peace delegation from the Lakota Sioux, while carrying a white flag, was killed by Crow scouts.
Sources: 110

MT22 *Battle of Wolf Mountain* • January 8, 1877
Location: Tongue River and Battle Butte Creek
War: Great Sioux War
Col. Nelson A. Miles moved up the Tongue River to Battle Butte Creek, causing Crazy Horse to move his people to a high ridge for protection. The soldiers camped, and Big Crow, a Cheyenne, walked back and forth between the soldiers and the ridge, still angry at the army for the attack on Dull Knife's village. After he was shot, the other warriors dragged him back to their position.

The Oglalas and Cheyennes held off the soldiers until the women were able to escape up the Tongue River toward the Little Bighorn. Their rear was guarded by He Dog, Crazy Horse, and two Cheyennes. A blizzard masked the fact that the warriors also departed. Big Crow died along the way.
Sources: 91, 110, 114, 197, 275, 380, 420

MT23 *Battle of Lame Deer* • May 7, 1877
Location: Little Muddy Creek
War: Great Sioux War
Col. Nelson Appleton Miles organized an attack on Lame Deer's village with the intent that no women or children were to be killed. He had Lt. E.W. Casey and 20 men stampede the native pony herd while Lt. Lovell H. Jerome's company rounded it up. Capt. Randolph Norwood chased the natives out of the camp and up a hill.

Lame Deer and warrior Iron Star approached the officers to shake hands while the other warriors laid down their weapons. A young soldier arrived on the scene and, mistaking it for something else, aimed his rifle at Lame Deer and fighting broke out. Lame Deer was shot 17 times and 16 other Lakota Sioux were killed. Miles took control of the camp, losing four soldiers in the fight. This marked the end of the Great Sioux War.
Sources: 4, 91, 114, 265, 275, 420

MT24 *Battle of the Big Hole* • August 9–10, 1877
Location: 10 miles west of Wisdom
War: Nez Perce War
The Nee Me Poo, called the Nez Perce by early French Canadian fur trappers, lived in the Wallowa Valley which also was desired by white settlers. The government sought to capture the natives and confine them to a reservation. Approximately 750 to 800 people led by Chief Joseph, including sick and elderly, moved their large horse herd and all of their baggage, over a 1,400 mile retreat from the troops.

They mistakenly believed that if they could cross through the Idaho panhandle and into Montana, they would be safe.

At their camp on the east bank of the north fork of the Big Hole River, they were attacked by 15 officers and 146 soldiers of the 7th Infantry led by Col. John Gibbon (One Who Limps), accompanied by 34 volunteers. Within minutes, several of the Nez Perce were dead. Chief Looking Glass ordered them to take up concealed positions, and their fire caused the soldiers to retreat across the river to the foot of Battle Mountain. The fire from the Nez Perce guns kept the soldiers pinned down for the rest of the day.

The army had 31 killed and 38 wounded. Of the 17 officers, 14 were killed or wounded. From 60 to 90 Nez Perce were killed, mostly women and children. On August 10, most of the survivors moved off toward the south. A handful of warriors kept the soldiers pinned down until nightfall, when they slipped off to join the rest of the tribe, which then sought to reach the Crow land in the Yellowstone country.

Monuments: (1) The site of a fort built in 1877 by Capt. Charles Rawn to protect the area from the Nez Perce is denoted by a marker on US 12, 6 miles west of Lolo; (2) Big Hole National Battlefield is located on SR 43 near Wisdom.

Sources: 5, 9, 33, 66, 70, 86, 91, 114, 147, 175, 191, 192, 197, 203, 236, 264, 285, 286, 288, 315, 350, 366, 378, 405

MT25 *Battle of Canyon Creek* • September 13, 1877
Location: North of Yellowstone River, near the confluence with Clark's Fork
War: Nez Perce War

As the 700 Nez Perce and 2,000 horses were crossing the plain north of the Yellowstone River, they were overtaken by the army commanded by Col. Samuel D. Sturgis. The warriors formed a protective defensive line, while the rest of the tribe attempted to flee into the nearby canyon.

With long-distance rifle fire, the warriors were able to keep the soldiers and Crow scouts away. Gradually, the number of Nez Perce defenders dwindled to one, and then he left to join the rest of his people who were leaving the area. Although they lost some horses, natives claimed that their casualties were limited to three slight wounds. The soldiers had three killed and 11 wounded. Sturgis claimed that they had killed 16 Nez Perce.

Sources: 86, 91, 175, 191, 197, 236, 285, 315

MT26 *Battles in Crow Country* • Late September, 1877
Location: Cow Island, Cow Creek Canyon
War: Nez Perce War

The Nez Perce who survived the action at Big Hole and the gruelling march into the wilderness reached the lands of their former friends, the Crows. However, as they found out during the several encounters with the army and their native scouts, the Crows had aligned themselves with the soldiers.

On September 14, a hundred Crows and Bannocks attacked the rear of the Nez Perce column. When the Nez Perce came upon a party of Crows hunting bison at Judith Basin, they killed several and captured the horses and meat. On September 23, they engaged a few white soldiers in long-distance shooting at a depot at Cow Island, resulting in one white killed and two injured.

The Nez Perce attacked a wagon train and killed two or three of the teamsters. Soldiers then appeared at the site of the attack. Led by Maj. Guido Ilgis, they briefly fought with the warriors, with one civilian and one soldier killed, before retreating.

The Crows attacked the Nez Perce several times until the Nez Perce left their country and headed toward Canada.

Sources: 5, 86, 147, 175, 191, 236, 285, 315

MT27 *Battle of Bear Paw* • September 30–October 5, 1877
Location: Snake Creek in the Bear Paw Mountains
War: Nez Perce War

Along Snake Creek within 40 miles of Canada, the Nez Perce were surprised by the army under the command of Col. Nelson A. Miles, who had traveled from Fort Keough in eastern Montana. With the soldiers were 30 Cheyenne and Sioux scouts. On the morning of September 30, they ran off the horses of Chief Joseph and his people.

Early action involved a party led by Capt. Owen Hale, who was killed at the outset. In the main part of the camp, 75 warriors held off the attack of 125 cavalry and 90 infantry. Miles, wishing to be promoted to the rank of brigadier general, wanted to win the battle before the arrival of reserves led by Col. Samuel D. Sturgis and Gen. Oliver O. Howard, with whom he might have to share the glory. He ordered another risky charge, but suffered 53 casualties within the 125-man 7th Cavalry. He then pulled back and surrounded the Nez Perce's position. The siege lasted five days and several were killed, including Lean Elk, Looking Glass, Toohoolhoolzote, Pile of Clouds and Ollokot.

Messengers were sent northward to inform Sitting Bull of their plight. However, they were killed by Assiniboins who wanted to show the soldiers that they were not aiding the Nez Perce. During a period of truce and talk, Miles had Joseph seized at the army camp and tied up. At the Nez Perce camp, Lt. Lovell H. Jerome was similarly seized. On October 2, the two captives were traded for each other and the shooting resumed.

Suffering from cold and hunger, on October 5 the Nez Perce surrendered to Gen. Howard and Col. Miles, believing that they were promised by Miles that they would be sheltered and fed for the winter at Fort Keough, and then would be returned to the Lapwai Reservation in their own country in Oregon. That night, 70-year-old White Bird and 300 others escaped to Canada to join Sitting Bull's camp. The rest were shipped to a malaria-ridden reservation near Fort Leavenworth in eastern Kansas, where many died of sickness.

Monuments: (1) The grave of Chief Joseph, located in the cemetery of Nespelem, WA, is marked by a marble gravestone erected by white admirers; (2) A marble Chief Joseph Battleground marker is in Bear Paw State Monument, located on CR 240 16 miles south of US 2 near Chinook.

Sources: 5, 9, 20, 13, 19, 33, 63, 66, 70, 86, 90, 91, 114, 135, 147, 175, 191, 192, 197, 203, 236, 254, 264, 265, 266, 285, 286, 315, 350, 366, 378, 380, 405, 420, 421

NEBRASKA

NE1   *Battle on the Platte River* • August 14, 1720
Location: Near Columbus
From Santa Fe, New Mexico, Gen. Don Pedro de Villasur led a force of 120 men, consisting of Spanish soldiers and native allies, through El Cuartelejo in Colorado and into the Kansas-Nebraska Territory. Their goal was to win the good will of the Pawnees, making contact through a Pawnee slave. They came to a large Pawnee mound village, but the slave messenger was ignored because he wore European clothing. They then communicated with written messages, some in French because Villasur believed there were anti–Spanish French among the Pawnees. The Spanish camped in the open, letting the native allies take care of security.
   One night, the Pawnees, some French, and a party of Otoes, surrounded the Spanish camp and at dawn 500 warriors charged. The Pawnees stampeded the horses and fought with arrows and French guns. From 25 to 50 of the Spanish party including Villasur were killed, and most of their native allies deserted. Only 14 made it all the way back to Santa Fe.
Sources: 103, 182, 204, 208, 213, 217, 219, 246, 261, 278, 281, 306, 307, 358, 410

NE2   *Attack on Pawnee Village* • May 21, 1847
Location: North of Platte River
Pawnees returned to their villages north of the Platte River under a promise of protection given by the Sioux. Shortly after they arrived, a Sioux party attacked and killed 23 Pawnees. Other Sioux raids occurred during the summer, causing the Pawnees to move south of the Platte. The army then made plans to drive them again north of the river.
Sources: 199

NE3   *Attack on the Omahas* • July, 1855
Location: Along Beaver Creek
In July, a Brule raiding party traveled to the lower Platte River country, and a few Oglalas went with them. They came upon an Omaha camp and stole their best horses. On the following day, while the Omahas were out looking for them, they attacked the camp. Omaha chief Logan Fontenelle was killed and Curly, an Oglala later known as Crazy Horse, killed an Omaha woman.
Sources: 110

NE4   *Battle of Ash Hollow* or *Battle of the Blue Water* • September 3, 1855
Location: Blue Water Creek
Gen. William S. Harney led 1,200 men from Fort Leavenworth, consisting of four companies of dragoons plus infantry and artillery, and camped at Ash Hollow. The action was in retaliation for the Grattan Massacre of 1854 in Wyoming.
   They were supposed to be supported by troops led by Gen. Edwin Sumner, but they turned back to Fort Leavenworth when they heard war drums along the route. While they were there, the Bois Brules led by Little Thunder attacked a wagon train and killed all 20 of its settlers.

Harney sent a demand to Little Thunder to turn over the warriors who were responsible for the killings, and Little Thunder responded that they were not under his control. Harney warned that he would have to punish the natives. A fierce charge pushed the warriors into a ravine that had only one other exit, a narrow pass that Harney had blocked with cavalry. The trapped natives, including women and children, were allowed to live as prisoners, rather than be slaughtered. Even so, 135 had been killed.

Little Thunder was impressed by Harney's mercy and, rather than attempting further retribution for what could have been senseless killing of noncombatants, worked for peace in the region.

Sources: 4, 70, 84, 91, 92, 109, 110, 114, 158, 182, 196, 154, 278, 315, 380, 407

NE5 *Attacks Along the Platte River* • Early August, 1864
Location: 35 miles east of Fort Kearny
War: Cheyenne-Arapaho War
Fourteen men were killed in attacks on three wagon trains, while women and children were taken prisoner. The wagons were robbed and burned.

Near Gilman's Ranch, just east of the confluence of the North and South Platte Rivers, three white men were killed, and on August 10 another killing of a settler was reported near Cottonwood Springs, across the river from North Platte.

On August 10, a party of Cheyennes raided the Little Blue River Valley about 170 miles east of Cottonwood Springs, killing at least 11. Six more were killed at Thirty-two Mile Creek. At the Liberty Farm station, keeper Joe Eubanks was killed and scalped and his two children were captured.

Sources: 278, 362

NE6 *Attacks in Nebraska* • January and February, 1865
Location: Platte River
War: Cheyenne-Arapaho War
War parties composed of Sioux, Cheyenne and Arapaho warriors conducted raids along the Platte River and both of its branches. They burned ranches and stage stations, tore down telegraph wires, and halted the mails, supply trains and stagecoaches. They effectively cut off Denver, Salt Lake City and San Francisco from communication with the eastern portion of the country.

They were pursued by the 11th Ohio Volunteer Cavalry led by Col. W.O. Collins, which fought the natives on February 6 near the present site of Sidney. On February 8, they again fought near present Bridgeport. The battles did little other than slow down the natives' movement toward the Powder River valley in Wyoming, where they spent the winter.

Sources: 147, 362

NE7 *Uprising at Horse Creek* • June 14, 1865
Location: Near Red Cloud Agency
At a camp along Horse Creek were soldiers and their native prisoners, in the process of relocation. In the morning, the soldiers began to move out in continuation of their travel, but the native wagons did not move. When the soldiers tried to hurry them along, two shots were fired and the officer in charge, Fouts, was killed along with five of his men. As revenge for this, the surviving soldiers scalped a crippled prisoner.

Sources: 109, 110

NE8   *Battle of Plum Creek* • August 17, 1867
Location: Lexington
A party of Southern Cheyenne led by Turkey Leg pried up the rails and caused the crash of a train, resulting in the deaths of fireman Hendershot and engineer "Bully Brooks" Bower. Maj. Frank North was ordered to the scene by Gen. Christopher C. Augur, who was the commander of the army north of the Platte River. He and his men arrived by train, and then their Pawnee scouts found a recent trail leading south toward the Republican River valley.

About ten days later, North and three other officers led a party of 48 Pawnees to the Cheyenne camp. They found 150 warriors and each side formed a battle linc across a small creek from each other. The Pawnees charged across the creek, sending the Cheyennes into retreat. By nightfall, the Pawnees had killed 15, taken two prisoners, and captured 35 horses and mules. The soldiers and Pawnees suffered no injuries.
Sources: 91, 201

NE9   *Attack at Elm Creek Station* • April 16, 1868
Location: Elm Creek
A band of Sioux led by Two Strikes sought to cripple the railroad heading through the state, attacking and killing five section men near the station and taking some livestock.

On the same day, the post at Sidney was attacked by part of the same band of Sioux. Conductors Tom Cahoon and William Edmundson were attacked, with Cahoon being shot and scalped, and Edmundson being both shot and hit by four arrows. Both survived.
Sources: 201

NE10   *Attack on Train* • September, 1868
Location: Between Alkali and Ogalalla
The same renegade band of Sioux that had attacked Elm Creek and Sidney pried up the rails to stop a train, resulting in a crash which sent the cars into a ditch and killed the fireman. The conductor and two or three passengers defended the train with arms that were carried aboard for protection against native attacks.

Maj. Frank North took a company of his Pawnee scouts in search of the Sioux and came upon them along the North Platte River. They killed two and continued on for 35 miles in search of the main body of Sioux. Some of the soldiers negligently tended their fires that night, starting an immense prairie fire which alerted the warriors to their presence. The soldiers then broke off the search.
Sources: 210

NE11   *Pawnee and Sioux Massacre* • August 5, 1873
Location: Massacre Canyon, near Lexington
The Pawnees who lived on a reservation near Columbus customarily went on a fall buffalo hunt. The Sioux living on the Pine Bluff Reservation had a grudge against them. At the Pawnee camp on Plum Creek, the Sioux drove a herd of buffalo toward the Pawnees, who began shooting the animals.

The Sioux then arrived, and the Pawnees fled down the canyon. The larger

band of Sioux followed them on either bank, killing about 10 men, 39 women and 10 children. The Sioux fled when the cavalry arrived on the scene.
Sources: 66, 201, 213

NE12   *Skirmish at War Bonnet Creek* • July 17, 1876
Location: Northwest corner of Nebraska, near Camp Robinson
War: Great Sioux War
The 5th Infantry led by Col. Wesley Merritt came upon a body of Cheyennes traveling from the Red Cloud Agency to the Powder River. The skirmish resulted in the warriors being turned back, toward the agency. It was important in that it prevented their meeting up with the forces of Sitting Bull and Crazy Horse.
Sources: 91, 420

NE13   *Battle at Fort Robinson* • January 9, 1879
Location: Near Crawford
The Northern Cheyennes led by Dull Knife and Little Wolf were on their exodus northward through Nebraska, when they were stopped by a snowstorm. They were also surrounded by soldiers, eventually surrendered and were taken to Fort Robinson, reaching it on October 25. They expected that they would be required to give up their weapons, so they dismantled the best five rifles and hid the parts, while turning in the broken ones.

After a long stay at the fort, they were ordered back to Oklahoma and refused to go. After five days of confinement in the barracks without food or wood for the heating stove, they reassembled the five remaining rifles. At 9:45 p.m., they shot the guards and burst out of the barracks through the windows, picking up the guards' weapons.

The Cheyennes headed toward a line of bluffs, with about a ten-minute head start on the mounted soldiers. The soldiers caught up with them and soon killed about half of the warriors, plus many women and children. Thirty-eight escaped and 65 were herded back into the fort the next morning. Of those who escaped, 29 were hunted down and killed, and the rest were taken prisoner.
Sources: 70, 91, 278

Nevada

NV1   *Pyramid Lake Massacre* • May 9, 1860
Location: Pyramid Lake
War: Paiute War
During the gold rush era, a party of miners captured some Paiute women, taking them to town to do domestic chores. The native men raised a force of 100 and rescued the women without a fight. The whites took offense at this and decided to wipe out the Paiute camp on the north shore of Pyramid Lake.

When the 105 volunteers arrived, they were ambushed by the warriors and 46 of them were killed by arrows.
Sources: 203

NV2   *Rout of Paiutes* • June 2, 1860
Location: Pyramid Lake
War: Paiute War
Texas Ranger veteran Col. Jack Hays assembled volunteers, two companies of infantry, dragoons and howitzers. They routed the Paiutes along the Truckee River, near the previous month's Pyramid Lake Massacre. One result of the war against the Paiutes was the establishment of Fort Churchill, east of Lake Tahoe.
Sources: 66, 91

NEW HAMPSHIRE

NH1   *Destruction of Native Villages* • Summer, 1675
Location: New Hampshire
War: King Philip's War
The first attacks in New Hampshire began at a settlement on the Oyster River, in what is now the town of Durham.

Capt. Samuel Moseley led a campaign against King Philip and his Wampanoags, attempting to put an early end to what is now known as King Philip's War. While in New Hampshire, the army burned two villages which were supposedly under the protection of the friendly sachem Wonnalancet.

Moseley also stormed into the Praying Indian villages of Nashobo (Littleton) and Okammakamest (Marlborough), where he took 15 prisoners and carried them off to Boston.
Sources: 280, 334

NH2   *Attack on Cocheco* • June, 1679
Location: Near Dover
Even before the formal declaration of King William's War in April, there was a series of raids by natives on settlements in New England. Edmund Andros, governor of Virginia, sent an expedition against the natives in Maine and established several forts.

After a reduction of the English forces, the raids were renewed, including one against the village of Cocheco. A large number of its residents was killed or captured.
Sources: 328

NH3   *Attack at Dover* • June, 1689
Location: Dover
War: King William's War

Three garrison houses were each visited by two squaws, who were invited to spend the night. They later opened the gates and let in bands of warriors who killed Maj. Waldron and his son-in-law, plus 21 others. Twenty-nine were taken captive and the houses were plundered and burned.
Sources: 280

NH4   *Attack at Oyster River* • July 18, 1694
Location: Durham
War: King William's War
At dawn, a party of warriors attacked the town of Oyster River, which is now known as Durham, and killed or captured approximately 100 settlers. One who survived was Thomas Bickford.

Bickford placed his wife, mother and children in a canoe and sent them down the river, while he defended his home by himself. The attackers tried to draw him out by making promises, and then threats, but he would not leave. He confused them by appearing at the windows in several outfits, making them believe that there was more than one defender in the house. They eventually left him alone.
Sources: 128, 274, 290, 328

NH5   *Battle at Wakefield* • February 20, 1725
Location: Wakefield
War: Dummer's War
Capt. John Lovewell and his soldiers fought with a party of natives. They scalped ten of the warriors and were paid 100 pounds for each in Boston. This was the first known instance of scalping by Europeans.
Sources: 133

NEW MEXICO

NM1   *Battle of Hawikuh* • July 7, 1540
Location: Hawikuh
War: Mixton War
This was the first formal military encounter between Europeans and natives, and it occurred near the town of Hawikuh near the present Arizona border. Francisco Vasquez de Coronado and his expedition were heading north in search of the seven cities of gold when they came upon Hawikuh, a typical Zuni pueblo. They decided to take possession of it.

The Zunis closed the road to the pueblo with a line of sacred cornmeal but the Spaniards charged across it. After an hour of battle, the rocks and arrows of the Zuni succumbed to the firearms of the Spanish cavalry. The Spaniards remained at Hawikuh until November.
Sources: 72, 75, 108, 281, 282, 283, 284, 314, 358

NM2   *Battle of Acoma* • December 4, 1598
Location: Acoma Pueblo, Western New Mexico
War: Onate Expedition
The Spanish court sent Don Juan de Onate into New Mexico to repeat the successes of Francisco Coronado and Francisco Pizarro, and in September of 1595
appointed him as the Governor and Captain General of New Mexico. Onate led
a band of 400, consisting of colonists, soldiers, friars and cattle, to an area north
of the Rio Grande. At Acoma, also known as Aku or Sky City, the expedition was
at first turned away, then welcomed into the virtually inaccessible settlement.
Although some, including Zutacapan, urged the Pueblos to prepare for war, elder
Chumpo convinced the leadership that if the Spaniards were treated fairly, they
would treat the natives the same way.
      On October 27, Onate made his usual demand that the natives pledge their
submission to him, and they did. A month later, Onate's nephew, Juan de Zaldivar,
demanded food for his troops at Acoma. This time, the men listened to Zutacapan
and refused, but after being offered hatchets in trade, agreed to grind the demanded
corn. After three days, Zaldivar led 16 armed men into Acoma and the confrontation turned violent. Zaldivar and 12 of his men were killed, as were an unrecorded
number of the Pueblo natives. By the end of the year, Onate formally declared war.
Sources: 20, 92, 108, 147, 199, 213, 246, 275, 277, 281, 283, 357, 358, 412

NM3   *Attack on Sky City* • January 21, 1599
Location: Acoma Pueblo
War: Onate Expedition
Vicente Zaldivar, the brother of the late Juan, led 75 men against the Acoma
mesa. Twelve dragged a cannon up a rock wall at the rear, then turned it against
the town and destroyed the adobe and stone houses. The main force rushed into
the town and killed more than 800 of the total population of 6,000. Five hundred women and children were taken prisoner, where they were tried by Gov. Don
Juan de Onate and convicted of treason. Many were sentenced to 20 years as
indentured servants, and others were publicly mutilated.
Sources: 20, 108, 147, 213, 275, 282, 283, 329, 348, 357, 380, 412

NM4   *Battle at Sky City* • August 10, 1680
Location: Acoma Pueblo
War: Pueblo Revolt
After its destruction by the Spanish in 1599, Sky City was rebuilt and for decades,
the area remained in relative peace. On the prearranged date of August 10, 1680,
all of the Pueblos (Taos, Santa Clara, Picuris and Santa Cruz) successfully revolted
under a Tewa leader named Pope, resulting in the deaths of 21 Franciscans and
375 Spaniards and their servants. With the Pueblos were some Jicarilla and
Mescalero Apaches and some Navajos, recruited by Pope.
      The bodies of the hated priests were stacked on the altars of the churches.
About 1,000 of the survivors fled to El Paso del Norte and Spain, once they were
convinced that the Apaches and Navajos were supporting the rebels. The entire
Spanish population of the area had only been about 2,500.
Monuments: (1) Sky City is located 12.5 miles southwest of the junction of Inter-
state 40 and SR 23; (2) Ruins of the destroyed Mission San Geronimo de Taos
are located 2.5 miles north of Taos Plaza, Taos.

Sources: 19, 20, 31, 48, 53, 66, 92, 102, 103, 104, 108, 135, 204, 213, 245, 275, 281, 282, 283, 284, 288, 297, 315, 329, 348, 356, 358, 380, 405

NM5 *Siege of Santa Fe* • August 15–21, 1680
Location: Santa Fe
War: Pueblo Revolt
Following the fighting at Sky City, about 1,000 Spaniards crowded into the Palace of the Governors in Santa Fe. The leadership of the 2,500 natives sent the governor Antonio de Otermin two crosses with one to be returned, white for surrender and red for continued fighting. He returned the red one and, on August 20, launched a counterattack.

The following day, they escaped and headed south to El Paso, where they were befriended by the Manso natives. The death toll was 380 soldiers and 21 priests. The Pueblos then converted the palace into a pueblo village by blocking the windows and doors and adding ladders that entered the buildings from the roof.

For 12 years, the Pueblos were free, and when the Spanish returned in 1692 Gen. Don Diego de Vargas and a 300-man army peacefully regained the area, so the conquerors and natives again lived in relative peace. That ended when they were reconquered by the Spanish in 1696.
Museum: The Palace of the Governors is located at Palace Ave., Santa Fe.
Sources: 20, 31, 35, 46, 48, 102, 103, 104, 108, 144, 245, 281, 282, 283, 315, 329, 348, 358, 415

NM6 *Conquest of Pueblos* • 1694
Location: New Mexico
War: Pueblo Uprising
Don Diego de Vargas, the Spanish governor, embarked on a campaign to reconquer the rebel pueblos, after he regained control of Santa Fe in December of 1693.

On March 4, he attacked the Tewa pueblo of San Ildefonso and in five hours of fierce fighting 20 Spaniards were wounded and 15 allied natives were killed. After attempting to carry on further attack from March 11 to 19, he withdrew.

On April 17, he and friendly Keresan natives captured La Cieneguilla, killing several and capturing hundreds. He unsuccessfully attacked Jemez in May.

In late June, the Spaniards marched on Taos, and the natives fled to a nearby canyon. While they were gone, Vargas took their corn and burned the town. On July 24, he led 120 Spaniards and several Keresans against Jemez again, killing 84 and capturing the town. On September 4, they attacked San Ildefonso along with allies from Pecos, Zia, Santa Ana and San Felipe. The siege was lifted on September 8, marking a Spanish victory.
Sources: 275, 329, 358

NM7 *Pima Uprising* • June 4, 1696
Location: Taos and several other villages
War: Pueblo Uprising
The Spaniards had Opatas as their assistants, but this strained relations with the Pimas because the Opatas considered them inferior. In 1695, the Pimas revolted, killing some Jesuit priests and the Opatas. The mission settlements of Altar and Caborca were destroyed.

Pima chief El Tupo agreed to turn over the individuals responsible for the killing of the priests, and when one perpetrator was identified, a Spanish officer beheaded him. The Pimas fled, but were chased by Spanish soldiers and allied Seris, who killed El Tupo and 50 others.

Sources: 48, 108, 275, 314, 329

NM8 *Raid on Taos* • 1716
Location: Taos
The Utes and Comanches staged a large raid on Taos, while Gov. Don Felix Martinez had most of the Spanish forces away on an expedition against the Moquis in Arizona. The natives also attacked the Tigua Pueblos and outlying Spanish settlements.

This resulted in the Spanish sending out a punitive expedition led by Don Juan de Padellano. He struck a Comanche camp and was victorious. He then released the captives he had taken and announced that the Spanish found peace and trade preferable to war.

Sources: 103, 204

NM9 *Attack on Pecos* • 1744
Location: Pecos
A band of Comanches attacked Pecos from the plains east of New Mexico. They killed a number of Pueblo natives and continued with their attack to Galisteo, 20 miles south of Santa Fe.

In June of 1746, the Comanches again struck Pecos and Galisteo, causing the friendly Apaches to flee the area.

Sources: 204

NM10 *Attack on Ute and Comanche Camp* • October, 1748
Location: Near Abiquiu
Gov. Rabal personally led a force of 500 men west of the Rio Grande and into the Chama River district, attacking a Ute and Comanche camp. They killed 107 and captured 200 natives and 1,000 horses. Three months later, Rabal and his army drove off a Comanche raiding party at Pecos.

Sources: 204

NM11 *Defeat of Comanches* • November, 1751
Location: Near Santa Fe
Following a battle at Galisteo Pueblo, about 20 miles south of Santa Fe, in which the Spanish repulsed 300 Comanches and killed six, Gov. Tomas Velez Cachupin assembled an army to fight back. Consisting of 54 soldiers, 30 militiamen and about 40 Pueblo auxiliaries, it set out toward the Galisteo Pueblo.

They came upon the Comanches and attacked during the daylight, gaining the advantage. They continued the fight after dark, but found that the dense brush and waist-deep water in the watering hole favored the natives. Velez had his men set fire to the thicket, providing light to reveal the hidden Comanches, who refused to surrender.

At midnight, individuals began to surrender and, finding that they were not killed immediately, called to the rest to turn themselves in. At 3 a.m., a group of warriors attacked and most were killed by musket fire. At dawn, they could find no live natives in the area except for those who had surrendered, and Velez set them free.

Only 49 of the 145 Comanches survived. Eight Spaniards had been wounded, one fatally. Velez and his men rode away with four hostages to trade for Spanish captives taken earlier by the Comanches.
Sources: 204, 246

NM12 *Attacks on Missions* • November 20, 1751
Location: New Mexico
Luis Oacpicagigua organized the natives near the Spanish missions located in the lands of the Northern Pimas. On the morning of November 20, they attacked missions and ranches, eliminating many ranch families. Some missions that had been warned by knowledgeable Jesuits were prepared and defended themselves for a few days before abandoning the missions.
Sources: 202, 314

NM13 *Attack at Villapando Ranch House* • August, 1760
Location: Near Taos
The Taos natives were allies of the Spanish and danced for them at a festival. They showed 15 Comanche scalps, which angered the Comanches, a band of which attacked a ranch house where several Spanish families gathered for their defense.

The Comanches battered their way into the building, losing 49 warriors in the process. They killed all of the white men and captured 56 women and children. They were unsuccessfully pursued onto the plains for 200 miles by the Spanish, aided by some Apaches.
Sources: 204, 246

NM14 *Skirmish at Ojo Caliente* • September, 1768
Location: 25 miles southwest of Taos
A band of 24 Comanches killed an unarmed settler, then rode by the settlement of Ojo Caliente and shot at it, but hit no one.

They were pursued by a party of soldiers, 16 settlers and some Ute warriors, and the Comanches entrenched themselves in a previously successful defensive position. However, this time they had 21 killed and two captured.
Sources: 246

NM15 *Attacks in Chama Valley* • Early July, 1774
Location: Chama Valley
In the Chama Valley and near the Santa Clara Pueblo, 1,000 Comanches attacked several locations. They killed seven, wounded several, and captured three boys.
Sources: 281

NM16 *Attack at Albuquerque* • Late July, 1774
Location: Albuquerque
About 1,000 Comanche warriors killed several Spaniards in Albuquerque. They also captured the town's horses and many of its sheep.
Sources: 281

NM17 *Attack at Pecos* • August, 1774
Location: Pecos
About 100 Comanches galloped into Pecos and attacked the settlers as they were working in their fields. They killed seven men and two women, capturing seven more. Gov. Mendinueta sent 114 men after them the next day, and they caught up with the warriors four days later about 180 miles from Santa Fe.

The Spanish attacked and initially had success, killing several Comanches and rescuing the single surviving captive. The Comanches continued to fight until late afternoon, and the fighting resulted in one Spanish soldier killed and 22 wounded. They estimated that they killed 40 warriors in the early fighting and several more throughout the day.

In September, Mendinueta sent out 600 men to punish the Comanches, and they killed or captured about 400 in an attack on a large Comanche camp.
Sources: 204, 246

NM18 *Attack at Pecos* • May, 1775
Location: Pecos
A band of Comanches attacked the Pecos natives as they worked in their fields. Each side had three killed. The same Comanches a week later killed a boy while he tended his oxen near Santa Fe. During the year, white losses to the Comanches, Gila Apaches and Navajos totalled 41.
Sources: 246, 281

NM19 *Attack Along the Gila River* • 1775
Location: Headwaters of the Gila River
Hugo Oconor and 1,500 troops attacked the Gileno Apaches, trapping them near the headwaters of the Gila River. They killed 138 warriors and captured over 100 women and children.
Sources: 48

NM20 *Raid on Taos* • Fall, 1779
Location: Taos
Cuerno Verde (also known as Kuhtsoo-ehkuh and Green Horn) led a Comanche raid against Taos. They were pursued by the 600-man Spanish army led by Col. Don Bautista de Anza, who trapped a party of 50 in a bog. Cuerno Verde and others died in the battle, and the bulk of the Comanche war party escaped. Only one Spanish soldier was wounded in the action.
Sources: 103, 246, 281

NM21 *Attack at Bent's House* • January 19, 1847
Location: Taos
Gov. Charles Bent's home was the site of a gathering mob, most of which had moved there from the local cantinas. Bent attempted to reason with them, but the natives wanted to regain control of the region. Bent was shot and stabbed. Through the back door escaped his wife, sister-in-law (Kit Carson's wife), his two children, and a Mrs. Boggs. Five other men were killed in Taos.
Sources: 230, 341

NM22 *White Massacre* • October, 1849

Location: Between Rock Creek and the Whetstone River

Mr. White and his wife and child were on their way to Santa Fe with the wagon train belonging to Mr. Aubrey. After passing through the area considered to be dangerous, they left the train with Mr. Lawberger and three others. While they camped, a party of Jicarillas arrived and demanded presents, and when they were refused they killed all but Mrs. White and her child, who were taken prisoner.

The wagons were then plundered by a party of Mexicans who happened on the scene. The natives were followed by a company of dragoons led by Kit Carson, who killed several of the Jicarillas. Mrs. White and her child were killed by the Jicarillas before they fled the area.

Sources: 254

NM23 *Battle of Cieneguilla* • March 30, 1854

Location: 25 miles southeast of Taos

A band of Jicarilla Apaches attacked a mail coach and its 60-soldier guard. They fought for three hours in a battle in which 23 soldiers died. The warriors were then pursued by a force led by Lt. Col. Philip St. George Cooke and guided by Kit Carson.

In a deep Ojo Caliente canyon, they again exchanged rifle fire and the Apaches were routed by mounted dragoons. Four or five warriors were killed.

Sources: 66, 91, 230

NM24 *Ambushes Near Pinos Altos* • July, 1861

Location: Southeast of Pinos Altos

War: Apache War

Mangas Coloradas, leader of the Chihenne (White Springs Apaches) was opposed to Americans for two main reasons. In 1837, a Kentucky entrepreneur killed at least 20 Apaches for their scalps, on which there was a bounty. In 1851, whites dug for gold near Pinos Altos, a practice the Apaches believed would anger Ussen, a symbol of the sun, and bring punishment against the inhabitants.

In retribution for these actions, Mangas laid siege to the gold camp in May and was joined by Cochise and his Chiracahuas (Chokonen) in July. They ambushed and killed about 100 miners and soldiers who passed near the slopes of Cooke's Peak.

Sources: 254, 298

NM25 *Battle of La Glorieta* • March 28, 1862

Location: Glorieta Pass

War: Apache War

A Confederate army led by Gen. Henry H. Sibley marched up the Rio Grande River and occupied Albuquerque and Santa Fe. They encountered a force of Apaches and the 1st Colorado Volunteers led by Col. John M. Chivington at Glorieta Pass and were soundly defeated. After losing 500 men, the Confederate army left New Mexico.

Monument: A marble plaque was erected on the site of the battle by the United Daughters of the Confederacy in 1939.

Sources: 48, 101, 171, 253, 277, 281, 283, 373, 405

NM26 *Massacre of Mescaleros* • Fall, 1862
Location: Near Gallina Springs
War: Apache War
Gen. James Henry Carleton led the California Column of Union soldiers to this area from the west to fight the Confederates, who instead fled to Texas. Carleton then looked for others to fight, and chose the Mescalero Apaches. By September, he ordered the killing of the men and the capture of the women and children, for relocation to a reservation along the Pecos River. Kit Carson, another Union officer, arranged for five Mescalero chiefs to meet with Carleton in Santa Fe. Along the way, two of the chiefs and their escorts encountered Capt. James Graydon and his men, who pretended friendship and gave them flour and beef for the journey. Shortly thereafter, Graydon encountered them again and was allowed to come into their camp, where the soldiers killed all the Mescaleros.

The remaining three chiefs, Cadette, Chatto and Estrella, met with Carleton in Santa Fe, where they were told that they had to move to the reservation where they would be confined by soldiers from Fort Sumner.
Sources: 70

NM27 *Nana's Raid* • June–August, 1881
Location: New Mexico
War: Victorio's Rebellion
After the near annihilation of the Chihenne at Tres Castillos in Chihuahua, Nana gathered the survivors together and began to rebuild his band. In June of 1881, they embarked on a campaign of fighting which had them riding 3,000 miles within two months. They won all seven serious battles with the cavalry.

Although they were chased by 1,000 soldiers and 300 to 400 civilians, they and about 30 to 40 Mescaleros who rode with them were able to remain free and attacked over a dozen ranches and towns. They captured over 200 horses and mules, and killed at least 35 whites, while suffering no serious casualties. When the long raid was over, Nana felt that he had avenged some of the injustice suffered by Victorio, and moved on to Sonora.
Sources: 298

NM28 *Chiricahua Raid* • March, 1883
Location: New Mexico
War: Apache War
A Chiricahua raiding party of 16 warriors came into New Mexico in a fashion similar to that led by Nana in 1881. They rode as many as a hundred miles a day and, in less than a week, killed 26 whites and stole dozens of horses. Only one Apache died in the fighting.

The identity of the leader of the raid is not certain, but many agree that it was Chatto. He later turned on the Chiricahuas and became an army scout.
Sources: 298

NM29 *Attack by Apaches* • December, 1885
Location: Alma
War: Apache War
Josanie and his Apache braves killed two settlers near Alma early in the month and then escaped into the mountains. They were attacked by the 8th Cavalry on

December 9 near Papanosas, escaping to ambush another band of soldiers, killing five and wounding two. Near Christmas time, they killed a freighter near Alma and on December 27 they took refuge in the Chiricahua Mountains.
Sources: 166

NEW YORK

NY1   *Battle on Lake Champlain* • July 30, 1609
Location: Lake Champlain
War: Champlain Expedition
At Trois-Rivieres, Samuel de Champlain joined a war party of 60 Hurons and Algonquins on the St. Lawrence River, portaged to the Richelieu River, then arrived at Lake Champlain at Rouses Point. They met a party of Iroquois (Kaniengehagas) who had never seen firearms, and he killed two chiefs with one shot. Others in his party shot from the woods and the Iroquois ran off.
Sources: 20, 92, 379, 412

NY2   *Attack on Raritans* • 1640
Location: Staten Island
War: Governor Kieft's War
Some pigs were killed on Staten Island and the Raritans were blamed, perhaps wrongly. A party of Dutch led by Van Tienhoven retaliated with torture and killings.
Sources: 16, 199, 290

NY3   *Swanneken Massacre* • September 1, 1641
Location: Staten Island
War: Governor Kieft's War
In retaliation for the attacks in 1640 by Van Tienhoven, a band of Raritan natives attacked the plantation of David de Vries. They killed four and burned the house and tobacco sheds.
Sources: 16, 53

NY4   *Massacre of Wappingers* or *Pavonia Massacre* • February 25, 1643
Location: Corlaer's Hook on Manhattan
War: Governor Kieft's War
Following the murder of Dutch farmer Gerrit Jansz Van Vorst, New Amsterdam governor Willem Kieft ordered the massacre of a friendly tribe that had come to the Dutch seeking shelter. They had come to Corlaer's Hook to escape from Mohicans or Mohawks. While they slept, the Dutch killed 80 to 120 Wappingers, decapitated them, and hung their heads on poles in the city. One captive was tortured and forced to eat his own flesh.
Sources: 16, 53, 92, 98, 126, 199, 237, 275, 284, 290, 380, 412

NY5   *Attack at Southhampton* • 1649
Location: Long Island
Southhampton, the first English settlement in New York, was attacked by a band
of Connecticut natives. They killed Phoebe Halsey, the wife of Thomas Halsey.
Sources: 98

NY6   *Attack at New Amsterdam* • September 15, 1655
Location: Manhattan and Staten Island
War: Peach War
Hendrick Van Dyck allegedly killed a squaw he caught stealing peaches from his
orchard. In retaliation, 500 armed Hackensack warriors attacked New Amsterdam, including Cornelius' Melyn's settlement on Staten Island. Sixteen settlers
were killed and 49 were captured. After 31 days, they were released upon the
payment of 1,400 guilders.
Sources: 16, 53, 98, 199, 412

NY7   *Skirmish at Esopus* • Early May, 1658
Location: Esopus, between New Amsterdam and Beverwyck
War: Esopus War
Settlers, ignoring the advice of Peter Stuyvesant to protect themselves with a wall
and blockhouse, spread themselves out on farms. Exchanges of furs for brandy
led to skirmishes with the natives. In one, the child of Jacob Adriaensen was lost.
     After becoming intoxicated, a band of warriors shot and killed Herman
Jacobsen. The same night, they burned the Adriaensen farm.
Sources: 16

NY8   *Attack at Esopus* • September 20, 1658
Location: Esopus (Wiltwyck)
War: Esopus War
Eight natives became drunk and fell asleep. A number of settlers attacked them,
shooting one and hitting another in the head with an axe. One was taken prisoner.
     The following day, 500 to 600 natives took revenge by destroying barns and
haystacks and killing livestock. They turned on captured settlers held in Fort
Wildmeet, tying eight to stakes, torturing them and burning them alive.
Sources: 16

NY9   *Attack at Wiltwyck* • June, 1663
Location: Wiltwyck
War: War at Wiltwyck
The Esopus natives again attacked the settlement, setting it on fire. Several set-
tlers were killed and others were captured. The settlers organized some resistance,
and chased the warriors away.
Sources: 16

NY10   *Attack on King Philip's Camp* • Late 1675
Location: Scaticook (Schaghticoke), north of Albany near Hoosick
War: King Philip's War
King Philip, leader of the Wampanoags, chose to leave Massachusetts and spend
the winter with his men at Schaghticoke (Scaticook) and the Hoosic River, and

use the opportunity to attempt to forge an alliance with the Mohegans. He also hoped to obtain additional weapons from people trading with the French.

Encouraged by the British governor Edmund Andros of New York, a band of Mohawks surprised the Wampanoag camp with an attack that killed all but 40 of Philip's 400 men. Those that survived were badly wounded, as was Philip's prestige among the natives in New England.

Sources: 315, 320, 334

NY11 *Destruction of Schenectady* • February 9, 1690
Location: Schenectady
War: King William's War
Three expeditions of French soldiers and native warriors were sent out from Montreal by its governor, Count Frontenac, against settlements south of the St. Lawrence River. One was directed against Albany, but instead resulted in the destruction of the Dutch settlement of Schenectady. About 60 were killed and 30 were taken captive. They were pursued by some of the townspeople, who were able to free some of the captives.
Sources: 92, 98, 133, 199, 274, 290, 328, 381

NY12 *Attack on Onondaga Village* • 1696
Location: New York
War: King William's War
About 1,000 French and an equal number of natives attacked an Onondaga village. The Onondagas fled, but first burned the village. While negotiations were being made for the Oneidas who desired peace to move to Canada, they were attacked by a force of 700 led by Gov. Pierre de Vaudreuil.

The Oneida village was burned, the immature maize was cut down, and several prisoners were taken. The Oneidas had agreed to move to Canada, but after the attack most decided to stay in New York.
Sources: 300

NY13 *Raid on Saratoga* • November 28–29, 1745
Location: Saratoga
War: King George's War
A force of 400 French and 200 natives burned the town of Saratoga, following the English success in enlisting the Iroquois to fight the French. More than 100 colonists were killed or captured.
Museum: The Iroquois Indian Museum, focusing on their culture, is located off Interstate 88 and SR 7 on Caverns Rd., Howes Cave, NY.
Sources: 19, 133, 290, 379, 381

NY14 *Attack on Hoosick* • August 27, 1754
Location: Hoosick
War: French and Indian War
The settlement of Hoosick was raided by a combined French and native force. About 20 settlers were either killed and burned in their homes, or were captured to serve as slaves. The local militia was placed on alert, and according to the governor of New Hampshire, the settlers' fear caused 30 new townships to be abandoned.
Sources: 55

NY15 *Battle of Lake George* • September 8, 1755
Location: Lake George
War: French and Indian War
The French had as their native allies some Mohawks, Onondagas and Senecas. Sir William Johnson, the British commander, was supported by about 200 to 400 other Mohawks led by Tiyanoga (Hendrick). Near the Narrows by Lake George, 600 French Canadians led by La Reine and Languedoc and 700 Iroquois laid an ambush for the approaching British column, but the British fought back well, especially after the French regulars were abandoned by their native allies.

Included in the captives was Comm. Jean-Armand Dieskau, second in command in New France under Gov. Pierre Rigaud de Vaudreuil de Cavagnial. This major British victory helped to ignite the worldwide Seven Years' War.
Sources: 20, 55, 115, 131, 135, 147, 237, 275, 284

NY16 *Lery's Raid* • March 27, 1756
Location: Between the Mohawk River and Lake Oneida
War: French and Indian War
The French force, led by Lt. de Lery, was very hungry, having not eaten for two days. After a march of 12 hours, they came near the Portage Road which the British used to supply their Oswego forts, and camped. At 10 a.m. the next morning, the French and their native allies ambushed a party of British and captured their sleighs of butchered meat. The natives were satisfied to have participated in the ambush and the feast, and some departed.

The French, Canadians and 20 natives continued on to Fort Bull and found the gates open. As the whites were approaching the fort (and hoping that their bedraggled appearance would mask the fact that they were the enemy of the British defenders), the natives rushed past in search of rum. Realizing that the attack had begun, Lery charged the fort just as the British closed the gate as the 260-man force reached it.

The Canadians chopped down the gate and the French entered and killed most of the British inside. Only 31 were spared. Before more soldiers could arrive from Fort William Henry, the French destroyed the fort and its munitions and supplies.
Sources: 55, 131

NY17 *Ambush Near Oswego* • July 3, 1756
Location: 9 miles south of Oswego
War: French and Indian War
The French attack on Fort Bull and the capture or destruction of supplies meant for the support of the Oswego Forts, resulted in a relief expedition led by Lt. Col. John Bradstreet. The French watched his fast movement to the fort with supplies, carried from Albany by 1,000 men in 350 boats.

On the way back from Oswego, Bradstreet was ambushed by the French and natives. The 300 members of the British advance guard were attacked as they rowed upstream, and then surprised the 700 French by charging them. The French tried to flee, and many were killed in hand-to-hand combat along or in the river.
Sources: 131

NY18 *Attack Against Oswego Forts* • August 14, 1756
Location: Forts Ontario and Oswego
War: French and Indian War
A French army left Fort Frontenac on August 4 and met up with Canadians and natives at a camp in Famine Bay, and the combined force traveled to the right bank of the Oswego River a half hour from Fort Ontario, near Fort Oswego. While his men prepared for an attack on Fort Ontario, Sieur de Combles was walking with a Canadian officer and noticed what appeared to be a friendly native a short distance away. The native mistook Combles for a British subject and shot him. A shot rang out from Fort Ontario, but the British were still unaware that the French were nearby.

A small French boat was found a mile and a half from the fort, and the vessels sent out by the British to destroy it were repulsed by French guns set up along the shore. On August 11–13, French soldiers cut a road through the woods toward Fort Ontario in preparation of a siege.

With scant gunfire from the fort, Col. Bourlamaque ordered an assault party to see what was going on inside. They reached the fort walls and climbed through, capturing it. They continued their trench-digging and other preparations for a siege against the nearby Fort Oswego and a fortified British camp across the river. Rigaud de Vaudreuil and his Canadian militia and natives were sent four miles upstream to cross the river and attack from the land.

Shortly after the bombardment of the fort on August 14, the British surrendered, after about 1,000 of their soldiers had been killed. The French took over the fort, substantial supplies and four naval vessels. After removing all that could be used, the French burned the fort. The British soldiers taken captive were shipped to Europe.
Monument: Fort Ontario State Historic Site is located three blocks north of SR 104 on E. 7th St., Oswego.
Sources: 19, 55, 90, 115, 131, 133, 290, 379, 381, 388, 412

NY19 *Attack at Fort Carillon* • January 21, 1757
Location: Lake Champlain
War: French and Indian War
Maj. Robert Rogers and his force, known as the Rangers, had set a trap for a sled convoy of French about five or six miles from Fort Carillon. When one of the sleds had pulled ahead of the rest, springing the trap, the remaining ten retreated to the fort. Eight successfully made it back. The soldiers in the fort readied for an attack.

The fort's commander, de Lusignan, sent out a ranger and fur trader, Charles de Langlade, with 100 men to meet the oncoming 73 with Rogers. They set up an ambush about two miles west of the fort and they began firing when the first Englishman came within five yards. After a brief exchange of fire, the armies settled in for a while, and then the French returned to the fort.

The English had 11 dead, while the French lost 14. The English left to camp on the shore of Lake George. On January 25, a rescue party arrived with sleds from Fort William Henry.
Sources: 55

NY20 *Attack on Fort William Henry* • March 18, 1757
Location: Fort William Henry

War: French and Indian War

English scouts discovered three long lines of French soldiers marching southward over frozen Lake George toward Fort William Henry. When the 1,500 regular soldiers and natives arrived early on March 18, Maj. William Eyre gave the order to fire. The cannon quickly prompted a French retreat.
Sources: 55, 115

NY21   *Attack on Vessels* • March 22, 1757
Location: Fort William Henry
War: French and Indian War
Rigaud de Vaudreuil, the brother of the French governor general, tried a final time to cripple the English at Fort William Henry. He sent Lt. Wolf and a party of Canadians to the ships anchored near the fort, and they burned one of the large vessels. They had hoped that the fire might spread to the fort, but there was no wind to carry the flames that far.
Sources: 55

NY22   *Action on Lake George* • July 21–24, 1757
Location: Lake George
War: French and Indian War
Among the islands in Lake George, a French scout was attacked. On July 21, the English, numbering 75 in five barges and 100 on Isle a la Barque, were chased out of the area by a Canadian patrol of ten in fast French canoes.

At dawn on July 24, the English barges were ambushed by musket fire from Potawatomis, Ottawas, Chippewas and Menominees. The English attempted to swim to safety and most of those that were not killed in the water were captured, killed, cooked and eaten.
Museum: Lake George Battlefield Park is located off US 9 in Lake George Village.
Sources: 19, 55, 324

NY23   *Attack on Fort Edward* • July, 1757
Location: Fort Edward
War: French and Indian War
Lt. Marin and a party of western natives and Canadian woods runners, totalling 100 men, quickly arrived at and surrounded Fort Edward. They killed and scalped all 32 of the English occupying the fort, taking no prisoners. After the attack, they returned to Fort Carillon.
Sources: 55

NY24   *Siege of Fort William Henry* • August 3–9, 1757
Location: Fort William Henry
War: French and Indian War
Gen. Louis Joseph Montcalm-Gozon led a contingent from Fort Carillon and met up with 3,000 men led by Chevalier de Levis who had headed south along the western shore of Lake George. On August 3, a British boat saw the army marching toward Fort William Henry and sailed there to sound an alarm.

Montcalm sent Levis ahead with a force of soldiers and 88 Potawatomis to meet any attack which Col. Daniel Webb might send out from the fort. They were involved in only scattered musket fire. The French took their positions to the east of the fort, and the natives settled in along the portage road leading south to Fort Edward. Trenches heading to the fort were begun.

The first bombardment of the fort took place on August 6 and continued for four days. The English returned fire, inflicting casualties. The trenches came to within 100 yards of the fort. An honorable surrender was proposed to Col. George Munro. A message from Gen. Webb encouraged him to surrender, as relief troops would not be forthcoming soon. On August 9, the British surrendered and departed the fort for a march to Fort Edward.

Along the way, a party of Abenaki attacked a group of New Hampshire militia at the back of the column, and many of the prisoners ran for their safety. The total killed by the Abenaki and those hunted down by the Potawatomis brought the English death toll to more than 200. An additional 200 were carried off by the natives. Levis had the British fort burned.

Museum: The Fort William Henry Museum is located on US 9 in the center of Lake George Village.

Sources: 19, 55, 92, 98, 133, 275, 284, 290, 324, 336, 381, 412

NY25 *Raid on the Palatine* • November, 1757
Location: Palatine, on the Mohawk River
War: French and Indian War
The German colony of the Palatine and its five forts were attacked by a force of 300 French, Canadians and natives. Mayor Johan Jost Petrie surrendered the town, and the attackers looted and burned. They killed the cattle, sheep and hogs, and took 150 prisoners by horseback.
Sources: 55, 290

NY26 *Attack on Fort Edward* • January, 1758
Location: Fort Edward
War: French and Indian War
The Hudson River flooded and carried away supplies kept on the island near the fort, including the soldiers' snowshoes. When a work party was attacked by natives who had traveled from Fort Carillon, they were unable to outdistance the warriors who used their own snowshoes adeptly. When the English dropped from exhaustion, they were scalped.
Sources: 55

NY27 *Battle of the Snowshoes* • March 13, 1758
Location: West of Lake George
War: French and Indian War
In retaliation for the slaughter of the beef herd at Fort Carillon, Sieur de Langy de Montegron led a party out from the fort on snowshoes to engage the force of Maj. Robert Rogers. They met in a valley behind a bald-faced mountain west of the northern tip of Lake George.

Rogers attacked Langy's advance party, then was attacked by Langy's main force. Rogers moved up the slope to where Lt. Crofton and Sgt. Phillips had taken a firm position, and were followed by the Canadians and natives. By the end of the day, the party led by Sgt. Phillips surrendered, and the men were tortured and beheaded.

Rogers took his men over the mountain to a prearranged rendezvous with Capt. Stark. About 130 English had been killed, and Langy celebrated with his men. They believed Rogers to be among the dead.
Sources: 55, 90

NY28 *Battle of Ticonderoga* • July 6–8, 1758
Location: Fort Carillon, Ticonderoga Peninsula
War: French and Indian War
A thousand boats carried 15,000 to 16,000 British soldiers on Lake George, and Gen. Louis Montcalm knew that they intended to attack Fort Carillon (also known as Fort Ticonderoga), on Lake Champlain. On July 6, they landed on the west shore of Lake George. Chevalier de Bourlamaque and Gen. Montcalm burned the bridge at the sawmill on the river connecting the two lakes, to slow the British advance.

A force of 350 men of the total 3,000 had been deployed to meet the British, but when they all landed together, rather than in smaller parties, they drew back into the woods. Led by Sieur de Trepezec, they fought with a British force in the woods. During the fight, Gen. Howe was killed, and his British column then ran away.

On July 7, the British army continued toward Fort Carillon, now led by Maj. Gen. James Abercromby. The French continued to dig trenches and build dirt parapets. On July 8, the British marched toward the French defenses and the first column attacked shortly after noon. Heavy fighting continued for about five hours, with the French lines holding. The final British attack came within the next hour, consisting of Highlanders and Royal Americans.

That charge did not dislodge the French and the British retreated to the woods. The French had scored a major victory, losing 106 to 122 and having 175 to 268 wounded. The British lost from 464 to 561 and 1,115 to 1,356 were wounded.
Museum: Restored Fort Ticonderoga is located one mile northeast of Ticonderoga on SR 74.
Sources: 19, 55, 90, 131, 133, 237, 284, 299, 336, 381, 412

NY29 *Siege of Fort Niagara* • July 13–25, 1759
Location: Fort Niagara, north of Niagara Falls
War: French and Indian War
Fort Niagara was besieged by a large British army commanded by Sir William Johnson, supported by 900 Iroquois including the very aggressive Senecas. The French had assembled a force of natives to attack Fort Pitt, but they were instead moved north to act as a relief column during the siege against Fort Niagara. About three miles from the fort, they were attacked by a force led by Lt. Col. Eyre Massey and Capt. James De Lancey and a party of Senecas, who pursued them for five miles after the column broke apart and routed them.

Five hundred of the French and their native allies were killed and 100 captured. Without reinforcement, Fort Niagara surrendered to the British and the troops departed on July 26. The natives allied with the French recognized the superior strength of the British, and many desired to switch their alliance to them. Some of the Ottawas, including chief Pontiac, returned to Detroit, but a significant number instead started a new settlement at the mouth of the Cuyahoga River at the present site of Cleveland.

Museum: The restored fort is located in Fort Niagara State Park off SR 18F in Youngstown, NY.
Sources: 19, 55, 115, 131, 135, 322, 379, 381

NY30 *Massacre at Devil's Hole* • September 14, 1763
Location: Along the Niagara River
War: Pontiac's Rebellion
Supplies from Fort Niagara at the mouth of the Niagara River were taken by boat to the foot of the falls, then were unloaded and carried to the top along a road to a place known as Devil's Hole, where there was a cave in the gorge wall. They were then taken overland to small boats, and then transferred to larger ones for the trip to Fort Detroit.

On September 14, from 350 to 500 Senecas hid beside the trail that was close to Devil's Hole, waiting for 25 empty wagons returning from depositing their supplies. As they approached, the Senecas opened fire. Some of the whites were tomahawked, some were shot, and some died when they plunged over the cliff. Only two escaped into the forest.

Two companies of soldiers positioned near the foot of the falls heard the initial volley and the 80 men advanced up the trail. The Senecas met them at a point about a mile below Devil's Hole, and their first volley dropped about half of the soldiers. A few escaped, but many were killed, scalped and stripped. Later, a relief column found the bodies of five officers and 67 men, and the Senecas probably lost no one.
Sources: 14, 90, 123, 315, 322, 379

NY31 *Attack on Portage Road* • October 20, 1763
Location: Near Fort Niagara
War: Pontiac's Rebellion
Along the road used for portaging around Niagara Falls to get from Lake Ontario to Lake Erie, Maj. John Wilkins led 600 men from Fort Niagara toward Detroit. They were attacked by natives who killed two officers and six others. They continued to Fort Schlosser to continue the journey by boat.

On November 7, they were caught in a sudden storm on Lake Erie and 70 drowned. The survivors returned to Fort Niagara.
Sources: 322

NY32 *Attack at Fort Stanwix* • June 25, 1777
Location: Rome
War: Revolutionary War
The garrison of Fort Stanwix (formerly known as Fort Schuyler), built by the British in 1758, contained the American army of 550 led by Col. Peter Gansevoort and Lt. Col. Marinus Willett, along with 60 Oneidas.

Capt. Gregg and Corp. Madison saw a flock of pigeons flying near the fort, and went out to do some hunting. They were ambushed by warriors who killed Madison. Gregg played dead while he was scalped, but lived.
Museum: Fort Stanwix National Monument includes a restored fort and film.
Sources: 19, 135, 199, 234, 412

NY33 *Attack at Fort Stanwix* • July 27, 1777
Location: Rome

War: Revolutionary War

Three young girls left Fort Stanwix to pick berries at the edge of a cedar swamp 500 yards away. They were attacked by warriors who killed two. The third sustained a wound but ran back to the fort. Col. Peter Gansevoort then sent the women and children to Fort Dayton at German Flats.

Sources: 412

NY34   *Battle of Oriskany* • August 3–22, 1777
Location: Rome
War: Revolutionary War

The garrison at Fort Stanwix was supplemented by 200 militiamen who arrived on August 2. Hours later, the fort was besieged by 1,300 British troops led by Col. Barry St. Leger and 400 Iroquois led by Theyendanegea, also known as Joseph Brant. On August 3, Col. Peter Gansevoort declined an offer of surrender, believing that a relief column led by Gen. Nicholas Herkimer and 900 militiamen were marching to his aid.

However, many of the British and their allies left to ambush the relief column at Oriskany, and while they were gone a contingent led by Lt. Col. Marinus Willet went to the undefended encampments of the British and Iroquois, looting and vandalizing. When they discovered this, they returned to the Fort Stanwix area.

A second relief column was formed and Gen. Benedict Arnold was placed in charge. It was a small column, but Arnold set free a captured mentally retarded Dutch man, Hon-Yost Schuyler, and had him tell St. Leger that the approaching Americans were "as numerous as the leaves on the trees." Arnold held Schuyler's family captive to insure his cooperation. The Iroquois knew the strange man and believed that he had supernatural powers. They and the American loyalists then deserted, leaving St. Leger with one-third of his former force. He called off the siege and withdrew to Fort Oswego.

Monument: A reproduction of the fort is located at Fort Stanwix National Monument, 112 E. Park St., Rome.

Sources: 3, 5, 32, 33, 83, 98, 123, 135, 199, 234, 275, 300, 395, 412

NY35   *Battle Near Oriskany* • August 6, 1777
Location: 6 miles southeast of Rome
War: Revolutionary War

Gen. Nicholas Herkimer mustered a force of 700 to 900 Tryon County militiamen at German Flats on the Mohawk River, and that relief column began a march to aid the Americans besieged at Fort Stanwix, 50 miles away. The British commander, Col. Barry St. Leger, found out about the relief column and sent a detachment of soldiers and natives to Oriskany and waited for them to arrive.

In the ambush and the hand-to-hand fighting that followed, nearly 500 American and Onieda lives were lost, as were about 200 of the opposing force. The British and Iroquois, led by Joseph Brant, withdrew after about six hours when they found that their encampments near Fort Stanwix had been looted and vandalized in their absence. The relief column broke off the march to Fort Stanwix.

This marked the beginning of a civil war of sorts, as both groups of natives had once been members of the Hodenosaunee Confederacy.

Monument: A granite shaft and audiovisual presentation are featured at Orsikany Battlefield, 6 miles east of Rome on SR 69.
Sources: 3, 12, 19, 33, 147, 412

NY36 *Burning of Cobleskill* • May 30, 1778
Location: Cobleskill
War: Revolutionary War
Joseph Brant (Thayendanega) led the Mohawks on a raid at Cobleskill, where they proceeded to burn it down. They were interrupted by a party of Schoharie militia, who were routed by the Mohawks and had 20 to 22 militiamen killed. Two people were taken prisoner and the fort was burned. Brant then withdrew only a few miles to plan his next attack.
Sources: 3, 83, 123

NY37 *Attack at Springfield* • June 18, 1778
Location: Springfield
War: Revolutionary War
The Mohawks organized by English Col. John Butler and led by Joseph Brant burned barns, wagons, houses and plows and drove 200 cattle away from the village. They then went to and ravaged the settlements near Otsego Lake.
Sources: 3, 83, 123

NY38 *Attack at Andrustown* • July 18, 1778
Location: Andrustown, at the head of Lake Otsego
War: Revolutionary War
Unadilla served as the chief town of the Mohawks and their leader, Joseph Brant. From it in July, they launched a raid on Andrustown.
Sources: 3, 12, 83, 379

NY39 *Attack at German Flats* • September 17, 1778
Location: Mohawk Valley
War: Revolutionary War
William Caldwell and Joseph Brant led a force of 500 natives and Tories to the fertile plain known as German Flats. They encountered four American scouts and killed three, but John Helmer ran back to the settlement with a warning. The residents packed into Forts Herkimer and Dayton, and watched the burning of their homes, barns and grist mills. Over 700 animals were killed or carried off. Fortunately, only three people were killed.
Sources: 3, 83, 123

NY40 *Burning of Unadilla* • October 6, 1778
Location: Unadilla
War: Revolutionary War
In retaliation for the Mohawk burning of Andrustown, German Flats and other settlements resulting in the killing or capturing of 294 settlers and their defenders, the Americans attacked the Mohawk chief town of Unadilla. The natives fled and the whites burned the homes. Few captives were taken.
Sources: 3, 12, 83, 123, 379

NY41 *Cherry Valley Massacre* • November 11, 1778
Location: Cherry Valley
War: Revolutionary War
Col. Ichabod Alden commanded Fort Alden in Cherry Valley, defended by 300 Massachusetts soldiers and 150 local militiamen. Walter Butler led the English and allied natives on a 150-mile march from Chemung toward Fort Alden to strike the strongest point on the New York border. With him were 200 Rangers, 50 regular soldiers and 400 warriors.

Along the way, they captured an American scouting party and on November 10, camped six miles from Cherry Valley. The snow prevented further travel that night. The following day, their shooting of two woodcutters gave the garrison some warning of the impending attack.

When the attackers ran from the woods toward the fort, Alden and 11 others were killed attempting to run to the fort from the Wells house 400 yards away. Lt. Col. William Stacey and 11 others were captured in the same mad dash. As the attack proceeded, most of the warriors, mostly Senecas and Cayugas led by Hiokatoo, broke off and sought easier targets in the area. That day's action resulted in the deaths of 31 or 32 Americans and the taking of 71 prisoners.

Without the support of the Senecas and Cayugas who had unexpectedly left the main attack, Butler pulled his soldiers and Mohawks back. He prepared for an attack from the Americans, which never came. No further significant action occurred on either side.
Monument: A marble marker surrounded by tombstones was dedicated in 1878 on the site of the fort.
Sources: 3, 19, 83, 123, 234, 275, 300, 379

NY42 *Burning of Onondaga Towns* • April 20, 1779
Location: Onondaga Castle
War: Revolutionary War
Brig. Gen. James Clinton sent Col. Goose Van Shaick with 580 regular soldiers and militia men from Fort Stanwix in an expedition against the Onondagas. They burned three native towns, capturing 38 women and children and killing 12 warriors.

The Ononodagas had previously been uninterested in the war, but the attack caused them to ready themselves for fights against the whites.
Sources: 3

NY43 *Battle of Newtown* • August 29, 1779
Location: 5 miles east of Elmira
War: Revolutionary War
Gen. George Washington sent Maj. Gen. John Sullivan and about 2,500 to 3,000 American soldiers into the Iroquois country. Brig. Gen. James Clinton met up with him with 1,500 men, and together they approached a ridge near the native village of Newtown. Walter Butler and his English soldiers and allied warriors set up a defensive position and waited for Sullivan's advance.

Rather than rush into a hand-to-hand battle, Sullivan spent hours studying the situation while his artillery weakened the English line. Joseph Brant attempted a counterattack with his Mohawks, and then ordered a general retreat while they were pursued by the Americans. The native force was dispersed, and most of the warriors headed back to their respective villages to protect their families.

The English reported five Rangers and 12 warriors killed, while the Americans had five killed and 36 wounded. Although there was little bloodshed, this was considered a tactical victory for the Americans, leaving the Iroquois homeland open and defenseless.

The Oneidas and Tuscaroras, which had allied with the Americans, were punished by Sullivan for their allegiance by Joseph Brant and the Mohawks, who burned their villages, cornfields, gardens and orchards. In 1780, 1781 and 1782, Brant and pro–British warriors laid waste to almost 50,000 square miles between the Mohawk and Ohio Rivers.

Museum: The Joseph Brant Museum is the restored home of the Mohawk chief, located at 1240 North Shore Blvd. E., Burlington, ON.

Sources: 3, 12, 19, 123, 135, 147, 234, 275, 284, 300

NY44 *Attack at Fort Schlosser* • July 4, 1813
Location: Across the Niagara Valley from Chippewa
War: War of 1812
A force of 34 natives and Canadian militia led by Lt. Col. Thomas Clark attacked the blockhouse known as Fort Schlosser. They seized it and took its supplies, then returned to Canada.
Sources: 397

NY45 *Ambush of Eldridge* • July 8, 1813
Location: Near Fort George
War: War of 1812
A party of natives attacked Lt. Joseph C. Eldridge and his 39 men who had left Fort George. All but five were killed.
Sources: 397

NY46 *Battle of Sandy Creek* • May 30, 1814
Location: 16 miles from Sackett's Harbor
War: War of 1812
An American flotilla led by Master Commandant Melancthon Woolsey carried 34 large naval guns from Oswego to Sackett's Harbor, under the protection of 150 riflemen and 200 Oneidas, who took cover in the woods near the creek. Capt. Stephen Popham and 200 British soldiers attacked, and were cut to shreds by the soldiers and Oneidas. Over 70 British soldiers died or were wounded and the rest were captured. The Americans had few casualties. The guns reached Sackett's Harbor and insured American parity on Lake Ontario.
Monument: Sackett's Harbor Battlefield State Historic Site is located in Sackett's Harbor.
Sources: 19, 397, 400

NORTH CAROLINA

NC1 *Attack on Aquascogoc* • July, 1585
Location: Eastern North Carolina
War: Raleigh Expeditions
In July of 1584, the Secotans were visited near the outer island of Hatarask (Roanoke) by two British vessels backed by Walter Raleigh and others, looking for a good place to establish a British settlement. They were met by chief Granganimeo of the Secotans, who allowed trading with the Europeans. Raleigh returned to England and was knighted.

In July of 1585, seven ships commanded by Ralph Lane arrived with 108 soldiers to erect a fortified settlement in the Secotan country. They landed on Wococon Island and left to explore the mainland. They traded in the town of Aquascogoc, but after discovering that a silver cup was missing, attacked and burned the town and its surrounding cornfields, with the natives fleeing to other towns. Lane convinced chief Pemisapan (Wingina) that his actions were justified, and was allowed to trade for corn and erect a fort on Roanoke Island.
Sources: 147, 247

NC2 *Attack on Dasemunkapeuc* • June 1, 1586
Location: Dasemunkapeuc
War: Raleigh Expeditions
For nearly a year, the Secotans put up with the arrogance of Ralph Lane and his men, and an epidemic brought by the British which killed many natives in the nearby towns. By late May, warriors began to gather at Roanoke to fight the British, but when Lane heard of the plan he attacked Dasemunkapeuc, the mainland town where chief Pemisapan was. The Secotans accepted Lane's invitation to a meeting, but when chief Pemisapan and his subchiefs arrived, they were shot down. Pemisapan, wounded twice, was run down and beheaded by two British soldiers.

The British slaughtered the rest of the inhabitants of Dasemunkapeuc, leaving the other Secotan villages in a state of shock and mourning. Ten days later, Sir Francis Drake arrived and found the British colonists nearly out of supplies. On July 18, they sailed back to England with Drake.
Sources: 147, 247

NC3 *Disappearance of Roanoke Settlement* • 1587–90
Location: Roanoke Island
War: Raleigh Expeditions
Led by John White, the artist who had accompanied Martin Frobisher to Baffin Island in 1577 and Ralph Lane to North Carolina in 1585–86, 118 men, women and children left England to settle in the Chesapeake area. However, when the ship arrived in the summer of 1587, it landed on Roanoke Island, well to the south. The colonists repaired and occupied the fort and cottages which had been abandoned by Ralph Lane and his men during the previous year. White, leaving his daughter and newborn granddaughter, Virginia Dare, sailed back to England with a plan to return in three months with supplies.

White's return was delayed by problems with the Spanish Armada and the loss of favor of Walter Raleigh. It wasn't until August 17, 1590, that White could raise the necessary funds and return to Roanoke with supplies. Upon arrival, White found no settlers, a wooden palisade in place of the houses, and carved on trees the words "Cro" and "Croatoan." Believing that the settlers may have gone to the outer island village of Croatan (Cape Hatteras), White left to search for them but a storm blew the ships far out into the Ocean, and the captain refused to return for them. White returned to England, never finding out what happened to his family and the rest of the colonists, who became known as the Lost Colony.

Several theories have been advanced for the colony's disappearance, including a massacre by natives. No definitive answer has yet been generally agreed upon, but in the 1650s the Croatoans migrated to the mainland, called themselves the Lumbees, and showed traits such as light hair, blue eyes, names of some of the original Roanoke settlers, and speech with some similarity to Elizabethan English.

Monument: A restored colony is located at Fort Raleigh National Historic Site, US 64, c/o Cape Hatteras National Seashore, Rt. 1, Box 675, Manteo, NC 27954.
Sources: 5, 19, 32, 126, 127, 133, 137, 147, 214, 247, 248, 289, 301, 310, 321, 345, 354, 381, 412

NC4   *Capture of von Graffenried* • September, 1711
Location: Neuse River
War: Tuscarora War
While on a pleasure river trip, Baron von Graffenried and Surveyor-General John Lawson were attacked by a Tuscarora war party led by King Hancock. The native leaders conferred regarding the disposition of the two captives, and they probably would have been released except for Lawson's arguing with the Coree king, Cor Tom. Von Graffenried bargained for his life and eventually escaped from Cotechny, King Hancock's town.
Sources: 146, 328, 332

NC5   *Tuscarora Massacre* • September 22, 1711
Location: Along the Neuse, Roanoke and Chowan Rivers
War: Tuscarora War
Spurred on by the harsh treatment of a Tuscarora native by a white man and encouraged by some Senecas, the Tuscaroras began a killing spree. Within two hours, they had killed 60 English and 70 Palatines, and had taken 30 captives. Others participating in the 500-warrior uprising were members of the Marmusekit, Wetock, Bory, News, Pamptego, Cor and Trent tribes. The Saxapahaws refused to join them, and the rebels killed 16 of their men and drove the rest from their plantations.

Two areas, Albemarle and Bath, were left unharmed because the friendly local Tuscarora chief chose not to join the others in the massacre.
Sources: 133, 146, 289, 300, 328, 332, 353, 381, 388

NC6   *Battle at Narhantes* • January 28, 1712
Location: Along the Neuse River
War: Tuscarora War
Col. John ("Tuscarora Jack") Barnwell led a force of white militia, Yamassees,

Apalachees, Yuchis, Cusabos, Santee, Cherokee, Wateree, Congaree, Catawba, Waxhaw, Sagarees and Suterees into the Saxapahaw country, occupied by the Tuscarora and Coree. Barnwell came upon a Tuscarora fort and attacked it, finding two fortified buildings inside. A charge killed at least ten within the fort, with light casualties to the whites. Several wounded Yamassees slowed things down.

 Several of the natives left the expedition with 30 captives, and Barnwell left to find the fort of King Hancock.
Sources: 133, 328, 332, 388

NC7 *Battle at Hancock's Town* • March 6–7, 1712
  Location: Cotechney Creek
  War: Tuscarora War
A force of 94 white men and 148 natives reached Hancock's Town on March 5 and prepared for battle by constructing two hundred fascines, which they used on March 6 for protection from the gunfire up to about ten yards from the fort. When the defending Tuscaroras in the fort saw the ineffectiveness of their fire, many threw up their arms and retreated, making them easy targets for the approaching English.

 Col. John Barnwell's force lost four and had 20 wounded. The battle temporarily ended because of a heavy rain, and the attackers set up a breastwork behind which they waited until the morning of March 7. At that time, the Tuscaroras handed over several captives and two canoes and agreed to talks for a more permanent peace, to be held on March 19. The natives failed to appear.
Sources: 146, 332

NC8 *Ruse at Hancock's Town* • March 29, 1712
  Location: Cotechney Creek
  War: Tuscarora War
When the Tuscarora did not show up for the appointed meeting to set the peace terms, Col. John Barnwell led a force back to Hancock's Town. He found that the fort had been enlarged to include the breastwork that his own men had constructed. He led a charge to within 300 yards of the fort which chased the Tuscaroras outside into the confines of the fort, but because his force was so small, Barnwell chose not to attack the fort.

 Barnwell retreated to Coree Town and built Fort Barnwell along the Neuse River, 20 miles from New Bern and seven from Fort Hancock.
Sources: 332

NC9 *Siege of Fort Hancock* • April 8, 1712
  Location: Cotechney Creek
  War: Tuscarora War
On the night of April 7, Col. John Barnwell led a force of 153 whites and 128 natives (nearly all Yamassee) back to Fort Hancock, and by the next morning had it surrounded. Their siege lasted ten days. It ended when the Tuscaroras agreed to release all white and black captives, horses, provisions, and King Hancock and other native leaders. Restrictions were placed on where the Tuscaroras could plant their corn.

 When the conditions were accepted, the English tore down the front wall of

the fort and retrieved the captives. However, King Hancock was in Virginia and could not be handed over. The peace did not last.
Sources: 332

NC10 *Attack at Fort Neoheroka* • March 20–23, 1713
Location: Cotechney Creek
War: Tuscarora War
Col. James Moore arrived at Fort Barnwell with a contingent of 33 white soldiers, and added 310 Cherokees commanded by Capts. Harford and Thurston of South Carolina. Col. Maurice Moore led 50 Yamassees. They were kept on the Pamlico River until March because of heavy snows. They then moved a few miles north of Fort Hancock to meet the Tuscaroras at Fort Neoheroka (Noo-her-oo-ka).

The Cherokees camped across the creek and created a battery toward the western wall of the fort. Opposite was a camp of 400 mixed natives and 88 whites from North Carolina. Above that was the Yamassee camp, and from there trenches were dug toward the fort. The fort stood up to attack, so it was ordered to be set on fire. That was successful with one bastion, and the same tactic was used on another and several buildings the following morning.

By 10:00 a.m. on March 23, the defenders were completely ousted, having made a final stand behind a palisade leading to the creek. The white attackers had 22 killed and 36 wounded, and their native allies had 35 killed and 58 wounded. Col. Moore reported that his force had scalped 192, burned 200 or more within the fort, another 166 killed outside the fort, and 392 captured.

This defeat essentially ended the Tuscarora War, which resulted in the deaths of about 1,400 Tuscaroras and the enslavement of nearly 1,000 more. Col. Moore easily defeated the remaining Cotechney, Coree and Matamuskeet. The Tuscaroras headed to Madison County, New York, to join the Iroquois Confederation.
Sources: 90, 133, 146, 300, 326, 328, 332, 380, 381, 388

NC11 *Battle at Echoe* • June 27, 1760
Location: Near Franklin
War: First Cherokee War
In retaliation for Cherokee attacks on Fort Prince George, South Carolina, and settlements from Georgia to Virginia, the British sent 1,200 soldiers to sack and burn Cherokee towns, cornfields and granaries, and kill and capture natives. Commanded by Col. Montgomery, they burned villages in South Carolina and then marched to the northwest to the Cherokee Middle Towns.

At Echoe, near present-day Franklin, they fought Cherokee warriors who killed 20 soldiers, wounded 76, and forced the Highland and Royal Scot regulars to retreat, before finally withdrawing from the area themselves.
Sources: 147, 332

NC12 *Battle Near Franklin* • June 10, 1761
Location: Within 2 miles of the previous June's battle
War: First Cherokee War
Col. James Grant mustered about 2,600 men and left from Fort Prince George on the route taken the year before by Col. Montgomery. Near the prior battle site, they fought with a party of Cherokees, which Grant defeated. English losses were

set at 50 to 60 killed and wounded. The Cherokees lost fewer men, but the defeat was a blow to their morale. Peace was negotiated before the end of the year.
Sources: 332

NC13 *Raid on Watauga* • July 21, 1766
Location: Near Sycamore Shoals
War: First Cherokee War
A party of Cherokees attacked the colonists at the Watauga Fort, and were initially driven off. They then set in for a two-week siege that was broken when Lt. Col. William Russell arrived with six companies of soldiers.
Sources: 332

NC14 *Destruction of Cherokee Towns* • September, 1776
Location: North Carolina
War: Second Cherokee War
Gen. Griffith Rutherford and 2,400 men of the Salisbury Militia, supported by the few remaining members of the Catawba tribe, became active in the campaign against the British-allied Cherokees. They scaled the mountains at Swannanoa Gap, then headed southward along what became known as Rutherford's Trace. By September 18, they had destroyed 36 of the Middle Towns and continued on to attack the Valley Towns.
     Near Echoe, Griffith's force was attacked from the sides of a mountain pass. Lt. Hampton is credited with rallying the troops to turn what seemed to be a defeat into a victory. Seventeen whites and 14 Cherokees were killed. After that, Griffith's march through and destruction of the Valley Towns proceeded with little resistance.
Sources: 3, 199, 332

NC15 *Battle of Guilford Courthouse* • March 15, 1781
Location: Greensboro
War: Revolutionary War
Several Catawbas served as scouts with the Americans during the Revolutionary War. Many fought in South Carolina, then went north with the army to Virginia, and then participated in the Battle of Guilford Courthouse.
Sources: 326, 332

NC16 *Attack at Deep Creek* • February 2, 1864
Location: Quallatown (Cherokee)
War: Civil War
Maj. Francis M. Davidson led the 14th Illinois Cavalry in an attack at Deep Creek, under orders to pursue Col. William Holland Thomas and his Cherokee soldiers. The 600 union soldiers surprised Thomas and his force of 250 and fought with them for an hour.
     The Union claimed that nearly 200 of the Confederates were killed and 22 Cherokees and 32 whites were captured. The Confederates claimed that a total of 20 to 30 were captured and that only one, a Cherokee, was killed. Col. Thomas also claimed that his men killed eight Union men and took one prisoner.
Sources: 60

NC17 *Murder of Barnes* • December 21, 1864
Location: Robeson County
War: Lowrie War
James P. Barnes, a wealthy planter and minor official who attempted to conscript natives into the Confederate army, accused the sons of Lumbee native Allen Lowrie of stealing and butchering two of his best hogs to feed Union prisoners. Barnes warned the Lowries to stay off his land or be shot, and he himself was shot by a Lumbee as he was on his way to the Clay Valley post office, where he was the postmaster.

   He lived long enough to accuse William and Henry Berry Lowrie as his attackers.
Sources: 60, 301

NC18 *Assassination of Harris* • January 15, 1865
Location: Robeson County
War: Lowrie War
James Brantly Harris had dealt in liquor with the Lumbees prior to the Civil War. He became a Home Guard officer and was charged with keeping the peace in his community and hunting for deserters and escaped Union prisoners.

   Harris was attracted to a Lumbee girl, whose Lumbee boyfriend threatened to kill Harris. Harris decided to kill him first and shot Jarman Lowrie, but he turned out to be the wrong man. Fearing Jarman's brothers who came home on leave from Fort Fisher, he arrested both on a charge of desertion. While he had them in handcuffs, he bludgeoned them to death, later claiming it was self defense.

   Harris was shot to death in a volley of gunfire and his body was thrown in a well and covered up. Henry Berry Lowrie and his group were accused of the killing.
Sources: 60, 301

NC19 *Raid on Argyle Plantation* • February 27, 1865
Location: Robeson County
War: Lowrie War
In a raid on the Argyle Plantation, Lowrie Band member and escaped Union prisoner Owen T. Wright was wounded. He and the rest of the band were then pursued by the Home Guard led by Capt. Hugh McGregor. Wright was later captured at the home of a local white schoolmistress sympathetic to the Lowries.
Sources: 60

NC20 *Execution of Lowries* • March 3, 1865
Location: Robeson County
War: Lowrie War
Home Guardsmen led by Capt. Hugh McGregor began arresting those blamed for the breakdown of law and order in Robeson County, including Allen, Mary, Calvin, Sinclair and William Lowrie and George Dial, another Lumbee. About 80 whites gathered and accused the Lowries of supporting Union soldiers, charges which the Lowries denied. William Lowrie attempted to escape, but was shot and brought back.

   The group set up a court, convicted the four Lowrie men, and ordered them shot. Two were allowed to live, but Allen and William were executed after they were forced to dig their own grave.

The Lowries and allies were involved in shootings and other acts of violence resulting in the deaths of several, including 18 in 1870–73. By late 1872, the once large Lowrie Band was reduced to just Andrew Strong and Steve Lowrie. Strong was killed by bounty hunters in December, 1872, as was Lowrie in late February, 1874.
Sources: 60, 301

NORTH DAKOTA

ND1   *Attack on Ashley Party* • June 2, 1823
Location: On the Missouri River near the South Dakota border
War: Arikara War
Arikara warriors attacked a white trading party led by Gen. Ashley and killed 13. Fearing what the whites would do in revenge, most of them hid out with the Pawnees in Nebraska for two years. When they returned to North Dakota, they resettled farther north, by 1851 as far north as the Heart River.

In 1862, they moved to Fort Berthold and in 1871 settled on a permanent reservation there with the Mandans and Hidatsas.
Sources: 134, 148, 376

ND2   *Attack at Fort Berthold* • December 24, 1862
Location: Fort Berthold
A Sioux war party of about 600 attacked Fort Berthold, intending to burn homes in the Arikara, Mandan and Hidatsa village to create a smokescreen within which they could attack the fort. This attempt failed, and the warriors from within the fort fought against and defeated the Sioux.

The fort and nearby village were badly damaged, so the three affiliated tribes moved to Fort Atkinson.
Sources: 376

ND3   *Battle of Whitestone* • September, 1863
Location: Kulm
Gen. Alfred H. Sully led an army into North Dakota from the south, intending to meet with a force commanded by Gen. Henry H. Sibley, but they missed each other. Instead, they found a Sioux band which Sully decided to pursue. After three days, he caught up with them and attacked, killing 150 Sioux.
Monument: The Whitestone Battlefield Historic Site is located at the intersection of CRs 2 and 3, southeast of Kulm.
Sources: 19, 376

ND4   *Attack at Fort Berthold* • June, 1869
Location: Fort Berthold

A force of 500 Sioux rushed the Arikara, Mandan and Hidatsa village at Fort Berthold. After a brief battle in which there were twice as many Sioux casualties as the others, the Sioux withdrew. The three affiliated tribes, being much smaller than the Sioux, were decreasing in numbers and could not afford many such "victories."
Sources: 376

ND5   *Attack on Fort Berthold* • January 2, 1870
Location: Fort Berthold
Two hundred Sioux attacked the native village at Fort Berthold, and were driven off by cannon fire from troops stationed at Fort Stevenson, about 17 miles to the east.
Sources: 376

OHIO

OH1   *Attack on Pickawillany* • June 21, 1752
Location: Near Piqua
The Twightwees/Miami village of Pickawillany on the Miami River contained 400 warriors and British traders. Charles Michel Langlade organized a party of 200 Ottawas and Chippewas to attack the village, and passing through Detroit picked up more Ottawas and Potawatomis.

They struck Pickawillany by surprise while most of the warriors were hunting elsewhere. Langlade persuaded the natives and British to surrender by promising them their freedom. Instead, Langlade had pro–English chief Memiska ("Old Briton" or "La Demoiselle") and a British trader killed and parts of their bodies eaten, and five others were taken captive.

The village was destroyed and survivors moved to an area along the Maumee River. The British provided no response to the attack.
Sources: 123, 131, 176, 292, 324, 412

OH2   *Capture of Fort Sandusky* • May 16, 1763
Location: Sandusky
War: Pontiac's Rebellion
Pontiac sent a party of Ottawa and Huron warriors to Fort Sandusky while the siege of Fort Detroit was going on, in order to obtain a quick victory and solidify his position as war chief of the Ottawas. With the local Hurons, they approached Fort Sandusky to request a council inside with its commander, Ensign Christopher Pauli. He allowed seven in, and when they sat for council they seized Pauli and killed his 15 soldiers and the traders who had been in the fort. Pauli was taken to Detroit, made to run the gauntlet, and was adopted by a native woman.

This action was part of a simultaneous attack engineered by Pontiac, which

also included Forts St. Joseph, Miamis, Ouiatenon, Michilimackinac, Presque Isle, Machault, Le Boeuf, and Edward Augustus.
Sources: 315, 322, 324, 374, 412

OH3   *Yellow Creek Massacre* • April 30, 1774
Location: Baker's Bottom, near Steubenville
War: Lord Dunmore's War
Tachnechdorus, also known as John Logan, was a prominent Cayuga-Mingo sachem who had been a friend of the British. Near the mouth of Yellow Creek on the Ohio River, Jacob Greathouse and his party welcomed ashore Taylaynee and his party of six warriors, two women and a child. Taylaynee was the brother of Logan, whose sister was one of the women.

The whites treated the Cayugas to rum and challenged them to a shooting match, betting more rum against beaver skins that the natives had brought.

Seven white hunters shot at the target, followed by the seven warriors. As soon as the Cayugas had shot, 26 concealed men opened fire and killed the warriors and one of the women. As about 15 Cayugas approached in canoes, the remaining woman screamed a warning and the whites opened fire on the canoes. All but two were killed, and then the pregnant woman and her unborn child were stabbed to death. Logan discovered the bodies the following day.

In retaliation, Logan and a small group of warriors wiped out a settlement of whites. This began a chain of attacks and retaliations.
Sources: 147, 275, 326, 374

OH4   *Siege of Fort Laurens* • January 23–March 28, 1779
Location: Tuscarawas River
War: Revolutionary War
Fort Laurens, named after Henry Laurens, had a garrison of about 150. In January, about 500 natives arrived at the fort, seeking food.

On January 23, Capt. Clarke was led 15 soldiers toward Fort McIntosh in Pennsylvania, when they were attacked by a party of 17 Wyandots and Mingos. With that group was Simon Girty, who was known to some of the soldiers. Two soldiers were killed initially, and a packhorse was killed along the way to the fort.

When they arrived at the fort, it was attacked by the warriors, whose numbers grew. Two nights later, a messenger sent by Col. Gibson left the fort in darkness to notify Gen. Lachlan McIntosh and get help, but a mile from the fort he was captured by Girty and taken to the British in Detroit.

On February 23, a party left the fort for the nearby woods because no natives could be seen. After traveling for only a half mile, they were attacked by Wyandots, Chippewas and Mingos. Sixteen soldiers were killed and the other two were captured. Two hundred warriors recommenced their firing on the fort, which then contained 106 men under the command of Maj. Frederick Vernon.

In late March, the siege was lifted when Gen. McIntosh arrived with 500 infantry as reinforcements.
Sources: 234, 293, 374

OH5   *Attack on Chalahgawtha* • July 30, 1779
Location: 50 miles south of Wapatomica
War: Revolutionary War

Col. John Bowman led a campaign from Kentucky into Ohio to fight the Shawnees. His goal was the village of Chalahgawtha on the Little Miami River, containing 3,000 Shawnees. When the army arrived, most of the 1,000 warriors were in Wapatomica, leaving only 35 defenders. The soldiers set fire to the buildings, but wasted time gathering loot.

They concentrated more on their plunder, and 10 were shot from the large council house, where the defenders were gathered. Bowman ordered a withdrawal, but not before taking the herd of about 144 horses. With the loot and horses, the trip back to Kentucky was very slow.

The Shawnee defenders caught up with the army after about 10 miles and, one by one, shot soldiers off of their horses. Bowman halted his men and formed a defensive square, and the natives vanished. When they resumed their march, the natives resumed their sniping. Two dozen warriors were able to control about 240 soldiers, causing them to stop and attempt to defend five times.

One hundred soldiers led by Capt. James Harrod put down their loot and charged the warriors, who returned to Chalahgawtha. The army, having lost 30 and having 60 wounded, reached Kentucky and called it a victory.

Sources: 374

OH6 *Burning of Chillicothe* • Summer, 1780
Location: Miami River
War: Revolutionary War

Brig. Gen. George Rogers Clark led expeditionary forces of riflemen from Virginia and Kentucky through what was then the western region of the U.S., in an attempt to secure it from the natives and the British. On the first of the three expeditions, Clark became drunk and disorganized, and after hundreds of his men deserted, the expedition was cancelled.

On the second expedition in 1780, he and a force of 800 sacked and burned Chillicothe and other principal Shawnee towns. They tortured, murdered and scalped the natives.

Although Clark's actions took control of the area from the British, the Shawnees began retaliatory raids in Kentucky, taking men and resources away from the war effort against England. They allied behind war chief Blue Jacket.

Sources: 3, 147, 234, 315

OH7 *Battle at Piqua* • August 8, 1780
Location: Piqua
War: Revolutionary War

After the Shawnees abandoned their main town at Chillicothe, they settled in the fortified town of Piqua. Upon the arrival there of Brig. Gen. George Rogers Clark and his army, the battle commenced. The natives were outnumbered three-to-one and had some early success, but were ultimately defeated. Without sufficient supplies, however, Clark was unable to continue the campaign and carry out Gov. Jefferson's order to exterminate the natives or at least move them beyond the lakes or the Illinois River.

American losses were 20 killed and 40 wounded, and they reportedly had scalped 73 Shawnees.

Sources: 3, 315

OH8   *Attacks on Settlers* • 1780s
Location: Ohio and Miami Rivers
War: Revolutionary War
Little Turtle and his Miamis, and Blue Jacket and his Shawnees, attacked homes and farms, killing settlers and attacking flatboats traveling down the Ohio River with new settlers and supplies. Maj. Gen. Arthur St. Clair tried to make peace, but was rejected by the natives.
   St. Clair assembled a force of 1,450 Kentucky and Pennsylvania recruits and placed it under the command of Brig. Gen. Josiah Harmar.
Sources: 147

OH9   *Burning of Coshocton* • Spring, 1781
Location: Coshocton
War: Revolutionary War
Col. Daniel Broadhead led 150 soldiers and 134 militiamen on an expedition to punish the Delawares, who had recently become belligerent. He surprised and burned the town of Coshocton. After they surrendered, Broadhead killed 15 of the warriors.
   The result was a hardening of the Delawares' hatred of the whites, and they responded by burning nine Kentucky prisoners.
Sources: 3

OH10   *Brady's Ambush* • October 12, 1781
Location: Kent
War: Revolutionary War
Capt. Samuel Brady led the unit known as Brady's Rangers, containing about 50 men. He took 40 of them up the Beaver River in search of a war party of what was believed to include Mingoes, Senecas and Wyandots. They followed the signs 20 miles up the Mahoning River and found 60 natives camped on Breakneck Creek.
   Brady set up an ambush, knowing that because of their superior numbers, the natives would pursue them after their initial gunshots. The plan was to shoot once, then scramble back to Fort McIntosh in groups no larger than two.
   Brady's group of 13 opened fire on the camp at about dawn and killed 10. The remaining 50 natives gave chase, and at one point the 13 turned around and waited for the warriors to come within about 50 yards. When a signal was given, all 40 Rangers opened fire, killing several natives and causing the rest to run back to camp. The soldiers hurried back to Fort McIntosh, but Brady was the sole Ranger taken prisoner, by five Wyandot hunters who were unaware of the ambush.
   Brady was ordered to run the gauntlet in the Mingo village of Honnia at the site of present-day Kent. He refused to remove his clothing and flattened a warrior with a punch when he attempted to strip off Brady's shirt. Brady then grabbed a baby from the crowd of onlookers and threw in into a fire. As the warriors rushed to rescue it, Brady ran northward, pursued by a band of warriors.
   The warriors knew that Brady could not outrun them, so they took no shots. After about a mile, Brady passed Standing Rock on the shore of the Cuyahoga River with the warriors about 60 yards behind him. After another 100 yards, he reached The Narrows and leaped across the river at a point where it was 22 feet

wide, with 20-foot-deep turbulent water below. Brady made it across the river but no warrior would attempt the jump. One shot him across the river and injured his thigh, but Brady ran to what is now called Brady Lake and hid in a hollow log until dark, when he limped back to the fort.

Sources: 374

OH11 *Moravian Massacre* or *Gnadenhutten Massacre* • March 10, 1782
Location: Gnadenhutten
War: Revolutionary War

A hundred Pennsylvania militiamen led by Col. David Williamson were in pursuit of Delaware marauders who had killed whites along the upper Ohio River. Williamson came upon the Moravian mission settlement of Gnadenhutten along the Tuscarawas River, where the pursued warriors had stopped for a while to trade. Before reaching the village, they had come upon the bodies of Jane Wallace and her infant daughter, impaled on saplings and left to be found by the militiamen, which included the husband and father of the dead.

The Delawares surrendered and turned over their weapons. Fifty Delawares came from Salem to join the 45 already at Gnadenhutten. The militia packed 90 of the 150 men, women and children into two cabins, then butchered them with a mallet and tomahawks and then cut off their scalps. One scalped adult and two children managed to escape, the latter two to Schoenbrunn. The Delawares there quickly departed, shortly before Williamson arrived and burned down the village.

Other natives used the killings as justification for attacks on white settlers along the frontier. Settlers and British soldiers were appalled at the killings.

Monument: The 9-acre Gnadenhutten Monument on US 36 about 10 miles east of Interstate 77 includes a marble obelisk, log church and cooper's cabin.

Sources: 3, 12, 19, 169, 275, 288, 324, 374, 380, 395

OH12 *Battle of Sandusky* • June 4–5, 1782
Location: Battle Island, north of Upper Sandusky
War: Revolutionary War

In retaliation for native attacks, which themselves were in retaliation for the massacre at Gnadenhutten, Col. William Crawford set out with a column of soldiers. As they traveled along the Sandusky River, from 600 to 1,000 Wyandots and Delawares led by Monakuduto, Wingenund and Punoacan came out of a ravine and began shooting. Crawford had his men retreat to a grove which they thought they could defend.

The battle raged all day on June 4, with many killed. During the night, 15 volunteers deserted, three wounded had died, and several of the other 19 wounded were close to death. Shooting began again at dawn, then tapered off. That night, with fires lit to fool the natives into thinking the army was in its camp, they instead intended to retreat.

Capt. John Hardin disagreed with Crawford, believing that the route selected would lead into an ambush. Before the wholesale retreat was to begin, Hardin left with his unit in another direction. When Crawford found out about the insubordination, he set out along Hardin's trail. Hardin's men were attacked as they tried to sneak through the warrior line, and the gunfire panicked the main body of soldiers who believed they themselves were being attacked, and rode off into the woods.

Crawford heard the Hardin gunfire and returned to the main camp, just as the army had left. He then rode deeper into the woods to search for three of his relatives who were under his command, gave that up and came upon Dr. John Knight, and the two of them attempted to get away from the area. The army was reforming and continuing its retreat under Col. David Williamson while they skirmished with parties of warriors along the way.

On June 6, Crawford and Knight were found by a party led by Capt. John Biggs, who joined them in their retreat. The following day near Bucyrus, Crawford and Knight were captured by the Delawares and on June 11 Crawford was tortured, scalped and killed.

Estimates of American deaths from the battle and subsequent pursuit range from 30 to 250.

Sources: 3, 12, 234, 324, 374

OH13   *Battle of the Olentangy* • June 6, 1782
Location: Olentangy River
War: Revolutionary War
Units of the army which had been led by Col. William Crawford were in the process of retreating under the leadership of Col. David Williamson. An advance group of seven led by Maj. John Rose was attacked and galloped back to the main army. Williamson called a halt when they reached the Olentangy River, but Rose recommended that they continue to some protective timber.

A party of warriors attacked, and within an hour there were three white dead and eight wounded. When there was a lull in the fighting, Williamson ordered the burying of the dead and a continuation of the retreat.
Sources: 374

OH14   *Capture of Chillicothe* • November 10, 1782
Location: Chillicothe
War: Revolutionary War
Brig. Gen. George Rogers Clark and about 1,000 Kentucky riflemen attacked and captured the British-allied Shawnee town of Chillicothe, in what some consider to be the war's final battle.
Sources: 90

OH15   *Attack at Ludlow's Station* • Early April, 1790
Location: Northeast of Cincinnati
War: Ohio Indian Wars
Israel Ludlow established a settlement on Mill Creek near Cincinnati. Near it Samuel Jeffers was tomahawked and scalped.
Sources: 374

OH16   *Attacks on Short Creek* • July, 1790
Location: Short Creek
War: Ohio Indian Wars
John Carpenter and his wife were working in their field when he was wounded by a band of warriors. She ran toward their cabin to alert their son, George, with warriors in pursuit. When George came out with a gun, they ran back to where John had been so they could take his scalp, but by then he had crawled into a cornfield. The warriors departed.

Also on Short Creek, the warriors attacked the McCoy home, killing George McCoy and his wife and capturing Richard Tilton and David Pusley. They tomahawked Pusley and took Tilton to Indian Cross Creek, where they also killed Thomas Van Swearingen and David Cox.
Sources: 374

OH17 *Attack at Stillwater Creek* • December 11, 1790
Location: 18 miles from Wheeling
War: Ohio Indian Wars
A deer hunting party of 14 crossed the Ohio River and headed along Indian Wheeling Creek for Stillwater Creek. They had a very good day of hunting, then camped for the night. At two or three o'clock in the morning, a party of Wyandots and Mingoes attacked. A hunter, Daniel C. Whitaker, estimated that it consisted of 20 to 30 warriors.

The warriors shot the 14 as they lay sleeping in their blankets around the fire, killing 13. No one shot Whitaker, and he pretended to be dead as they went to the others, taking scalps, guns and other possessions. When they got to him, he sprang to his feet, threw his blanket over the warriors, and ran off barefoot through patches of snow, taking a thrown tomahawk in the shoulder.

Whitaker ran into a low-hanging branch and knocked himself out. When he came to after sunrise, he headed toward Wheeling. After spending the night in a hollow log, he finally reached the Ohio River, built a raft, and made it to Fort Henry.
Sources: 374

OH18 *Big Bottom Massacre* • January 2, 1791
Location: Stockport
War: Ohio Indian Wars
The Big Bottom settlement on the Muskingum River was approached by warriors who crossed the river in the dark. They surrounded the blockhouse and shot and killed twelve, capturing the rest. Asa and Eleaszer Bullard, who lived about a hundred yards from the stockade, escaped to Waterford.
Memorial: Big Bottom State Monument, located one mile southeast of Stockport on SR 266, has a marble obelisk on a three-acre site.
Sources: 19, 176, 412

OH19 *Attack at Dunlap's Station* • January, 1791
Location: 18 miles north of Cincinnati
War: Ohio Indian Wars
Three hundred Potawatomis, Miamis, Delawares and Shawnees attacked Dunlap's Station, killing several Americans. Surveyor Abner Hunt was captured and was slowly burned to death within sight of the station. The natives were eventually repulsed by the defenders.
Sources: 169, 324

OH20 *Attack Near Fort Hamilton* • November 3–4, 1791
Location: Later site of Fort Recovery
War: Ohio Indian Wars
After the defeat of Brig. Gen. Josiah Harmar, the army was put under the command

of Maj. Gen. Arthur St. Clair. A force of 2,300 men, plus 200 women to attend to them, left on October 4 from Fort Hamilton on the Great Miami River. By November, the force dwindled to about 1,400. On November 3, they camped along a tributary of the Wabash River. The following morning, they were attacked by Little Turtle (Michikinikwa), Blue Jacket, and 1,000 warriors.

The militiamen across the stream from the main camp were taken by surprise and many were killed with hatchets and knives. Survivors fled across the stream to the main camp, which was soon charged and engaged in hand-to-hand fighting. Artillerymen were wiped out by a charge of Shawnees led by Blue Jacket and Delawares led by Buckongahelas. Five hundred surviving soldiers retreated through the forest. The casualty list included the deaths of 832 soldiers and civilians, 271 seriously wounded, and the loss of all supplies and artillery, making this the worst military defeat of all time for a U.S. army at the hands of natives. The victors had only 21 to 150 killed and 40 wounded.

This battle is considered by many to be the greatest native defeat of an American army in all of history. The victory caused Little Turtle and his warriors and allies to believe themselves invincible, especially because they were promised support by the British.

Two years later, Fort Recovery was built on the same site.

Memorial: Fort Recovery State Memorial, 1 Fort Site Street, Fort Recovery, OH, is located on SR 49 at SR 119.

Sources: 19, 20, 34, 56, 91, 123, 135, 147, 172, 176, 189, 257, 284, 292, 293, 315, 323, 324, 339, 349, 364, 374, 381, 383, 393, 412

OH21 *Attack at Big Bottom* • December 20, 1791

Location: 40 miles above Marietta

War: Ohio Indian Wars

Twenty-one settlers stopped briefly at Marietta and told the residents there that they intended to establish a new settlement at Big Bottom. Since Fort Harmar was only 24 miles away, they felt they could flee there for refuge in case natives attacked.

Under Blue Jacket, the warriors attacked the uncompleted settlement. The first firing killed 11 men, a woman and two children. Four surrendered and three ran away to safety in Marietta.

Monument: Big Bottom State Monument, SR 266, Stockport, OH, includes a marble obelisk on a 3-acre site.

Sources: 19, 374

OH22 *Delaware Massacre* • March 10, 1792

Location: Schoenbrunn Village

War: Ohio Indian Wars

The Delawares invited the Moravians to establish a mission in the Ohio country, which they did at Schoenbrunn Village in 1772. During the Revolutionary War, the Moravians and native converts intended to remain neutral, but were hassled by both the Americans and British. They dismantled Schoenbrunn and moved to Gnadenhutten and Lichtenau.

In 1781, the British forced the Delawares to relocate to a site on the Sandusky River. About 100 were allowed to return in 1792 to the Tuscarawas to obtain their possessions and harvest corn, but on the way they met American Col. David

Williamson and 90 militiamen. The unarmed pacifist Delawares were captured for their supposed help to the British and 96 were massacred.
Monument: Reconstructed Schoenbrunn Village, SR 259, New Philadelphia, OH, has 17 reconstructed log buildings and the original mission cemetery.
Sources: 19, 199, 284, 349

OH23 *Attack on Supply Train* • October 17, 1793
Location: 7 miles from Fort St. Clair
War: Ohio Indian Wars
Blue Jacket led 250 warriors in an attack against an army supply train which was accompanied by 100 mounted riflemen at a place known as the Forty Foot Pitch. Killed were Lt. John Lowry and 14 regular soldiers.
Sources: 19, 374

OH24 *Attack at Holt's Creek* • December 2, 1793
Location: 32 miles below Maysville
War: Ohio Indian Wars
A party of natives crossed the Ohio River on about November 20 to steal horses and was pursued by a scouting patrol led by Simon Kenton. On December 2, Kenton overtook them near the mouth of Holt's Creek. Although Capt. William Hardin was wounded, six Shawnees were killed, the rest were scattered and the horses were recovered.
Sources: 374

OH25 *Attack on Fort Recovery* • June 30, 1794
Location: Fort Recovery
War: Ohio Indian Wars
Gen. "Mad Anthony" Wayne, known to the natives as "Blacksnake," while waiting for supplies to arrive to support his campaign against the natives in Ohio, had his troops build advance posts at Forts Greenville and Recovery. On June 20, Blue Jacket led 1,200 allied warriors against Fort Recovery and had early success against it before they were driven off by cannon fire. Blue Jacket suffered heavy losses.

The Miamis and Shawnees concluded that Wayne was more competent than Brig. Gen. Josiah Harmar and Maj. Gen. Arthur St. Clair, who were easily beaten by them in prior encounters. Realizing that they could not count on support from the British, Little Turtle decided to attempt to make peace with the whites. Blue Jacket still felt that they could defeat the soldiers.
Museum: Fort Recovery State Memorial is located at SRs 49 and 119, Fort Recovery, OH, includes museums. Also, a monument is located at SR 49 and W. Butler St., Fort Recovery.
Sources: 19, 34, 91, 147, 324, 374

OH26 *Battle of Fallen Timbers* • August 20, 1794
Location: 2 miles west of Maumee
War: Ohio Indian Wars
Gen. Anthony Wayne and 2,000 to 2,200 infantry regulars plus 1,000 to 1,500 Kentucky militia cavalry led by Maj. Gen. Charles Scott headed toward the native villages on the Maumee River. Along the way, they built Fort Defiance at the

junction of the Auglaize and Maumee Rivers. They then started down the Maumee in search of the natives. Little Turtle, Turkey Foot and Blue Jacket with 1,400 to 2,000 warriors prepared to meet them in a large clearing where a tornado had blown down many of the large trees.

Wayne's army entered the clearing on August 20, led by 150 Kentucky cavalrymen ahead of four infantry regiments. In the woods on one side of the clearing were the Miamis and Delawares, in the center were the Ottawas, Potawatomis and other Great Lakes tribes, and on the third side were Shawnees, Wyandots, and 70 whites who had come from Canada to help the natives.

The groups in the center prematurely attacked the soldiers, who gave way and fled. Upon Wayne's order, they reformed and fought the Ottawas. Bayonet charges dislodged the tribes on either side. An American sharpshooter killed the principal war chief of the Ottawas, beginning a withdrawal of that group and eventually the rest of the natives. The battle, lasting less than an hour, resulted in 31 soldiers and 40–50 natives killed. It was considered a crushing defeat for Blue Jacket and a psychological disaster for the Ohio tribes.

The fleeing natives went to Fort Miamis, five miles from the battlefield, to seek help from the British. It was denied, and the fort's commander ordered his men to shoot any native who tried to enter over the fort's walls. When Wayne's men arrived at the fort, the natives fled to the western shore of Lake Erie.

Monument: A marker showing the site of the battle is located on SR 24, west of Maumee.

Sources: 14, 26, 27, 34, 43, 44, 56, 91, 109, 119, 120, 123, 133, 135, 144, 147, 169, 170, 176, 181, 199, 231, 256, 257, 275, 284, 287, 289, 292, 293, 315, 323, 324, 339, 349, 374, 380, 381, 383, 386, 389, 390, 393, 398, 399, 412

OH27 *Attack Near Fort Greenville* • December 18, 1812
Location: Greenville
War: War of 1812
Lt. Col. John B. Campbell led a column of 600 men from Dayton toward Fort Greenville to attack the Delawares and Miamis. Leaving on December 14, they attacked a native village three days later and killed eight, taking 42 prisoners. They also shot the cattle and burned three native towns.

Prior to dawn on December 18, the remaining natives attacked the soldiers. After an hour's fight, they were repulsed. Forty soldiers were crippled by the cold and the fighting resulted in 10 dead and 48 wounded soldiers and 107 dead horses. Severe frostbite cases were left behind, and the rest continued to Fort Greenville.

Monument: The Garst Museum at 205 N. Broadway, Greenville, has displays including relics of the wars with the local natives.

Sources: 396, 397

OH28 *Sieges of Fort Meigs* • April 25–May 9 and late July, 1813
Location: Maumee River
War: War of 1812
Tecumseh ("Crouching Tiger") led 1,200 Potawatomis and other natives and accompanied 900 to 1,000 British soldiers against the American Fort Meigs, built under the command of Gen. William Henry Harrison. The 550 Americans were successful in defending it both times, improving the army's morale despite the loss of Detroit and other British victories.

The fort was saved through the action of a relief force of 1,100 to 1,200 Kentucky militiamen, half of whom were killed or captured in an ambush by Tecumseh and his warriors on the way to the fort on May 5.

The July siege involved a force of 5,000 British regulars, militia and natives. They were unsuccessful in luring the American defenders out of the fort.
Monument: A reconstructed 10-acre fortification with 7 blockhouses, cannon, and earthen traverses is located on SR 65, Perrysburg, OH.
Sources: 19, 26, 32, 91, 144, 149, 181, 293, 315, 324, 349, 396, 398, 400

OH29 *Attack on Fort Stephenson* • August 2, 1813
Location: Sandusky River
War: War of 1812
Unable to take Fort Meigs, British Maj. Gen. Henry Procter attacked Fort Stephenson, which was defended by 160 men under the command of Maj. George Croghan. Gen. William Henry Harrison ordered the 21-year-old major to abandon the fort, but he refused. Harrison relented, although he felt the fort was not defensible.

Procter attacked with 400 soldiers and a group of natives. Kentucky sharpshooters cut them down at the edge of the fort, so the British retreated to Canada. Procter blamed the defeat on the natives, who he said disappeared when the fighting began.
Monument: The Memorial Monument, 423 Croghan St., Freemont, OH, includes Croghan's grave and the single cannon used by the Americans in the battle.
Sources: 91, 144, 181, 400

OKLAHOMA

OK1 *Battle at Twin Villages* • Early October, 1759
Location: Red River
Col. Don Diego Ortiz de Parilla, the commander of the Spanish fort at San Saba, Texas, marched an army north to punish the Comanches and Kiowas and expel the French. His 300 soldiers attacked Twin Villages, which were defended by the French and Taovaya traders, forcing the Spanish to retreat after a day-long battle.
Sources: 294

OK2 *Battle of Claremore Mound* • October, 1817
Location: Verdigris River
John McLamore led a combined force of Cherokees, Choctaws, Chickasaws, Peorias and Pawnees against the village of Osage chief Clermont. They killed 83 women, children and old men while the warriors were away on a hunt. They also captured 103 children for sale as slaves. The attackers burned the village and the fields, then returned to their camps on the Arkansas River.

The Cherokees persuaded the U.S. government to pressure the Osages to give up (to the Cherokees) a portion of their territory as spoils of war.

The Osages responded with a raid on the Cherokees. Other natives scheduled for relocation in what is now Oklahoma refused to go until the Osages and other tribes were willing to allow them to settle peacefully.

Sources: 173, 208, 294, 304

OK3 *Battle Along the Canadian River* • May 11, 1858
Location: Canadian River
John S. ("R.I.P") Ford was the most experienced Texas Ranger still in service, and was appointed as the senior captain and supreme commander for all state armed forces. He raised an army of 102 men and set up his base camp, called Camp Runnels, near the Brazos Reservation. Indian agent L.S. Ross raised a force of 113 warriors, mostly Tonkawas, to help fight the Comanches.

The army crossed the Red River and came upon a Comanche camp along the Canadian River. While Ford considered what to do, some Tonkawas attacked a small camp about three miles from the main concentration, and two Comanches fled on horseback to spread an alarm to the rest. Ford ordered a hard ride right at the main camp.

The 300 warriors led by Iron Jacket stood their ground. Iron Jacket was shot dead by several Texans, and Ford ordered a charge. The battle stretched over a six-mile area, with the Texans having superior weaponry. Charging warriors brandishing spears and arrows were knocked from their mounts by repeating pistols. When the Comanches retreated, the cavalry pursued them for seven hours. The Rangers killed 76 and lost only two of their own, while capturing 18 women and children and about 300 horses.

Rather than authorize Ford to continue on his campaign to destroy the Comanches, the government disbanded the army.

Sources: 103, 294

OK4 *Battle of the Wichita Village* • October 1, 1858
Location: 5 miles southeast of Rush Springs
Capt. Earl Van Dorn led a portion of the 2nd Cavalry from Fort Belknap and 135 friendly Wacos, Caddoes and Tonkawas. He encountered the Comanches and Wichitas at Rush Creek. In about five hours of fighting, about 70 of the Comanches were killed.

When his scouts located a Comanche camp, Van Dorn rode out with his cavalry, leaving the infantry behind, and traveled 90 miles in 37 hours to meet the 500 Comanches. They attacked at dawn, killed 56, burned the lodges, and took about 300 horses. However, most escaped and were able to inflict damage on the soldiers.

Afterwards, the Comanches moved to the Arkansas River and joined the Kiowas, while the Wichitas asked for sanctuary at Fort Arbuckle. Van Dorn and his troops went to Camp Radziminski for the winter.

Sources: 91, 103, 227, 294

OK5 *Battle of Round Mountain* or *Battle of Round Mounds* • November 19, 1861
Location: Near the mouth of the Cimarron River
Opothle Yahola (also called Ho-po-eith-le-yo-ho-la) and Halleck Tustennuggee

led their Loyal Creeks, those not wishing to become involved in the Civil War, from their home in Oklahoma north toward a safe region in Kansas. On November 19, they were engaged in battle by Col. Douglas H. Cooper and Confederate soldiers near Round Mountain, near the meeting of the Arkansas and Cimarron Rivers.

With Cooper was an ex-chief of the Creeks, McIntosh, and other Creeks, Choctaws, Seminoles, Cherokees and Chickasaws who had aligned themselves with the Confederacy. The outcome of the battle was indecisive, and the Creeks slipped away during the night.
Sources: 58, 105, 112, 173, 294, 335, 340

OK6 *Battle of Caving Banks* • December 9, 1861
Location: Bird Creek at Chusto Talasah, north of Tulsa
War: Civil War
Col. Douglas H. Cooper and 500 of Col. Drew's Cherokee regiment again came upon Opothle Yahola and the Creeks on December 9. Again, the Creeks and other pro–Union natives were able to repel the attackers and slip away from Cooper, with only 27 killed.
Sources: 60, 105, 173, 335, 340

OK7 *Battle of Chustenahlah* or *Battle of Patriot Hills* • December 26, 1861
Location: Osage Hills
War: Civil War
Col. Douglas H. Cooper's Confederate force was able to rout the Creeks led by Opothle Yahola in a four-hour battle, because the natives' ammunition failed. They abandoned all of their possessions at the camp and fled during the night to Kansas. Many died in the intense cold and some were eaten by wolves.

In addition to the Loyal Creeks, heading north were some of the Seminoles, Cherokees, and another band of Creeks, who chose to take their chances with the weather rather than be governed by the Confederacy. The fleeing party was estimated at between 6,000 and 10,000. They were pursued by Confederate Cherokees led by Stand Watie, who killed 20 or 21 and captured 75.
Sources: 60, 105, 112, 173, 294, 330, 335, 340

OK8 *Battle at Locust Grove* • July 3, 1862
Location: Locust Grove
War: Civil War
The 1st Federal Indian Expedition was formed of Delawares and other natives allied with the Union and was led by Col. Benjamin Weer. Near Locust Grove, they surprised and surrounded the Confederate Missouri force led by Col. James J. Clarkson. As a result of the confrontation, 100 Confederates were killed, Clarkson and 110 of his men were captured, and 60 ammunition wagons were seized.

As a result of the Union victory, many natives allied with the Confederacy deserted, some joining Col. Ritchie's 2nd Kansas Indian Home Guards.
Sources: 60, 105

OK9 *Battle of Bayou Menard* • Summer, 1862
Location: Seven miles northeast of Fort Gibson
War: Civil War

Maj. William A. Phillips and the 1st Kansas Indian Home Guard Regiment left from Park Hill on three roads which met at Bayou Menard (Bayou Bernard). Col. Stand Watie's Confederate regiment had come to the area to take revenge on Cherokee traitors who had switched to pro–Union allegiance. The Union Cherokees surrounded the Confederates, taking them by surprise.

The Confederates had 32 killed and 25 captured, plus 68 wounded. Included in the dead were Lt. Col. Thomas Fox Taylor and Capt. Hicks, plus two Choctaw captains.

Sources: 105

OK10 *Battle of Honey Springs* • July 17, 1863
Location: Honey Springs
War: Civil War
The 1st Creek Regiment was led by Col. D.M. McIntosh and the 2nd was led by Col. Chilly McIntosh. Col. Douglas H. Cooper led Choctaws, Chickasaws, Cherokees and the Creeks, and located them at Honey Springs, along with some Texas cavalry. His plan was to march up the Texas Road and capture the Union's Fort Gibson commanded by Gen. James Blunt.

Before Cooper's army left to attack the fort, soldiers from the fort attacked him. When the Southern forces ran out of ammunition, they were routed. The Creeks withdrew to the area along the Red River, forming refugee camps within Choctaw and Chickasaw territory.

Sources: 8, 105, 275, 294, 340

OK11 *Raid on Tahlequah* • October 29, 1863
Location: Tahlequah
War: Civil War
Stand Watie led a party of Cherokees to the Cherokee capital at Tahlequah, burning the council house, killing a few Pins, and capturing some Union Cherokees.

They then attacked Park Hill and burned Rose Cottage, the home and plantation of chief John Ross. They killed four Union soldiers and a Cherokee Unionist, and captured some of the Ross slaves.

Sources: 60

OK12 *Capture of the Ferry* J.R. Williams • June 10, 1864
Location: Near Pleasant Bluff on the Arkansas River
War: Civil War
Stand Watie and his Confederate Cherokees, Creeks and Seminoles attacked the Union ferry steamboat *J.R. Williams* as it headed with supplies toward Fort Gibson. It was guarded by an escort of 26 Union soldiers.

Confederate gunfire hit the smokestack, pilot house, boiler and pipes, causing a release of steam which blinded the Union soldiers, who deserted it and set up a defense on a sandbar. They were overrun by the Confederates, who then plundered the boat. Having no wagons, they burned the supplies that they could not carry individually.

Sources: 60

OK13 *Attack Near Sand Town* • September 16, 1864
Location: Verdigris River

War: Civil War

The Confederate forces planned to attack a massive wagon train heading for Fort Gibson and moved its soldiers and native warriors into position for the battle. Along the way, they came upon 185 Union troops from the 2nd Kansas Cavalry and the 1st Kansas Colored Infantry, who were busy cutting hay for the Fort Gibson livestock.

The Confederates attacked them with canister and grapeshot, killing 110 and taking the rest as prisoners. They also burned 100 tons of hay and destroyed the mowing equipment.

Sources: 60

OK14 *Second Battle of Cabin Creek* • September 19, 1864
Location: Cabin Creek
War: Civil War

Scouts of Confederate Gen. Stand Watie found a Union supply train of 300 wagons traveling from Fort Scott, Kansas, to Fort Gibson, escorted by a heavy mounted guard. Along with the wagons were 250 armed teamsters, 300 Indian Home Guards including some Cherokee Pins, and 430 regular soldiers from Forts Gibson and Scott.

The Confederates, including allied Cherokees, attacked at the Cabin Creek crossing and defeated the Union guard, driving the train from the Cherokee lands into Confederate territory. The Union force suffered over 200 casualties and the loss of 120 prisoners and over $1.5 million worth of supplies, including 129 wagons and 740 mules. The Confederates had seven Texas troops and one Seminole killed. The Confederate-allied Cherokees were accused of massacring and mutilating wounded prisoners who were Cherokee Unionist Pins.

The captured clothing, food, medicine and blankets were shared with the natives living along the Red River.

Sources: 60, 294

OK15 *Battle of the Washita* • November 27, 1868
Location: Washita River near Cheyenne

In the fall of 1868, Black Kettle gave in and brought his Southern Cheyenne band to a reservation on the Washita River. With many of the young men having stayed with the more warlike Northern Cheyenne, the village consisted mostly of women, children, and the elderly.

Lt. Col. George Armstrong Custer and the 7th Cavalry were sent into the southern plains to bring in the natives who had not peaceably settled on the reservations. They followed a Cheyenne raiding party that went to Black Kettle's village, and at dawn on November 27 attacked the sleeping village while the soldier band played "Gary Owen," the 7th Cavalry's regimental song.

Black Kettle went out to meet the soldiers and talk to them of peace and avoid a massacre like that at Sand Creek. They killed him, his wife, and 101 Southern Cheyennes. They captured 53 women and children to take back to Gen. Philip Sheridan.

From a nearby village, Arapahos joined the Cheyennes in a rear guard action, surrounding 19 soldiers led by Maj. Joel Elliott and killing all of them. By midday, Kiowas and Comanches also began to arrive, so Custer left with his men and captives to return to the temporary base at Camp Supply on the Canadian River.

Monument: A monument marking the site of the battle is located on SR 47A about 25 miles north of Interstate 40 from the Sayre exit, near Cheyenne.
Sources: 19, 24, 32, 91, 92, 109, 135, 145, 178, 227, 235, 247, 250, 271, 284, 288, 294, 299, 305, 328, 355, 362, 380, 417

OK16 *Battle of Soldier Spring* • Late November, 1868
Location: Canadian River
War: War of 1868-69
Maj. A.W. Evans marched his troops from Fort Bascom, New Mexico, toward Antelope Hills and the camp of the Nokoni Comanches near the Wichita village. Arrowpoint led the Comanches in a charge against the soldiers, but when he was wounded, his men retreated. Also taking part in the battle were Kiowas from Woman's Heart village at Sheep Mountain.
    The Comanche village was destroyed and one soldier was killed.
Sources: 227

OK17 *Attack on Wagon Train* • July 3, 1874
Location: Hennessey
A wagon train led by Patrick Hennessey was attacked and burned by Arapahos and Cheyennes.
Sources: 227

OK18 *Battle Near Cimarron River* • September 13, 1877
Location: North of the Cimarron River
Little Wolf and Dull Knife led their Northern Cheyennes south to Oklahoma, where they understood that they were to look at and consider a reservation at Fort Reno to be shared with the Southern Cheyennes, or they could return to their home in the north. Finding it to be inadequate, they chose to return home, but were prohibited by soldiers from doing so. On September 9, they left anyway and headed north.
    After crossing the Cimarron, they positioned themselves behind cedar breaks in an area where four canyons crossed. Capt. Joseph Rendlebrock's Arapaho scout brought back Little Wolf's message that they were not going to return to Fort Reno, and soon after that, the army attacked. They entered the canyons and opened fire and were pinned down until the following morning by well-positioned warriors behind the cedars.
    On September 14, the Cheyennes headed north and the soldiers retreated. For the rest of September, the Cheyennes carried on a running battle as they traveled north through Kansas and Nebraska. Ten thousand soldiers and 3,000 volunteers picked off the young and old who fell behind. They lost 34 on the trek, mostly to the soldiers' bullets.
Sources: 70, 201

OK19 *Skirmish at Muskogee* • December 25, 1878
Location: Muskogee
In Muskogee, the peacekeeping force was largely black, and on Christmas day they disarmed John and Dick Vann, a pair of Cherokees who were passing through the town. Another individual decided to ally with the Cherokees against the blacks, and a fight broke out. It resulted in the death of one of the blacks and three others were wounded.

In August of 1879, another fight took place in the same town between the Cherokees and blacks. John Vann was killed, as was a white working in a store who was hit with a stray bullet. Several blacks were also wounded. Whites who wanted the Cherokees out informed the tribe of the scuffle, so that a larger fight would break out and measures would have to be taken against the natives. However, Indian agent Vore persuaded the Cherokees to allow proper legal processes to prevail.
Sources: 340

OK20 *Raid on Marshalltown* • July 26, 1880
Location: Marshalltown
Marshalltown, located a few miles north of Muskogee, was a settlement of blacks, many of whom were allied with the Creeks. It was a rough area, inhabited by horse and cattle thieves who often took the law into their own hands if they felt the proper channels would take too long to bring justice.

In 1880, Cherokees made several raids into Marshalltown, shooting into blacks' homes and killing several residents. On July 26, a party of mixed-blood Cherokees abducted two blacks whom they accused of being horse thieves, carried them over the district line to the Cherokee jurisdiction, and hanged them. On July 27, a party of blacks rode across into Cherokee territory and a running battle ensued, going back and forth over the boundary line.

Several on both sides were wounded and William Cobb, a Cherokee, was killed. Tempers flared and further violence was avoided by penalties being handed out by the judicial system.
Sources: 340

OK21 *Killing of Lighthorsemen* • July, 1881
Location: Wewoka
War: Green Peach War
A follower of Isparhecher was arrested near Wewoka by two lighthorsemen, police selected by Creeks. They disarmed the natives in attendance at an armed political meeting and arrested Heneha Chupco, allegedly for resisting an officer. He was rescued when a party followed the lighthorsemen and killed them.

A thousand militiamen were assembled by Principal Chief Samuel Checote, and they skirmished with Isparhechers followers, resulting in few casualties. By August, the matter was over, some of the men involved were arrested, and the leaders fled into the lands of the Seminoles and Cherokees.
Sources: 112

OK22 *Battle Near Okmulgee* • December 24, 1882
Location: About 20 miles southwest of Okmulgee
Tuckabatchee Harjo led a force of insurgent Creeks and several Seminole volunteers into the Cherokee territory from the west, on the way toward Nuyaka. He came upon a party led by lighthorse captain Jim Larney and the judge of the Wewoka District, Tulwa Fixico (a.k.a. Joseph Dunston or Dunsey).

They fought, resulting in seven of Larney's party being killed. The Creeks then withdrew back to the west.
Sources: 340

OK23 *Encounter East of Wichita* • April 23, 1883
Location: 9 miles east of Wichita Agency
Creek insurgents camped at a strong position on a hill, apparently ready for a battle. Maj. J.C. Bates led a force from Fort Gibson and picked up reinforcements from Fort Sill. Ready to take on Isparhecher and the 400 to 500 Creeks he had with him, they came upon the insurgents and offered them an opportunity to surrender and be given safe passage home.

     Their answer was evasive, and the cavalry moved into position for an attack. The Creeks then retreated, breaking and running. Within days they were rounded up.
Sources: 340

OREGON

OR1 *Umpqua Massacre* • July 14, 1828
Location: Umpqua River
War: Smith Expedition
Jedediah Smith and 17 other men had traveled through the brush and canyons of the Klamath and Trinity Rivers, and then headed north toward the Rogue River. They were hungry and sick and had eaten their last dog.

     On June 24, they came upon a native village of 10 to 12 lodges, whose inhabitants fled when they saw the whites approach. They saw four natives on July 3 who avoided the white party. About a week later, they camped along the Coos River, about four miles from the ocean.

     On July 14, their camp was stormed by a party of Kalawatsets, who killed 14 and took 728 beaver pelts and 228 horses and mules. The sole survivor was Arthur Black, who made his way nearly 200 miles north to Fort Vancouver, Washington, arriving there on August 8. Two days later, Smith and two companions who were away from the camp during the massacre also reached Fort Vancouver.
Sources: 10, 213, 337

OR2 *Raid on Fremont Party* • May 8–9, 1846
Location: Klamath Lake
War: Fremont Expedition
John Charles Fremont led an exploring and surveying party through the lands of the Modocs in December of 1843 without incident. When he returned in May of 1846, his party (including four Delaware warriors) was attacked by Klamaths who wanted the whites' horses. During a nighttime raid on their camp, three of Fremont's party were killed and one was wounded.

     The survivors, including Kit Carson and Dick Owens, responded with an attack on the warriors on the north shore of the lake and burned the Klamath village on May 13.
Sources: 10, 163, 171, 228, 230, 262

OR3   *Attacks on Wagon Trains* • Summer, 1847
Location: Southern Oregon
Jesse and Lindsay Applegate headed a party of explorers who traveled through the Southern Oregon Modoc country, establishing a shorter route for settlers heading to the area. Called the Applegate Trail, it was in use by October of 1847. The Modocs were angered because the settlers scared game away, so they attacked wagon trains along the trail. During the summer of 1847, they killed a total of 24 settlers.
Sources: 262

OR4   *Skirmish Near Fort Lee* • January 8, 1848
Location: The Dalles
War: Cayuse War
Twenty-three natives, including eight Cayuses and some Teninos, ran off a herd of cattle at The Dalles and were pursued by 17 military volunteers. The two parties skirmished for two hours with native casualties being three killed and one wounded. The natives kept the 300 cattle.
    Oregon militia began gathering at The Dalles under the leadership of Col. Cornelius Gilliam, but this did not stop the Cayuses from killing settlers. Some drove the whites' horses to a hillside and when their owners arrived to retrieve them, the Cayuses killed two of the men.
Sources: 81

OR5   *Battle on the Deschutes River* • January 29, 1848
Location: 35 miles from The Dalles
War: Cayuse War
Maj. Henry A.G. Lee and 20 scouts fought with a band of Cayuses and Teninos. After charging and killing one warrior and capturing two women and some horses, Lee and his men withdrew into a ravine. The warriors spent the rest of the day rolling rocks down on them.
Sources: 81

OR6   *Battle of Sand Hollow* • February 24, 1848
Location: 8 miles east of Wells Springs on the Oregon Trail
War: Cayuse War
Cayuses, Coeur d'Alenes and Pend Oreilles met Col. Cornelius Gilliam's 300 volunteers and refused to talk to three commissioners who approached under a flag of truce. The battle began when shaman Grey Eagle and Five Crows rushed the troops. Grey Eagle was shot by Capt. Thomas McKay and bludgeoned by Baptiste Dorion. Five Crows was wounded in the arm, and the natives fell back.
    Twenty minutes later, a series of native charges began. The troops responded with a nine-pound cannon which frightened many of the attackers. After three hours of fighting, the natives had eight of their men killed. With the high number of casualties and some dissention among themselves, they broke off the battle.
Sources: 81, 361

OR7   *Battle of the Abiqua* • Early March, 1848
Location: Abiqua River
War: Cayuse War

White settlers attacked the camp of a band of Molallas, who had been joined by some Klamath warriors. Over a two-day period, 13 Klamaths were killed and one was wounded. Only one white was wounded in a surprisingly easy victory.
Sources: 132

OR8   *Attacks in the Rogue Valley* • June 1 and 2, 1851
Location: Near the Rogue River
War: Rogue River War
On June 1, a party of Rogues ambushed 26 whites at a point 20 miles south of the Rogue River ford. The whites escaped, killing one Rogue in the process.

On June 2, the Rogues attacked four miners at the same location, taking their packs and animals but killing none. On the same day, the Rogues fired on the pack train of I.B. Nichols, wounding one. At about the same time, they ambushed and killed four white travelers.
Sources: 337

OR9   *Attack on McBride Party* • June 2, 1851
Location: Bear Creek
War: Rogue River War
A party of Rogues attacked 32 miners returning from California under the leadership of Dr. James McBride. They fought for four hours, injuring only one miner. Seven Rogues were killed and several were wounded. Horses and packs containing gold dust were taken by the attackers.
Sources: 337

OR10   *Attack at Battle Rock* • June 10, 1851
Location: Port Orford
War: Rogue River War
Capt. William Tichenor hoped to found a settlement at the present site of Port Orford, and sailed there with a crew of nine on the *Sea Gull*. With a cannon, the men put ashore to begin setting out a townsite and camped atop what became known as Battle Rock. The ship was scheduled to return about 13 days later.

Approximately 100 natives who had performed a war dance nearby approached the camp and were repulsed by a blast of the cannon. While confusion reigned, the whites rushed the natives and caused them to retreat. Seventeen natives were killed and more were wounded. Two of the white party were wounded by arrows. They fled from the area to safety with the natives at Coos Bay.
Sources: 337

OR11   *Attack on Wagon Train* • June 17, 1851
Location: South side of Klamath River
War: Rogue River War
In response to the attacks on various native settlements by a band of white volunteers organized in Yreka, California, a party of Shastas attacked the pack train of Ford, Penny, Homan & Company between Indian Creek and the Scott River. Three of the packers were killed.
Sources: 337

OR12   *Attack on Kearny Party* • June 17, 1851
Location: Up the Rogue River from Table Rock
War: Rogue River War
Maj. Philip Kearny and 28 soldiers entered the Rogue Valley on their way to San Francisco, and were attacked by a band of Rogue warriors. Capt. James Stuart was mortally wounded and two other soldiers received less serious wounds. At least 17 natives were killed.
Sources: 337

OR13   *Skirmishes in the Rogue Valley* • June 23–26, 1851
Location: Near the Rogue River
War: Rogue River War
Maj. Philip Kearny was supported by volunteers led by settler Joseph Lane, and together they skirmished with the Rogues on June 23, 25 and 26. Including the attack on June 17, Lane's estimate of native casualties was at least 50 killed or wounded.
Sources: 337

OR14   *Attack on Coquille River* • September 14, 1851
Location: Coquille River
War: Rogue River War
William G. T'Vault led a party in an attempt to establish a route from the Port Orford settlement to Fort Umpqua. While they were on the south fork of the Coquille River, they were attacked by Coquille warriors coming from a village on the north bank. Several of the explorers were wounded, and reached Port Orford two days later.
Sources: 337

OR15   *Attack on Coquille River* • November 22, 1851
Location: Coquille River
War: Rogue River War
In early November, troops led by Col. Silas Casey moved to the mouth of the Coquille River in preparation for a campaign against the Coquille natives. About 150 warriors exchanged rifle fire with the soldiers on November 5, but no one was killed or wounded.

While some soldiers continued upriver by boat, others quietly approached the Coquille village on foot. When the natives opened fire on the boats, they were overrun by foot soldiers who chased them into the brush. About 15 warriors were killed, as were two soldiers.
Sources: 337

OR16   *Attacks in the Rogue Valley* • August 17, 1853
Location: Rogue River Valley
War: Rogue River War
On August 13, farmers from the Bear Creek area fled to the cabins of Dunn and Alberding. On August 17, those cabins were attacked by Rogue warriors. On the same day, the Rogues killed John Gibbs, William Hudgins and three others.

The Rogues also opened fire on 15 immigrants who were entering Oregon on the Applegate Trail. Hugh Smith was killed and five others were wounded.
Sources: 337

OR17 *Attack Near Evans Creek* • August 24, 1853
Location: Jacksonville, near Evans Creek
War: Rogue River War
Col. John E. Ross, Lt. Alden and Gen. Lane led parties of soldiers along Evans Creek and the Rogue River in search of natives. They came upon recently abandoned camps on August 23 and stopped for the night.

The next morning, they surprised the Rogues at their new camp. In the first attack, Lt. Alden and Capt. Pleasant Armstrong were killed. Soon after, Gen. Lane was seriously wounded. After about four hours of fighting, natives told Lane that they wanted peace, and they met with the soldiers about a week later and agreed to terms.

Eight Rogues died during the battle, and seven more died later from their wounds.
Sources: 91, 337

OR18 *Skirmishes on the Illinois River* • September, 1853
Location: Illinois River
War: Rogue River War
On September 12, warriors attacked prospectors at the placer bars on the river. On the same day, Robert Williams led a group of volunteers in a battle with warriors on the Applegate Trail and wounded about 12 natives, but was not able to get them to surrender.

On September 22, Capt. Smith of Camp Alden sent troops to the area, and they found the natives at their camp in the Siskiyous. In their attack, they killed about 15 natives, took 16 horses, and burned much of the warriors' personal possessions. Two soldiers were wounded, and four more were wounded in an ambush later in the day.
Sources: 337

OR19 *Nasomah Massacre* • January 29, 1854
Location: Coos County, at the mouth of the Coquille River
War: Rogue River War
Miners in this area gathered to share complaints about the Nasomah band of the lower Coquilles. After a second such meeting, 40 of them reassembled at dawn under the leadership of George H. Abbott and attacked the village while its natives slept. The whites killed 15 men and one woman, and wounded two others.
Sources: 337

OR20 *Attack at the Chetco River* • February 15, 1854
Location: Near the mouth of the Chetco River
War: Rogue River War
A band of Coquille natives had operated a ferry on the Chetco River for decades, until A.F. Miller arrived in late 1853. Despite their protests, he built a cabin in the midst of one of their two villages and announced that he was going to control the ferry. After he promised peace, the natives gave up their guns.

Miller and friends from the Smith River attacked the two villages and killed 12 men, allowing most of the women and children to escape.
Sources: 337

OR21 *Attack Along the Illinois River* • January, 1855
Location: Illinois River
War: Rogue River War
Nineteen out-of-work miners from Sailor's Diggings planned attacks at snow-bound native villages along the Illinois River. At one, they found only seven women and three children. They shot one woman nine times and killed the children.
Sources: 337

OR22 *Attack on Wagon Train* • September 25, 1855
Location: Siskiyou Mountains
War: Rogue River War
A band of natives led by Tipsey stole a horse in August and ambushed the white pursuers. In September, they burned fence rails at Vannoy's Ferry, stole from a settler named Walker, and shot cattle at Tuft's Ranch.
On September 25, they attacked a wagon train, killing two men and chasing the survivors along the trail.
Sources: 337

OR23 *Attacks in the Rogue Valley* • October 9, 1855
Location: Near Grants Pass and Simcoe Valley
War: Rogue River War
A band of Rogues on their reservation murdered William Guin, an agency employee. Some then went to Fort Lane to seek protection from its commander. Others began a series of attacks in the Rogue Valley.
On October 9, they attacked Jacob B. Wagner's ranch and murdered his wife and daughter and visitor Sarah Pellett. They attacked the ranch of George W. Harris and killed him and wounded his daughter. Frank Reed and David Harris were killed by their cabin. Four were killed at the Haines place, as were J.K. Jones and his wife. At Evans Ferry, they killed Isaac Shelton. Mr. Hamilton was killed by the river crossing near Jewett's claim and four teamsters were killed in the Willamette Valley.
Sources: 91, 132, 337

OR24 *Battle at Skull Bar* • October 17, 1855
Location: Mouth of Galice Creek
War: Rogue River War
A band of Rogues attacked the cabin and temporary breastwork at a miner's camp near Skull Bar. The fight lasted eight hours until dark, when the natives withdrew. Of the 40 miners and packers, four died and 11 more were wounded.
Sources: 337

OR25 *Attack on Supply Wagons* • October 24, 1855
Location: Cow Creek
War: Rogue River War
The Rogues attacked hog drovers and supply wagons, killing Hollen Bailey. They then continued down the creek and burned barns, cabins and fences, driving the settlers from the area.
Sources: 337

OR26 *Attack at Looking Glass Prairie* • October 25, 1855
Location: Umpqua River
War: Rogue River War
A band of white volunteers attacked a peaceful native village, killing at least five. This band of natives had previously lived peacefully along with their white neighbors.
Sources: 337

OR27 *Battle of Hungry Hill* • October 31–November 1, 1855
Location: Grave Creek
War: Rogue River War
On October 24, soldiers from Fort Orford were ambushed by a party of Rogues. Lt. Kautz was shot in the chest, but was saved when the ball struck his pocket diary. The troops retreated to Fort Lane, leaving two dead soldiers.

When the party returned, Capt. Smith left Camp Stewart with 105 soldiers and other companies met up with them at the crossing at Grave Creek. Together, the 250 men headed toward the ambush site. On October 31, they charged the Rogues, who were on the summit of a bald peak. Arrows and bullets forced the soldiers back down the mountain.

On November 1, the Rogues surrounded and rushed the soldiers' camp, but were forced back after four hours of fighting. The soldiers left the area and stayed two days at Camp Allaston on Grave Creek. The volunteers took their wounded to Six Bit House, an inn and tavern on Wolf Creek.

The volunteers had seven killed and 20 wounded, the soldiers had four killed and seven wounded, and about 20 warriors were killed.
Sources: 91, 337

OR28 *Attack at Whiskey Creek* • November 25, 1855
Location: Rogue River
War: Rogue River War
Maj. James Bruce led a contingent of 286 soldiers in an effort to attack the natives' stronghold near Little Meadows. They were discovered chopping wood to build rafts for the trip across the Rogue River, and were attacked by the Rogues. A day-long exchange of gunfire resulted in the death of one white and four wounded, while the Rogues had about two or three casualties.
Sources: 337

OR29 *Raid on Fort Henrietta* • December 4, 1855
Location: Butler Creek
War: Cayuse War
The soldiers constructed Fort Henrietta, named after James Heller's wife, near the confluence of Butler Creek and the Umatilla River. At the beginning of December, Col. James K. Kelly led most of his troops from the fort to Fort Walla Walla and up the Walla Walla River, where he planned to attack the Cayuses by surprise.

While they were away from the fort, warriors attacked and killed a horse guard, Pvt. William Andrews. They took both his scalp and the facial skin including his beard. They also stole the post's pack animals.
Sources: 81

OR30 *Fort Miner Massacre* • February 22, 1856

Location: Gold Beach

The Gold Beach volunteer guard had planned an all-night dance to celebrate the birthday of George Washington. A party of Tututni attacked near dawn.

Nine of the 14 men present were shot down at the first charge. The other five dived into the brush and escaped. Some leaving from the party heard the cries of the warriors and screams of the volunteers, and paddled their canoe away as fast as they could. Others in Gold Beach rushed across the Rogue River and took refuge in a half-completed stockade, working on it during that night. They called it Fort Miner.

Including a sweep through nearby settlements, the natives killed 23 and burned nearly every building they found. The survivors at Gold Beach waited for help from other locations. Eight of the Port Orford volunteers rowed down the coast to see the damage, but they overturned in the surf and six drowned.

During the first week of March, seven of the survivors hiked to a potato field and were ambushed, with only two making it back to Fort Miner.

Sources: 337

OR31 *Ambush at the Pistol River* • March 18, 1856

Location: South bank of the Pistol River

War: Rogue River War

George H. Abbot led a group of volunteers who were anxious to be the first to arrive at Fort Miner and assist the besieged settlers. They walked into an ambush in the dunes on the southern shore of the river and engaged the Rogues in a day-long battle. Only one man was killed.

On March 21, government troops, the Crescent City Guard and men from Port Orford arrived to give the settlers freedom from attack.

Sources: 337

OR32 *Battle with Rogues* • March 22, 1856

Location: Near Skookum House Prairie

War: Rogue River War

On March 19, troops led by Capt. Christopher C. Augur burned villages at the Rogue and Illinois River fork and in a skirmish with the Shasta Costas, killed five. Troops from Fort Lane arrived on March 22 and exchanged gunfire with the Rogues, suffering two casualties.

Col. Robert C. Buchanan sent Capts. E.O.C. Ord and DeLancey Floyd-Jones with 112 men to the principal Mikonotunne village near Skookum House Prairie. When they started to burn abandoned stores and plank houses, the Rogues opened fire. In close combat, at least five warriors died, and three drowned attempting to flee in canoes. Rather than risk casualties in a chase, Buchanan chose to return to Fort Miner.

Sources: 182

OR33 *Attack on Pack Train* • March 23, 1856

Location: Between Crescent City and the Illinois Valley

War: Rogue River War

A party of Rogues attacked a pack train, killing four men and taking 28 mules carrying ammunition and supplies.

Sources: 337

OR34 *Raid on Fort Henrietta* • April 20, 1856
Location: Butler Creek
War: Cayuse War
Sixty natives raided the area around Fort Henrietta, killing and scalping horse guard Pvt. Lot Hollinger and running off the post's horses.
Sources: 81

OR35 *Ambush on Lobster Creek* • April 22, 1856
Location: Mouth of Lobster Creek
War: Rogue River War
A company of Gold Beach Guard headed up the Rogue River to the mouth of Lobster Creek and concealed themselves behind boulders. Two canoes came down the creek shortly after sunrise, carrying 12 men and three women. The volunteers opened fire and killed 12 of the natives.
Sources: 337

OR36 *Attack at the Chetco River* • April 29, 1856
Location: Chetco River
War: Rogue River War
Col. Robert C. Buchanan bought supplies for his men in Crescent City and ordered Capt. E.O.C. Ord and his troops to accompany the packers on their trip from headquarters to the boundary of California. As they crossed the Chetco River, they were attacked by natives. Although the troops chased 70 from their initial position, they continued to fire on the men and mules in the river.

Several natives were killed, as was an army sergeant who lost in hand-to-hand combat with a warrior he had forced into the water.
Sources: 91, 337

OR37 *Battle of Big Bend* • May 27–28, 1856
Location: Big Bend
War: Rogue River War
The Rogues agreed to peace terms with Col. Robert C. Buchanan, and he sent soldiers toward Big Bend to accept their surrender. While the natives were on their way to the surrender point, a company of volunteers attacked them. Several wounded and defeated warriors were shot down in their canoes or on the trails along the river.

The Rogues now believed that instead of marching to surrender, they were about to be exterminated. When they reached the Big Bend surrender point on May 27, they charged the ridge and killed four soldiers, wounding 15.

The next morning, the attack began again and the battle raged for 12 hours. Fresh troops led by Capt. Christopher C. Augur chased the Rogues to the river bank, where they surrendered. Army casualties consisted of seven killed and 20 wounded.
Sources: 91, 254, 337

OR38 *Attack Near Big Meadows* • May 27, 1856
Location: Near Big Meadows
War: Rogue River War
Five hundred thirty-five men commanded by Maj. James Bruce and William

Latshaw camped at Little Meadows, and found many natives between there and Big Meadows. They sent small parties to try and draw the natives into a weak position, but they refused to take the bait.

On April 27, 100 volunteers marched through the mountains and descended the bluffs to fire on the village from across the river. They surprised the natives, who ran for the woods. One volunteer and 20 to 30 natives were killed.
Sources: 337, 380

OR39 *Burning of Village* • June 5, 1856
Location: Near Copper Canyon
War: Rogue River War
While the Rogues were still assembling at the Big Bend surrender point, soldiers went downstream to force remaining hostile bands from the Copper Canyon area. Led by John Reynolds, they burned a Shasta Costa village and killed four natives who were fishing.

At about the same time, volunteers from the Gold Beach Guard went to Painted Rock and killed eight men, seized four canoes, and took 12 women and children captive.
Sources: 337

OR40 *Battle of the Grande Ronde* • July 17, 1856
Location: 8 miles southeast of Elgin
War: Cayuse War
While along the Grande Ronde River to harvest roots, several Cayuses and Walla Wallas were visited by militia led by Capt. John, and a heated exchange of words resulted. The volunteers formed a line and charged, causing the Cayuses to flee. As they ran for cover, the troops killed old men, women and children. Twenty-seven were killed in the initial attack area, and about 13 more were killed in the area as they tried to escape. The whites had five killed and four wounded.
Sources: 81, 285

OR41 *Battle of Lost River* • November 29, 1872
Location: Northwest corner of Tule Lake, at the mouth of the Lost River
War: Modoc War
The warlike Modocs raided other native tribes, and starting in the 1850s, the white settlers who were coming into their homeland along the border of Oregon and California. In 1864, they were placed on a reservation with the Klamaths, their historic enemies. A band of Modocs left the reservation in 1865 under the leadership of Kintpuash (Captain Jack). He returned in 1869, and soon the tribe had insufficient food and left again with 371 warriors. In 1872, the new agent decided to move them back to the reservation by force.

Captain Jack led his Modocs off of their Klamath reservation when they became hungry, and established a camp in the Lost River Valley. They were ordered back to the reservation, but instead requested their own reservation in the valley. That was refused, and the army was assigned the task of moving the Modocs back to the reservation by force.

Capt. James Jackson led 38 soldiers from the 1st Cavalry to the Modoc camp and ordered the warriors to place their guns on the ground near the soldiers. Captain Jack did so, and instructed his men to follow suit. They did, but Scarfaced

Charlie refused to give up his pistol. Tempers flared, and shots were exchanged by Scarfaced Charlie and Lt. Frazier Boutelle. The warriors picked up their rifles and about five minutes of gunfire erupted. The soldiers retreated after having one killed and seven wounded.

While this action took place, the women and children were paddling south toward Tule Lake. The warriors traveled along the shore and met up with them later.

Sources: 69, 70, 91, 197, 254, 262, 263, 397

OR42 *Battle of Big Camp Prairie* • Spring, 1878
Location: Big Camp Prairie
War: Bannock War

A large party of warriors raided the Big Camp Prairie. Afterwards, Buffalo Horn and Egan headed toward the Malheur Reservation to meet dissident Paiutes led by Otis. They then headed north toward the Columbia River in an attempt to recruit others to fight against the whites.

Sources: 132

OR43 *Battle of Pilot Rock* • July 8, 1878
Location: Birch Creek north of Pendleton
War: Bannock War

Troops from Fort Boise commanded by Gen. Oliver O. Howard caught up with the Bannocks and Northern Paiutes near Birch Creek. They were dislodged by the soldiers from the steep bluffs and warriors attempted to hide out at the Umatilla Reservation.

Unfortunately for the warriors, the Umatillas were allied with the whites and killed Egan. Oytes turned himself in during August, and a group of Bannocks who had made it to Wyoming were captured in September.

Sources: 66, 91, 134

OR44 *Attack at John Day River* • July 20, 1878
Location: North Fork of John Day River
War: Bannock War

Brevet Brig. Gen. James W. Forsyth arrived from Chicago to command the 1st Cavalry. They flanked the natives out of a strong position in a canyon, causing the defenders to break and scatter. This ended the Bannock War.

Sources: 66, 91

PENNSYLVANIA

PA1 *Skirmish at Jumonville Glen* • May 27–28, 1754
Location: 7½ miles northwest of Great Meadows
War: French and Indian War

Lt. Col. George Washington led a small band of Virginia militiamen to build a military road into the Ohio Valley, in preparation for a campaign against the French by Lt. Gov. Robert Dinwiddie. They were accompanied by Monakaduto and 150 Seneca scouts. En route, the Senecas reported that a party of 32 French soldiers commanded by Joseph Coulon de Villiers, Sieur de Jumonville, was camped nearby.

Washington took his 40 men, along with Monakaduto and seven warriors, and surrounded the French camp. Early in the morning, they opened fire and rushed in with bayonets, catching the French off guard. Ten were killed, 21 were captured, and one escaped. The French dead were scalped by the Senecas, and Washington presented Monakaduto with Jumonville's scalp to take to the natives as an encouragement for them to ally with the British.

The British lost only one and had three wounded in the 15-minute battle, ended by a French surrender. They returned to Great Meadows and built Fort Necessity.

Monument: The preserved battlefield is reached by driving west from the Fort Necessity Visitors Center 4.9 miles on US 40 to Mount Summit, turning right on Jumonville Rd. (LR 26115), and continuing north for 2.5 miles.

Sources: 5, 19, 32, 33, 34, 55, 123, 131, 133, 164, 316, 318, 374, 381, 412

PA2   *Attack on Fort Necessity* • July 3–4, 1754
Location: Farmington
War: French and Indian War
In April, Lt. Col. George Washington and 120 men had come to this part of the Ohio Valley to protect the 40 Virginia frontiersmen erecting a British fort at the present site of Pittsburgh. Seneca chief Tanaghrisson, also known as the Half King, had supported and advised the fort builders, and protected them from the French.

The fort was attacked on July 4 by 600 French and 100 natives, attempting to avenge what they characterized as the assassination of the French party at Jumonville Glen. They were led by Louis Coulon de Villiers. The natives with the French included Wyandots, Ojibwas, Abenakis, Nipissings, Ottawas, Algonquins and Iroquois. After eight hours of fighting and at least 40 English casualties, the natives deserted and Washington agreed to a surrender, turning the fort over to the French. They allowed the British to depart for Virginia on July 4, and then destroyed the fort.

Monument: A reconstructed fort and museum are located at Fort Necessity National Battlefield, US 40E, P.O. Box 528, Farmington, PA.

Sources: 5, 14, 19, 33, 34, 55, 78, 131, 147, 164, 293, 316, 318, 324, 374, 389, 412

PA3   *Rout of Braddock* or *Battle of the Monongahela* • July 9, 1755
Location: 6 miles east of Pittsburgh
War: French and Indian War
Maj. Gen. Edward Braddock insulted several tribes, including the Shawnees and Delawares, who then sided with the French. They comprised about two thirds of the 850 to 900 fighters who attacked Braddock and his men as they approached Fort Duquesne, as part of a grand plan to end the war. The French were led by Capt. Pierre de Contrecoeur, who was also supported by Ottawas and Potawatomis from the Detroit area.

Braddock's forces, including eight Mingos led by Monacatootha, traveled westward from Fort Cumberland in Maryland through a dark pine wood called "The Shades of Death" to begin a siege on Fort Duquesne. A force led by Daniel Hyacinthe de Beaujeu, consisting of 250 Canadian soldiers and 500 natives, headed south to meet the approaching British.

Braddock's force, slowed by fever and dysentery, became trapped in a narrow ravine largely because he chose not to fight with irregular lines and concealment from the enemy. Initially, he could not even see his adversaries, who were well concealed. Beaujeu was cut down early by British gunfire, and was succeeded in command by Capt. Jean-Daniel Dumas. The British suffered heavy casualties before retreating to Fort Necessity. Braddock died five days later from the wounds incurred in the battle and was buried about a mile west of the Fort Necessity ruins.

Braddock's aide de camp, George Washington, had two horses shot out from under him, but was not himself injured. When Braddock went down, Washington took command.

The French and their allies suffered only 16 casualties, while 977 of Braddock's 1,459 men were killed or wounded. The 500 horses and 100 oxen of the British became the prize of the French. The road cut by Braddock's army over what had been the Nemacolin Trail became a main route for westward-bound settlers for the next 75 years.

Braddock's defeat nearly drove the Iroquois to ally with the French, because of doubts about the ability of England to protect them.

Monument: Braddock's grave is on US 40, a mile west of Fort Necessity National Battlefield in Farmington.

Sources: 19, 20, 27, 32, 33, 34, 55, 65, 67, 78, 99, 119, 120, 123, 126, 147, 164, 210, 214, 221, 238, 242, 243, 257, 284, 293, 300, 304, 305, 310, 316, 318, 323, 324, 336, 339, 364, 369, 374, 381, 388, 389, 391, 412, 415

PA4   *Attack on Moravian Village* • November, 1755
Location: Northampton County
War: French and Indian War
A Moravian village two miles northeast of Bethlehem on the Lehigh River was attacked by natives. This was one of a series of attacks in Northampton County, resulting in the deaths of 115 settlers by September of 1757.
Sources: 412

PA5   *Capture of Fort Granville* • August 2, 1756
Location: Fort Granville
War: French and Indian War
A force led by Captain Jacobs, the leader of the Delawares, and French officer Coulon de Villiers, captured and burned British Fort Granville.
Sources: 55

PA6   *Raid on Kittanning* • September 8, 1756
Location: Kittanning
War: French and Indian War
In Kittanning on September 7, the Delawares danced and celebrated their capture and destruction of British Fort Granville. They were watched by a party

from Lt. Col. John Armstrong's 2nd Pennsylvania Battalion, consisting of 300 men.

Shortly after dawn on September 8, the soldiers advanced upon the homes and killed the waking natives with muskets, bayonets and fire. After a brief exchange of gunfire with a small party of French soldiers, the battle ended when all of the surviving defenders left the area. Casualties included 40 dead Delawares and 30 burned homes.

Sources: 55

PA7   *Defense of Fort Duquesne* • September 14, 1758
Location: Near Pittsburgh
War: French and Indian War
In 1758, Ottawas and Potawatomis helped defend the French fort in another British attack, led by Swiss mercenary Col. Henry Bouquet. Bouquet was persuaded by Maj. James Grant to allow him to rush the fort with a force of 842 soldiers and 27 Catawba scouts, but when he reached the fort he closed ranks and marched with the accompaniment of bagpipers. The natives set an ambush and killed 270, wounding 42 and taking 100 prisoner, including Grant and Maj. Andrew Lewis.

The natives felt that their service to the French was complete and returned to Detroit. From November 19–24, with an army led by Gen. Forbes approaching, the French burned Fort Duquesne and moved to Fort Venango on the Allegheny River. The British moved in, erected temporary palisades in 1759, and then rebuilt the fort on 17½ acres, naming it Fort Pitt.

Museums: (1) The Pennsylvania Military Museum, US 322, Boalsburg, PA, has exhibits illustrating Pennsylvania's participation in the French and Indian War; (2) Fort Pitt Museum is located at 101 Commonwealth Pl., Point State Park, Pittsburgh.

Sources: 19, 55, 90, 131, 299, 317, 318, 322, 332, 336, 374, 381

PA8   *Raid on Loyalhannon* • October 12, 1758
Location: Loyalhannon Creek
War: French and Indian War
A force of 440 French Canadians and 150 natives attacked the English position on Loyalhannon Creek on the east side of the Allegheny River, led by Charles Phillipe d'Aubry. They intended to hurt the English morale and delay their advance into the area.

The French were met by 60 rangers set out from Fort Ligonier by commander Col. Burd. They were supposed to determine the strength of the oncoming force, but the party was defeated. When Burd sent out 500 more men, the French drove them back. Burd shelled the French with mortars and howitzers, with little effect. The French rounded up the few horses that they could find near the fort.

Sources: 55

PA9   *Massacre at Dunkard Creek* • Early 1759
Location: Dunkard Creek
War: French and Indian War
After the fall of Fort Duquesne in September of 1758, settlers from Virginia and

eastern Pennsylvania streamed into the area between the Allegheny Mountains and the Monongahela and Allegheny Rivers. The Dunkard Creek settlement was established where it emptied into the Monongahela by the three Eckerley brothers, and within six months natives destroyed it and killed two of the brothers. Dr. Thomas Eckerley was spared only because he was away on a fur trading excursion.
Sources: 374

PA10   *Assassination of Teedyuscung* • April 19, 1763
Location: Wyoming
War: French and Indian War
Arsonists, probably men of Connecticut's Susquehannah Company, burned the Delawares' cabins that had been built for them by the Quakers. Their inhabitants were driven away except for Teedyuscung, leader of the eastern Delawares, who burned to death in his cabin.
Sources: 131

PA11   *Attack on Clapham Settlement* • May, 1763
Location: 25 miles southeast of Pittsburgh
War: French and Indian War
Col. William Clapham set up a new settlement about 25 miles southeast of Fort Pitt in the Monongahela valley. They were attacked by a party of 20 Delawares led by Chief Wolf, resulting in the death of Clapham, one of his men, a child and two women.
Sources: 374

PA12   *Siege of Fort Pitt* • May 27–August 1, 1763
Location: Pittsburgh
War: Pontiac's Rebellion
Pucksinwah's Shawnees, Delawares and Mingos from Ohio laid siege to Fort Pitt, garrisoned by Capt. Simeon Ecuyer and 338 men, some of whom were suffering with smallpox. On June 24, two Delawares met with him and told of the fall of the other forts, suggesting that he surrender before the other tribes arrived to form a massive force to bring down Fort Pitt. The natives broke off the siege when they learned that Col. Henry Bouquet and 460 soldiers were on the march toward them.

   In the first recorded instance of germ warfare, Ecuyer gave the Delawares a gift of blankets and a handkerchief taken from smallpox patients. Having essentially no resistance to the disease, the members of these three tribes quickly spread the epidemic.
Sources: 131, 147, 187, 315, 324, 336, 349, 374, 412

PA13   *Siege of Fort Ligonier* • June, 1763
Location: Ligonier
War: French and Indian War
Fort Ligonier was attacked on June 4 at 5:00 a.m. by warriors shooting from the edge of the woods. Inside, under the leadership of Lt. Archibald Blane, were the inhabitants of Bushy Run and Stony Creek. Over the next few days, some of the horses were stolen.

Communications were cut off from Fort Pitt on June 17, and four days later some soldiers were allowed to leave the fort to pursue the natives. Four hundred yards from the fort, a hundred waited in ambush, but none of the party of soldiers was hit. This was the only small fort in the region which did not fall to attacks.
Sources: 234, 412

PA14   *Attack at Fort Venango* • June 16, 1763
Location: 80 miles north of Pittsburgh
War: Pontiac's Rebellion
A war party of Senecas and Shawnees attacked Fort Venango and wiped out the contingent of soldiers stationed there. Years later, a Seneca who claimed to have been there said that they had gotten into the fort on the pretense of talking to its commander. They then killed all but the commander, Lt. Gordon. He was brought out each evening and was partly roasted over a slow fire until he died on the fifth day.
Sources: 123, 315, 324, 336, 412

PA15   *Capture of Fort LeBoeuf* • June 18, 1763
Location: North of Fort Venango
War: Pontiac's Rebellion
Ensign George Price, two corporals and 11 soldiers occupied the blockhouse known as Fort LeBoeuf. Shawnees and Senecas arrived from the direction of Presqu' Isle and demanded ammunition, which Price denied. Other natives took positions around the blockhouse, shot flaming arrows and burned it down. Price and his men escaped through a window and walked to Fort Venango, only to find it reduced to ashes.
Sources: 234, 315, 324, 336, 412

PA16   *Destruction of Fort Presqu' Isle* • June 20–21, 1763
Location: Erie
War: Pontiac's Rebellion
This fort was attacked by 200 Senecas, Ottawas, Hurons and Chippewas who shot at the blockhouse all day. On the next day, they attacked and entered the fort, getting as far as the commanding officer's room on the parade, which they burned. The Hurons suggested that the soldiers surrender, and agreed to let them leave with six days' provisions if they did.
    Ensign John Christie led his men out, but the warriors massacred all but three. Christie and the two other survivors fled into the woods.
Sources: 315, 412

PA17   *Battle of Bushy Run* • August 5, 1763
Location: Edge Hill, east of Pittsburgh
War: Pontiac's Rebellion
Following the French and Indian War, the British held Fort Pitt, later to become Pittsburgh, and although it was strong, it was exposed. Col. Henry Bouquet was ordered to bring supplies and reinforcements to it. As they came within 26 miles of the fort after a 17-mile march, they were attacked by Delawares, Mingoes, Hurons and Shawnees at Bushy Run. After dark, they built a fort of flour bags on top of a grassy knoll called Edge Hill.

After a sleepless night, the British feigned a retreat over the top of Edge Hill. As the natives advanced to take advantage of it, they found themselves in a trap. The soldiers killed many with inaccurate "Brown Bess" muskets and bayonets and caused the rest to flee. Eight officers and 116 soldiers were killed. Native losses totalled 22.

Four days later, the troops reached the fort and were successful in lifting the siege which had been laid by the natives. Bouquet's plan to continue the fight against the natives was put on hold because he lacked the manpower to do more than help reinforce the existing forts. More than a year later, he launched an expedition westward which involved the negotiation of the release of prisoners and peace with several tribes.

Monument: A limestone memorial with a bronze plaque is located on Edge Hill in the 183-acre Bushy Run Battlefield on Bushy Run Rd., Jennette, PA.

Sources: 14, 19, 90, 120, 131, 133, 139, 234, 318, 322, 374, 388

PA18 *Massacre of Christian Susquehannocks* • December 14, 1763
Location: Conestoga
War: French and Indian War
During the winter of 1763, four upper Susquehanna villages were destroyed by an expedition planned by Sir William Johnson and led by Andrew Montour, consisting largely of Mohawk and Oneida volunteers.

The 20 last surviving Susquehannocks attempted to live peacefully under the protection of the Pennsylvania government. The Paxton Boys, a mob of border ruffians led by a hysterical elder of the Presbyterian Church, murdered six of the Susquehannocks a few miles north of Harris' Ferry as revenge for Pontiac's War. The remaining 14 were taken to a workhouse in Lancaster for protection.

The Paxton Boys, 57 Scotch-Irish Presbyterian men from Paxton along the Susquehannock River, followed them and on December 27, broke into the workhouse and slaughtered them all.

Sources: 3, 90, 92, 131, 135, 147, 199, 275, 299, 380, 412

PA19 *Attack Along the Ohio River* • May, 1765
Location: Ohio River
War: Pontiac's Rebellion
Sir William Johnson assigned Indian agent Maj. George Croghan to bring Pontiac to the treaty council and formally end the hostilities. He stayed at Fort Pitt, assembling a balanced delegation of Delawares, Shawnees and Senecas to go with him. Pontiac had finally been convinced that the Ohio natives had made their peace, and that the French had confirmed that they had made peace with the British.

Between the leaving of an advance party on March 22 and Croghan's departure on May 15, some of the natives began to vacillate, the French spread rumors, and hostile acts continued to occur. When Croghan and his party were on the Ohio River, he lost two whites and three natives. The attackers had been told by the French that the natives accompanying Croghan were Cherokees, enemies from the south. When they discovered their mistake, they made peace with the British and gave them back their forts.

Croghan and Pontiac met at Fort Ouiatenon to discuss the terms of a treaty. Pontiac wanted it to provide that the lands still belonged to the natives, and that the British would only occupy it as their guests. Croghan agreed, even though he knew that his superiors back east would not allow this. They then met with other tribes' representatives at Fort Detroit on August 17, and agreed to the same condition.

Pontiac was killed on April 20, 1769, by a member of the Peoria tribe. He was unarmed and was struck from behind with a war club and then stabbed as he exited a trading post in Cahokia, Illinois.

Sources: 322

PA20   *Attack at Forty Fort* or *Wyoming Massacre* or
            Battle of Wyoming • July 3, 1778
Location: Near the intersection of River and Fort Sts., Kingston
War: Revolutionary War
English Col. John Butler brought a column of 450 from New York into the Wyoming Valley, capturing and burning two stockades without a fight. As they approached Forty Fort, a force of American defenders rushed to attack them.

Hundreds of Iroquois sprang from concealment and attacked the Americans, causing them to panic and flee. As they retreated, many were killed by tomahawks. Others were burned or tortured to death. The English reported 227 scalps and five prisoners taken, with a death toll perhaps as high as 400. English casualties were reported as three deaths and eight Iroquois wounded.

The survivors in the fort surrendered the following day and were permitted to leave the area unharmed.

Monument: A marker for the battle is located five miles from Wilkes-Barre, PA, on the west bank of the Susquehanna River, reached via SR 11.

Sources: 3, 83, 123, 234, 288, 325, 379

PA21   *Attack on Fort Hand* • April 26, 1779
Location: Along the Kiskeminetas River, about 8 miles from the Allegheny River
War: Revolutionary War
Fort Hand, under the command of Capt. Samuel Moorehead and Lt. William Jack, was manned with poorly trained militia. Although they successfully resisted the superior force of 100 Senecas and Mingoes, Sgt. Philip McGraw was killed and Sgt. Leonard McCauley was severely wounded.

Sources: 374

PA22   *Attack on Sykes Cabin* • April 26, 1779
Location: Near Redstone
War: Revolutionary War
A party of Delawares attacked the home of George Sykes along the Monongahela River. Sykes had traveled to Brownsville for supplies, and when he returned the same day, his cabin had been burned down and his wife and six children were missing. They were released 16 years later.

Sources: 374

PA23   *Attack on Sanford Cabin* • Spring, 1779
Location: Southwest of Potter's Fort
War: Revolutionary War
A party of Wyandots attacked the home of Abraham Sanford on Bald Eagle Creek,

130 miles east of Pittsburgh. Sanford and one daughter escaped through a window, but seven other members of his family were killed.
Sources: 374

PA24 *Ambush at Brady's Bend* • August 25, 1779
Location: Allegheny River
War: Revolutionary War
Col. Daniel Broadhead led a force up the Allegheny River and sent Capt. Samuel Brady ahead with an advance unit. As guides, Brady used Jonathan Zane and Thomas Nicholson. Four Delawares joined them, totalling 30 in the advance unit.

When they reached Brady's Bend, they took cover and were passed by a war party of 40 Wyandots, Munceys and Senecas with rifles, tomahawks and knives, led by Bald Eagle. The warriors reached the main party of Broadhead and, in the face of gunfire, retreated back the way they came. As they came by the advance unit, Brady shot and killed Bald Eagle. Four more were killed and others were wounded. The rest ran out of range before the soldiers could reload.
Sources: 374

PA25 *Battle at Brokenstraw Creek* • Early September, 1779
Location: Allegheny River
War: Revolutionary War
Col. Daniel Broadhead's army traveled along the Allegheny River, burning the villages they found, including Venango on French Creek next to Fort Machault. About three miles downstream from the mouth of Dagahshenodeago (Brokenstraw Creek), Capt. Samuel Brady's advance party sighted a war party of Senecas and Munceys, led by Dehguswaygahent ("The Fallen Board") and Dayoosta ("It Is Light To Be Lifted"). Tom Nicholson volunteered to lure them to shore.

When they left their canoes on the river bank, one warrior sighted a different white man, so Nicholson ducked behind a tree and Brady's party opened fire. In the early shooting, Seneca subchief Dahgahgahend ("White Eye") was killed, as was Dehguswaygahent. Fifteen were killed and 14 were wounded, while the whites had none killed and only a few wounded.

The soldiers scalped the dead and took their weapons and the wounded were sent to Fort Pitt.
Sources: 374

PA26 *Destruction of Hannastown* • July 13, 1782
Location: Hannastown
War: Revolutionary War
Hannastown was attacked and burned by 100 Senecas and 60 Canadian Rangers who had arrived by canoes on the Allegheny River. Sixty settlers with nine rifles retreated to a stockade and unsuccessfully attempted to defend their village.
Sources: 90, 123

PA27 *Attacks at Dunkard Creek* • March, 1789
Location: Dunkard Creek
A party of warriors attacked the homes of William Thomas and Joseph Cambridge. Thomas and the entire Cambridge family were killed.
Sources: 374

PA28   *Attack at Dunkard Creek* • May 1, 1791
Location: Dunkard Creek
War: Ohio Indian Wars
Susan, Elizabeth, Christiana and Catherine Crow were attacked while bringing in their cows from the pasture between Dunkard and Grave Creeks. Seven Delawares leaped from cover with three rifles and four tomahawks. They ordered the girls to come with them and they did, but after about a 30-yard walk, they broke into a run. As they did, Susan was shot and killed and Catherine was wounded with a tomahawk. Elizabeth and Christiana were killed by tomahawks. Catherine, the only survivor, hid in a hollow tree until she was found by her brothers and father.
Sources: 374

PA29   *Attack on Conneaut Outlet* • June 15, 1795
Location: French Creek
A party of surveyors was attacked at the Samuel Hulings settlement. Three natives believed to be Senecas tomahawked and scalped James Finley and Barney McCormick and captured James Thompson.
Sources: 374

RHODE ISLAND

RI1   *Raid on Pawtuxet* • January 19, 1675
Location: Pawtuxet
War: King Philip's War
Natives staged an early morning raid on the settlement of Pawtuxet and destroyed several buildings. The Carpenter garrison house was saved from fire. Hours after the action, Capts. Samuel Moseley and Sill arrived at the scene, but decided not to follow the natives.
    A band of natives lying in the brush beside a road ambushed Toleration Harris and a black servant, both of whom were killed. The band then burned 50 wagonloads of hay and killed 50 cattle and 80 horses.
Sources: 34, 152

RI2   *Attack at Nipsachuck* • August 1, 1675
Location: 12 miles northwest of Providence
War: King Philip's War
English attackers aided by Mohegan warriors were aware that more troops led by Capt. Daniel Henchman were on their way to increase their numbers, but decided to attack the Wampanoags without further delay. They surprised the warriors led by Onecas at Nipsachuck, and they left their village and abandoned their possessions to the attackers.
    The English and Mohegans continued the attack, which ended at about 9:00

a.m. when the Wampanoags retreated to a swamp. When Henchman arrived he could have pushed the attack and perhaps have finally defeated the Wampanoags, but he delayed until the next day, giving them time to escape.
Sources: 34, 152

RI3   *Attack at Wickford* • December 15, 1675
        Location: Wickford (Smith's Garrison)
        War: King Philip's War
        Stonewall John, a Narragansett native, came to the army headquarters at Wickford supposedly to discuss peace. He aggravated the officers and was told that if there was to be a meaningful discussion, it was the sachems that would have to be involved.
        A few minutes after Stonewall John left the headquarters, a party of natives killed or mortally wounded three of the nearby soldiers. Later in the day, two men in Capt. James Oliver's command were killed at a house about three miles away. Gov. Josiah Winslow sent three companies of soldiers to bring back the company of Capt. Samuel Appleton and on the way, they skirmished with the natives. One native was killed.
        Sources: 152, 188

RI4   *Attack at Bull's Garrison* • December 16, 1675
        Location: Pettaquamscut
        War: King Philip's War
        Most of the people in the garrison house of Jirch Bull, located at Pettaquamscut, were killed by natives and the building was burned down. This was discovered by soldiers sent out by Gov. Josiah Winslow to look for soldiers from Connecticut, who were supposed to be in Rhode Island to help protect the settlers.
        Sources: 152

RI5   *Great Swamp Fight* • December 19, 1675
        Location: South Kingstown Township
        War: King Philip's War
        Josiah Winslow, the governor of Plymouth Colony, and a force of 1,000 United Colonies troops and 150 Mohegans came upon a picket party of natives, with whom they exchanged brief gunfire. They followed them over the frozen swamp and attacked the Narragansetts at their winter fort on a five to six acre island in the middle of the Great Swamp. They were lucky, in that they came upon the fort commanded by Canonchet at its one uncompleted corner, the one weak area of defense.
        The English charged at the corner, and early casualties included Capts. Johnson and Davenport. Some soldiers pushed into the fort, but they were forced out again into the swamp. As other companies arrived, they were able to gain ground inside the stockade. At about 4:00 p.m., the soldiers left the fort to spend the night at Wickford, arriving at about 2:00 a.m. Six hundred to over 1,000 native men, women and children inside the fort had been killed and the village was destroyed. About 300 were taken prisoner and the blacksmith forge was destroyed, temporarily preventing the natives from repairing their guns. About a month later the survivors fled to the Nipmuck country.
        This was the first victory of the war for the colonists, although it was costly

in the loss of seven of the 14 company commanders, plus 70 men killed and 200 injured. With no further decisive action happening, Winslow disbanded his forces on February 5, 1676.

Monuments: (1) There is a plaque commemorating the battle at the northwest end of the Great Swamp, which borders the northwest shore of Worden Pond, 4 miles southwest of West Kingston on SR 136; (2) A statue of King Philip is located just west of SR 1A in the center of Narragansett.

Sources: 34, 53, 96, 125, 135, 150, 152, 188, 199, 226, 251, 268, 270, 272, 274, 284, 288, 310, 315, 334

RI6 *Attack Along Pawtuxet River* • March 26, 1676
Location: 5 miles north of Providence
War: King Philip's War
Capt. Michael Pierce, along with a company of 65 Plymouth Colony men and 20 friendly natives, headed north from Rehoboth to locate a band of the enemy. Expecting trouble, Pierce sent a messenger to Providence to request additional troops, but the messenger waited until after worship services to deliver the message. When he did, Capt. Andrew Edmunds hurried to reach Pierce, but arrived too late.

Pierce's force fought a band of 26 Narragansetts, which surrounded the soldiers. Forty-two of the soldiers died and the survivors barely escaped.
Sources: 34, 152, 188, 315

RI7 *Destruction of Providence* • March 29, 1676
Location: Providence
War: King Philip's War
Following heavy settler losses at Marlboro on March 26 and at Rehoboth on March 29, a band of Narragansetts attacked and destroyed the town of Providence. Roger Williams, a friend of the tribe, considered this to be a betrayal. Williams confronted them on the outskirts of town, and found that one of the reasons the natives gave for the attack was that God favored them.
Sources: 270, 290

RI8 *Attacks on Frontier Towns* • February to May, 1676
Location: Seekonk, near Mount Hope
War: King Philip's War
Wampanoags and Narragansetts attacked the settlement of Providence on March 30, burning much of it.

On April 11, a force of Englishmen led by Capt. George Denison, plus Pequots, Mohegans and Niantics raided the area near Pawtuxet. They killed about 50 and captured 40, including Canonchet (Quononshot or Myantonomy), the son of Miantonomo, who had been previously killed by the Mohegans. Canonchet, the Narragansett sachem, was taken to Stonington, Connecticut, where he refused to swear allegiance to the British. He was shot by the Pequots, beheaded by the Mohegans, and cut up and burned by the Niantics. His head was saved as a trophy and sent to Hartford.
Sources: 125, 225, 226, 274, 315

RI9 *Late Actions* • July to August, 1676
Location: Eastern Rhode Island

War: King Philip's War

Maj. Bradford and Capt. Benjamin Church commanded forces in Massachusetts to patrol the area and protect the settlers from native attacks, which were decreasing in frequency. On July 2, a Connecticut force led by Maj. John Talcott killed 170 natives in a spruce swamp near Pautucket. Those killed included the old squaw sachem, Quaiapen. On their way home, Church's men met and killed another 60.

Sources: 150, 212, 226

RI10   *Battle at Nipsachuck* • July 20, 1676
Location: Northern Rhode Island
War: King Philip's War
A June campaign by the Massachusetts and Connecticut forces combed the Connecticut River valley northward to Northfield, but produced nothing. Afterwards, the Connecticut soldiers had some successes at Nipsachuck against the Narragansetts who had returned to the area.
Sources: 125, 268

RI11   *Death of Philip* • August 12, 1676
Location: Cold Spring, near Mount Hope
War: King Philip's War
Capt. Benjamin Church organized an ambush of King Philip at the chief's headquarters. With Maj. Peleg Sanford and Capts. Golding and William and their 80 men, they approached the camp, leaving an Englishman and a native hidden behind trees. Gunfire into the camp caused the natives to flee, and Philip ran toward the pair who were concealed behind the trees.

Philip was shot and killed by the native, Alderman. As required by English law for those guilty of high treason, Philip was beheaded. After the severed head was carried on a pole through the streets of Plymouth on August 17, it and one of Philip's hands was awarded to Alderman. By autumn, the fighting in this area finally ended.

Monuments: (1) An engraved stone monument south of Bristol, reached via SR 136 (Metacom Ave.) was placed 100 feet east northeast of the spot where Philip fell by the Rhode Island Historical Society in December of 1877; (2) A stone pile known as King Philip's Chair is located on the grounds of the Haffenreffer Museum of Anthropology, which also has exhibits on King Philip.

Sources: 34, 125, 150, 152, 188, 225, 251, 270, 272, 275, 284, 288, 290, 310, 315

SOUTH CAROLINA

SC1   *Battle at San Juan* • November, 1566
Location: Foot of Blue Ridge Mountains
War: Pardo Expedition

Capt. Juan Pardo led an expedition up the Savannah River to northwestern South Carolina and found many natives willing to become subjects of the Spanish government. The Spanish built Fort San Juan, which was garrisoned by 30 soldiers led by Sgt. Boyano.

After Pardo returned to his starting point at Santa Elena on Port Royal Sound, he learned of fighting at San Juan in which more than 1,000 natives were killed. Fifty native homes were burned, and the Spanish only had two wounded. Boyano then sent 20 of his men into the mountains to fight chief Chisca and his people. They set fire to a native fort, burning to death its inhabitants.

Fort San Juan was destroyed and its soldiers were massacred by April of 1584.

Sources: 232, 360

SC2 *Attack at Santa Elena* • 1576
Location: Port Royal Sound
War: Spanish Exploration
The Spanish fort commander at Santa Elena was concerned with his low food supply and sent Lt. Boyano and 21 men to the cacique of Escamucu, between Port Royal and Charleston. The soldiers captured the natives' food supply, and most of the residents fled.

The cacique responded with an attack which killed all but one of the soldiers. Calderon, the only one to escape, carried the news back to Santa Elena.

Sources: 232

SC3 *Attack on Port Royal* • 1686
Location: Port Royal
A colony of Scots was established at Port Royal, and allegedly sent Caleb Westbrooke and Aratomahan, a native, to the Yamassee tribe to encourage them to make war with the Timechos. The latter had been Christianized, and had a chapel and Spanish friar with them. The Scots furnished weapons, which the Yamassees used to kill 50 Timechos and take 22 prisoners. They also burned the Timechos' town and chapel and killed the friar.

In reprisal, 153 Spanish soldiers, natives and mulattoes arrived at Port Royal in a galley and two pirogues, commanded by Capt. Tomas de Leon. They burned and plundered the Scots' homes, and most of those whom they did not kill went to Charles Town to live under the protection of the English.

The Spaniards continued with their damage, attacking Edisto plantations and burning the homes of Gov. Morton and Paul Grimball. A hurricane thwarted their plan of attacking Charles Town, when it wrecked two of the Spanish vessels.

Sources: 310, 328, 332

SC4 *Attacks by Tuscaroras* • 1712
Location: Neuse River
War: Tuscarora War
John Lawson, a friend of the local natives, aroused suspicions among the Tuscaroras when he began surveying and marking lands which they claimed. The whites were expanding their territory into that of the Tuscaroras. They captured Lawson and killed him by driving fat pine splinters into his body and burning them.

Afraid that the whites would retaliate, the natives decided to strike first. They began with the settlers in the northern part of the colony, killing 130.
Sources: 100

SC5   *Rout at the Tar River* • December, 1712
Location: Tar River
War: Tuscarora War
Col. John Barnwell brought temporary peace to the area after his army killed or enslaved many of the Tuscarora warriors. After making a treaty, he left for Charles Town.

As soon as Barnwell left, the Tuscaroras resumed the killing. Gov. Craven sent Col. James Moore with 40 whites and 800 friendly natives into the area, and they killed 200 and captured 800 along the Tar River.
Sources: 100

SC6   *Attack at Chestowee* • Spring, 1714
Location: Chestowee
Alexander Long, a trader, hated the Yuchis following an altercation with a Yuchi warrior. With his friend, Eleazar Wiggan, he obtained the support of Middle Cherokee chiefs Flint and Caesar. The force they raised surrounded the Yuchi village of Chestowee and in the attack they killed several and burned the buildings.

The Yuchis attempted to take refuge in the town house. To avoid capture, the warriors killed the women and children, and then killed themselves.
Sources: 332

SC7   *Pocotaligo Massacre* • April 15, 1715
Location: Pocotaligo
War: Yamassee War
White traders in South Carolina were accused of improper treatment of the natives. They reportedly robbed their native clients, forced them to carry animal skins great distances for little pay, raped the women while the men were away on errands, and beat up any who protested. The natives decided to strike back.

A party of Yamassees attacked Port Royal, beginning with the white agent, Thomas Nairne, and several traders including John Wright. Many were tortured and houses were burned. A total of about 90 whites died that day. Others, including John Cochran, were captured and killed later. Nairne was subjected to piercing by lightwood splinters which were burned, prolonging the torture for several days.

Capt. Burroughs and a trader escaped and warned the 400 inhabitants at Port Royal, who boarded a smuggler's vessel in the harbor as the Yamassees arrived to burn their houses.
Sources: 133, 135, 199, 326, 332, 353, 381

SC8   *Attack at St. Bartholomew* • April 15, 1715
Location: Between the Edisto and Combahee Rivers
Sources: Yamassee War
A band of natives attacked and sacked St. Bartholomew's parish, capturing about 100 whites. Most of the town's inhabitants escaped with their possessions to

Charles Town before nearly all of the homes in St. Bartholomew's were destroyed. The attackers included Apalachees, Catawbas and Creeks.

Sources: 332

SC9   *Battle Near Salkehatchie* • Late April, 1715
Location: Salkehatchie
Sources: Yamassee War

Gov. Craven, desiring to protect his province, mobilized the militia of Colleton County and moved to the home of Capt. Woodward where a temporary fortification was constructed. A force of natives attacked, but the garrison held them off. As the engagement began, Cols. John Barnwell and Mackay were sent by water to notify Pocotaligo. Craven then led his men to meet up with Barnwell and Mackay.

When they reached Salkehatchie, Craven's 240 whites and a few settlement natives fought with 500 warriors. After an hour of heavy fire, Craven rallied his troops to rout the Yamassees. John Snow was the only white who was killed, but the Yamassees lost several of their leaders.

Craven followed the Yamassees into a dense swamp, then turned back and returned to Charles Town.

Sources: 332

SC10   *Capture of Pocotaligo* • Late April, 1715
Location: Pocotaligo
War: Yamassee War

Col. Mackay, sent out with a party of militia from Capt. Woodward's house, captured Pocotaligo and recovered many English possessions which had previously been taken by the Yamassees. The natives retreated into a strong fort which was defended by 200 warriors.

Mackay attacked with 140 whites, scaling the wall and killing several, but was required to retreat. A second attack was led by a young man named Palmer, and this time the Yamassees were dislodged and forced from the area.

Sources: 332

SC11   *Massacre at Herne Plantation* • June, 1715
Location: 30 miles from Goose Creek
War: Yamassee War

A party of 400 natives from the eastern Carolina rivers, allies of the Sioux including 70 Cherokees, traveled through the region of the Santee settlements. They appeared at the settlement of John Herne and talked of making peace. They ate dinner with Mr. Herne and then killed him with a tomahawk.

Capt. Thomas Baker responded by gathering 90 men on horseback to fight the natives, but rode into an ambush that resulted in the death of Baker and 26 of his men. Refugees swelled the population of Charles Town.

Sources: 332

SC12   *Battle at Schenkingh Cowpen* • June, 1715
Location: Santee Area
War: Yamassee War

Most of the Santee area was deserted by the whites, but one garrison of 70 whites

and 40 blacks remained at the cowpen of Benjamin Schenkingh. They were attacked by a larger force of natives led by Redwood, who then proposed a discussion of peace. The whites set down their arms and allowed the natives to come among them, and then the natives pulled out knives and tomahawks and killed 22 of the defenders. The garrison was then plundered and burned.
Sources: 332

SC13   *Attack at Plantation* • July 19, 1715
        Location: Near Ponds
        War: Yamassee War
        Capt. George Chicken led 120 men from the Ponds to a plantation about four miles away, then divided into three parties to surround a band of natives and prevent them from fleeing into a swamp. When the militia was discovered by two native scouts, they shot them and then attacked the band of natives. Chicken's men killed 40, wounded several, and took back four white prisoners that the Yamassees had been holding.
        The Yamassees eventually headed south to Georgia and Florida, where they supported the Spanish against the British.
        Sources: 332, 381

SC14   *Attack on New London* • July, 1715
        Location: New London
        War: Yamassee War
        A force of 500 warriors, mostly Apalachees but supported by some Savannahs and Yuchis, crossed the Edisto River at Pon-pon Bridge and attacked the village of New London. The garrison there was able to repel them.
        The natives then broke into smaller raiding parties and attacked the Stono River plantations. At least 20 in St. Paul's Parish were destroyed. They destroyed a ship at Boone's Landing. As they returned across the Edisto, they burned the Pon-pon Bridge.
        Sources: 332

SC15   *Battle at Dawfuskey Island* • Autumn, 1715
        Location: Dawfuskey Island
        War: Yamassee War
        Learning that a band of Yamassees was destroying plantations near Combahee, Col. Fenwick marched his men to the Ponds Bridge. First, they repaired the bridge, and then continued to Combahee to the Jackson house where he engaged a party of 16 natives. The Yamassees had nine killed and two taken prisoner, while Fenwick had one white killed and one black wounded. The whites also captured four of their boats.
        Fenwick met up with Capts. Stone and Burroughs, and they led their men to Dawfuskey Island and waited for the Yamassees to come by. When Capt. Palmer came upon the natives, they leapt overboard and swam for shore. They landed where Fenwick and the others waited for them, killing 35 and taking two prisoners. A few other natives escaped without weapons.
        Sources: 332

SC16   *Attack Near Port Royal* • August 1, 1716
Location: Near Port Royal
War: Yamassee War
The area's settlers welcomed more whites from England, even those with differing politics, because more defenders were needed to protect all from the Creeks and their allies. In one attack near Port Royal, they killed Maj. Henry Quintyne, Thomas Simons and Thomas Parmenter, and scalped Dr. Rose, who recovered.
Sources: 332

SC17   *Attacks on St. Helena* • June, 1720
Location: St. Helena
War: Yamassee War
In June, a Yamassee war party attacked St. Helena and killed one white settler. They also took as prisoners Mr. June, a tanner, and 12 slaves, who wound up in St. Augustine.
Sources: 332

SC18   *Attack on Edwards Home* • September, 1726
Location: Seven miles from Port Royal
War: Yamassee War
A small Yamassee party, allegedly with supplies provided by the Spaniards, attacked the Edwards home on the Combahee River. They killed John Edwards, captured three blacks as prisoners, and plundered the home.
Sources: 332

SC19   *Attack on English Settlements* • June, 1727
Location: South Carolina
War: Yamassee War
Spanish Indians, likely Yamassees, came into the English settlements and killed two whites, John Sparks and William Lavy. They spared the rest of the families, but warned them that there was a large party coming from St. Augustine with orders from the Spanish governor to spare no one.
Sources: 332

SC20   *Attack at Smallwood's Store* • July 23, 1727
Location: Near Fort King George
War: Yamassee War
A party of Yamassees attacked five white traders in their boat along the Altamaha River near the trading post of Matthew Smallwood. He was killed, along with Albert and John Hutchinson, John Annesley, and Charles Smith. The attackers also took their goods, then broke into the store and took more.

      The same party was soon found in the English settlements, where they killed Henry Mishoe and Hezekiah Wood and captured ten slaves. They were pursued by Capt. John Bull and his force of fifteen, who caught them and killed six natives and a Spaniard.
Sources: 111, 332

SC21   *Attack on Dawson House* • September, 1727
Location: French's Island
War: Yamassee War

The home of Alexander Dawson was attacked by a party of natives and fugitive black slaves, who killed or abducted four adults and four children. The blacks talked them out of killing and scalping them on the spot. As with most of the other prisoners taken during the decade by the Yamassees, they wound up in St. Augustine.
Sources: 332

SC22   *Attack Along the Savannah River* • 1752
Location: Along the Savannah River
After a party of Cherokees and Savannahs killed a Chickasaw and took two women captive, a Chickasaw war party retaliated and took ten Cherokee scalps and three prisoners.
    By April 26, the Chickasaws and a few Creek allies had killed 30 Lower Cherokee warriors. Their former allies, the Northern Cherokees, also turned against them.
Sources: 332

SC23   *Attack in York County* • 1754
Location: York County
A party of natives, likely Savannahs, attacked a group of settlers, killing 16 and capturing five. Only one was shot, with the rest being killed by arrows or toma-hawks.
Sources: 332

SC24   *Attack on Fort Prince George* • Late 1759
Location: Fort Prince George
War: First Cherokee War
In October of 1759, Oconostota and a party of 31 important Cherokees went to Charles Town to restore peace to the area. Instead of talking with the party, the governor of South Carolina arrested them and sent them to Fort Prince George. They were kept in a small room intended for six people. The governor freed Oconostota and several others upon receipt of substitute hostages, whom he executed.
    The Cherokees began attacking settlements from Virginia to Georgia and laid siege to Fort Prince George. They killed the post's commander who allegedly took part in a drunken rape of Cherokee women, and the soldiers retaliated by killing the imprisoned Cherokees.
    By the end of January, they had killed 14 white men at a trader's house about a mile away from the fort.
Sources: 147, 332, 364

SC25   *Long Canes Massacre* • February 1, 1760
Location: Long Canes
War: First Cherokee War
The settlers of Long Canes, fearing for their safety, were in the process of moving to Augusta when they were attacked by the Cherokees. The first estimate of the attacking force stated that there were 100 natives on horseback, who killed 40 settlers. Later, the casualty figures were increased to 50 whites and the loss of 13 loaded wagons and carts. Another report placed the number at 56, with several taken as prisoners.

Monument: A monument was placed at the site of the attack and notes the number of white deaths as 23, including the mother of Patrick Calhoun.
Sources: 332

SC26 *Attack on Fort Prince George* • February 16, 1760
Location: Fort Prince George
War: First Cherokee War
Fort Prince George was commanded by Lt. Cotymore, who was unpopular with the natives. On February 16 at about 8 a.m., two women came near the fort and talked with a Mr. DuCharty, and were joined by a Cherokee warrior. Lt. Cotymore joined them for a discussion, and upon the signal of the warrior, 25 to 30 Cherokees concealed by the river bank opened fire on the officer.
    The natives ran, and one was killed by a soldier. The soldiers went into the fort, and the natives opened fire on it. The fire was returned with cannon. The dead Lt. Cotymore was replaced by Lt. Miln. In retaliation for the attack, the native hostages, who had been held at the fort, were butchered.
Sources: 332

SC27 *Attack on Ninety Six* • March 6, 1760
Location: Ninety Six
War: First Cherokee War
Twenty-eight English militiamen gathered to defend the fort at Ninety Six, and were attacked by a party of Cherokees. Post commander Capt. James Francis reported that several of the attackers were killed and scalped.
Sources: 332

SC28 *Burning of Lower Towns* • June 1, 1760
Location: Oconee County
War: First Cherokee War
Gen. Amherst organized an army of 1,200 men, including a battalion of Highlanders and four companies of Royal Scots, and placed Col. Montgomery in command. The army sacked and burned Little Keowee, Estatoe, Sugar Town, and other Cherokee villages, while killing about 60 and capturing about 40. Orchards, granaries and cornfields were destroyed.
Sources: 332, 364

SC29 *Attack at Long Canes* • December 27, 1761
Location: Long Canes
War: First Cherokee War
A party of seven Creeks who were living with the defeated Lower Cherokees went into the Long Canes region and killed 14 white settlers. The Creeks had protested the incursion onto native lands by "Virginians," as they called the frontiersmen.
Sources: 111

SC30 *Ambush at Twelve Mile Creek* • 1763
Location: Twelve Mile Creek
Seven Shawnees came onto the lands of the Catawbas and set an ambush along the road leading from the Waxhaws to Catawba Old Town. Catawba chief King

Haigler, returning from the Waxhaws, was riddled with bullets and scalped. The Shawnees escaped.
Sources: 332

SC31 *Battle of Fort Moultrie* • June 28, 1776
Location: Charleston
War: Revolutionary War
A company of Catawba warriors fought in this battle, serving with the rangers led by Col. Thompson. They helped to guard the inlet between Sullivan's Island and the Isle of Palms, keeping the large British force from attacking the fort by land.
Sources: 100, 326, 332

SC32 *Attack at Ludley's Fort* • July 15, 1776
Location: Near Robbin's Creek
War: Revolutionary War
Beginning in July, war parties of Cherokees and some Creeks attacked settlements along an arc stretching from southern Virginia, through the western Carolinas, and into northern Georgia.

Near Robbin's Creek, a blockhouse was attacked by 28 natives and 102 English soldiers, many of whom were painted to look like natives. The force of 40 Americans led by Maj. Andrew Williamson had been joined the night before by 150 men led by Maj. Downs, and together they were able to hold off the attackers and kill several. From the English force, they captured 13 and sent them to Ninety Six.

This American victory may have discouraged the settlers in the area from choosing to ally with the English.
Sources: 3, 332

SC33 *Battle at Seneca Ford* • August 1, 1776
Location: Seneca
War: Revolutionary War
Maj. Andrew Williamson's army grew to 1,151 men. He took a detachment of 300 and marched to the town of Seneca on the Oconore Creek, in search of the British force. Reaching Seneca at 2 p.m., the army was met by gunfire from Tories and Cherokees from within the town walls.

A charge led by Col. Samuel Hammond forced the defenders out of the palisade and across the river. The casualty count for the army was 94 killed and wounded. The next day, the Americans burned the town and destroyed its corn and provisions.
Sources: 3, 332

SC34 *Attacks on Lower Towns* • August, 1776
Location: South Carolina
War: Revolutionary War
The American force, led by Maj. Andrew Williamson and headquartered at Twenty-Three Mile Creek, carried out a massed attack on the Cherokee Middle Towns. Beginning on August 4, a party led by Capt. Tutt destroyed Sugar Town, Soconee and Keowee. Starting on August 8, Williamson led a detachment of 640

and destroyed Estatoe and Tugaloo, including a successful skirmish with the natives on August 10. Williamson then went on to destroy Brass Town on August 11 and Tamassee, Cheowee and Eustaste on August 12.

A little later, Maj. Samuel Jack took 200 men and burned all of the Lower Towns between the Tugaloo and Chattahoochee Rivers.

Sources: 3, 162, 332

SC35   *Attacks on Lower Towns* • January, 1782
Location: Oconee County
War: Revolutionary War
At a time when massacres of Americans by Cherokees were reported, Gen. Andrew Pickens and Col. Robert Anderson began to patrol the native frontier. Soon, a campaign was launched against the southeastern portion of the Cherokee Nation, especially the 13 Lower Towns which had been rebuilt and occupied by the natives.

Pickens succeeded in destroying all 13 towns, killing 40 Cherokees and taking about 40 captive. Using specially smithed short swords, they hacked to death unarmed villagers. Their only casualties were two wounded men.

Sources: 326, 332

SC36   *Ambush Near Charleston* • June, 1782
Location: 40 miles from Charleston
War: Revolutionary War
Gen. Anthony Wayne spent a portion of the winter and spring of 1782 in South Carolina, and was ambushed by a war party of Creeks. Wayne was able to defeat the warriors and kill the chief.

Sources: 395

SC37   *Sacking of Columbia* • December, 1864
Location: Columbia
War: Civil War
Accompanying Union Gen. William Tecumseh Sherman on his March to the Sea and capture of Atlanta were Oneidas, frequently praised for their sharpshooting. They also participated in the sacking and burning of Columbia.

Sources: 60

SOUTH DAKOTA

SD1   *Attacks on Sioux* • June, 1863
Location: Dakotas
Gen. John Pope led expeditionary forces into the Dakotas, searching for the Santees who had caused problems for the government in Minnesota. They found peaceful camps of Yanktonais, Hunkpapas and other western Sioux and killed many, even though they had nothing to do with the fighting in Minnesota.

Gen. Henry H. Sibley attacked Sitting Bull's party of western Sioux, who had crossed to the east of the Missouri River because of drought in the west. In retaliation, Sitting Bull attacked a wagon train near Apple Creek and ran off a mule.
Sources: 147, 346

SD2   *Attack on American Horse's Village* or
           Battle of Slim Buttes • September 9, 1876
Location: Slim Buttes
War: Great Sioux War
During an army campaign of killing natives north and west of the Black Hills, Gen. George Crook needed supplies and headed south to the mining camps to obtain them. A contingent led by Capt. Anson Mills came upon a 40-lodge village of Oglalas and Minneconjous led by American Horse (Iron Plume), and attacked. The natives had left Crazy Horse and were on their way back to their reservation.

The Sioux drove the army back, and Mills waited for reinforcements from Crook. While he waited, all of the natives escaped except for a small group trapped in a cave at the end of a small canyon.

The main column of soldiers led by Crook came to the canyon and began firing into the cave. American Horse and his four soldiers returned the fire, but later surrendered. American Horse soon died of his wounds.
Sources: 4, 70, 91, 110, 224, 346

SD3   *Clash at Daly's Ranch* • December 12, 1890
Location: Mouth of Battle Creek
War: Ghost Dance War (Fourth Sioux War)
Rancher George Cosgrove and 12 cowboys, accompanied by *Omaha Bee* reporter Will Cressey, set an ambush behind a woodpile at Daly's Ranch. In about half an hour, a party of Sioux approached the ranch. When one came through the gate, cowboy Fred Thompson fired and hit him. More fire was exchanged until nightfall, with three Sioux killed and one cowboy seriously injured.
Sources: 235

SD4   *Skirmish at Stronghold* • December 15, 1890
Location: East of the Black Hills
War: Ghost Dance War (Fourth Sioux War)
Col. H.M. Day and 62 ranchers and cowboys in the South Dakota militia patrolled the Cheyenne River, looking for a fight. After some clashes with warriors, 18 of the men crossed the Cheyenne River and rode up Battle Creek Draw toward the Stronghold, a natural fortress made by a table area connected to a main plateau by a narrow land bridge.

They were met by a force of Sioux, who drove back the militia.
Sources: 235

SD5   *Clash at Phinney's Ranch* • Mid-December, 1890
Location: Between Spring and Battle Creeks
War: Ghost Dance War (Fourth Sioux War)
Col. H.M. Day and ten regular soldiers clashed with and held off a party of Sioux for four hours. The natives set fire to the corral and the surrounding prairie. A wind shift saved the soldiers and the Sioux withdrew.
Sources: 235

SD6 *Skirmish on the Grand River* • December 15, 1890
Location: Grand River
War: Ghost Dance War (Fourth Sioux War)
In a skirmish with U.S. soldiers, one of those killed was Sitting Bull. Many of his followers then sought refuge with Hump, an ex–Ghost Dancer.
Sources: 133, 141

SD7 *Wounded Knee Massacre* or *Big Foot Massacre* • December 29, 1890
Location: Pine Ridge Indian Reservation
War: Ghost Dance War (Fourth Sioux War)
Three hundred fifty Miniconjou Sioux led by ailing Big Foot were pursued 150 miles by the army for their practice of the Ghost Dance religion, which was believed to bring back ancestors and the old ways of life. Unknown to the whites, many of the band had already turned away from that religion. The Miniconjou had hoped to find a safe place to live with Red Cloud and the Oglala Sioux on the reservation.

On December 28, they encountered the 7th U.S. Cavalry, were surrounded by them, and were promised by Maj. Samuel M. Whitside that if they surrendered they would be allowed to live. Big Foot agreed, and the Miniconjou spent the night at the soldiers' camp on Wounded Knee Creek (Chankpe Opi Wakpala). On a hill overlooking the Sioux, a battery of four Hotchkiss rapid-fire guns was trained on them.

On the following morning, a panic was started by an accidental shot from the rifle of a deaf warrior, Black Coyote, who had not heard the initial order for all to surrender their weapons. It went off when a soldier tried to take it from his hands, and several other shots rang out and a major fight ensued. When the smoke cleared 20 minutes later, Big Foot and 150 to 250 of his band were dead and 50 were injured. The army had 25 killed and 39 wounded. Others died in a tremendous blizzard which struck three days later. The massacre marked the end of the natives' hopes of freedom in this country.
Monument: Wounded Knee, a National Historic Landmark, is located north of US 18 on Reservation Rd. from a point eight miles east of Pine Ridge.
Sources: 4, 13, 28, 31, 32, 34, 62, 66, 68, 70, 90, 91, 92, 109, 114, 126, 141, 147, 159, 182, 197, 199, 201, 203, 213, 235, 224, 275, 288, 315, 380, 381, 405, 419

SD8 *Battle at Drexel Mission* • December 30, 1890
Location: Drexel Mission
War: Ghost Dance War (Fourth Sioux War)
Oglala Sioux warriors who had attacked a wagon train, and who were frightened off by the approach of the 7th Cavalry, headed northward toward the Holy Rosary Catholic Mission operated by Father Jutz. Near the mission, also known as the Drexel Mission, they set fire to the schoolhouse. The smoke from it was seen by the troops, and a contingent led by Col. James W. Forsyth headed toward the mission.

After pausing at the mission for food, the soldiers headed to a valley below it where the Sioux camp was believed to be. On the way there, they encountered a party of warriors. After putting the horses in a safe place, they exchanged ineffective long-distance fire for about two hours. A messenger was sent for relief troops commanded by Maj. Guy V. Henry.

Forsyth forgot to guard his flanks, and the Sioux sent warriors into positions on surrounding bluffs. With artillery, they were able to push them out and the warriors returned to their camp. The soldiers returned to the agency from which they had come.

Sources: 144, 235

SD9 *Battle at White River* • January 1, 1891
Location: Five miles north of the mouth of Wounded Knee Creek
War: Ghost Dance War (Fourth Sioux War)
Sioux warriors, still angry from the massacre days before, rode along the bluffs overlooking the White River. The 6th Cavalry was camped at the mouth of Wounded Knee Creek and the regimental train was coming down the valley on the other side of the river, guarded by Capt. John B. Kerr's Troop K.

The Sioux rode down the slope and crossed the river, causing Kerr to circle the wagons and open fire. The sound of the battle was heard by a small encampment of cavalry commanded by Col. Eugene A. Carr, and they rode up to attack the warriors at the rear. The Sioux retreated, and as they left the soldiers shot six of them. Others were found and killed later. The white losses were one horse killed and another wounded.

Sources: 91, 235

TENNESSEE

TN1 *Siege of and Attack on Fort Loudon* • August, 1760
Location: Fort Loudon
War: French and Indian War
Fort Loudon was built in 1756 under the supervision of military engineer William Gerard DeBrahm. James Bullen and other Catawba warriors served as scouts under George Washington in an attack on it in May.

War chief Oconostota and his Cherokee warriors captured Fort Loudon, following the ending of the siege of the British Fort Prince George in South Carolina. Assisted by Chickasaws, a force of British soldiers arrived and defeated the Cherokees. The soldiers then marched through the Cherokee territory and reduced 15 native towns to ashes.

On August 8, 1760, Capt. Raymond Demere was allowed to lead his 200 men from the fort, which then was taken over by the Cherokees. After they left, the natives discovered that Demere had not complied with his promise to hand over all munitions, as he had hidden some under the fort and had thrown some into the river. As a result, the 700 Cherokees attacked the soldiers on August 9 at their camp, killing Demere and 29 others and capturing the rest.
Museum: A restored palisaded fort, rebuilt powder magazine, and museum are located on US 411 one mile east of Vonore, TN.
Sources: 55, 90, 92, 133, 146, 147, 199, 234, 332, 371, 381, 388, 418

TN2   *Battle at Island Flats* • July 20, 1776
      Location: Island Flats, on the Holston River
      War: Second Cherokee War
      Dragging Canoe of the British-allied Cherokees decided to punish the column
      of settlers coming into the Holston River country. Some of the whites had
      sufficient warning of the approaching war party to get into the stockades. The
      fort was garrisoned by 170 soldiers led by officers Thompson, Buchanan, Shelby,
      Campbell, Cocke and Madison. The army came out of the fort to battle with the
      natives, who had about the same number.
           The superior weaponry of the soldiers resulted in 13 dead Cherokees on the
      initial exchange of fire, and the wounding of Dragging Canoe. They settlers lost
      nine pack horses. The natives withdrew from the fight.
      Sources: 3, 332, 354, 355

TN3   *Battle at Fort Caswell* • July 20, 1776
      Location: Fort Caswell
      War: Second Cherokee War
      A war party of Cherokees arrived at the fort while a number of the settlement's
      women were in a nearby meadow, milking their cows. The women ran to the fort,
      found the gate closed and Lt. Col. John Sevier (Nolichucky Jack) leaned down
      from the fire step and instructed Catherine Sherrill to jump into his arms, so he
      could bring her into the fort. She did, and they later were married.
           The attacking Cherokees inflicted several casualties among the 40 soldiers
      stationed at Fort Caswell, also called Fort Watauga. This is the same event as TN4,
      although accounts vary slightly with the different titles.
      Sources: 3

TN4   *Attack at Watauga Fort* • July 20, 1776
      Location: Watauga
      War: Second Cherokee War
      The fort at Watauga was surrounded and attacked. It was defended by Ameri-
      cans led by Sevier and Capt. James Robertson for three weeks. They lost 18 men,
      two women and several children while killing 26 natives. Soon after the Chero-
      kees gave up the siege, reinforcements arrived.
      Sources: 332

TN5   *Battle of Boyd's Creek* • December 8, 1780
      Location: Along the French Broad River
      War: Revolutionary War
      Lt. Col. John Sevier and 250 North Carolinians battled with a party of Cherokees
      along the French Broad River, and inflicted heavy casualties while losing only one.
           This was one of a series of battles involving Sevier and 300 North Carolina
      volunteers, plus Col. Arthur Campbell and 400 Virginians. The campaign
      resulted in the deaths of 29 Cherokees and the destruction of 1,000 homes, 50,000
      bushels of corn, and other provisions.
      Sources: 199

TN6   *Attack at Nashborough* • April, 1781
      Location: Nashborough

Dragging Canoe and a party of Chickamaugans attacked Nashborough, ambushing Capt. James Robertson and 20 mounted men. Cut off from the fort, they were saved when the warriors were distracted by a pack of dogs from the fort, released by Mrs. Robertson.
Sources: 371

TN7   *Battle at Lookout Mountain* • September, 1782
Location: Base of Lookout Mountain
War: Revolutionary War
The Cherokee Nation was substantially reduced and, by treaty, was required to surrender much of its lands. However, several hundred warriors led by Dragging Canoe refused to go along with the terms of peace and settled a new town at the base of Lookout Mountain, along Chickamauga Creek north of the border with Georgia.

They continued to be hostile toward the Americans, and an expedition was formed by John Sevier and 250 Tennessee horsemen for the expressed purpose of the destruction of their settlements. They accomplished this, and the Cherokees relocated and established the new settlements of Long Island, Crow Town, Nickajack, Running Water and Lookout Mountain.

Others who settled in these towns were Creeks, Shawnees and white Tories, and they persisted in their raids of American settlements. In 1794, these new towns were destroyed by the Americans.
Sources: 3, 332, 382

TN8   *Raid on Middle Towns* • Summer, 1783
Location: Eastern Tennessee
Nearly 200 white men invaded the Cherokee Middle Towns, burning six of them and taking 15 scalps and several prisoners.
Sources: 332

TN9   *Massacre at Cavitt's Blockhouse* • September, 1783
Location: Near Knoxville
John Watts and Doublehead led a force of Cherokees and Creeks toward Knoxville, attacking the blockhouse known as Cavitt's Station. All men, women and children who had gathered there for protection were killed.

In retaliation, Lt. Col. John Sevier followed this party with 700 men as far as Ustanali in Georgia, which they burned.
Sources: 332

TN10   *Expeditions Against Valley Towns* • 1786 and 1788
Location: Holston River area
In retaliation for a raid against white settlers which had been led by the mixed-blood chief, John Watts, Lt. Col. John Sevier attacked the Valley Towns and burned three of them.

A second expedition took place in 1788 after Cherokees had killed 11 members of the Kirk family. Sevier burned several towns along the Little Tennessee River, ravaging the countryside. When chiefs were invited to come in and talk, two friendly ones, Abraham and Old Tassel, were murdered. This resulted in a Cherokee massacre of 28 whites at Gillespie's Station in October, 1788.
Sources: 332, 382, 412

TN11 *Battle at Buchanan's Station* • September 30, 1792
Location: Near Nashville
War: Lower Cherokee War
Led by John Watts, a band of Lower Cherokees, Creeks and Shawnees attacked Buchanan's Station. The garrison defended well, and the natives became discouraged and withdrew, leaving many of their belongings.
Sources: 332, 355

TN12 *Attack Along the Tennessee River* • June 25, 1794
Location: Between Nickajack and Running Water
The settlements along Chickamauga Creek and the Tennessee River harbored and encouraged the Creeks, who attacked a boat and killed the whites on it. They captured several blacks and provisions.
Sources: 332

TN13 *Destruction of Nickajack* • September 12, 1794
Location: Sequatchee Creek
In response to the attack on the boat in June, Col. Whiteley and Maj. Ore took 550 mounted men on an expedition against the Chickamauga towns. They attacked and destroyed Nickajack, taking 18 prisoners and killing nearly all of the rest of the population of 200 to 300.

A mile up the river, they plundered and destroyed the town of Running Water. The force returned to Nashville and was disbanded, and peace was negotiated by mid–November.
Sources: 332, 355

TN14 *Battle of Baptist Gap* • September 13–15, 1862
Location: Rogersville
War: Civil War
Union troops were attempting to pass through the Baptist Gap south of the Cumberland Mountains, to get into eastern Tennessee. Cherokees led by Confederate Lt. Terrell routed them.

The initial charge was led by 2nd Lt. Astoogatogeh, and the Union soldiers panicked. Astoogatogeh was killed, and his men scalped several of the enemy in return.
Sources: 60

TN15 *Skirmish at Gatlinburg* • December 10, 1863
Location: Gatlinburg
War: Civil War
Cherokee soldiers of the Thomas Legion, led by Col. William Holland Thomas, were attacked along a ridge by the 15th Pennsylvania Cavalry led by Col. William Jackson. They captured one, wounded three and forced the rest to retreat through the mountains.
Sources: 60

TEXAS

TX1   *Massacre at Ft. St. Louis* • Early 1689
Location: Fort St. Louis
War: La Salle Expedition
Rene Robert Cavelier, Sieur de La Salle, after travelling down the Mississippi
River, put ashore at Matagorda Bay in Texas on January 20, 1685. His intention
was to establish a colony to form the beginning of a French empire. They explored
portions of eastern Texas until La Salle was killed by a member of his party on
March 18, 1687, near Navasota. Some of the surviving members of his party
walked to Canada and returned to France in October of 1688.
     Six others headed for Ft. St. Louis in Texas and never made it. In 1689, the
fort was attacked by the Karankawas, who killed all except for a few children. The
ruins were found by Alonzo de Leon in late April during his attempt at coloniz-
ing the area.
Sources: 373

TX2   *Defeat of Apaches* • 1723
Location: North of the Wichita River
Apaches lived in Texas and Oklahoma north of the Canadian River until 1723,
when they were defeated by the Comanches in a nine-day battle. The Apaches
then moved farther south.
Sources: 135

TX3   *Attack on San Antonio* • 1730
Location: San Antonio
During the 1720s, Apaches killed many of the Coahuiltecan natives along the San
Antonio River, and the latter allied with the Spanish for their protection.
     During 1730, an Apache war party attacked the garrison at San Antonio,
resulting in the deaths or wounding of 15 soldiers. The rest were driven off to
hike into the town. Sixty head of cattle were driven off and butchered by the
Apaches.
     Bustillo y Cevallos led a punitive expedition against the Apaches and found
a native encampment along the San Saba River. Although not all of the inhabitants of the camp may have been involved in the attack, the Spanish claimed to
have killed 200 natives in the encounter.
Sources: 103

TX4   *Siege of San Saba Mission* • March 16–20, 1758
Location: San Saba River
The mission was guarded by 17 soldiers from the nearby Fort San Luis, who were
surprised on the morning of March 16 when they were surrounded by 2,000
Comanches, Wichitas, Tonkawas, Bidais and Tejas who had formed an alliance
with the French. The priest in charge, Padre Terreros, refused to give an order
to fire. A warrior rode to the mission gate, opened it, and let in a horde of riders. The priests brought out gifts and offered friendship.

The warriors demanded that the fort also be opened. A party of Spanish soldiers rode from the fort to reinforce the mission, and during a brief battle, they were all lanced or shot. Only one wounded soldier escaped.

The Comanches set fire to the mission and killed the soldiers and priests, with only four crawling to safety. After four days of siege and fighting, the Spanish losses totalled ten.

Sources: 92, 103, 246, 358, 373

TX5 *Attack on Tonkawa Village* • August, 1759
Location: Due north of San Antonio on the Red River
Col. Don Diego Ortiz de Parilla followed a route north of San Antonio, along the fringe of the Great Plains. He chose to avoid a march across the plains, where Spanish armies had not fared well in the past. With him were 139 regular soldiers, 241 militiamen, 120 Tlaxcaltecan and mission natives and 134 Apaches.

Although they were searching for Comanches who had burned the San Saba Mission, Parilla chose not to distinguish among the varied native peoples. He came upon a Tonkawa village and killed 60 warriors, taking 150 women and children prisoners.

Sources: 103, 358

TX6 *Battle at Red River* • October, 1759
Location: Red River
Present-day Texas was considered to be a Spanish province, while the land across the Red River in what is now Oklahoma was French territory. Col. Don Diego Ortiz de Parilla reached this border in his search for Comanches, and found his route blocked by breastworks guarding a Taovayas village flying a French flag. He also found several thousand natives on horseback, including Comanches, Red River Caddoans, Wichitas, perhaps Osages, and others.

Parilla ordered an attack and his native allies vanished. The Mexican militia who rode with him hesitated, and the Spanish ran for their lives, leaving the cannon and supply train. Parilla's force had 19 killed and 14 wounded and the rest made it back to San Antonio because the warriors chose not to pursue them.

Despite the loss of few men, it was a moral defeat, and inflated the feeling of power shared by the Comanches and Wichitas. Parilla was court-martialled.
Sources: 103, 246, 358

TX7 *Attack on Laredo* • 1771
Location: Laredo
A new community on the north bank of the Rio Grande was attacked by Comanches and the settlers were driven away. It was rebuilt as Nuevo Laredo on the better protected southern side.
Sources: 103

TX8 *Attack at Bexar* • September 18, 1780
Location: Southeast of San Antonio
A Comanche war party of about 80 warriors attacked a military outpost near San Antonio de Bexar, killing three soldiers and driving off a portion of the post's horse herd. Twenty-three men remained in the post without hope of receiving reinforcements from a depleted Spanish army.
Sources: 213, 246

TX9   *Massacre at Canon de Uvalde* • 1780
      Location: Uvalde, west of San Antonio
      Brig. Gen. Ugalde assembled a large force of Comanches and Wichitas who had
      come into Spanish territory to fight against the Apaches. With some Spanish
      lancers, they trapped several hundred Apaches in a canyon on the Nueces River.
      In a cul de sac, they were slaughtered, eliminating the Apaches as a serious prob-
      lem in that part of Texas.
      Sources: 103

TX10   *Attack at the Medina River* • December, 1780
      Location: Medina River
      Gov. Cabello sent 172 men led by Alferez Marcelo Valdes to track down and fight
      the Comanches, which they did at the Medina River. Eighteen of the 60 warriors
      were killed, including the chief, while only one soldier was wounded.
      Sources: 246

TX11   *Battle Along the Guadalupe River* • July, 1784
      Location: Guadalupe River
      In response to the stealing of two of the governor's best horses in San Antonio
      de Bexar, Francisco Amangual and Alferez Marcelo Valdes led a party of 79 men
      to punish the Taovayas and Wichitas who had been involved. Along the way,
      they encountered a Comanche war party on the way to San Antonio. In an eight-
      hour battle, 10 of the 40 warriors were killed.
          The Spaniards returned to Bexar with four wounded and several captives,
      plus horses taken from the Comanches.
      Sources: 246

TX12   *Attack at Arroyo de Soledad* • 1790
      Location: West of San Antonio
      A large party of Comanches attacked a group of Mescaleros, Lipans and other
      Apaches. As a follow-up action, Spanish commandant Brig. Gen. Ugalde led a
      force of Spanish soldiers and seven Comanche chiefs leading 140 warriors, against
      the Athapascans.
          The Apaches had two chiefs and 28 warriors killed, along with 28 women
      and a child. Thirty women and children and 800 horses were captured.
      Sources: 246

TX13   *Attack at Parker's Fort* • May 19, 1836
      Location: Limestone County
      The Parker family moved to Texas in 1834 from Virginia, by way of Tennessee
      and Illinois, and built a log stockade. Other settler families joined them, creat-
      ing a settlement of about 30. On May 19, a large party of natives appeared at the
      fort while most of the men were working in the cornfields outside.
          Benjamin Parker went outside the fort to communicate with the natives,
      most of which were Comanches from north of the Red River, plus some Wichi-
      tas, Kiowas and Caddoans. They demanded food and water. Parker reported this
      to the others inside the fort, then returned to the parley where he was killed by
      lances. The war party rushed into the fort and killed several, hunting down those
      who fled.

The men returned from the fields and joined the fight, so the natives departed. They had killed five men and two women, raping and mauling several others. Two women and three children were taken as captives. The survivors fled east to the nearest settlement.
Sources: 103, 246

TX14   *Raid on Kiowas* • Summer, 1837
Location: Fort Elliott
The Kiowas were preparing for a Sun Dance on a tributary of Scott Creek, a branch of the North Fork of the Red River, when they were attacked by 48 Cheyennes. All of the Cheyennes were killed, as were six of the Kiowas.
Sources: 227

TX15   *Attack by Comanches* • August 10, 1838
Location: Texas
A war party of 200 Comanches attacked Col. Henry Karnes and 21 soldiers. Karnes was wounded, but the soldiers defeated the warriors and forced them to retreat.
Sources: 246

TX16   *Attack on Kickapoo Town* • October 16, 1838
Location: Northeastern Anderson County
Kickapoos led by Wapanahkah (Benito) attacked settlers after being promised by the Mexicans that the tribe could own the land it then occupied. Gen. Thomas J. Rush responded with an attack on a Kickapoo town. After three days of fighting, Vincente Cordova and the Mexicans he had there fled to Mexico.
   Some of the Kickapoos led by Pacana agreed to peace and others led by Benito, expecting to fight again, followed Cordova to Mexico.
Sources: 223

TX17   *Attack Near San Antonio* • October 20, 1838
Location: 5 miles from San Antonio
A group of surveyors were attacked by a Comanche war party as they worked about five miles from town, and two were killed. Thirteen residents rode from town to find out what had happened, and they were attacked by about 100 Comanches about three miles from the surveyors.
   The whites charged, but were surrounded by the Comanches. Eight of the San Antonio residents were killed and four were wounded.
Sources: 246

TX18   *Attack on Quapaws* • July 15–16, 1839
Location: Near Red River
Texas governor Mirabeau B. Lamar considered the Quapaws to be a menace and supported their removal. The Texas army commanded by Joseph E. Johnston attacked and defeated them decisively, pushing them across the Red River into Choctaw territory.
Sources: 330

TX19   *Attack at El Paso* • Summer, 1839
Location: El Paso

About 20 Kiowas led by Guadalonte traveled toward El Paso to fight with the Mexicans there. At Hueco Tanks they were attacked by Mexicans and Mescalero Apaches, who killed the horses. After being penned in a cave, the Kiowas were able to climb out and escape, abandoning some of their wounded.
Sources: 227

TX20 *Attack on Victoria* • August 7, 1840
Location: Victoria
Buffalo Hump assembled a war party of 1,000 including at least 400 warriors, and headed south from the Edwards Plateau toward the level plains near the Gulf of Mexico. They passed near San Antonio during the night of August 4. Texas Ranger Capt. Ben McCulloch recognized their broad, beaten path near Gonzales and alerted the countryside. Armed men were assembled on August 6, while the Comanches were surrounding the town of Victoria.

The warriors killed black slaves as they worked in the fields and stole horses and cattle. On August 7, they rode into town and set fire to buildings. They were met by gunfire, and retreated. Along the way they drove off about 2,000 horses and mules and killed 15 people.
Sources: 103, 246

TX21 *Great Linnville Raid* • August 8, 1840
Location: Linnville
After leaving Victoria, Buffalo Hump and his people crossed the Guadalupe River and followed Peach Creek, forming a crescent heading toward the Gulf of Mexico. They killed settlers and burned homes along the way. On August 8, they came to the town of Linnville.

The captured a granddaughter of Daniel Boone and killed her baby, and killed three more whites and two blacks. They took others captive and looted and burned the town. The livestock which they could not drive off was killed for sport.

Rather than the usual Comanche practice of riding fast and far to avoid being caught, Buffalo Hump and his people traveled north slowly, so they would not have to abandon their great amount of plunder.
Sources: 103, 246

TX22 *Skirmish Near Linnville* • August 9, 1840
Location: Near Linnville
Capt. Ben McCulloch came to Victoria on August 8, and men from the town joined his force, increasing it to 100. They headed toward the coast and on August 9 came upon one of Buffalo Hump's scouting parties. In a brief encounter, one Texas Ranger was killed.
Sources: 103, 246

TX23 *Battle of Plum Creek* • August 12, 1840
Location: Big Prairie
Buffalo Hump and his Comanches continued northwest toward the high country, and Capt. Ben McCulloch determined that they would have to cross Big Prairie near Plum Creek, a tributary of the San Marcos River. He ordered a small group to continue following and harassing the Comanches, while the rest headed

for Plum Creek. Others from Gonzales, Victoria, Lavaca, Cuero and other villages headed toward the planned battle scene.

The force that was formed at Plum Creek was led by Brig. Gen. Felix Huston of the Texas Army. Fourteen Tonkawa warriors arrived on foot to serve as scouts. When the Comanches were close, Huston gave the order to charge, killing several and stampeding the horse herd. Some Comanche warriors could not maneuver their horses out of the mess, and some fell and were trampled. Other made easy targets for the soldiers and volunteers.

Also killed at the battle were several Kiowas who had accompanied the Comanches on the raid along the Texas coast.

Many who tried to flee on foot were chased down and killed. The rest abandoned their loot and attempted to escape, being chased for 15 miles. Along the way, they killed the prisoners they had taken in Linnville. The only surviving captive was the widow of Maj. Watts, whose whalebone corset saved her from death by an arrow that hit her. About 80 warriors were killed.
Sources: 103, 227, 246

TX24 *Attack on Comanche Camp* • Late October, 1840
Location: Near the Concho River
Col. John H. Moore led a force of 90 buckskinned riders and 12 Lipan Apache scouts westward, across the Concho River and the Red Fork of the Colorado River. They came upon a large camp of Pehnahterkuh Comanches. After midnight, Moore approached their camp and deployed riflemen along the most likely escape route across the adjacent river.

At dawn, the riders approached within 200 yards of the camp before they were discovered. They stampeded the horse herd and shot Comanches indiscriminately, without regard to age or sex. Those who tried to flee were cut down by the sharpshooters. Fifty were killed in the camp and 80 in the river. No prisoners were taken. Only one Texan was killed.
Sources: 103

TX25 *Fight with Texan–Santa Fe Expedition* • August 30, 1841
Location: South of the Red River
War: Santa Fe Expedition
Arapahos aligned with the Kiowas attacked Pawnees at White Bluff along the upper Canadian River, killing all of them. Soon after, the Kiowas were attacked by American soldiers, who lost five men in the battle. The Kiowas took the horses and left, and when they returned a few days later, they killed another soldier.
Sources: 108, 227, 372

TX26 *Skirmishes in Central Texas* • Early 1856
Location: Central Texas
War: 2nd Cavalry Campaign
The first U.S. cavalry regiment, designated as the 2nd Cavalry, was formed in March of 1855 in Louisville, Kentucky, for operations in Texas. In the fall of that year, it marched from Jefferson Barracks, Missouri, to the Texas border.

In late February, G Company tracked down and killed several in a party of Wacos, having only two men wounded. Shortly thereafter, C Company ambushed some Lipan Apaches returning from a San Antonio raid, killing several warriors

and horses. On May 1, Capt. Oakes and C Company caught up with a Comanche war party after trailing it for over 300 miles, and killed several natives without incurring any casualties.
Sources: 103

TX27 *Skirmishes in Central Texas* • Late 1856
Location: Central Texas
War: 2nd Cavalry Campaign
Lt. Jennifer and B Company attacked a party of Comanches along the Llano River, scattering the warriors and capturing their equipment and horses. Also in November, Capt. Bradfute skirmished with a party of Comanches along the Concho River, killing four, wounding several, and capturing one plus some horses.
Sources: 103

TX28 *Attack Near the North Concho River* • February 12, 1857
Location: North Concho River
War: 2nd Cavalry Campaign
In February, Lt. Wood of the 2nd Cavalry took a Delaware scout and 15 soldiers along a trail and came upon Comanche warriors near the North Concho River. He was wounded leading a mounted charge, but killed three and captured the rest.
Sources: 91, 103

TX29 *Battle at Devil's River* • July 20, 1857
Location: Devil's River
War: 2nd Cavalry Campaign
Lt. John Hood left Fort Mason on a hunt for Comanches with 24 soldiers and a Delaware scout. After 12 days, they found a trail which the scout estimated was left by 20 Comanches. After four days, they came close to the Comanche party, which was now estimated at 50.

They came upon the Comanches on a bluff by the Devil's River, waving a white sheet as a flag of truce. Hood rode to meet them, well ahead of the rest of his men. As he did, the Comanches threw down the flag and charged on foot toward him. Other natives set the grass on fire between Hood and his men. Thirty mounted warriors appeared and fired on the cavalry's flanks. Hood shot two warriors who rushed at him, and then rode back to join his men.

The soldiers, armed with Colt revolvers, were able to hold off the 50 or so warriors. Later Comanche estimates put the number at nearly 100, of which the soldiers killed 19 and wounded many. Two soldiers were killed and four were seriously wounded. Hood had taken an arrow through his left hand.
Sources: 91, 103

TX30 *Elm Creek Raid* • October 13, 1864
Location: Young County, about 10 miles above Fort Belknap
Little Buffalo, spreading the word that the soldiers had left and that they could ignore the few remaining Rangers, amassed a force of about 1,000 Comanches and Kiowas. They crossed the Brazos River at its junction with Elm Creek, and rode up both banks of the creek.

The area was populated with about 50 settlers, many of whom they killed or mutilated, while looting and burning their homes. The homes attacked included those of Elizabeth Fitzpatrick, Tom Hamby, Thomas Wilson and George Bragg. Other settlers were taken captive.

Lt. N. Carson rode from Fort Belknap with 14 militiamen of Bourland's Border Regiment, and attacked about 300 warriors. Five of Carson's men died at once, several were wounded, and the rest fled. Militia from Decatur, 80 miles away, arrived too late to prevent the damage.

Sources: 103, 227, 373

TX31   *Battle of Adobe Walls* • November 25, 1864
Location: Canadian River
Col. Christopher ("Kit") Carson marched from Cimarron, New Mexico, with over 321 mounted soldiers, 14 officers, 72 Ute and Jicarilla Apache warriors and two Ute women. They followed Ute Creek to the Canadian River, then turned east into Texas. On November 24, the native scouts reported an encampment of 176 lodges 15 miles away at Adobe Walls, near the old abandoned trading post of Bent and St. Vrain. Continuing through the night, Carson reached the Kiowa Apache camp at dawn.

The army attacked with 250 cavalry across a two-mile-wide valley. The Utes and Jicarillas tried to steal the horse herd. As the army approached, the warriors formed a skirmish line and the women and children ran for the ridges behind the river. The defense was organized by Dohasan (To'hau-sen, or Little Mountain), who also sent for help from other Kiowa and Comanche lodges downstream.

The cavalry pushed the attack against the warriors for about four miles, reaching the adobe buildings that gave the area its name. As they did, they saw a Comanche village of 500 lodges less than a mile away. From it came thousands of warriors. Kiowas were also arriving.

Howitzer fire moved the natives out of range, and Carson declared the battle over. Soon, they were surrounded by 1,000 warriors, but were able to inflict damage and hold them off for several hours with cannon fire. The soldiers rode off and burned the Kiowa Apache camp, rejoining the supply column they had left before the first attack. The warriors did not follow, perhaps because they were concerned about the howitzers. Native losses included many dead and 150 wounded. The army had two killed and 10 wounded.

Sources: 103, 114, 227, 228, 229, 230, 294, 357

TX32   *Attack at Dove Creek* • January 8, 1865
Location: 16 miles south of San Angelo
Four hundred Confederate soldiers from Fort Chadbourne attacked the Kickapoo camp on Dove Creek, capturing the natives' horses. They responded with a counterattack that won them back their horses and caused the Texans to retreat. Figuring that there would be another thrust from the army, the warriors broke camp and rushed across the border into Mexico.

Twenty-six soldiers were killed and 60 were critically wounded. The Mexican band of Kickapoo welcomed the warriors into their homes and the Mexican government gave them land and agricultural supplies. After the end of the Civil War, the Kickapoos conducted several attacks into Texas lasting three to four days each.

Sources: 223

TX33 *Raids in Panhandle* • 1868
Location: Northern Texas
War: Outbreak of 1868
In January, parties of natives killed 25, scalped nine and captured 14 children, all of whom froze to death in captivity. In February, seven were killed, 50 mules and horses were stolen and five children were captured, two of which were returned to Agent Leavenworth.

Satanta's band attacked Montgomery County and killed one and captured three McElroy children. They returned to Eureka Valley on June 10. In July, a party raided a settlement on the Brazos River and scalped four. Thirteen Comanches and Wichitas invaded Spanish Fort on September 1, killing one woman and three or four of her children.

On October 14, Satanta led a party against a wagon train on Sand Creek, Colorado.
Sources: 66, 227

TX34 *Battle Near Seymour* • July 12, 1869
Location: Seymour
War: War of 1868–69
On June 12, White Horse led a raid on Fort Sill which resulted in the capture of 70 mules. The natives returned to the area, killing a woodcutter, wounding Levi Lucans, and killing a Mexican near the agency corral. They also attacked a party of Texans accompanying a herd of cattle, killing one.

A party of 100 led by Kicking Bird robbed a mail coach at Rock Station in Jack County. Troops led by Capt. Curwen B. McClellan followed the natives and, on July 12, a fight broke out. Outnumbering the soldiers two to one, the natives killed three and wounded 12. After dark, the natives retreated.
Sources: 227

TX35 *Attack on Wagon Train* • January 24, 1871
Location: Butterfield Trail, between Weatherford and Fort Griffin, Young County
A party of Kiowas led by Mama'nte and Quitan crossed the Red River into Texas and came down Salt Creek. They ambushed a wagon train which was manned by four black teamsters, all of whom were killed and scalped.

Through April of that year, 14 people were known to have been killed by natives in Young County, including some very close to Fort Richardson.
Sources: 103, 227

TX36 *Salt Creek Wagon Train Massacre* or
      Salt Creek Prairie Massacre • May 18, 1871
Location: Near Vernon
Satanta (White Bear), Satank (Sitting Bear), Big Tree and Mamanti (Sky Walker), and a Kiowa raiding party, all totalling 100 warriors, entered Texas and attacked Warren's mule train consisting of ten freight wagons of corn. Seven of the 12 teamsters were killed and 41 mules were captured. They had nearly attacked another train which was escorting Gen. William Tecumseh Sherman who had come to see how well the natives were being pacified. A vision Owl Prophet had reported the night before instructed them to leave the first party of white men alone and massacre the second, which they did.

Five days later, Sherman went to Fort Sill on the Kiowa reservation and ordered the arrest of Satanta, Satank and Big Tree. A fight erupted and the three chiefs were jailed. While they were being taken for trial for the murder of the teamsters, Satank was killed. The other two were found guilty and sentenced to hanging, but their sentences were commuted and they were released on parole.
Sources: 66, 70, 103, 147, 197, 227, 380, 403

TX37 *Attack on Wagon Train* • April 20, 1872
Location: Howard Wells, Crockett County
A party of Kiowas led by Big Bow and White Horse from the Comanches crossed the Red River into Texas and attacked a government wagon train in Crockett County. They killed 16 whites and held off two companies of cavalry led by Capt. N. Cooney before retreating to the Indian Territory. One officer and one soldier were killed.
Sources: 103, 227

TX38 *Raids on Fort Sill* • June 4 and 15, 1872
Location: Fort Sill
On June 4, Satank's son, An-pay-kau-te, led a party of Kiowas which killed Frank Lee, a cowboy, taking his scalp and an ear. On June 15, Tenawerka and a party of Comanches raided Fort Sill and stole 54 mules and horses.
Sources: 227

TX39 *Attack on Lee Home* • June 9, 1872
Location: Camp Cooper on the Brazos River
A war party organized by White Horse, to avenge the killing of his brother, attacked the home of Abel Lee. They killed Mr. Lee and a child, scalped Mrs. Lee, and captured three children. The natives fled to the Kiowa reservation, pursued by the soldiers.
Sources: 227

TX40 *Attack at McClellan Creek* • September 29, 1872
Location: North Fork of the Red River
Gen. Ranald Slidell Mackenzie, the commander of the 4th Cavalry, operated out of Forts Richardson, Griffin and Concho. They patrolled the region and believed that the Comanches would be vulnerable during their fall hunting season. Mackenzie led 222 soldiers and 20 Tonkawa scouts on an expedition in western Texas, coming across the village of Bull Bear and his Comanches along McClellan Creek, a branch of the Red River.
The soldiers attacked the village, killing over 50 while losing 20 to 23 of their own. They took 130 women and children captive. The black Buffalo Soldiers, called that by the natives to distinguish them from the white men, burned the homes, possessions and food supply. They also captured the horses, but some were retaken by warriors during the following night. Eventually, the natives got them all back.
Sources: 70, 91, 103, 227

TX41 *Battle at Adobe Walls* • June 27, 1874
Location: Hutchinson County in the Texas Panhandle
War: Red River War

Satanta and Lone Wolf of the Kiowas and Quanah Parker of the Kwahadi Comanches led a force of 700 Kiowas, Kiowa-Apaches, Comanches, Cheyennes and Arapahos in an attempt to eliminate the white hunters from the plains south of Kansas. They attacked the hide hunters' base near the crumbling ruins of an old adobe trading post.

The 28 hunters and one woman held off the natives, who suffered losses. On the third day of the battle a warrior was shot by a hunter with a Sharps rifle at a range of one mile, and the natives withdrew. Nine warriors had been killed, along with three of the defenders.

The natives broke into smaller groups and attacked whites across the plains from Colorado to Texas. Some eventually went onto the reservations. Satanta was arrested in November of 1874 for violating his parole, and four years later it was reported that he had committed suicide by jumping out of a prison hospital window.

Sources: 66, 70, 103, 147, 197, 220, 227, 246, 357

TX42   *Lost Valley Fight* • July 16, 1874
Location: Salt Prairie
War: Red River War
Texas Rangers looking for Comanches who had killed a cowboy at Oliver Loving's ranch fought with a party of Kiowas led by Mama'nte, between Flat Top Mountain and Cox Mountain. Twenty-five natives charged and killed David Bailey and wounded others.
Sources: 227

TX43   *Attack at Palo Duro Canyon* • September 28, 1874
Location: Staked Plain
War: Red River War
Lone Wolf and his Kiowas, along with some Comanches and Cheyennes, opted not to settle on a reservation and instead headed for their former secluded camping grounds in the Palo Duro Canyon. The canyon was almost unknown to the whites, but was found by an army column which descended the steep trail and attacked the camps spread along two miles of the canyon floor.

Initially, they attacked the natives' horse herd and then exchanged fire with the warriors. The natives resisted for a while, and then fled. The soldiers remained to burn and destroy the camps and kill the 1,400 horses and mules. Only four Comanches died, while Col. Ranald S. Mackenzie lost hundreds.

Nevertheless, in the long run it was a victory for the soldiers. With all of the destruction, the natives were forced to settle on the reservations to avoid death during the oncoming winter. During the weeks following the battle, natives attempting to get to the reservation were attacked and killed by Mackenzie and his men in 25 small actions.
Sources: 15, 66, 70, 103, 147, 227, 246, 308, 380

UTAH

UT1   *Fancher Party Massacre* or
       Mountain Meadows Massacre • September 7, 1857
       Location: Mountain Meadows
       A band of about 200 Paiutes attacked a wagon train traveling from Carroll County, Arkansas, bound for California, killing 128 emigrants. Some individuals who were from Missouri had shouted insults at the Mormons and named one of their oxen Brigham Young.
            The Mormons, who considered themselves at war with the United States because of political persecution, had incited the natives. The Mormon militiamen killed the men after they had laid down their arms, and then the natives killed the women and children. Only 17 young children were spared.
            John D. Lee, the Mormon in charge of Indian affairs in the southern part of Utah, was convicted of murder and was executed at Mountain Meadows on March 23, 1877. Lee had attempted to justify the killings as retaliation against Pres. James Buchanan's removal of Brigham Young as governor of Utah.
       Monument: A historic marker is located off SR 18 in Mountain Meadows.
       Sources: 8, 52, 133, 196, 254, 269, 348, 362, 381, 405

UT2   *Attack on Stagecoach* • May, 1863
       Location: Eight Mile Station
       A party of Goshute natives attacked a stagecoach near the Utah-Nevada border, killing the driver. Maj. Egan, a passenger, took the reins and brought the stage in. Previously, the Goshutes had been generally peaceful, but went on the warpath when they learned that the soldiers had been withdrawn from the area.
            Another coach was fired on as it neared Salt Lake City, with the driver and messenger being scalped and the mail destroyed.
       Sources: 362

UT3   *Ambush at Canyon Station* • July 8, 1863
       Location: Western Utah
       A party of Goshutes hid by the station before dawn until the keeper and his four men stacked their guns and departed for breakfast. The warriors attacked and killed all five, scalping four and taking the beard of the one who was bald.
       Sources: 362

UT4   *Ambush Near Moab* • 1881
       Location: Near Moab
       A party of renegade natives killed a rancher in Colorado, then ambushed an approaching posse near Moab. Eight members of the posse were killed.
       Monument: The graves of the eight are located at Pinhook Battleground off La Sal Rd. in the Manti-La Sal National Forest.
       Sources: 348

VIRGINIA

VA1 *Attack on the Kiskiacks* • Spring, 1572
Location: Tidewater Region of Virginia
War: Aviles Expedition
The Kiskiacks, one of a number of groups associated through a common Algonquian language, were visited by a Spanish ship in 1561. A boy from a ruling family was captured and taken to Spain and then Mexico, where he was baptized and given to the Dominican friars. In 1566, he offered to join an expedition to return to his country and establish a mission. That expedition did not make it to North America, but in 1570 he arrived with another. After they camped along the York River, he escaped and returned to his people. After five months, he and other Kiskiacks attacked the mission and killed all of the Spaniards, except for a boy whom they adopted.

    In 1572, Pedro Menendez de Aviles arrived with soldiers to punish the natives and retrieve the boy. Many Kiskiacks were killed and a chief was captured. Menendez agreed to trade the chief for the Spanish boy, but when the boy was produced the Spaniards opened fire on the Kiskiacks and killed several. The Spanish then left the Chesapeake Bay area for good. When the British arrived in 1584, the Kiskiacks killed and wounded several, and that expedition was abandoned.
Sources: 147, 321

VA2 *Attack on Jamestown* • May 26, 1607
Location: Jamestown
War: First Anglo-Powhatan War
A British expedition of 105 colonists established a settlement in the area inhabited by the Powhatans, who viewed the new people as a threat. After they had been there two weeks, James Fort was attacked by 400 Powhatans led by Wahunsonacock, as retaliation for the striking of a native who had tried to steal a hatchet from a settler. Two colonists were killed and 14 were wounded.

    They held off the natives with adequate muskets and cannon, the latter knocking a tree bough on them and scaring them off. In June, the English ship returned to England to pick up supplies and more colonists.
Museum: The village of Jamestown, with many original and restored structures, is located at the western end of Colonial Pkwy.
Sources: 32, 92, 147, 214, 233, 284, 412

VA3 *Skirmish at the James River* • Fall, 1607
Location: Kecoughton
War: First Anglo-Powhatan War
Capt. John Smith and several colonists traveled upriver to trade for food with the natives. When they encountered the Powhatans at the town of Kecoughton, the natives wanted their firearms, but the colonists refused. The disagreement resulted in a fight in which several Powhatans were killed.

    The British took enough corn from the natives' supplies to fill their boat and left trinkets and hatchets in exchange. This action, plus bullying for corn in other towns, angered the Powhatans. In mid–December, Smith was seized by Pamunkey

warriors along the Chickahominy River, and was taken to Wahunsonacock. To preserve the British as a potential source of weapons and metal, Wahunsonacock treated Smith well, adopted him as son, and returned him to James Fort.
Sources: 147

VA4   *Siege of James Fort* • Fall, 1609
Location: Jamestown
War: First Anglo-Powhatan War
When full-scale war broke out, Pamunkey warriors led by Opechancanough came back from early British successes to hold the colonists in check. The Powhatans laid siege to James Fort and were close to eliminating the British from the area. Capt. John Smith was injured in an accidental gunpowder explosion and sailed back to England.

Additional colonists arrived, the siege was lifted, and the British went on the offensive during the summer of 1610. For a year, they battled the Powhatans, killing many in a crusade against non–Christians.

This war ended in 1614 following the kidnapping of Pocahontas and a devastating raid by the English against the Pamunkeys.
Sources: 147, 321, 326

VA5   *Jamestown Massacre* • March 22, 1622
Location: James River
War: Second Anglo-Powhatan War
After the death of Wahunsonacock, his half brother, Opechancanough (Opechankano) succeeded him as the leader of the Powhatans and planned the destruction of the British. In March, his adviser, Nemattanew, was murdered by an Englishman. Two weeks later, Opechancanough began launching surprise attacks at 31 separate settlements and plantations along the river. On the first day, 347 to 400 white colonists were killed out of a total population of 1,200. The town of Henrico and its college for native children were destroyed.

At Martin's Hundred, 78 of the 140 settlers were killed, and only two houses and a part of a church were left standing.

The London Company, the force behind the colony, ordered the extermination of the powerful Powhatan Confederacy. The majority of the fighting happened in the first three years, but continued on for ten. In 1624, Opechancanough led 800 warriors in a two-day battle which showed their strength, but could not defeat the British. Peace was declared in 1632.
Museum: Ruins and reconstructed buildings are located on Jamestown Island.
Sources: 20, 27, 32, 34, 53, 92, 107, 133, 135, 147, 199, 212, 214, 233, 275, 284, 310, 321, 326, 380, 391, 412

VA6   *Raid on Powhatan Village* • July, 1624
Location: Eastern Virginia
War: Second Anglo-Powhatan War
A raiding party led by Capt. William Tucker set off to arrange for the release of English prisoners. Along the way, they fired on a Powhatan village led by Itopatin and killed at least 40 of its inhabitants. They attended the peace negotiation meeting and brought poisoned wine which they used to kill 200 natives. The soldiers killed an additional 50 with weapons.
Sources: 107, 321

VA7   *Attacks Against Settlements* • April 18, 1644
Location: Several points along the frontier
War: Powhatan Uprising
Opechancanough, said to then be near 100 years old, led a band of Powhatans, Wey-
anocks, Nansemonds, Pamumkeys and Chickahominies against settlements and
tobacco plantations, killing 400 to 500 of the 2,000 colonists. Their focus included
the upper section of the York River down to the south shore of the James River.
 Further fighting went on for two years, but the natives could not defeat the
British. Opechancanough was captured and exhibited publicly by the British. He
was then shot in the back while imprisoned, marking the end of the Powhatan
Confederacy and an obstacle in the way of British expansion.
Sources: 27, 53, 92, 133, 135, 147, 199, 214, 233, 310, 321, 326, 391

VA8   *Battle Along the James River* • 1656
Location: Near the waterfalls
The Virginia Assembly decided to remove by force the Rechahecrians who had
settled by the falls of the James River. Col. Edward Hill, 100 soldiers, and
Pamunkey allies led by Totopotomoi, attempted to eject the natives. Most of the
Pamunkeys became casualties and Hill was severely criticized for failing in his
mission. Not long afterward, the Rechahecrians left the area on their own accord,
probably settling along the Savannah River.
Sources: 332

VA9   *Raid on Mathews' Plantation* • July, 1675
Location: Stafford County
War: Susquehannock War
A band of Doegs from across the Potomac River in Maryland raided the planta-
tion of Thomas Mathews, killing his overseer. The settlers retaliated with attacks,
and the natives counterattacked. The settlers were led by Virginia's Lt. Col. John
Washington and by Maryland's Gov. Thomas Truman. When they caught the
Susquehannocks entrenched in a palisade near Fort Washington, five chiefs came
out to talk with the officers. The chiefs were seized and killed.
 The last action was an attack by Susquehannocks at plantations near the
James River falls. That action resulted in the death of an overseer on the land of
Nathaniel Bacon and three men on the plantation of William Byrd.
Sources: 310, 391

VA10   *Attack on Occoneechee Town* • May, 1676
Location: Eastern Virginia
War: Susquehannock War
Nathaniel Bacon led an English force that intimidated the Pamumkeys and forced
them to abandon their town. They arrived at the fort of the friendly Occo-
neechees, who helped the English by killing some Susquehannocks who were
camped nearby.
 The English then turned against the Occoneechees, killing most of them.
Sources: 321

VA11   *Attack on Oneidas* • 1727
Location: Eastern Virginia

An Oneida Iroquois party attacked a Catawba village in South Carolina while the warriors were away, taking the women and children as prisoners. While on their way back home, they were overtaken by the pursuing Catawba warriors. They fought for two days, with the Catawbas finally victorious.

The Catawbas killed 57 and took several prisoners. The Virginia government wanted to recover the captives to avoid the wrath of the Iroquois, who might exterminate the Catawbas. They could not get an agreement on this issue, straining the relations between the Catawbas and the Tuscaroras, who were allied with the Iroquois.
Sources: 332

VA12 *Attacks in Halifax and Bedford Counties* • Early May, 1758
Location: Halifax and Bedford Counties
War: First Cherokee War
A party of natives claiming to be Shawnees plundered and stole horses in two Virginia counties. In one encounter, the whites killed three before they retreated, leaving one settler mortally wounded. Soon after, two white men sent to negotiate for a return of the horses were severely beaten, and a party was raised to ambush the natives. Two of them were killed in an attack at a pass.
Sources: 332

VA13 *Raid on Eaton's Station* • July 20, 1776
Location: Holston River
War: Revolutionary War
A band of Cherokees raided the white settlement of Eaton's Station, located near Long Island. This was part of a Cherokee campaign which included Creek support, extending from southern Virginia through the western Carolinas to northern Georgia.
Sources: 3

VA14 *Battle of Fair Oaks* • May 31–June 1, 1862
Location: Seven Pines
War: Civil War
Included in Company K of the 57th Pennsylvania Volunteer Infantry were 12 Iroquois. One, Cornelius Plummer, was killed in action at Fair Oaks.
Sources: 60

VA15 *Seven Days Battles* • June 25–July 1, 1862
Location: Charles City
War: Civil War
Company K of the 57th Pennsylvania Volunteer Infantry participated in this series of actions, and Onondaga soldier Levi Turkey Williams was killed. From the original 12 Iroquois in Company K, two were killed in battle, one died of tuberculosis, four left with service-related disabilities, and two were considered deserters.
Sources: 60

VA16 *Second Battle of Bull Run* • August, 1862
Location: Manassas
War: Civil War

Catawbas of South Carolina were loyal to the Confederacy and some served as part of Company H of the 12th South Carolina Volunteer Infantry led by Capt. Cadwalader Jones. They participated in the rout of the Union army led by Gen. Philip Kearny.

Sources: 60

VA17 *Battle of the Wilderness* • May 5, 1864
Location: Near Chancellorsville
War: Civil War

The 1st Michigan Sharpshooters, led by Col. Charles V. DeLand, participated in the Battle of the Wilderness as part of Gen. Ulysses S. Grant's Army of the Potomac. That unit included Ottawas and Ojibwas recruited in the summer of 1863 in Oceana and Mason Counties, Michigan. They successfully withstood a charge by a force twice as large as theirs.

Sources: 60

VA18 *Battle of Spotsylvania* • May 11–12, 1864
Location: Near Chancellorsville
War: Civil War

The 1st Michigan Sharpshooters, including Ottawas and Ojibwas, suffered heavy losses from raking fire on May 11. They then were strengthened by Col. Charles V. DeLand and moved out of range. That night, the lines were reinforced and in the early evening of May 12, they charged the Confederate line. Under heavy fire, they advanced about 500 yards to a position about 50 yards from the enemy, paused, and then continued to the Confederates' front line.

They captured that, but then were exposed to vicious cross-fire which prevented advance or retreat. They held their position for an hour, then charged the Union line twice before they were driven back.

The total killed in Company K in the Wilderness and Spotsylvania was 34, of which 13 were natives.

Sources: 60

VA19 *Battle of Petersburg* • June 14–18, 1864
Location: Petersburg
War: Civil War

Native sharpshooters formed part of the force led by Gen. Ulysses S. Grant against that of Gen. Robert E. Lee at Petersburg. The Union army was five times larger than that of the south.

On June 17, the natives as part of Gen. Robert Brown Potter's 2nd Division, 9th Corps, carried out a surprise attack on the sleeping Petersburg defenders. The Union army captured 600 troops at Shand House east of the city.

The 1st Michigan Sharpshooters were also cited for their gallantry in repulsing two vigorous charges, in which they captured two officers and 86 soldiers. Twelve of the native sharpshooters were captured and of those, seven died as prisoners of war at Andersonville, with one other listed as missing in action. Two were killed in action, including 2nd Lt. Garrett A. Gravaraet.

Sources: 60

VA20 *Battle of the Crater* or *Battle of Petersburg Mine* • July 30, 1864
Location: Petersburg
War: Civil War
The 1st Michigan Sharpshooters, including Oneidas and Ojibwas, were involved in the Battle of the Crater, a Union defeat. They were fired on from all directions and had little ammunition. At least four of the natives died in the battle.
Sources: 60

WASHINGTON

WA1 *Attack on Salish Village* • July, 1828
Location: Vancouver
Local natives, likely Umpquas or Coast Salish, killed a group of people from the Hudson's Bay Company and took one woman prisoner. In retaliation, John McLoughlin of the Company sent four clerks and 59 servants to attack the natives, of which they killed eight.

When the natives refused to return the prisoner, the Company people fired on them, killing one and wounding one. After three days of cannon fire from Lt. Aemilius Simpson's gunboat, the natives traded their prisoner for a wounded native.
Sources: 72

WA2 *Attack on Fort Misqually* • 1844
Location: Puget Sound
Fort Misqually, commanded by Roderick Finlayson, included a farm for cattle and sheep. Coast Salish killed and ate the cattle, and Finlayson demanded payment. Instead, they and members of other tribes attacked the fort. Finlayson fired on them and drove them away.
Sources: 72

WA3 *Whitman Massacre* or *Wailatpu Massacre* • November 29, 1847
Location: Walla Walla
War: Cayuse War
In 1834, Methodist minister Rev. Jason Lee established a mission in the Willamette Valley. He was followed in 1843 by Dr. Marcus Whitman, who built a mission near the bend of the Columbia River and attempted to cure children suffering from measles. When the Cayuse native children died but the whites lived because they had better resistance to the disease, about 40 natives participated in the killing of Whitman, his wife Narcissa, and 11 or 12 others.

Whitman's home was visited by Cayuse chief Tilokaikt (Tilaukait, Tiloukakt), who distracted Whitman while he was tomahawked from behind by Tomahas (Tamahas, Tamsucky). Narcissa was shot, taken outside and shot several times more, dumped in the mud, and beaten.

Memorial: The Whitman Mission Historical Site is west of Walla Walla on US 12.

Sources: 8, 9, 10, 25, 81, 90, 129, 132, 136, 175, 203, 206, 213, 216, 250, 254, 285, 286, 288, 392, 393, 404, 405, 407, 410, 411

WA4 *Touchet Fight* • March 15, 1848
Location: Touchet River
War: Cayuse War
The troops led by Capt. Thomas McKay camped near the Touchet River, harassed by Cayuses and Palouses. On the morning of March 15, the natives continued their chase of the whites, who positioned themselves on a hilltop. To keep them from fording the Touchet River two miles away, they began an hour-long battle in which about four warriors were killed and 14 were wounded. The whites had none killed, about ten wounded, and they were all able to make it across the river in their quest to apprehend the murderers of the Whitman Mission.

They were caught, tried, convicted, and hanged on June 3, 1850, in Oregon City.
Sources: 9, 81, 285

WA5 *Attack Along Toppenish Creek* • October 6, 1854
Location: Near the Yakima River
Maj. Granville O. Haller led 100 men from The Dalles to round up a band of dissident Yakimas who resisted peaceful coexistence with white settlers. They fought for three days and, after five of his men were killed and 17 were wounded, Haller and what remained of his command slipped away.
Sources: 66

WA6 *Assassination of Bolon* • October 3, 1855
Location: Eastern Washington
War: Yakima War
Indian agent for the Yakimas, Andrew J. Bolon, went unaccompanied to a group of Yakimas and ate lunch with them. They then killed him, and Maj. Granville Haller left the fort at The Dalles with 84 men to teach the Yakimas a lesson.

The soldiers were defeated, having five killed and several wounded. The natives captured many wagonloads of supplies. The Yakimas reported that two of their warriors were killed and four were wounded.
Sources: 236, 285

WA7 *Haller's Fight* • October 5–6, 1855
Location: Toppenish River
War: Cayuse War
Subagent Bolton traveled to the Yakima River to investigate the Yakima killing of eight miners, and on his return to The Dalles he was also killed by Yakimas.

The army retaliated by sending Maj. Granville O. Haller with 104 men and a howitzer to the Toppenish River. They were met by 1,500 Yakimas led by Kamiakin and Qualchin and Columbia River Salish led by Quil-ten-e-nock, who beat them in a two-day battle. Five soldiers and two natives were killed.
Sources: 9, 81, 285

WA8 *Union Gap Fight* • November, 1855
Location: Union Gap
War: Cayuse War
Maj. Gabriel J. Rains commanded an army of 335 regular soldiers, mounted volunteers, and citizen companies, for a total of 700 men. With three howitzers, they headed into Yakima country. The Yakimas were told that there were more soldiers than had been with Maj. Granville O. Haller, so they planned to join with the Cayuses, Umatillas and Walla Wallas to form a larger defensive group.

In a battle at Union Gap, Rains successfully drove the natives eastward across the Columbia River.
Sources: 81, 213, 285

WA9 *Touchet River Fight* • December 7–10, 1855
Location: Touchet River
War: Cayuse War
Scouts from the Oregon volunteers of Col. James K. Kelly skirmished with Cayuses in the Walla Walla Valley on December 4. The following day, Peopeomoxmox and 40 to 50 warriors surrendered, likely as a delaying tactic to allow the rest of his people to escape. The rest of the Cayuses abandoned their camp on December 6.

When the troops reached the mouth of the Touchet River, they were attacked by 300 warriors and the fighting lasted most of the day. The warriors withdrew to the east to the La Roque farm near Wailatpu. When Capts. Alfred Wilson and Bennett arrived with their men, most of the warriors retreated.

The troops attempted to tie up Chief Peopeomoxmox and the rest of the prisoners, who resisted. The troops killed and scalped 20 and cut off the chief's ears and hands. The battle continued the following day with 500 warriors, at least 50 of whom died in battle. Two days later, they withdrew and the troops left to build a fort two miles above Wailatpu.
Sources: 9, 18, 81, 129, 236, 285

WA10 *Attack on Seattle* • January 26, 1856
Location: Seattle
War: Yakima War
Chief Leschi and a band of Nisqually warriors, plus some allies from other tribes, attacked Seattle. Natives friendly to the white settlers informed them of the plans, allowing them to prepare for a defense. The attack was thwarted by shelling from warships in the harbor.
Sources: 206

WA11 *Tucannon River Fight* • Mid-March, 1856
Location: Tucannon River
War: Cayuse War
Volunteer troops from Oregon led by Col. Thomas R. Cornelius moved north into the Palouse country, killing natives and seizing their animals. Nine warriors were killed near the mouth of the Tucannon River.
Sources: 81, 285

WA12 *Attacks in Columbia Valley* • March 26, 1856
Location: South of the Naches River
War: Cayuse War
Col. George H. Wright arrived from San Francisco to lead 350 men from The Dalles into Yakima country on a peacekeeping expedition. On March 26, Yakimas and Klickitats, joined by remnants of Chinookan bands, killed 15 in the cascades of the Columbia River valley before troops from The Dalles and Fort Vancouver were able to drive them away. Wright was criticized for failing to adequately guard the Cascades portage, leaving the area vulnerable.

Wright and his troops arrived at the Naches River on May 9, and the Yakimas decided that they wanted peace instead of another fight. Kamiakin disagreed, but his warriors were insufficient to launch an attack, so they rode away to Palouse country. The rest settled with the army and were rounded up to be relocated.
Sources: 66, 81, 91, 285

WA13 *Attack on Steptoe Camp* • September 19, 1856
Location: Walla Walla
War: Cayuse War
Col. Edward J. Steptoe took four companies of soldiers to support Gov. Isaac Ingalls Stevens, who attempted to resolve tensions in the area through talking. On September 17, the talks broke off and Stevens formed columns for a march to The Dalles. His 69 volunteers, 50 teamsters and herders, 50 Nez Perce led by Spotted Eagle and 500 horses were threatened by natives who positioned themselves for an attack which did not happen.

Stevens positioned his men and wagons in a defensive formation, and Steptoe sent Col. B.F. Shaw and 24 mounted volunteer dragoons and a mountain howitzer in case the warriors were to attack while they retreated. They began to leave during the night, and at first light a party of natives attacked and were driven off by a dragoon charge and the howitzer. The whites reportedly lost one man and had one serious injury, and the warriors had 13 killed or wounded. The warriors kept up their fire while the train continued on to Steptoe's command post.
Sources: 81, 236, 285

WA14 *Battle of Rosalia* • May 16–17, 1858
Location: Rosalia, southeast of Spokane
War: Spokane War
Timothy (Tamootsin), a Christian Indian, saw a column of 158 dragoons commanded by Col. Edward J. Steptoe near his farm at the confluence of the Alpowa Creek and the Snake River. Timothy and other Nez Perce helped the soldiers and their 85 pack animals across the Snake River and some of the Nez Perce joined the soldiers as scouts.

When they arrived near the present site of Spokane, they were attacked by 600 to 1,000 Spokanes, Coeur d'Alenes, Cayuses, Yakimas, Palouses and Sinkiuses, and the encounter developed into a series of skirmishes and running battles. The whites and their scouts made it back to and across the Snake River after 25 were killed.
Sources: 9, 66, 81, 91, 203, 236, 254, 285, 361, 380, 404

WA15 *Battle of Four Lakes* • September 1, 1858
Location: Thirteen miles from present Spokane
War: Spokane War
A force of 680 to 700 well-trained soldiers led by Col. George Wright, aided by 30 Nez Perce scouts, were able to defeat 500 Yakimas, Coeur d'Alenes, Palouses and Spokanes in a battle of revenge for the attack on Col. Edward J. Steptoe's force in May. It occurred at a high hill near one of the lakes.

While two companies of dragoons led by Maj. Grier went around one side to cut off retreat, two companies of riflemen accompanied by a howitzer and the Nez Perce went around the other side. Capt. Keyes led four companies of infantry on a charge at the hill. Native losses were estimated at 17 to 20 killed and 40 to 50 wounded. There were no soldier casualties. Nez Perce warrior Utsinmalikin was cited for his bravery during the battle.
Sources: 9, 66, 81, 91, 203, 236, 254, 285, 361

WA16 *Battle of Spokane Plains* • September 5, 1858
Location: Spokane
War: Spokane War
Col. George Wright led 680 to 700 soldiers and 30 Nez Perce scouts in another battle against Yakimas and Spokans. The soldiers lost none, destroyed a large quantity of supplies and captured 130 horses. Afterwards, Spokan Garry negotiated for peace for his tribe. The military power of the tribes was broken and Wright hanged some of the warriors to show what would happen if they ever again challenged the whites.
Sources: 9, 81, 91, 203, 236, 254, 285, 361

WA17 *Execution of Natives* • 1858
Location: Columbia River
War: Spokane War
Gen. George Crook captured five natives who confessed to having killed some prospectors. Crook had them executed, but found the act "exceedingly distasteful." He delegated the executions to Lt. Turner, who "rather enjoyed that kind of thing."
Museum: The General George Crook House Museum is located at the intersection of 30th and Fort Sts., Omaha, NE.
Sources: 19, 298

WEST VIRGINIA

WV1 *Massacre at Draper's Meadows* • July 8, 1755
Location: Draper's Meadows
War: French and Indian War
Subchief Black Wolf and a war party of 40 Shawnees were on a raid along the New

River, attacking isolated cabins. They traveled further up the river than they had previously been and came upon the settlement of Draper's Meadows.

The surprise attack was first seen by Bettie Draper, near her cabin. Before she could reach the cabin a warrior took and killed her baby. Col. James Patton shot and killed two Shawnees before they killed him and entered his cabin. Several others were tomahawked, knifed, or captured.

Sources: 374

WV2 *Massacre at Muddy Creek* • July 8, 1755
Location: Near the Greenbrier River
War: French and Indian War

Hokolesqua led a war party of 80 Shawnees in a raid along Muddy Creek, killing the Filty Yolkum and Frederick Lea families. Then following the creek to its mouth at the Greenbrier River, they attacked about 50 people who had gathered at the home of Archibald Clendenin. They killed all of the men and several of the women and children.

They completed the sweep with raids on settlements along Jackson Creek.

Sources: 374

WV3 *Massacre at Decker's Creek* • Early 1759
Location: Decker's Creek
War: French and Indian War

After the fall of Fort Duquesne in September of 1758, settlers from Virginia and eastern Pennsylvania streamed into the area between the Allegheny Mountains and the Monongahela and Allegheny Rivers. The Decker's Creek Settlement was established by Thomas Decker, and within six months natives destroyed it and killed all of its settlers.

Col. John Gibson and a force from Fort Pitt pursued the attackers, ten Mingos led by Kiskepila (Little Eagle). Gibson used his sword to lop off the head of Little Eagle, one soldier was wounded by a gunshot meant for Gibson, and the natives retreated.

Sources: 374

WV4 *Stroud Massacre* • Spring, 1772
Location: Gauley River

Adam Stroud of Philadelphia settled with his wife and five children at The Glades, near the Gauley River. They were discovered by a party of Cherokees, who killed them all. This concerned the settlers along the nearby Kanawha River and all along the Ohio River.

A party was assembled by William White and William Hacker and set off to seek revenge, but the Cherokees were gone. When they came upon the Delaware village of Bulltown, they assumed that they were the natives that had killed the Strouds. They killed about 20 natives, including Captain Bull and five families. The rest escaped to establish a new village on the White River.

Sources: 374

WV5 *Skirmish at Captina Creek* • April 25, 1774
Location: Mouth of Captina Creek on the Ohio River
War: Lord Dunmore's War

Capt. Michael Cresap and his party of about 30 traveled down the Ohio River to the Mouth of Captina Creek, located on the Ohio side of the river. They found a Mingo camp and prepared for battle, but a rifle went off prematurely and the 20 natives picked up their weapons. In the battle which ensued, three natives were killed and about two others were wounded. The rest escaped.
Sources: 374

WV6   *Battle of Point Pleasant* • October 10, 1774
Location: Point Pleasant
War: Lord Dunmore's War
Lord Dunmore and from 1,100 to 1,200 militia from Virginia defeated Cornstalk (Hokolesqua) and his Shawnees, plus Delawares, Wyandots, Senecas, Cayugas and Mingos, at the northeast corner of the junction of the Ohio and Great Kanawha Rivers. Included in Cornstalk's force of 900 was Logan, who was reported to have taken 13 British scalps in retaliation for the murder of the 13 members of his family six months earlier at Yellow Creek.

Included in the dead was Col. John Field, and Gen. Andrew Lewis was wounded. The warriors lost chief Picksinwah and many others. The natives retreated north of the Ohio and in November, Cornstalk signed a treaty with the British relinquishing hunting grounds in Kentucky.

In 1777, Cornstalk returned to Point Pleasant with another leading Shawnee on a peace mission when they were captured and threatened with death. When his son came to the fort, he was also captured. On the next day, a company of soldiers entered the fort and killed all three. The Shawnees, who had previously decided to remain neutral in the American Revolution, changed their position and instead allied with the British.
Monument: The Point Pleasant Monument State Park is located at 1 Main St., Point Pleasant, WV, and includes an 84-foot-high granite shaft to commemorate the battle.
Sources: 14, 19, 32, 120, 123, 147, 199, 221, 234, 288, 293, 315, 326, 339, 374, 409

WV7   *First Siege of Wheeling* • September 1–3, 1777
Location: To the rear of the stores presently fronting on the west side of Main St., half a block from the intersection with 11th St., Wheeling
War: Revolutionary War
At about 6:00 a.m., Dr. David McMahan directed his slaves, Sam and Ezra, to hire a pair of men to help them round up his seven horses which were grazing next to Wheeling Creek near Fort Henry (previously known as Fort Fincastle). They hired two off duty militiamen, John Boyd and Jacob Greathouse. About a half hour later as they were returning to the fort with the horses, four men came out of the brush and shot and killed Boyd. Two others grabbed Ezra and pulled him into the brush.

At Fort Henry, the soldiers and settlers readied for an attack, and Col. Shepherd concluded that what was coming was just a small hit-and-run raiding party. He sent Capts. Samuel Mason and Ogle and 24 men to scout the area and bring back the two bodies. Three more left shortly thereafter, leaving 33 men in the fort.

The scouting party rode into an ambush, and about 200 Mingoes, Wyandots, Delawares and Shawnees opened fire, killing most of the soldiers. Only a few survived, generally with serious wounds. Other soldiers near the fort ran to the sound of the shots and entered the fort. A British officer also appeared and offered Col. Ebenezer Zane a surrender, but he refused, choosing instead to fight to the death. Gunfire continued at the fort, the Zane house, and the blockhouse 60 yards away. Near the end of the day, some of the soldiers who had survived the ambush of Meason's party had alerted others in the area, and reinforcements were on their way to the fort.

Using tomahawks, the natives hollowed out a log as makeshift artillery. They aimed it at the fort and lit the charge, but the log exploded and killed three warriors, injured 17 others, and did no damage to the fort. They began to burn the buildings and kill the livestock. By the end of the day, about 20 natives had been killed, and none of the people in the fort had even been injured.

The reinforcements arrived the following morning, only to find that the attacking force had left during the night.

Sources: 3, 234, 374

WV8 *Ambush at The Narrows* • September 22, 1777
Location: Grave Creek Settlement
War: Revolutionary War
Two men had been sent out from Fort Henry to investigate the status of the Tomlinsons at the Grave Creek settlement on the shore of the Ohio River, about 12 miles from Fort Henry. As they were returning before dawn on September 1, they were killed by the natives preparing for the attack on the fort. Col. Shepherd still needed to find out about Grave Creek.

Three weeks after the attack on the fort, he sent out Capt. William Foreman and 45 riflemen and 20 volunteers who were happy to find that Tomlinson's cabins and blockhouse were still standing, although the settlers had moved to another settlement. They camped for the night, and in the morning prepared to return to the fort along the same route. Capt. William Linn expressed concern about passing back through an area called The Narrows, as he felt it would be easy to stage an ambush there.

Foreman disagreed, but left it up to each individual to choose whether to go through The Narrows or take a much longer route with Linn. Only three opted to go with Linn. The rest were ambushed in The Narrows by at least 40 Wyandots. Foreman and several others were immediately killed, and the rest took cover. Linn and the three with him heard the shooting and rushed loudly down a hill which they had climbed, unsuccessfully trying to make the natives believe that reinforcements had arrived. By the end of the next day, 18 survivors made it back to the fort. Twenty-two stripped and mutilated bodies were located and buried, and some were never found.

Sources: 3, 14, 374

WV9 *Attacks on Short Creek* • September 25, 1777
Location: Up Short Creek from Fort Vanmetre
War: Revolutionary War
Maj. Sam McCulloch of Fort Vanmetre sent John Burkey upstream to check on the status of the Bendure family. While he was on the way, a party of five Wyandots attacked the settlement. They shot John Bendure, but his dog kept the attack-

ers away so he could escape. His wife and three girls were captured, and two were killed and mutilated. His wife and one daughter were never found.
Sources: 374

WV10 *Raids in the Kanawha Valley* • July, 1780
Location: Kanawha River
War: Revolutionary War
On July 14, a party of Shawnees killed Hugh McIver and his wife in their cabin on the Greenbrier River. On July 15, a war party mortally wounded John Pryor and took his wife and daughter captive as they crossed the Kanawha River. On July 16, 30 Shawnees attacked three cabins a mile upstream from the Little Levels Settlement, killing Thomas Drennon, Jacob Smith and Henry Baker, and capturing their families. Leaving that area, they encountered William Munday, whom they killed, and Capt. and Mrs. Samuel McClung, who escaped.

On July 17, they killed William Griffith and his daughter, with his wife and son being taken captive. The Seneca party broke into smaller ones, and a party of whites followed one up Elk River, Little Sandy Creek and Aarons Fork. They fired on a camp of two men and a boy, killing one of the men, while the other escaped. The man who was killed was a white renegade, and they named the tributary White Man's Branch. The rescued boy was James Griffith, but his mother was with another party.
Sources: 374

WV11 *Second Siege of Wheeling* • September, 1781
Location: Wheeling
War: Revolutionary War
About 100 warriors appeared at Fort Henry, and the first casualties were 10-year-old Johnny Ryan, who was tomahawked, and 12-year-old David Glenn, who was captured. George Reagan was shot, but managed to get into the fort.

The natives traveled to Middle Wheeling Creek, 14 miles above the fort, and killed two more settlers. The next day, they attacked the cabin of Jacob Peek, killed two or three, and captured three. On September 9, they killed William Huston in his cornfield. The same day, they killed Jesse Cochran, Benjamin Rogers, William Ayres, and Capt. Sam Leter, in separate attacks.
Sources: 374

WV12 *Third Siege of Wheeling* • September 11–13, 1782
Location: Southeast corner of 11th and Main Sts., Wheeling
War: Revolutionary War
Col. Ebenezer Zane was concerned about episodes of violence and the sightings of warriors in and near Wheeling. His spies reported that 400 warriors were on the Ohio side of the Ohio River, but heading for Wheeling. Zane had the two dozen men and the rest of the settlement move into his fortified house and Fort Henry, 60 yards away. He also sent Capt. William Boggs 25 miles away to the town of Washington and requested that Col. David Williamson bring his army to defend the area.

Warriors effectively surrounded Wheeling and began light shooting. Ebenezer turned over the fort to his brother, Silas, and moved into his house to provide two locations from which to shoot. Silas was offered the opportunity to surrender by Capt. John Pratt of the Queen's Rangers, but he declined.

The warriors found a log and cannonballs, but remembered the mistake which had been made five years earlier, when the makeshift cannon blew up. In the blacksmith shop, they reinforced it with iron and aimed it at the fort. When they fired it, the back blew out with a squishing sound, and they abandoned the idea.

During the night, several attempts to scale the fort's walls were unsuccessful. Sporadic firing occurred throughout the day. During the night of the 12th, Williamson left Washington with about 40 men. By the morning of the 13th, the natives left the area and Williamson's men arrived. They searched unsuccessfully for someone to fight, and returned to Washington two hours later.

The Wheeling defenders had only two minor wounds, while killing an undetermined number of warriors and British militia.

Sources: 3, 374

WV13 *Attack at Fort Vanmetre* • March, 1789
Location: Mouth of Short Creek
A party of warriors attacked Fort Vanmetre and killed some of the members of the John Vanmetre family. Others were captured.
Sources: 374

WV14 *Attacks on Monongahela River* • March, 1789
Location: Near Clarksburg
A party of natives attacked and killed the families of John Mauck, Jethro Thompson, William Johnson, John Simms and William Stalzer, with a total of eight killed.
Sources: 374

WV15 *Attack at Kennedy's Bottom* • Mid-March, 1789
Location: Kennedy's Bottom
In an attack at Kennedy's Bottom, Maj. William Bailey was killed and the entire five-member Jason Quick family was captured.
Sources: 374

WV16 *Attack Near Maysville* • March, 1790
Location: Maysville
War: Ohio Indian Wars
Three men headed to Maysville from Blue Licks were ambushed by Shawnees and two were killed. The third, Peter Livingston, was captured and then rescued by Simon Kenton.
Sources: 374

WV17 *Attack on King's Creek* • Late April, 1790
Location: King's Creek
War: Ohio Indian Wars
John Martin established a sugar camp near the mouth of King's Creek. His children, Sarah, Moses and Thomas Martin, were being visited by Mary and Margaret Castleman when a party of Wyandots attacked. John was killed and the five children were taken to Half King's Town on the Upper Sandusky River.
Sources: 374

WV18 *Attack on Purdy Cabin* • Early May, 1790
Location: Wheeling
War: Ohio Indian Wars
The under-construction cabin of the Robert Purdy family was entered by a party of warriors who attacked them in their bed. Mr. Purdy was killed, and his infant son was killed while Mrs. Purdy tried to escape with him. Mrs. Purdy was knocked unconscious, and when she came to her two daughters had already been captured and taken across the Ohio River.
Sources: 374

WV19 *Attack at Clendenin's Fort* • Mid-May, 1790
Location: Near the confluence of the Kanawha and Elk Rivers
War: Ohio Indian Wars
James Hale was shot and scalped by a warrior as he was fetching cool water for a sick fiancée, and she also soon died. Nearby a few days later, a Shawnee rifle ball killed Charles Staten as he drank from a stream.
Sources: 374

WV20 *Attack at Buffalo Creek* • May 29, 1790
Location: 16 miles above Wheeling
War: Ohio Indian Wars
Rebecca Van Buskirk was captured by natives on her way to the village of Washington, but her horse returned to her home on Buffalo Creek. Her husband, Lawrence, organized a group to ambush the natives, but one man made too much noise and alerted Rebecca's captors. They immediately tomahawked her and disappeared.
Sources: 374

WV21 *Attack on Grave Creek* • July, 1790
Location: Grave Creek
War: Ohio Indian Wars
Robert Carpenter was visiting his uncle, Joseph Tomlinson, when Robert was shot in the shoulder by a party of Wyandots. They captured him, but were unsuccessful in capturing the Tomlinson horses. Robert offered to help, but when he got near the horses he escaped into the underbrush. He made it to the home of Nathan Masters and the Wyandots gave up and crossed to the north bank of the Ohio River.
Sources: 374

WV22 *Attack at Tackett's Fort* • Summer, 1790
Location: Mouth of Coal River, just below Fort Clendenin
War: Ohio Indian Wars
A party of Shawnees attacked Tackett's Fort while John and Lewis Tackett and their mother were harvesting turnips in a nearby field. All three were captured. The warriors attacked the fort, tomahawking Christopher Tackett and capturing Sam Tackett, a small boy, and Betsy and George McElhany. Before they left, they killed George McElhany and burned the fort.
Sources: 374

WV23 *Attack at Wheeling* • September 27, 1790
Location: Wheeling
War: Ohio Indian Wars
A pair of Shawnee warriors captured Henry and John Johnson, aged 13 and 11, who had been sent out to bring in the cows. When the captors made camp for the night, the boys were ordered to sleep between them, but they only pretended to sleep. They took the captors' rifle and tomahawk and killed one, severely injuring the other. When they returned to Wheeling, Jacob Wetzel organized a party to track down the injured native.

    As they searched, two Wyandots attacked Wetzel but he was able to overpower and scalp both.
Sources: 374

WV24 *Attack at Wheeling Creek* • September 6, 1794
Location: Wheeling Creek at the mouth of Bruce's Run
War: Ohio Indian Wars
A small party of Wyandots attacked George Tush, who was out feeding his hogs. Although severely wounded, he ran back to his cabin but curiously continued on to the home of neighbor Martin Wetzel. While he was there, the natives killed all five children and captured Mrs. Tush. After about a two-mile walk, they tomahawked and scalped her, too.

    The Wyandots then came upon William and Sam Beckham, who had gone out to fetch horses. They were captured and taken to a camp at Grave Creek, and during the night both were tomahawked. Neither died and William went for help. When the warriors returned, they killed Sam.
Sources: 374

WISCONSIN

WI1 *Attack by Iroquois* • 1653
Location: Door Peninsula
War: Beaver Wars
Iroquois tribes from New York attacked the Neutrals, Hurons and Petuns, and survivors and tribes such as the Potowatomis moved westward. Many settled in Wisconsin, and built the fortified village of Mitchigami, meaning "Great Lake."

    Iroquois armed with guns obtained from the English and Dutch attacked the defenders, who were armed only with bows and arrows, lances and clubs. The Iroquois were tired and hungry and were unable to capture the fort. The tribes agreed to a cease-fire and a feast, in which the Potowatomis fed them poisoned corn.

    Sick and weak, the Iroquois attempted to flee, but they were pursued and nearly annihilated.
Sources: 323

WI2   *Battle Near Prairie du Chien* • July 21, 1814
          Location: Mississippi River
          War: War of 1812
          American troops led by Lt. Col. McKay traveled to the old trading town of Prairie
          du Chien at the mouth of the Wisconsin River to construct a fort in the Sauk and
          Fox area. Before it was finished, British troops drove them away and captured
          the site.
               American reinforcements attempting to get to the fort were trapped by Black
          Hawk. In heavy fighting, 34 Americans were killed or wounded and one of their
          ships was burned, causing them to retreat back down the Mississippi River.
          Sources: 91, 315, 349

WI3   *Attack at Prairie du Chien* • June 26, 1827
          Location: Prairie du Chien
          War: Winnebago War
          During 1826, two white farming families were murdered by a band of Winneba-
          gos, and in June of 1827, a group of whites kidnapped and raped seven native
          women.
               Chief Red Bird, Chichonsic and Wekau obtained some whiskey and ammu-
          nition from a trader in Prairie du Chien and walked two miles to the cabin of
          Registre Gagnier, who had been offensive to the natives. They killed Gagnier and
          Solomon Lipcap and scalped his baby daughter. The three Winnebagos then
          went to another cabin where they killed seven.
               Troops stationed at Fort Howard in Green Bay and led by Maj. William
          Whistler put down the rebellion led by Red Bird, who was captured and held as
          a prisoner.
          Sources: 90, 292, 415

WI4   *Battle of Wisconsin Heights* • July 21, 1832
          Location: Southeast of Sauk City
          War: Black Hawk's War
          A Winnebago spy informed frontier fighter Col. Henry Dodge of Black Hawk's
          flight into Wisconsin. The army followed them through the present site of Madi-
          son to a point near Sauk City. The Sauk and Fox warriors stood their ground and
          fought until nightfall, while the women and children escaped across the Wis-
          consin River. During the night, the warriors also left. The Americans had one
          killed and estimated that they killed 40 natives. Black Hawk claimed that he had
          lost only six.
               They had obtained canoes from the Winnebagos and hoped to obtain per-
          mission to pass Fort Crawford and disembark on the Iowa side of the river. How-
          ever, regular soldiers attacked and killed several. Any not drowned or captured
          were massacred by Menominees led by white officers.
          Memorial: A state historical marker indicates the site of the battle on US 12, two
          miles southeast of Sauk City.
          Sources: 189, 195, 315, 349, 375, 384, 386, 414, 415, 422, 423

WI5   *Battle of Bad Axe* or *Bad Axe Massacre* • August 2–3, 1832
          Location: 2.5 miles north of DeSoto
          War: Black Hawk's War

Gen. William Harney led 50 men on a search for Black Hawk and wanted to take 300 friendly Potowatomis with him, but they were not interested. Instead, he had a few Menominiee scouts, who left him before they got to Black Hawk and his Sauk and Fox warriors. He tracked them down at an old trading post along the Wisconsin River.

About 1,300 soldiers were dispatched from Fort Armstrong under the command of Gen. Henry Atkinson, Col. Henry Dodge, and Col. Zachary Taylor. With Taylor were Harney and Capt. Abraham Lincoln. On the prairie, the soldiers with long rifles and the natives with muskets exchanged hours of fire. Along Black Hawk's rear, there was also fire from the river steamer *Warrior*.

Sharpshooters on the *Warrior* killed several Sauk and Fox women as they were driven onto mud flats and islands in the Mississippi River near the confluence with the Bad Axe River. Twenty-one soldiers were killed and seven were wounded. Native deaths were estimated from 300 to 350, and the soldiers took 39 prisoners. Sixty-eight of those who successfully made it to the western bank of the Mississippi were killed and scalped by 100 Sioux led by Wabasha, and the rest were taken prisoner by them.

Black Hawk had escaped with nearly 50 of his people, but was captured two days later by Lt. Jefferson Davis and was brought to Fort Atkinson.

The Winnebagos, former allies of Black Hawk, deserted him. He surrendered to the army on August 27 and was taken on a tour in the east to convince him of the whites' power. This defeat marked the virtual elimination of the Sauk and Fox tribe.

Monuments: (1) There is a historical marker on SR 35, about 4 miles south of Genoa, at the probable site of the battle; (2) There are exhibits on the Black Hawk War at the Hoard Historical Museum and Dairy Shrine, 407 Merchants Ave., Fort Atkinson, WI.

Sources: 7, 34, 90, 91, 92, 133, 135, 144, 195, 196, 211, 315, 349, 365, 375, 381, 384, 386, 414, 415, 422, 423

WYOMING

WY1 *Siege of Mateo's Fort* • 1829
Location: Powder River
Antonio Mateo established the first store in Wyoming in 1828, 400 miles south of the next nearest trading post. The following year, he was attacked by Sioux or Blackfeet. His 200-foot square stockade was besieged for 40 days until the warriors departed.
Sources: 325

WY2 *Battle of Pierre's Hole* • July 18, 1832
Location: Near Jackson
Massachusetts ice dealer Nathaniel Wyeth and a combined party of trappers, at

the southern end of Pierre's Hole, encountered a large party of Gros Ventres returning from a visit with Arapahos in Colorado. Allied with the trappers were Nez Perce and Flatheads, and they pinned the Gros Ventres in a grove of willows and cottonwoods from which they were able to escape after dark.

Killed were more than 25 Gros Ventres, five trappers and seven Nez Perce.
Sources: 10, 229, 285

WY3   *Grattan Massacre* • August 19, 1854
Location: East of Fort Laramie
Gen. William "White Whiskers" Harney was sent north from Fort Leavenworth across the Platte River in response to an incident involving a white man's cow. He had left it with the peaceful Bois Brule on his way to the California gold fields, to be sent on with the next wagon train. Before that occurred, the Bois Brules were visited by a band of the Oglala Sioux who hunted and killed the cow.

A force of 30 Fort Laramie soldiers led by Lt. Grattan visited the Bois Brule camp of Black Beaver to investigate the incident. Conquering Bear, chief of the Brules, offered the pick of their herd in return, but Lt. Grattan wanted to arrest the offender, a Minneconjou who had been staying in the village as a guest.

The soldiers brought cannon to the camp, and when the offending Minneconjou was not produced he opened fire. The shooting of Conquering Bear was witnessed by a young Sioux called Curly, later known as Crazy Horse, who decided to fight the whites to avenge the attack. Grattan was shot by Straight Foretop and hacked to pieces by the warriors. The rest of the soldiers were shot by the warriors.
Sources: 4, 20, 62, 66, 91, 110, 114, 158, 159, 182, 213, 315, 325, 392, 407

WY4   *Fight with Snakes* • June 20, 1861
Location: Sweetwater River
An Oglala and Lakota raiding party led by Hump sought out a band of natives who lived in grass houses, believed by them to be a sign that they would not be good fighters. They were reputed to be relatives of the Snake tribe, but their language was different.

The battle lasted for two hours, with the Lakotas losing some horses and having one warrior injured. They killed one or two Snakes, but could not dislodge them from their position. Curly individually charged the enemy's position twice on horseback, killing two warriors with his bow. He dismounted long enough to scalp them in full view of the Snakes. The Lakotas and Oglalas departed. Among the casualties was Washakie's son.
Sources: 110

WY5   *Attacks on Stage Stations* • April, 1862
Location: Between Casper and Fort Bridger
A band of Bannocks attacked several stage stations including Split Rock Station, driving off 60 horses and mules, destroying mail and killing several men. These included an attack during April on the Sweetwater River midway between Rawlins and Lander, the present route of US 287. Ten to 12 natives attacked a party of nine whites, who then walked eight miles to the Three Crossings station for safety.
Sources: 159, 362

WY6   *Attack at Cooper's Creek Station* • July 5, 1863
Location: 25 miles northwest of Laramie

A band of Utes attacked the relay station and ran off all of the mules. They then went to the Medicine Bow station located within 20 miles for Fort Halleck and stole the stock, firearms, ammunition and provisions, and stripped the keeper and his men.

Six companies of the 1st Colorado Volunteer Cavalry responded, led by Maj. Edward W. Wynkoop. About 30 miles from Fort Halleck they were found behind log breastworks on a hillside, and a battle resulted in 20 to 60 Utes killed. One soldier was killed and four were wounded.
Sources: 362

WY7   *Attack at Fort Laramie* • January 7, 1865
Location: Fort Laramie
War: Sioux War

Fort Laramie was commanded by Capt. N.J. O'Brien, defended by one company of the 7th Iowa Cavalry and two artillery pieces. On January 7, 1,000 Cheyenne and Sioux warriors appeared at the fort after killing one at the Julesburg stage station.

O'Brien left 13 in the fort and rode out with the 28 others to engage the natives in battle about a mile from the fort. The warriors charged and killed several, then surrounded the survivors. The artillery kept them from killing all of the soldiers.

The next morning, the soldiers searched for the bodies of the dead and found them severely mutilated. Later, the natives stated that 63 of theirs had been killed.
Sources: 159, 201

WY8   *Attack at Fort Laramie* • February 2, 1865
Location: Fort Laramie
War: Sioux War

Cheyenne and Sioux warriors came again to the fort and burned the stage company's station house, stores, one or two houses, and other fort outbuildings.

In Devil's Dive, a ravine about five miles below the station, Capt. N.J. O'Brien and four or five men were escorting the stage toward the station when they came upon the scene. O'Brien rode up to a bluff where natives were, took the blanket of one, and swung it around his head. The warriors took this as O'Brien's signal for a large force to attack, and the natives began to retreat. The stage driver quickly made it to the fort and the artillery helped hasten the warriors' retreat.

The whites were able to inflict little damage on the Cheyennes and Sioux, other than making them drop some of their plunder as they left. However, the action of Capt. O'Brien prevented a full-scale attack on the fort by a native force with superior numbers.
Sources: 201

WY9   *Battle at Platte Bridge Station* • July 24–26, 1865
Location: Platte River
War: Cheyenne-Arapaho War

As revenge for the massacre at Sand Creek, several chiefs decided to attack at the northernmost army outpost along Bozeman's Trail. The Southern Cheyenne were led by Roman Nose, and he was joined by Red Cloud, Dull Knife, and Old-Man-Afraid-of-His-Horses. With 3,000 warriors, they reached the hills overlooking the bridge crossing the North Platte River on July 24. About 100 soldiers were within the stockade across the bridge.

They sent ten warriors to the stockade, but the soldiers would not come out. On July 25, decoys drew the soldiers only as far as the bridge. On July 26, a platoon of cavalry came out and crossed the bridge. The Cheyenne and Sioux attacked, killing Lt. Caspar Collins, with some escaping to join a rescue party on the bridge. Cannon fire from the fort ended the attack.

Soon after, a wagon train arrived. Apparently that was what the cavalry had left the fort to meet. The natives surrounded the wagons, charged, and killed all of the soldiers. The chiefs, believing that they had taught the white men a lesson, departed with their warriors to the Powder River country.

Museum: The Fort Caspar Museum is located at 4001 Fort Caspar Rd. in Casper, and has exhibits relating to local history.

Sources: 32, 114, 133, 159, 178, 230, 350

WY10 *Battle of Tongue River* • August 29, 1865
Location: Ranchester
War: Sioux War

Brig. Gen. Patrick Connor and Col. J.J. Kidd led the army in a surprise raid against the Arapaho village of Black Bear and Old David. Eight soldiers were killed as well as 35 Arapaho warriors. The army captured 500 horses and burned 200 lodges.

Sources: 275, 325, 350

WY11 *Action Along the Powder River* • August, 1865
Location: Along the Powder River
War: Sioux War

In July, Brig. Gen. Patrick E. Connor led three columns of soldiers to march from the south to trap natives between armies in South Dakota and Montana. Another unrelated column was heading west toward the Powder River on the way to the Montana gold fields. The existence of the fourth column, headed by civilian James A. Sawyers, became known to the Cheyenne and Sioux on August 14 or 15. Red Cloud, Dull Knife, George Bent and about 500 warriors rode out to meet them.

The warriors spread out on two hills, between which the wagon train and 300 cattle were heading. When they began firing at the soldier escorts, the wagons circled. A few warriors came close and opened fire over the next two to three hours, and they were met with howitzer fire. It was basically a stalemate, with the wagon train being immobile but well defended.

Upon the urging of the chiefs, a conference was held with the officers to determine why they had come into native territory. The soldiers wanted to know why the natives had fired on peaceful white men, and it was explained that it would continue to occur until the government hanged Col. John M. Chivington, the officer responsible for the Sand Creek Massacre. The chiefs offered to let Sawyers proceed west, but by a different route.

When Sawyers protested because the route would not take him by the fort which Gen. Connor was building on the Powder River, the chiefs became aware of the impending invasion from the south. Red Cloud and Dull Knife allowed the wagon train to take the route they desired in exchange for some food and supplies. Sawyers and his men had to put up with harassment from a second band of Sioux, but Red Cloud and Dull Knife took their warriors away.
Sources: 70, 109

WY12 *Fighting Along the Bozeman Trail* • July 17, 1866
Location: South of Sheridan
War: Red Cloud's War
Col. Henry B. Carrington established three forts along the Bozeman Trail, a shortcut route promoted by John M. Bozeman which ran from the Oregon Trail near Fort Laramie to western Montana. Carrington, known to the natives as Little White Chief, used Fort Phil Kearny as his headquarters.

While it was being built, it was visited by a party of Cheyennes which included Black Horse and Two Moons. They concluded that the fort was too strong to attack, and that the soldiers would have to be lured out of it for the natives to be successful.

On July 17, a party of Red Cloud's Oglala Sioux stampeded 175 mules and horses from the fort's herd. As the soldiers pursued over a 15-mile route, they suffered the first casualties in this area. Throughout the summer, the fort's builders were harassed by Crazy Horse, High Back Bone, Yellow Eagle and other warriors who also attacked wagon trains, settlers and messengers along the trail. Forts were raided to drive off animals and kill soldiers who went outside the protective walls. The forts were essentially in a state of siege.
Sources: 20, 64, 70, 147, 161, 254

WY13 *Attack Near Fort Connor* • August 16, 1866
Location: 60 miles south of the mouth of Crazy Woman Fork
War: Sioux War
Gen. Patrick E. Connor established a fort and named it after himself. With his men was a company of Pawnee scouts commanded by Capt. Frank North. They had enlisted for pay so they could fight the Sioux, Cheyennes and Arapahos. While the white soldiers were cutting logs for the construction of Fort Connor, the Pawnees searched the area for their enemies.

A small party of Cheyennes, including Yellow Woman, was seen approaching from the south. When Yellow Woman and four men in an advance party saw the natives, she thought they were also Cheyennes, or perhaps Sioux. The Pawnees signalled that they were friends, and the party approached. When they came close enough, the Pawnees attacked and killed the advance party.
Sources: 64, 70, 114, 325

WY14 *Skirmish Near Fort Phil Kearny* • December 6, 1866
Location: Near Buffalo
War: Red Cloud's War
Two Oglala Sioux, High Back Bone and Yellow Eagle, took about 100 warriors and positioned them along the road from Fort Phil Kearny to the area where the

fort's woodcutters worked. Red Cloud took other warriors to the ridgetops. The leaders communicated with mirrors to signal the movement of Col. Henry B. Carrington's troops.

The soldiers and natives exchanged rifle fire, and the army appeared to be in a state of confusion. Once, Crazy Horse appeared on the trail in front of one of the officers, who led several soldiers in pursuit. As they ran down the road, they were easy targets. Lt. Horatio S. Bingham and Sgt. G.R. Bowers were killed and several others were severely wounded.

Museum: The Fort Phil Kearny Museum is located off Interstate 90, between Sheridan and Buffalo.

Sources: 70, 90, 109, 114, 161, 254, 350

WY15 *Fetterman Massacre* or *Battle of Fort Phil Kearny* or
Battle of the Hundred Slain • December 20–21, 1866

Location: Seventeen miles south of Sheridan

War: Red Cloud's War

After Col. Henry B. Carrington's forts were under siege and the Bozeman Trail was rendered unsafe for use, Red Cloud decided that it was time to seriously battle the white soldiers. In a camp near Fort Phil Kearny, over a thousand lodges from the Sioux, Cheyenne and Arapaho drew together. An ambush was set up in the hills, but the soldiers refused to follow a mixed 10-warrior decoy group into the area. Red Cloud chose not to attempt a direct assault against the fort. Carrington also wanted to have some real action.

The Sioux trapped a party of the fort's woodcutters, and Capt. William J. Fetterman was sent out on December 21 with 80 men to rescue them. They chased decoys led by Crazy Horse and fell into an ambush, and all 81 were killed by 2,000 Sioux, Arapaho and Cheyenne warriors led by Little Horse. The natives suffered almost 200 casualties in their victory.

Museum: Fort Fetterman, ten miles west of Douglas off of SR 93, contains exhibits about the early days of the fort. At the battle site, on US 87 south of Sheridan, is a stone monument marking the location of the massacre.

Sources: 4, 19, 20, 62, 64, 66, 70, 90, 91, 92, 109, 110, 114, 115, 147, 159, 161, 197, 201, 213, 220, 254, 265, 278, 288, 315, 325, 346, 350, 380

WY16 *Battle of Wagon Box* • August 2, 1867

Location: Little Piney River, 1 mile south of Story

War: Red Cloud's War

Red Cloud personally led a war party of 1,500 to 2,500 against Fort Phil Kearny. They had intended to lure the rest of the soldiers out of the fort with their decoys, but several Sioux let themselves be seen too early, and the soldiers stayed in the fort.

They then turned on a party of 32 woodcutters and soldier escorts who fought from within a circle of 14 wheelless iron wagon beds. The soldiers led by Capt. James W. Powell had breech-loading repeating Springfield rifles, and the Sioux soon retreated.

Eventually, the government decided that the opening of the Bozeman Trail was not worth the expense and fighting. In 1868, the army abandoned the forts, which were then burned by the natives. The honor of burning Fort Phil Kearny in late August of 1868 went to Little Wolf's Cheyennes.

Monument: Fort Phil Kearny State Historic Site includes a self-guided tour past the site of the fight, and is reached by following signs from Interstate 90, exit 44W.
Sources: 64, 66, 70, 91, 110, 114, 147, 159, 161, 197, 201, 220, 254, 265, 315, 325, 350, 380, 392, 407

WY17 *Attack on Dull Knife's Village* • November 25, 1876
Location: Battle Creek, near the North Fork of the Powder River
War: Great Sioux War
"Three Star" Gen. Crook assembled an army of about 1,000, with 168 wagonloads of rations and 400 pack mules loaded with powder and ammunition. He was looking for Crazy Horse and came through the Powder River country attacking all natives in his path.

A camp of Northern Cheyennes led by Dull Knife spending the winter in Wyoming was set upon by a portion of Crook's army, led by Gen. "Three Fingers" Ranald S. Mackenzie. They took their positions during the night and attacked at dawn, with Pawnee mercenaries leading the charge toward the 150 lodges. Several were killed, the homes were burned, and the ponies were herded against a canyon wall and shot.

The survivors headed for Crazy Horse's village on Box Elder Creek. That night, 12 Cheyenne babies and several elderly natives froze to death. After three days in the snow they reached Crazy Horse's camp.
Sources: 4, 66, 70, 91, 110, 114, 401, 418, 420

WY18 *Attacks in Yellowstone* • August 22–31, 1877
Location: Yellowstone National Park
War: Nez Perce War
After the Battle of Camas Meadows, the Nez Perce crossed the Targhee Pass into Montana and entered the new Yellowstone National Park on August 22. Bands of Nez Perce captured two tourist parties (the Shively/Radersburg and Helena Parties) totalling 19 individuals. Near Mammoth Hot Springs, they burned a cabin while chasing off some horses and killed two whites in the park.

The captives were not harmed and some escaped. The reputation of Chief Joseph grew and he was looked on by some as a hero.
Monument: A marker inside the park shows the location of the August 24 capture of the Radersburg party.
Sources: 70, 86, 175, 191, 236, 285, 286, 315, 366, 378

CANADA

CN1 *Battle at Bloody Point* • 1577
Location: Niountelik Island, near Baffin Island, Northwest Territories
War: Frobisher Expedition

In the summer of 1576, Martin Frobisher sailed from England to find the Northwest Passage from the Atlantic to the Pacific Oceans, when he came upon Niountelik Island. The Inuits welcomed him and brought goods to trade. An Inuit agreed to guide the British through the area and Frobisher sent five of his men with him in a skiff, but they rowed away and did not reappear, presumably having been captured.

Frobisher abducted one Inuit and his kayak and sailed to England with his remaining crew of 13. Although the Inuit died in England, Frobisher was sent back in 1577 because a mineral he had found turned out to contain gold. On his second trip, Frobisher brought soldiers and had a peaceful session of trading. However, they decided they needed interpreters and tried to capture two of the Inuits. A fight broke out, with Frobisher being wounded.

The following day, 40 soldiers attacked 18 Inuit men, women and children and killed most of them. They also sacked the Inuit camp. In August, they returned to England with three captives, who died there. In 1578, Frobisher made a final trip to Baffin Island, but the natives avoided contact with him.
Sources: 147

CN2   *Huron Massacre* • March 16, 1649
Location: Georgian Bay, Ontario
War: Beaver Wars
The first Jesuits landed at Quebec in 1625 and began decades of missionary work, befriending the Hurons north of Lake Ontario. They permitted the Ste. Marie Mission to be established along the Georgian Bay on Lake Huron and were involved in the fur trade which had pelts moving to Dutch traders in Fort Orange (Albany, New York).

The Hurons acted as middlemen in the fur trade between the Ottawas and the French. There then developed competition for the French from the Dutch and British who had befriended the Iroquois. When the latter ran out of furs on their own land, they tried to buy them from the Hurons, who refused. This made it difficult for the Iroquois to obtain British weapons and other goods, and they attacked Huron fur fleets to steal their pelts. The Hurons retaliated with attacks against Iroquois villages.

The Iroquois struck back with an attack that nearly annihilated the Hurons. At sunrise, 1,000 Iroquois natives attacked a Huron village near the shore of the bay, scrambling over the walls of the protective stockade. They killed many of the inhabitants and took as captives Fathers Jean de Brebeuf and Gabriel Lalemant, who were there to say mass for the Huron converts. They were tortured to death.

The Hurons then abandoned and burned 15 of their villages on May 1 and from 6,000 to 8,000 of them took refuge on Christian (St. Joseph) Island, while others joined neighboring tribes. All but a few hundred of those on Christian Island died the following winter.

The Ottawas attempted to assume the middleman role in the trading with the French, but the Iroquois also attacked them, so they fled to Green Bay, Wisconsin, to live with the Potawatomis. The Iroquois continued warfare against other tribes, including the Neutral Nation in 1651 and the Eries in 1656.
Monument: The Martyrs' Shrine on Hwy. 12 on the east side of Midland, ON, is a monument to the eight missionaries killed by natives between 1642 and 1649.

Across the street is Sainte-Marie Among the Hurons, a re-creation of the Jesuit mission.
Sources: 19, 135, 178, 275, 284, 300, 310, 315, 323, 380

CN3   *Assault on Montreal* • 1660
       Location: Ottawa River, Quebec
       War: Beaver Wars
       From the beginning of the French colonization of Canada, the Iroquois laid siege to the settlements along the St. Lawrence River. Throughout the 1650s, they harassed Montreal, ending with a major assault in 1660.
           The native force was beaten off by Adam Dollard and a small group of followers who staged a fight to the death at the Long Sault Rapids along the Ottawa River.
       Sources: 178

CN4   *Destruction of LaChine* • 1687
       Location: LaChine, Quebec
       Iroquois relations with the French were not good, and warriors destroyed LaChine and attacked Montreal.
       Sources: 135

CN5   *Raid on LaChine* • August 5, 1689
       Location: Just Outside Montreal, Quebec
       War: King William's War
       A large Iroquois war party made several raids against French settlements on the upper portion of the St. Lawrence River. Several hundred were butchered or captured at LaChine, near Montreal.
       Sources: 92, 199, 290, 328

CN6   *Attack Near Montreal* • 1692
       Location: Just outside Montreal, Quebec
       Several Oneida warriors, including many of their principal chiefs, were in a house near Montreal. Nearly all were killed in a surprise attack by the French, who were accompanied during the attack by a Cayuga chief and several Caughnawaga Iroquois.
       Sources: 300

CN7   *Raid on Quebec* • June, 1747
       Location: Montreal, Quebec
       New York's Governor William Johnson, in response to the Iroquois grand council's policy of neutrality, instigated a Mohawk raid against the French in Montreal. The attackers suffered great losses in an ambush.
       Sources: 131

CN8   *Attack on Fort Beausejour* • June 2, 1755
       Location: Near Amherst, New Brunswick
       War: French and Indian War

On June 2, a 40-ship British fleet sailed into Chignecto Bay to capture Fort Beausejour, and were seen by the French defenders before they disembarked at Fort Lawrence, across the Missaquash River. The 5,100 men were under the command of Col. Robert Monckton. The French readied for an attack with only 150 soldiers, plus 1,200 Acadian laborers and several Micmacs.

On June 4, 250 British soldiers crossed the river at Pont a Bout and were met by French gunfire. Shortly thereafter, the French retreated with their native allies and burned down their blockhouse. Monckton moved his men into position east of the fort. The adjacent town and church were burned to provide a field of fire.

On June 8, British Lt. Alexander Hay was captured near Pont a Bout by a party of natives working for the French. The French tried some long-range shooting, and one evening Capt. de Bailleul took a patrol out of the fort and into a skirmish with the British.

On June 16, a 13-inch shell from a British mortar hit the curtain wall next to the main gate. Its explosion killed Lt. Hay, Sieur Rambaut, and the native interpreter, and wounded two other officers. The French surrendered and left the fort, which was then occupied by Col. Monckton and renamed Fort Cumberland.

Sources: 55

CN9   *Capture of Fort Frontenac* • August 26–27, 1758
Location: Fort Frontenac, Ontario
War: French and Indian War
Small British boats were seen heading toward the fort on August 25, and British gun batteries were being dug the following day by Col. Corsa and his men from Long Island. On the evening of the 26th, mortar fire came from the fort, but the digging continued.

On August 27, the main gun was in place and was used to break a hole in the fort wall. Soon, Payan de Noyan surrendered the fort to Lt. Col. John Bradstreet, who took over 76 cannons, two sailing vessels which the French had previously captured, and supplies which were then shipped to the western forts.

The elimination of this French post destroyed their shipping in the area, and hurt their ability to feed their soldiers and buy the loyalty of the natives. The fall of the fort concerned the natives and made them reconsider who had the real military strength.

Sources: 55, 133

CN10 *Attack on Odanak* • 1759
Location: St. Francis, Ontario
War: French and Indian War
Robert Roger's Rangers attacked the village of Odanak at the present site of St. Francis. Rogers sustained heavy casualties on the trek home.

Sources: 284

CN11 *Battle at Montmorency* • July 31, 1759
Location: Beauport, east of Quebec, Quebec
War: French and Indian War

Gen. Louis Montcalm came to Quebec on May 22 and surveyed its defenses, expecting an attack by the British from the water. He had five battalions (10,800 men) of regulars and militia build the Beauport lines. In addition, he had a force of sailors, gunners and natives. The village of Beauport served as his field head-quarters when the British arrived by ship. Maj. Gen. James Wolfe saw the defen-sive line and decided to approach elsewhere. His troops camped on Ile d'Orleans and east of the Montmorency River, across from Beauport.

During July, the British ships put a strain on the city's lifeline to the out-side, threatening its food supply. On July 21, Col. Carleton raided the village of Pointe aux Trembles, only 18 miles west of Quebec.

On July 31, Wolfe attacked but found that there were underwater boulders which prevented the large troop transport ships from reaching the shore. It took 75 minutes to locate an acceptable channel, and a storm erupted while 7,000 British soldiers prepared for battle. Natives and Canadians patrolled along the Montmorency River.

By the time the storm cleared, the British were in despair. They retreated after suffering 430 casualties, being sure to take their dead to prevent mutilation by the French-allied natives.

Monument: A redoubt built by Wolfe's forces is in the park at Montmorency Falls on Rte. 440 near Quebec.

Sources: 19, 34, 55, 80, 131, 170, 178, 336

CN12 *Attacks Near Quebec* • August, 1759
Location: Near Quebec City, Quebec
War: French and Indian War
Gen. Louis Montcalm concluded that the likely place for the British to attack was at Pointe aux Trembles, 18 miles west of Quebec, so he set up his headquarters there. Col. Bougainville was organizing a mobile counterattack force and before he was ready, Adm. Holmes brought a brigade across the river, commanded by Brig. Gen. James Murray. They landed where Montcalm had predicted and were met by French dragoons, then regulars, and more dragoons. The British hastily retreated with only 140 casualties.

On August 18, Holmes and Murray attacked the town of Deschambault, 28 miles west of Quebec. This time, the dragoons were ineffective and the British plundered the personal possessions of the French troops and left before Col. Bougainville arrived with the regulars.

Sources: 55

CN13 *First Battle of the Plains of Abraham* • September 13, 1759
Location: West of Quebec City, Quebec
War: French and Indian War
Maj. Gen. James Wolfe decided to cross on September 7 from Ile d'Orleans between Pointe aux Trembles and St. Augustin, drifting upriver with the night tide. Heavy rain, however, postponed the action for days. While they waited, they studied the north bank and saw a path leading upward to the Plains of Abraham.

During the night of September 12–13, the soldiers crossed the St. Lawrence, passing by the mouth of the St. Charles River northeast of Quebec. Sentries on the cliffs, believing the ships to carry supplies for the French, let them pass. No one believed that the British would attempt to scale the face of the cliff. The light infantry did just that, climbing 175 feet to the open plain without resistance from anyone.

When the advance party reached the top, a sentry challenged them and was subdued. Musket fire broke out, but the British party led by William Howe and Capt. Delaune continued and caused the French in their camp to flee. Three waves of soldiers were to come across by boat but shortly after dawn cannon fire began from the Samos Battery, on the cliff about a half mile away.

Gen. Louis Montcalm sent Capt. Jean-Daniel Dumas with the militia to hit the British on their left, and a force of natives and more militia to hit them on their right. Montcalm assembled his army to attack from the front. The French moved in, standing up and making considerable noise. The British were lying down and firing, moving forward silently. The French-allied natives were involved in the fighting along the British right flank.

After fierce fire, the French broke ranks and ran. Gen. Wolfe was mortally wounded, and as his last act ordered the French to be cut off from the bridge back to the Beauport lines. The battle also saw the deaths of British Col. Robert Monckton and French Gen. Montcalm. On September 18, de Ramezay capitulated and gave Quebec to the British.

Monument: National Battlefields Park is located between rue Bougainville and Champs-de-Bataille, Quebec.

Sources: 19, 32, 34, 55, 65, 80, 115, 131, 133, 336, 389

CN14   *Second Battle of the Plains of Abraham* • April 28, 1760
Location: West of Quebec City, Quebec
War: French and Indian War
The French unsuccessfully attempted to retake Quebec, and were met in the lower town by British muskets late on January 30. On February 24, they tried again with a force of 800 but were repulsed by Brig. Gen. James Murray and three regiments.

To break the British naval blockade of the St. Lawrence River, Gen. de Levis had to retake Quebec as soon as the river ice broke. They needed to be ready for the French fleet, which waited for the thaw. At the end of April, the British force in the city numbered 5,600, of which 2,300 were on sick lists.

On April 27, Levis used St. Luc de la Corne's native warriors to form a screen to protect the French soldiers as they came ashore at St. Augustin and headed toward Quebec. The force of 8,000 French, Canadians and natives formed a battle line on the Plains of Abraham, and Murray formed his to meet it. He hoped that his large artillery would balance the French superiority in numbers.

The battle raged along the plains to the top of the cliff, where Capt. Donald McDonald and most of his hundred men were killed and scalped by the French-allied warriors. The French line moved forward, and Murray drew his men back to the walled city of Quebec. He had lost 1,000 men and 20 big guns. Levis had lost about 100 officers and 1,000 men.

Sources: 55

CN15   *Skirmish at Ile-Sainte-Helene* • October 30, 1775
Location: Ile-Sainte-Helene, Quebec
War: Revolutionary War
Sir Guy Carleton led a force of about 800 Canadians, 130 troopers and 80 Iroquois

natives against the Americans who held the shore at Longueuil. As the Canadian boats approached, 130 Americans opened fire on the shore, leaving 30 to guard the fort. After an exchange of rifle fire in which three natives were killed and two were captured, Carleton led his army back to Montreal.
Sources: 77, 377

CN16 *Battle of the Cedars* • May 20, 1776
Location: 25 miles north of Montreal, Quebec
War: Revolutionary War
Joseph Brant, a Mohawk war chief, was the commander of several hundred Seneca, Cayuga and Canadian natives. Their presence on the battlefield supporting the British, making a force of 650, frightened the American officers, causing them to retreat after a holdout of less than an hour.
Sources: 3, 123, 234

CN17 *Invasion of Canada* • July 12, 1812
Location: Fort Malden, Ontario
War: War of 1812
U.S. Gen. William Hull crossed the Detroit River with 3,000 men to attack 300 British at Fort Malden. He defeated a small party of British and natives, but was ambushed by Tecumseh and 150 warriors.
At about the same time, Capt. Henry Brush and 230 American soldiers were protecting a supply convoy on the way from Ohio to Detroit. Brush asked for some relief troops from Hull, who on August 4 sent him 200 men. Tecumseh trapped them south of Detroit and killed several, sending the rest back to Hull.
Brush then withdrew to the south, behind the Raisin River. Hull abandoned his invasion of Canada and returned to the U.S.
Sources: 315

CN18 *Battle of Monguaga* • August 8, 1812
Location: South of Detroit, Ontario
War: War of 1812
Gen. William Hull sent a relief column of 600 men to rescue the force of Capt. Henry Brush, waiting along the Raisin River. They were intercepted by a party led by Tecumseh and composed of natives and British troops.
Heavy fighting occurred and Tecumseh was wounded in the leg. The British and warriors retreated to the Canadian side of the Detroit River, but Brush's supply convoy remained in a defensive position south of the Raisin River.
Sources: 181, 315

CN19 *Attack on Detroit* • August 14, 1812
Location: Near Detroit, Ontario
War: War of 1812
Maj. Gen. Isaac Brock brought 300 British reinforcements to Fort Malden and asked Tecumseh for advice. Tecumseh urged an immediate attack on Detroit. Brock sent a message to Gen. William Hull, who refused to surrender. The British opened fire on Fort Detroit and the warriors crossed the Detroit River.
A British courier whom Brock allowed to be captured told Hull that 5,000 more Chippewa warriors were on the way to join Tecumseh. This happened just

after 350 more Americans had left Detroit to attempt to rescue Capt. Henry Brush's supply column on the Raisin River. Tecumseh marched his warriors by the fort three times in single file, tricking Hull into believing that the reinforcements had arrived. Hull then surrendered Detroit to the British.
Sources: 181, 315

CN20 *Battle of Queenstown Heights* • October 13, 1812
Location: Queenstown Heights, Ontario
War: War of 1812
A force of British soldiers and natives defeated the American army commanded by Gen. Stephen Van Rensselaer. U.S. losses were about 1,000. British deaths included Gen. Isaac Brock.
Memorial: Queenstown Heights Park, seven miles north of Horseshoe Falls, includes a 210-foot monument to honor Gen. Brock.
Sources: 19, 79, 133

CN21 *Battle of Beaver Dams* • June 24, 1813
Location: Southwest of St. Catharines, Ontario
War: War of 1812
Mohawks from Upper Canada plus men from the St. Regis, Caughnawaga, and Lake of the Two Mountains reserves from Lower Canada, defeated an American force led by Dr. Cyrenius Chapin. The battle began with the natives, led by Capt. Francois Dominique Ducharme, killing all of the members of the American advance guard. At the first musket volley the Mohawks, allies of the Americans, fled the area.

The rest of the American force led by Lt. Col. Charles Boerstler was driven back to a coulee, surrounded, and forced to surrender.
Sources: 79, 149, 379, 400

CN22 *Battle of the Thames* or *Battle of Moraviantown* • October 5, 1813
Location: Thamesville (Moraviantown), Ontario
War: War of 1812
A year after Tecumseh allied himself with the British and successfully defeated the Americans at Fort Detroit, he found out about the British plans to retreat into Canada. An American force of 3,000 to 3,500 led by Gen. William Henry Harrison was advancing on Detroit, and with British Col. Henry Procter planning on going to Ontario, Tecumseh had to join him or risk defeat.

The 1,000 warriors took their position in a swampy thicket, and Col. Richard M. Johnson and his 1,200 to 1,500 mounted Kentucky riflemen appeared with a midafternoon cavalry charge. The British soon retreated, leaving the natives who fought and lost. Tecumseh was killed in battle, with the kill attributed to Johnson, and the warriors retreated into the forest. All of the 700 British were either killed or captured.

After Tecumseh's death, bands of Wyandots, Chippewas, Delawares and Miamis left the British side and made their peace with Gen. Harrison. This battle ended the hopes of many natives who had sought a unified resistance to the Americans.
Monument: The life of Tecumseh is portrayed in a historical outdoor drama at Sugarloaf Mountain Amphitheatre, Delano Rd., Chillicothe, OH.

Sources: 8, 14, 19, 26, 30, 37, 79, 91, 92, 126, 133, 144, 147, 149, 169, 181, 195, 199, 223, 231, 257, 293, 299, 301, 311, 315, 323, 370, 380, 382, 389, 390, 393, 396, 397, 398, 406, 415

CN23 *Battle of Lundy's Lane* • July 25–26, 1814
Location: West side of Niagara River, Ontario
War: War of 1812
On July 25, British Maj. Gen. Phineas Riall set up a defensive line of 950, north of the American force camping on the Chippewa battlefield. The line was strung along Lundy's Lane, about three miles from the 2,600 Americans. American reinforcements crossed from the east at Lewiston. In the afternoon, Brig. Gen. Winfield Scott attacked along the Queenstown Road. His 1,000 men fought until darkness with 1,600 to 1,800 British.

About 9:00 p.m., the Americans were strengthened by the 1,300-man 2nd Brigade led by Brig. Gen. E.W. Ripley, which included Porter's militia and native brigade.

The Americans retreated on the morning of July 26, after suffering 171 deaths and 572 wounded. The British had 84 killed and 559 wounded. Each side had captured or missing about 860 men.
Museum: Lundy's Lane Historical Museum is located at 5810 Fery St., Niagara Falls, ON.
Sources: 19, 396, 397

CN24 *Encounter in Saskatchewan* • 1885
Location: Western Saskatchewan
War: Riel Rebellion
Louis Riel was a mixed-blood, or Metis, who desired to establish a form of self-government for his people and their full-blooded relatives in the western provinces of Canada. He led hostilities in Manitoba in 1869 and a second relatively bloodless encounter in 1885. He was executed after it, and that ended the conflict between the natives and the Canadian government.
Sources: 20

MEXICO

MX1 *Raid on Tamaulipas* • Winter, 1837
Location: Tamaulipas
A Kiowa raiding party ventured into Mexico to attack the Timber Mexicans. Among the Kiowa casualties was K'inahiate.
Sources: 227

MX2 *Attack on Raiding Party* • January, 1851
Location: Sonora

An Apache raiding party of about 250 was driving a large herd of stolen cattle when they were attacked by Ignacio Pesqueira and 100 troops. The soldiers had 26 killed and then Pesqueira's horse was killed. The soldiers assumed that their leader was lost, so they withdrew. A few days later, Pesqueira walked into Arizpe and was acclaimed by his men as a hero.

Sources: 48

MX3   *Battle at Pozo Hediondo* • January 19, 1851
Location: Pozo Hediondo, Sonora
About 20 miles east of Arizpe and Pozo Hediondo (Stinking Wells) an attack was carried out by a band of Apaches. Mangas Coloradas was identified by some as its leader, but there are discrepancies in the accounts which bring this into doubt. This encounter may have been confused with a battle which Geronimo claimed over 50 years later had occurred later in 1851 and closer to Arizpe.

Sources: 298

MX4   *Janos Massacre* • March 5, 1851
Location: Janos, Chihuahua
Just outside Janos, Geronimo camped with his mother, Alope, his three children, and other Bedonkohe Apaches. In charge of the band was Mangas Coloradas.

While most of the men were in town trading, 400 Mexican soldiers from Sonora, commanded by Col. Jose Maria Carrasco, attacked the camp. They killed the 16 warriors who stayed behind to guard the camp, took all of the weapons and ponies, destroyed supplies, and killed many of the women and children. Included in the dead were Geronimo's mother and children.

Geronimo claimed that the massacre was unprovoked, and his later action near Arizpe was in retaliation for it. Official Mexican records show the action at Pozo Hediondo coming first, and that Carrasco's action at Janos was in retaliation for the earlier, unprovoked, attack by the Apaches.

Sources: 298

MX5   *Attack Near Arizpe* • 1851
Location: Near Arizpe, Sonora
A party of Chiricahua Apaches led by Geronimo as a guide, but commanded by Mangas, Cochise and Juh, camped in northern Sonora near the town of Arizpe. When eight Mexicans came from the town to talk, the Apaches killed them all.

The following day, the Chiricahuas fought with two Mexican cavalry companies consisting of about 100 soldiers. Geronimo wanted revenge on the soldiers who had killed his family in the Janos Massacre, and he believed these were those men. Geronimo directed the natives to form a hollow circle near a river among some trees.

When the cavalry came within 400 yards, he led a charge which resulted in the deaths of several of the soldiers. The battle lasted for over two hours. The Mexicans lost 26 and had 46 wounded.

Sources: 298

MX6   *Attack at Kaskiyeh* • Summer, 1858
Location: Kaskiyeh, Chihuahua
War: Apache War

A band of Bedonkohe Apaches on their way to Casa Grande stopped at the town of Kaskiyeh, staying for several days in tents outside of the town. Daily, some would go into town to trade while the camp was left with only a small guard.

One day, the camp was attacked by Mexican soldiers who killed all of the women, children, and the warriors left there as a guard. They also stole the ponies and weapons and destroyed the Apaches' supplies. Without the capability of fighting back, Mangus Coloradas moved the survivors back to their homes in Arizona. Geronimo swore vengeance against the Mexican army.
Sources: 47, 166

MX7   *Battle Near Arizpe* • Summer, 1859
Location: Near Arizpe, Sonora
War: Apache War
Three bands of Apaches, the Bedonkohe led by Mangus Coloradas, the Chokonen led by Cochise, and the Nednhi led by Whoa, prepared for battle against the Mexican army. Geronimo acted as their guide into Mexico.

They camped near Arizpe and killed eight Mexican soldiers who rode out to them to talk. A larger contingent of soldiers appeared the next day, and fighting lasted most of the day.

On the next day, two companies each of cavalry and infantry arrived, and Geronimo directed the battle which lasted a few hours. The Apaches were victorious, killing several of the soldiers. They felt they had avenged the massacre at Kaskiyeh the year before.
Sources: 47

MX8   *Attack in Sierra de Sahuaripa Mountains* • Summer, 1860
Location: Sahuaripa Mountains, Sonora
War: Apache War
Geronimo and 25 warriors laid in ambush in the Sierra de Sahuaripa Mountains and attacked a column of Mexican soldiers. The army dismounted and arranged the horses as breastwork, which the Apaches charged from all directions. Hand-to-hand fighting resulted in the death of all of the Mexicans. Geronimo had been knocked unconscious by the butt of a Mexican carbine, but he survived and recovered with a scar.
Sources: 47

MX9   *Attack on Mule Train* • Spring, 1861
Location: East of Casa Grande, Chihuahua
War: Apache War
Geronimo led a party from Arizona and attacked a pack mule train. The Mexicans rode away without loss of life, abandoning their animals and possessions.
Sources: 47, 168

MX10   *Attack in Sierra de Sahuaripa Mountains* • Spring, 1862
Location: Southern portion of Sierra de Sahuaripa Mountains, Sonora
War: Apache War
Geronimo and eight warriors returned to Mexico to attack pack mule trains. One with four drivers sighted the Apaches and fled, leaving their mules, blankets, tobacco, calico and loaf sugar. Another loaded with cheese fled for the mountains.
Sources: 47, 168

MX11 *Attack Near Pontoco* • Winter, 1864
Location: Near Arizpe, Sonora
Twenty warriors led by Geronimo attacked several settlements in Mexico and headed north toward their home in Arizona. As they reached Pontoco, they attacked a pack train and killed one of its three drivers. They then became drunk on the mescal they captured from the train.

On the following day, they captured some cattle and drove them home. The Apaches remained peaceful for the remainder of the winter.
Sources: 47, 168

MX12 *Attack Near Arizpe* • Autumn, 1865
Location: Near Arizpe, Sonora
Geronimo led nine warriors on foot into Mexico, where they attacked several settlements south of Casa Grande and captured several horses. On the way back to Arizona, they camped in the mountains near Arizpe and turned the horses loose in a canyon.

Mexican troops approached the camp at the end of the canyon, and troops opened fire on them as they went to get the horses. The Apaches scattered, met up three days later in the Sierra Madre Mountains, and then returned to Arizona.
Sources: 47, 168

MX13 *Attack Near Gulf of California* • Late Autumn, 1865
Location: Near the Yaqui River, Sonora
Geronimo took four warriors to the Gulf of California, which they believed to be a large lake. They attacked several settlements and captured 60 cattle northwest of Arizpe. When they reached home in Arizona, they butchered the cattle and dried and packed the meat.
Sources: 47, 168

MX14 *Attack in Sierra de Sahuaripa Mountains* • Early Summer, 1866
Location: Sierra de Sahuaripa Mountains, Sonora
Geronimo led 30 mounted warriors through Chihuahua to Santa Cruz, through the Sierra Madre Mountains and followed a river to the Sierra de Sahuaripa Mountains. Along the way, they captured horses, mules and cattle and drove them to Arizona. During this expedition, the Apaches killed about 40 Mexicans.
Sources: 47, 168

MX15 *Attack Near Arizpe* • 1867
Location: Near Arizpe, Sonora
Mangas, having succeeded to the leadership of the Apaches after the death of his father, Mangas Coloradas, led eight mounted warriors including Geronimo into Mexico. In a skirmish with cowboys, two warriors were killed but they gained possession of the cattle and drove the herd northward.

They were attacked by Mexican soldiers and rode off without the cattle, dismounted and took cover in a timbered area. The soldiers caught up with them and took their ponies after a brief battle.
Sources: 47, 168

MX16 *Attacks on Arizpe* • 1867
Location: Arizpe, Sonora
After Mangas and the survivors of the earlier raid returned home, Geronimo headed south on foot with six warriors to Arizpe, camping in the Sierra de Sahuaripa Mountains. They made several night raids and captured horses, mules, saddles and provisions. Traveling at night, they reached Arizona without a confrontation with soldiers.
Sources: 47

MX17 *Raids in Sonora* • 1868
Location: Sonora
Mexican soldiers raided a settlement near Geronimo's camp in Arizona, rounding up cattle, mules and horses. Shortly thereafter, two Mexican scouts were found in the area and were butchered. Other Mexican troops began gathering the Apaches' animals, and Geronimo led 20 warriors on foot to a ranch near Nacozari, Sonora. They attacked the troops and killed two, released the animals from the pen, and drove them back toward Arizona.
      They were followed by nine Mexican soldiers, and while they slept at a camp near the Arizona border, the animals were retaken by the Mexicans. The Apaches gave up and went home.
Sources: 47, 168

MX18 *Attack on Kickapoo Village* • May 18, 1872
Location: Sonora
Col. Ranald S. Mackenzie led his men into Mexico from Fort Clark after he heard that the Kickapoo warriors had gone west for a hunt. They crossed the border near El Moral and continued on back trails for 70 miles to the village.
      The natives fought back until the soldiers set fire to the homes and then retreated. Nineteen Kickapoos were killed and 40 women and children were captured and taken to San Antonio.
Sources: 223

MX19 *Battle of White Hill* • 1873
Location: Nacori, Sierra Madre Mountains, Sonora
The Nednhi Apaches led by Whoa returned to Mexico and went into hiding in the Sierra Madre Mountains near Nacori. As they prepared to initiate a raid, they were attacked by two companies of Mexican cavalry. The soldiers dismounted and opened fire, and were surrounded by 60 warriors. The Apaches killed all of the Mexican horses and charged on foot. When the soldiers attempted to run away, the Apaches killed and scalped them. The Apaches moved their camp eastward through the Sierra Madre Mountains into Chihuahua, then returned to Arizona.
Sources: 47, 168

MX20 *Attack Near Santa Rosa* • May 18, 1873
Location: Bolson de Mapimi region of Coahuila
Gen. Ranald Slidell Mackenzie and the 4th Cavalry were ordered by Gen. Philip Sheridan to proceed to Fort Clark and take action to halt the raiding which was going on in the area. Mackenzie understood this to include the crossing of the

Rio Grande, which he had Seminole scouts do to locate the raiders near Santa Rosa, 80 miles inside Mexico.

They attacked three Kickapoo-Apache settlements in a valley, killing many with sabers and gunfire. Those that were not killed were captured and the villages were burned. Mackenzie immediately turned north to cross back into Texas.

Upon the order of Indian Agent J.M. Haworth, the captives were released in June and began raiding again.

Sources: 103

MX21 *Raid Near Eagle Pass* • Fall, 1873
Location: Olmos, Sonora
A party of Kiowas and Comanches conducted a raid below Eagle Pass, killing 14 Mexicans, taking two prisoner, and capturing 150 horses and mules.

Lt. Charles L. Hudson found the animals near Fort Clark and became involved in a fight with the natives which resulted in the deaths of nine natives and the wounding of one soldier. Fifty of the horses were recaptured by the soldiers.

Sources: 227

MX22 *Battle of Skolata* • 1880
Location: South of Casa Grande, Chihuahua
Geronimo was camped with about 30 warriors south of Casa Grande when they were attacked by about 24 Mexican soldiers. The first volley killed two Apaches and caused the warriors to run for the nearby timber. Intending to scatter the troops, Geronimo ordered an attack which resulted in the deaths of all of the soldiers. The Apaches buried their 12 dead and headed toward the northwest.

Sources: 47, 168

MX23 *Attack at Nokode* • 1880
Location: Near Nacori, Sonora
About 80 Bedonkohe and Nednhi Apaches were attacked by three companies of Mexican soldiers at Nokode, near Nacori. the warriors scattered and kept firing, losing the pursuing soldiers in the Sierra Madre Mountains.

Sources: 47

MX24 *Massacre at Casa Grande* • 1880
Location: Casa Grande, Chihuahua
At a meeting at Casa Grande to negotiate a peace treaty, the Mexicans provided a band of Apaches with mescal. When they became drunk, they were attacked by two companies of Mexican soldiers. Twenty died, many were captured, and the rest fled.

Sources: 47

MX25 *Battle at Tres Castillos* • October 15–16, 1880
Location: East of the Sierra Madre, Chihuahua
War: Victorio's Rebellion
Victorio led his Chihenne Apaches away from their reservation in September of 1877, and by 1880 they were in Chihuahua. While he sent Blanco and Kaytennae on an expedition to secure ammunition for the warriors, Victorio and his people

camped among three hills on the plains, believing that the army would look for them in the mountains instead. They planned to break camp soon and move west to the Sierra Madre.

He did not know that he had been followed by Joaquin Terrazas and a force of 260 Mexican regular soldiers, volunteers and Tarahumara natives. On October 15, Terrazas attacked at sunset with the Tarahumaras in the front. The Apaches were low on ammunition and constructed breastworks of rock. At midnight, the Apaches began a two-hour death song.

At sunrise, the battle resumed with hand-to-hand combat. By 10:00 a.m., the battle ended was over 78 dead Apaches, including Victorio, plus 68 women and children taken prisoner. Seventeen escaped. Terrazas lost three and had ten wounded. The Mexicans credited Tarahumara Mauricio Corredor with killing Victorio, while the Apaches claim he committed suicide after running out of ammunition.

Sources: 46, 47, 48, 70, 92, 135, 298, 380

MX26 *Ambush at Galeana* • November, 1882

Location: 20 miles southeast of Casa Grandes, Chihuahua

War: Geronimo's Rebellion

The last joint effort of the free Chiricahuas, led by Juh, Geronimo and Nana, occurred near the town of Galeana. A party of Apache raiders was sent along the main road to the town in which a patrol of Mexican cavalry was stationed. They came to the edge of the town, stole some horses, and headed north. Twenty-three cavalrymen followed, led by Juan Mata Ortiz.

When the Mexicans appeared to nearly catch up with the fleeing horse thieves, the rest of the Chiricahuas rose out of a ravine along the side of the road. The cavalry retreated to a small hill and constructed breastworks, and then were surrounded by warriors. The Apaches crawled up the hill under the cover of rifle fire, and then battled the Mexicans in hand-to-hand combat.

The one surviving Mexican was allowed to escape, so he would tell his story and have other soldiers come to fight. It turned out that the remaining soldiers in Galeana were too afraid to fight, and that probably saved their lives. The hill is still known as Cerrito Mata Ortiz.

Monument: In the courtyard in Galeana, a stone pyramid and plaque with the names of the 22 soldiers killed was dedicated in 1986.

Sources: 167, 169, 298

MX27 *Pursuit of Apaches* • May, 1883

Location: Sierra Madres, Sonora

War: Apache War

Gen. George Crook led a troop of the 6th Cavalry into Mexico, supported by 193 Apache scouts wearing red headbands so they would not be confused with the ones they were seeking. The scouts were also Apaches, representing bands of Chiricahua, White Mountain, Yuma, Mojave and Tonto.

They crossed the border on May 1 and found their first Chiricahuas on May 14. On May 15, a party led by Capt. Emmet Crawford fought with a small and harmless group in a canyon, killing nine mostly old men and women, and taking five children captive. Other warriors escaped.

They came across the camp of Chatto and another leader and, although they were elsewhere raiding villages, their possessions became the prize of the soldiers.
Sources: 25, 45, 46, 135, 168, 298, 380, 385

MX28 *Attack at Bavispe Mountains* • June 22, 1885
Location: Northeast of Oputo, Sonora
War: Apache War
Capt. Emmet Crawford and a company of soldiers, joined by Chief of Scouts Al Seiber, Capt. Kendall and Lts. Elliot and Hannah with a portion of the 6th Cavalry, met up with Lt. Britton Davis at Skeleton Canyon to pursue Geronimo.
On June 22, Davis, Elliot, Seiber and about 50 scouts attacked the camp and killed one Apache, wounded at least one, and captured about 15. The soldiers did an incomplete job of surrounding the camp, and the rest escaped. There were no army losses.
Sources: 46, 47, 166

MX29 *Battle at Devil's Backbone* • January 10–11, 1886
Location: Sierra Madres, Chihuahua
War: Apache War
Capt. Emmett Crawford led his men across the border into Mexico on December 11 and spent three weeks in Sonora before finding a Chiricahua trail near the Aros River. On January 9, they camped 12 miles away from Geronimo. They attacked at dawn the next day.
The Chiricahuas fled into the surrounding mountains, known as Devil's Backbone, leaving behind their horses, food and supplies. Later in the day, a messenger brought word that Geronimo and Naiche wished to have a meeting with Crawford the next day.
On the morning of January 11, a large party approached, and at first it was believed to be reinforcements sent by Gen. George Crook. Instead, it turned out to be 150 Mexicans who had also been hunting the Chiricahuas, and mistook Crawford's scouts for hostile Apaches. Shouting in Spanish, the officers were able to bring a halt to the shooting, and then Crawford climbed on top of a rock, waving his handkerchief. A shot rang out, hitting him in the head.
The American scouts opened fire and the battle lasted about an hour. Four on the American side were wounded, and the Mexicans had four killed and five wounded. The Mexicans finally surrendered. Crawford was comatose, and died seven days later.
Sources: 46, 47, 166, 298, 406

MX30 *Uprising at Villa de Ayala* • 1911
Location: Villa de Ayala, Sonora
War: Mexican Revolution
Natives rose up under the mestizo Emiliano Zapata. Beginning March 11, 1911, in a decade of bloody fighting they destroyed the power of the haciendas, overthrowing the white elite which had controlled the churches, banks, newspapers, businesses and the land.
Sources: 130, 198, 255, 313, 424, 425

MX31 *Battle of Zacatecas* • June 17–23, 1914
Location: Chihuahua
War: Mexican Revolution
Mestizo Doroteo Arango (Pancho Villa) led a war in northern Mexico. the turn-
ing point was in 1914 at the Battle of Zacatecas, at the site of La Bufa, the first
Mexican silver mine, which had used native labor.
Sources: 130, 198, 255, 313, 394, 424, 425

MX32 *Capture of Agua Prieta* • November 1–4, 1915
Location: Yaqui Valley, Sonora
War: Yaqui War
The Yaqui natives were at war with Mexico. In August, they killed a colonel of
Pancho Villa, claiming that he had killed a Yaqui. In November, as they crept
through barbed wire to attack Agua Prieta, Plutarco Calles and his defenders
switched on searchlights and caught them. Thousands were killed.
     The Yaquis were defeated in April of 1916 near Tonicki, Sonora, by Mexi-
can forces led by Gen. Rajaci Estrada.
Sources: 92, 135, 281, 312, 313, 424

Bibliography

1   *A Brief History of the Pequot War*, by John Mason (University Microfilms, 1966).
2   *A Cheyenne Sketchbook*, by Cohoe (University of Oklahoma Press, 1964).
3   *A Company of Heroes: The American Frontier 1775–1783*, by Dale Van Every (William Morrow, 1962).
4   *A Good Year to Die*, by Charles M. Robinson III (Random House, 1995).
5   *A Guide to National Monuments and Historic Sites*, by Jill MacNeice (Prentice Hall, 1990).
6   *A History of Georgia*, by Kenneth Coleman (The University of Georgia Press, 1977).
7   *A History of the American People, Volume II Since 1865*, by Harry J. Carman, Harold C. Syrett and Bernard W. Wishy (Alfred A. Knopf, 1961).
8   *A History of the Indians of the United States*, by Angie Debo (University of Oklahoma Press, 1970).
9   *A History of the Pacific Northwest*, by George W. Fuller (Alfred A. Knopf, 1966).
10 *A Life Wild and Perilous: Mountain Men and the Paths to the Pacific*, by Robert M. Utley (Henry Holt and Company, 1997).
11 *A Little History of the Navajos*, by Oscar H. Lipps (The Torch Press, 1989).
12 *A Short History of the American Revolution*, by James L. Stokesbury (William Morrow, 1991).
13 *A Shovel of Stars: The Making of the American West 1800 to the Present*, by Ted Morgan (Simon & Schuster, 1995).
14 *A Sorrow In Our Heart: The Life of Tecumseh*, by Allan W. Eckert (Bantam Books, 1992).
15 *A Strange and Distant Shore: Indians of the Great Plains in Exile*, by Brent Ashabranner (Cobblehill Books, 1996).
16 *A Sweet and Alien Land: The Story of Dutch New York*, by Henri and Barbara van der Zee (Viking, 1978).
17 *A Treasury of Florida Tales*, by Webb Garrison (Rutledge Hill, 1989).
18 *A Way Through the Wilderness*, by William C. Davis (HarperCollins, 1995).
19 *AAA TourBook Series* (American Automobile Association, 1997).
20 *After Columbus: The Smithsonian Chronicle of the North American Indians*, by Herman J. Viola (Smithsonian Books, 1990).
21 *Alabama: A Bicentennial History*, by Virginia Van der Veer Hamilton (W.W. Norton, 1977).
22 *Alabama: Mounds to Missiles*, by Helen Morgan Akens and Virginia Pounds Brown (Strode, 1966).
23 *Alachua County, Florida Historical Tour Series (Rochelle, Cross Creek, Island Grove, Hawthorne, Campville, Windsor)* (Alachua County Historical Commission, 1984).
24 *Alaska: A Bicentennial History*, by William R. Hunt (W.W. Norton, 1976).
25 *The American Heritage Book of Great Adventures of the Old West* (American Heritage Press, 1970).
26 *The American Heritage History of the Making of the Nation 1783–1860*, by Francis Russell (American Heritage, 1968).

27 *American History, Vol. 1: To 1877*, by Nelson Klose (Barron's Educational Series, 1965).

28 *American History, Vol. 2: Since 1865*, by Nelson Klose (Barron's Educational Series, 1965).

29 *American Indians in Colorado*, by Donald Hughes (Pruett, 1977).

30 *The American Past*, by Roger Butterfield (Simon & Schuster, 1966).

31 *America's Fascinating Indian Heritage* (Reader's Digest, 1978).

32 *America's Historylands: Landmarks of Liberty*, (National Geographic Society, 1962).

33 *America's National Battlefield Parks*, by Joseph E. Stevens (University of Oklahoma Press, 1990).

34 *America's Wars & Military Excursions*, by Edwin P. Hoyt (McGraw-Hill, 1987).

35 *The Anasazi*, by J.J. Brody (Rizzoli International, 1990).

36 *Andrew Jackson*, by Robert V. Remini (Harper & Row, 1966).

37 *Andrew Jackson*, by William Graham Sumner (Chelsea House, 1980).

38 *Andrew Jackson*, by Herman J. Viola (Chelsea House, 1986).

39 *Andrew Jackson and Pensacola*, by James R. McGovern (University of West Florida, 1974).

40 *Andrew Jackson and the Course of American Empire, 1767–1821*, by Robert V. Remini (Harper & Row, 1977).

41 *Andrew Jackson and the Search for Vindication*, by James C. Curtis (Little, Brown, 1976).

42 *Andrew Jackson: Hero*, by Donald Barr Chidsey (Thomas Nelson, 1976).

43 *Anthony Wayne*, by Harry Emerson Wildes (Harcourt, Brace and Company, 1941).

44 *Anthony Wayne: Soldier of the Early Republic*, by Paul David Nelson (Indiana University Press, 1985).

45 *Apache Campaign in the Sierra Madre*, by John G. Bourke (Charles Scribner's Sons, 1958).

46 *The Apache Indians*, by Frank C. Lockwood (University of Nebraska Press, 1966).

47 *Apache Wars: An Illustrated Battle History*, by E. Lisle Reedstrom (Sterling, 1990).

48 *The Apaches: Eagles of the Southwest*, by Donald E. Worcester (University of Oklahoma Press, 1979).

49 *Apalachee: The Land Between the Rivers*, by John H. Hann (University Presses of Florida, 1988).

50 *Archaeology, History, and Custer's Last Battle*, by Richard Allan Fox, Jr. (University of Oklahoma Press, 1993).

51 *The Arkansas*, by Clyde Brion Davis (Rinehart, 1940).

52 *Arkansas: A Bicentennial History*, by Harry S. Ashmore (W.W. Norton, 1978).

53 *Atlas of the North American Indian*, by Carl Waldman (Facts On File Publications, 1985).

54 *The Battle at the Loxahatchee River: The Seminole War*, by John B. Wolf (Loxahatchee Historical Society, 1989).

55 *Battle for a Continent: The French and Indian War 1754–1763*, by Harrison Bird (Oxford University Press, 1965).

56 *The Battle of Fallen Timbers, August 20, 1794*, by John Tebbel (Franklin Watts, 1972).

57 *The Battle of the Washita*, by Stan Hoig (Doubleday, 1976).

58 *Battlefields of the Civil War*, by John Bowen (Chartwell Books, 1986).

59 *Bent's Fort*, by David Lavender (Peter Smith, 1968).

60 *Between Two Fires: American Indians in the Civil War*, by Laurence M. Hauptman (The Free Press, 1995).

61 *The Billy Bowlegs War*, by James W. Covington (Mickler House, 1982).

62 *Black Hills/White Justice: The Sioux Nation Versus the United States 1775 to the Present*, by Edward Lazarus (HarperCollins, 1991).

63 *Blackfeet and Buffalo: Memories of Life Among the Indians*, by James Willard Schultz (University of Oklahoma Press, 1962).

64 *The Bloody Bozeman: The Perilous Trail to Montana's Gold*, by Dorothy M. Johnson (McGraw-Hill, 1971).

65 *The Bold and Magnificent Dream: America's Founding Years 1492–1815*, by Bruce Catton and William B. Catton (Doubleday, 1978).

66 *The Book of the American West*, by Jay Monaghan (Bonanza Books, 1963).

67 *Braddock at the Monongahela*, by Paul E. Kopperman (University of Pittsburgh Press, 1977).

68 *Buckskin and Blanket Days*, by Thomas Henry Tibbles (Doubleday, 1957).

69 *Burnt-Out Fires: California's Modoc Indian War*, by Richard Dillon (Prentice-Hall, 1973).

70 *Bury My Heart at Wounded Knee: An Indian History of the American West*, by Dee Brown (Bantam, 1972).

71 *Cabeza de Vaca's Adventures in the Unknown Interior of America*, by Cyclone Covey (University of New Mexico Press, 1961).

72 *California*, by John Walton Caughey (Prentice-Hall, 1953).

73 *California: A Bicentennial History*, by David Lavender (W.W. Norton, 1976).

74 *California: A History*, by Andrew F. Rolle (Thomas Y. Crowell, 1969).

75 *California: A History of the Golden State*, by Warren A. Beck and David A. Williams (Doubleday, 1972).

76 *California: An Interpretive History*, by Walton Bean (McGraw-Hill, 1968).

77 *Canada & the American Revolution 1774–1783*, by Gustave Lanctot (Harvard University Press, 1967).

78 *Canada: The War of the Conquest*, by Guy Fregault (Oxford University Press, 1969).

79 *The Canadian Indian: A History Since 1500*, by E. Palmer Patterson II (Collier-Macmillan Canada, 1972).

80 *The Capture of Quebec*, by Christopher Lloyd (Macmillan, 1959).

81 *The Cayuse Indians: Imperial Tribesmen of Old Oregon*, by Robert H. Ruby and John A. Brown (University of Oklahoma Press, 1972).

82 *Cherokee Chief: The Life of John Ross*, by Electa Clark (Crowell-Collier, 1970).

83 *The Cherry Valley Massacre, November 11, 1778*, by David Goodnough (Franklin Watts, 1968).

84 *The Cheyennes: Indians of the Great Plains*, by E. Adamson Hoebel (Holt, Rinehart and Winston, 1960).

85 *The Chickasaw*, by Duane K. Hale and Arrell M. Gibson (Chelsea House, 1990).

86 *Children of Grace: The Nez Perce War of 1877*, by Bruce Hampton (Henry Holt, 1994).

87 *Children of the Raven: The Seven Indian Nations of the Northwest Coast*, by H.R. Hays (McGraw-Hill, 1975).

88 *Chippewa Trails and Indian Tales*, by Mary Cobb Langley (Thumb, 1968).

89 *The Choctaw Before Removal*, by Carolyn Keller Reeves (University Press of Mississippi, 1985).

90 *Chronicle of America*, (Chronicle, 1989).

91 *Chronological List of Engagements Between the Regular Army of the United States and Various Tribes of Hostile Indians Which Occurred During the Years 1790 to 1898, Inclusive*, by George W. Webb (AMS Press, 1939).

92 *Chronology of the American Indian*, (American Indian Publishers, 1994).

93 *Civil War on the Western Border 1854–1865*, by Jay Monaghan (Bonanza, 1955).

94 *Coacoochee: Made of the Sands of Florida*, by Arthur E. Francke, Jr. (E.O. Painter, 1986).

95 *Colonial Connecticut: A History*, by Robert J. Taylor (KTO Press, 1979).

96 *Colonial Massachusetts: A History*, by Benjamin W. Labaree (KTO Press, 1979).

97 *Colonial New Jersey: A History*, by John E. Ponfret (Charles Scribner's Sons, 1973).

98 *Colonial New York: A History*, by Michael Kammen (Charles Scribner's Sons, 1975).

99 *Colonial Pennsylvania: A History*, by Joseph E. Illick (Charles Scribner's Sons, 1976).

100 *Colonial South Carolina*, by Eugenia Burney (Thomas Nelson, 1970).

101 *Colorado: A Bicentennial History*, by Marchall Sprague (W.W. Norton, 1976).

102 *Colorado: A History of the Centennial State*, by Carl Abbott (Colorado Associated University Press, 1976).

103 *Comanches: The Destruction of a People*, by T.R. Fehrenbach (Alfred A. Knopf, 1974).

104 *The Coming of the White Man*, by Herbert I. Priestley (Quadrangle, 1971).

105 *The Confederate Cherokees: John Drew's Regiment of Mounted Rifles*, by W. Craig Gaines (Louisiana State University Press, 1989).

106 *The Connecticut*, by Walter Hard (Rinehart, 1947).

107 *The Conquest of Paradise: Christopher Columbus and the Columbian Legacy*, by Kirkpatrick Sale (Alfred A. Knopf, 1990).

108 *Conquistadores and Pueblos: The Story of the American Southwest, 1540–1848*, by Olga Hall-Quest (E.P. Dutton, 1969).

109 *Crazy Horse and Custer: The Parallel Lives of Two American Warriors*, by Stephen E. Ambrose (Doubleday, 1975).

110 *Crazy Horse: The Strange Man of the Oglalas*, by Mari Sandoz (University of Nebraska Press, 1961).

111 *The Creek Frontier, 1540–1783*, by David H. Corkran (University of Oklahoma Press, 1967).

112 *The Creek People*, by Donald E. Green (Indian Tribal Series, 1973).

113 *Creeks and Seminoles: Destruction and Regeneration of the Muscogulge People*, by J. Leitch Wright, Jr. (University of Nebraska Press, 1986).

114 *Custer in 76: Walter Camp's Notes on the Custer Fight*, by Kenneth Hammer (Brigham Young University Press, 1976).

115 *The Custer Reader*, by Paul Andrew Hutton (University of Nebraska Press, 1992).

116 *Custer's Last*, by Don Russell (Amon Carter Museum, 1968).

117 "Dade Battlefield State Historic Site," flier by Florida Department of Parks.

118 *Dade's Last Command*, by Frank Laumer (University Press of Florida, 1995).

119 *Daniel Boone: The Life and Legend of an American Pioneer*, by John Mack Faragher (Henry Holt, 1992).

120 *Daniel Boone: Wilderness Scout*, by Stewart Edward White (Doubleday, 1972).

121 *De Soto and the Conquistadores*, by Theodore Maynard (Longmans, Green, 1930).

122 *De Soto Didn't Land at Tampa*, by Rolfe F. Schell (Island Press, 1966).

123 *The Death and Rebirth of the Seneca*, by Anthony F.C. Wallace (Alfred A. Knopf, 1970).

124 *The Destruction of California Indians*, by Robert F. Heizer (Peregrine Smith, 1974).

125 *Diary of King Philip's War, 1675–1676*, by Colonel Benjamin Church (The Pequot Press, 1975).

126 *Don't Know Much About History*, by Kenneth C. Davis (Crown Publishers, 1990).

127 *The Early American Wilderness As the Explorers Saw It*, by Bill Lawrence (Paragon House, 1991).

128 *The Eastern Frontier: The Settlement of Northern New England, 1610–1763*, by Charles E. Clark (University Press of New England, 1983).

129 *Eden Seekers: The Settlement of Oregon, 1818–1862*, by Malcolm Clark, Jr. (Houghton Mifflin, 1951).

130 *Emiliano Zapata*, by John David Ragan (Chelsea House, 1989).

131 *Empire of Fortune: Crowns, Colonies & Tribes in the Seven Years War in America*, by Francis Jennings (W.W. Norton, 1988).

132 *Empire of the Columbia*, by Dorothy O. Johansen (Harper & Row, 1967).

133 *The Encyclopedia of American Facts & Dates*, by Gorton Carruth (Harper & Row, 1987).

134 *Encyclopedia of Native American Tribes*, by Carl Waldman (Facts on File Publications, 1988).

135 *The Encyclopedia of North American Indian Tribes: A Comprehensive Study of Tribes from the Abitibi to the Zuni*, by Bill Yenne (Arch Cape Press, 1986).

136 *The Era of Expansion: 1800–1848*, by Don E. Fehrenbacher (John Wiley & Sons, 1969).

137 *The European and the Indian*, by Hale G. Smith (Florida Anthropological Society, 1956).

138 *Everyman's Eden: A History of California*, by Ralph J. Roske (The Macmillan Company, 1968).

139 *Expedition Against the Ohio Indians*, by William Smith (University Microfilms, 1966).

140 *Explorers of the Mississippi*, by Timothy Severin (Alfred A. Knopf, 1968).

141 *Eyewitness at Wounded Knee*, by Richard E. Jensen, R. Eli Paul, and John E. Carter (University of Nebraska Press, 1991).

142 *Fantasies of the Master Race: Literature, Cinema and the Colonization of American Indians*, by Ward Churchill (Common Courage Press, 1992).

143 *Fearless & Free: The Seminole Indian War 1835–1842*, by George Walton (Bobbs-Merrill, 1977).

144 *The Final Challenge: The American Frontier 1804–1845*, by Dale Van Every (William Morrow, 1964).

145 *First Encounters: Spanish Explorations in the Caribbean and the United States, 1492–1570*, by Jerald T. Milanich and Susan Milbrath (University of Florida Press, 1989).

146 *First on the Land: The North Carolina Indians*, by Ruth Y. Wetmore (John F. Blair, 1975).

147 *500 Nations: An Illustrated History of North American Indians*, by Alvin M. Josephy, Jr. (Alfred A. Knopf, 1994).

148 *Five Indian Tribes of the Upper Missouri: Sioux, Arickaras, Assiniboines, Crees, Crows*, by John C. Ewers (University of Oklahoma Press, 1961).

149 *Flames Across the Border: The Canadian-American Tragedy, 1813–1814*, by Pierre Berton (Little, Brown, 1981).

150 *Flames Over New England: The Story of King Philip's War, 1675–1676*, by Olga Hall Quest (E.P. Dutton, 1967).

151 *Flashbacks: The Story of Central Florida's Past*, by Jim Robison and Mark Andrews (*The Orlando Sentinel*, 1995).

152 *Flintlock and Tomahawk: New England in King Philip's War*, by Douglas Edward Leach (W.W. Norton, 1958).

153 *Florida Historic Markers & Sites*, by Floyd E. Boone (Gulf, 1988).

154 *Florida's Family Album: A History for All Ages*, by Cora Cheney and Ben Partridge (San Marcos, 1993).

155 *Florida's Past: People and Events That Shaped the State, vol. 2*, by Gene M. Burnett (Pineapple, 1988).

156 *Florida's Past: People and Events That Shaped the State, vol. 3*, by Gene M. Burnett (Pineapple, 1991).

157 *Florida's Peace River Frontier*, by Canter Brown, Jr. (University of Central Florida Press, 1991).

158 *The Forgotten Sioux: An Ethnohistory of the Lower Brule Reservation*, by Ernest L. Schusky (Nelson-Hall, 1975).

159 *Fort Laramie and the Sioux Indians*, by Remi Nadeau (Prentice-Hall, 1967).

160 *Fort Mellon 1837–42: A Microcosm of the Second Seminole War*, by Arthur E. Francke, Jr. (Banyan, 1977).

161 *Fort Phil Kearny: An American Saga*, by Dee Brown (G.P. Putnam's Sons, 1962).

162 *Four Centuries of Southern Indians*, by Charles M. Hudson (The University of Georgia Press, 1975).

163 *From Wilderness to Empire: A History of California*, by Robert Glass Cleland (Alfred A. Knopf, 1959).

164 *George Washington: The Virginia Period 1732–1775*, by Bernhard Knollenberg (Duke University Press, 1964).

165 *Georgia: A Bicentennial History*, by Harold H. Martin (W.W. Norton, 1977).

166 *The Geronimo Campaign*, by Odie B. Faulk (Oxford University Press, 1969).

167 *Geronimo: The Man, His Time, His Place*, by Angie Debo (University of Oklahoma Press, 1976).

168 *Geronimo's Story of His Life*, by S.M. Barrett (Corner House, 1980).

169 *God Gave Us This Country: Tekamthi and the First American Civil War*, by Bil Gilbert (Atheneum, 1989).

170 *Great Lakes County*, by Russell McKee (Thomas Y. Crowell Company, 1966).

171 *Great Westerner: The Story of Kit Carson*, by Bernice Blackwelder (Caxton, 1962).

172 *Handbook on Indiana History*, by Donald F. Carmody (Indiana Sesquicentennial Commission, 1963).

173 *Harlow's Oklahoma History*, by Victor E. Harlow (Harlow, 1967).

174 *The Havasupai People*, by Henry F. Dobyns and Robert C. Euler (Indian Tribal Series, 1971).

175 *Hear Me, My Chiefs! Nez Perce History and Legend*, by L.V. McWhorter (Caxton, 1986).

176 *The Heartland: Ohio, Indiana, Illinois*, by Walter Havighurst (Harper & Row, 1974).

177 *Hernando de Soto: Knight of the Americas*, by Miguel Albornoz (Franklin Watts, 1986).

178 *The History of Canada*, by Kenneth McNaught (Praeger Publishers, 1970).

179 *History of Delaware*, by John A. Munroe (University of Delaware Press, 1984).

180 *History of Florida*, by Caroline Mays Brevard (The Florida State Historical Society, 1924).

181 *History of the Late War in the Western Country*, by Robert Breckinridge McAfee (University Microfilms, 1966).

182 *History of Nebraska*, by James C. Olson (University of Nebraska Press, 1966).

183 *History of the Ojibway Nation*, by William W. Warren (Ross & Haines, 1974).

184 *History of Orange County, Florida*, by William Fremont Blackman (The Mickler House, 1973).

185 *History of Orlando*, by E.H. Gore (1951).

186 *The History of St. Augustine, Florida*, by William W. Dewhurst (G.P. Putnam's Sons, 1885).

187 *History of the Second Seminole War 1835–1842*, by John K. Mahon (University of Florida Press, 1967).

188 *History of the State of Rhode Island, Vol 1, 1636–1700*, by Samuel Greene Arnold (D. Appleton, 1859).

189 *History of the Westward Movement*, by Frederick Merk (Alfred A. Knopf, 1978).

190 *Hunters of the Stormy Sea*, by Harold McCracken (Doubleday, 1957).

191 *"I Will Fight No More Forever": Chief Joseph and the Nez Perce War*, by Merrill D. Beal (University of Washington Press, 1963).

192 *Idaho: A Bicentennial History*, by F. Ross Peterson (W.W. Norton, 1976).

193 *Illinois: A Bicentennial History*, by Richard J. Jensen (W.W. Norton, 1978).

194 *Illinois: A History of the Prairie State*, by Robert P. Howard (William B. Eerdmans, 1972).

195 *Indian America: The Black Hawk War*, by Miriam Gurko (Thomas Y. Crowell, 1970).

196 *Indian Foe, Indian Friend*, by Jules Archer (Crowell-Collier, 1970).

197 *The Indian Frontier of the American West 1846–1890*, by Robert M. Utley (University of New Mexico Press, 1984).

198 *Indian Givers: How the Indians of the Americas Transformed the World*, by Jack Weatherford (Crown Publishers, 1988).

199 *The Indian in America*, by Wilcomb E. Washburn (Harper Torchbooks, 1975).

200 *Indiana: A Bicentennial History*, by Howard H. Peckham (W.W. Norton, 1978).
201 *Indians as the Westerners Saw Them*, by Ralph W. Andrews (Bonanza, 1963).
202 *Indians of the American Southwest*, by Bertha P. Dutton (Prentice-Hall, 1975).
203 *Indians of the Great Basin and Plateau*, Francis Haines (G.P. Putnam's Sons, 1970).
204 *Indians of the High Plains: From the Prehistoric Period to the Coming of Europeans*, by George E. Hyde (University of Oklahoma Press, 1959).
205 *Indians of the Pacific Northwest*, by Karen Liptak (Facts on File, 1991).
206 *Indians of the Pacific Northwest: From the Coming of the White Man to the Present Day*, by Vine Deloria, Jr. (Doubleday, 1977).
207 *Indians of the Southeast: Then and Now*, by Jesse Burt and Robert B. Ferguson (Abingdon Press, 1973).
208 *Indians & Pioneers: The Story of the American Southwest Before 1830*, by Grant Foreman (University of Oklahoma Press, 1936).
209 *Indians, Settlers, & Slaves In a Frontier Exchange Economy: The Lower Mississippi Valley Before 1783*, by Daniel H. Usner, Jr. (University of North Carolina Press, 1992).
210 *Invisible Armies: The Impact of Disease on American History*, by Howard N. Simpson, M.D. (Bobbs-Merrill, 1980).
211 *Iowa: A Bicentennial History*, by Joseph Frazier Wall (W.W. Norton, 1978).
212 *The Invasion of America: Indians, Colonialism and the Cant of Conquest*, by Francis Jennings (W.W. Norton, 1975).
213 *"It's Your Misfortune and None of My Own": A New History of the American West*, by Richard White (University of Oklahoma Press, 1991).
214 *Jamestown, 1544–1699*, by Carl Bridenbaugh (Oxford University Press, 1980).
215 *Journey Into Wilderness*, by J.R. Motte (University of Florida Press, 1963).
216 *The Kalispel People*, by Robert C. Carriker (Indian Tribal Series, 1973).
217 *The Kansa Indians: History of the Wind People, 1673–1873*, by William E. Unrau (University of Oklahoma Press, 1971).
218 *Kansas: A Bicentennial History*, by Kenneth S. Davis (W.W. Norton, 1976).
219 *The Kaw People*, by William E. Unrau (Indian Tribal Series, 1975).
220 *Keep the Last Bullet for Yourself: The True Story of Custer's Last Stand*, by Thomas B. Marquis (Two Continents, 1976).
221 *Kentucky: A Bicentennial History*, by Steven A. Channing (W.W. Norton, 1977).
222 *The Kentucky Encyclopedia*, by John E. Kleber (The University Press of Kentucky, 1992).
223 *The Kickapoo People*, by George R. Nielson (Indian Tribal Series, 1975).
224 *Killing Custer*, by James Welch with Paul Stekler (W.W. Norton, 1994).
225 *King Philip's War, 1675–76: The New England Indians Fight the Colonists*, by Louise Dickinson Rich (Franklin Watts, 1972).
226 *King Philip's War Narratives*, (University Microfilms, 1966).
227 *The Kiowas*, by Mildred P. Mayhall (University of Oklahoma Press, 1962).
228 *Kit Carson*, by Stanley Vestal (Houghton Mifflin, 1928).
229 *Kit Carson: A Pattern for Heroes*, by Thelma S. Guild and Harvey L. Carter (University of Nebraska Press, 1984).
230 *Kit Carson: A Portrait in Courage*, by M. Morgan Estergreen (University of Oklahoma Press, 1962).
231 *Lake Erie*, by Harlan Hatcher (Bobbs-Merrill, 1945).
232 *The Land Called Chicora*, by Paul Quattlebaum (University of Florida Press, 1956).
233 *Land Where Our Fathers Died: The Settling of the Eastern Shores, 1607–1735*, by Marion L. Starkey (Doubleday, 1962).
234 *Landmarks of the American Revolution*, by Mark M. Boatner III (Stackpole, 1973).
235 *The Last Days of the Sioux Nation*, by Robert M. Utley (Yale University Press, 1963).
236 *Let Me Be Free: The Nez Perce Tragedy*, by David Lavender (HarperCollins, 1992).
237 *Life Along the Hudson*, by Allan Keller (Sleepy Hollow Restorations, 1976).
238 *The Life and Adventures of Daniel Boone*, by Michael A. Lofaro (The University Press of Kentucky, 1986).
239 *Life in a Narrow Place: The Havasupai of the Grand Canyon*, by Stephen Hirst (David McKay, 1976).
240 *The Life of Andrew Jackson*, by Robert V. Remini (Harper & Row, 1977).
241 *Like Beads on a String: A Cultural History of the Seminole Indians in North Peninsular Florida*, by Brent Richards Weisman (The University of Alabama Press, 1989).

242 *The Long Hunter: A New Life of Daniel Boone*, by Lawrence Elliott (Reader's Digest, 1976).

243 *The Longman History of the United States of America*, by Hugh Brogan (William Morrow, 1985).

244 *Looking for DeSoto: A Search Through the South for the Spaniard's Trail*, by Joyce Rockwood Hudson (The University of Georgia Press, 1993).

245 *Lords of the Earth: A History of the Navajo Indians*, by Jules Loh (Crowell-Collier, 1971).

246 *Los Comanches: The Horse People, 1751–1845*, by Stanley Noyes (University of New Mexico Press, 1993).

247 *The Lost Colony*, by Dan Lacy (Franklin Watts, 1972).

248 *The Lost Colony in Fact and Legend*, by F. Roy Johnson (Johnson, 1983).

249 *Maine: A Bicentennial History*, by Charles E. Clark (W.W. Norton, 1977).

250 *Marcus and Narcissa Whitman: Pioneers of Oregon*, by James Daugherty (Viking, 1961).

251 *Massachusetts: A Bicentennial History*, by Richard D. Brown (W.W. Norton, 1978).

252 *Massacre!*, by Frank Laumer (University of Florida Press, 1968).

253 *Massacre At Sand Creek*, by Irving Werstein (Charles Scribner's Sons, 1963).

254 *Massacres of the Mountains: A History of the Indian Wars of the Far West*, by J.P. Dunn, Jr. (Capricorn, 1969).

255 *Memoirs of Pancho Villa*, by Martin Luis Guzman (University of Texas Press, 1965).

256 *Michigan: A Bicentennial History*, by Bruce Catton (W.W. Norton, 1976).

257 *Michigan In Four Centuries*, by F. Clever Bald (Harper & Brothers, 1961).

258 *Michigan Off the Beaten Path*, by Jim DuFresne (Globe Pequot, 1988).

259 *Minnesota: A History of the State*, by Theodore C. Blegen (University of Minnesota Press, 1975).

260 *Mississippi: A Bicentennial History*, by John Ray Skates (W.W. Norton, 1979).

261 *The Mississippi Valley Frontier: The Age of French Exploration and Settlement*, by Anthony Caruso (Bobbs-Merrill, 1966).

262 *The Modoc*, by Odie B. Faulk and Laura E. Faulk (Chelsea House, 1988).

263 *The Modocs and Their War*, by Keith A. Murray (University of Oklahoma Press, 1959).

264 *Montana: A Bicentennial History*, by Clark C. Spence (W.W. Norton, 1978).

265 *Montana: A History of Two Centuries*, by Michael P. Malone and Richard B. Roeder (University of Washington Press, 1976).

266 *Montana: An Uncommon Land*, by K. Ross Toole (University of Oklahoma Press, 1959).

267 *Month of the Freezing Moon: The Sand Creek Massacre, November 1864*, by Duane Schultz (St. Martin's, 1990).

268 *Mount Hope: A New England Chronicle*, by George Howe (Viking, 1959).

269 *The Mountain Meadows Massacre*, by Juanita Brooks (University of Oklahoma Press, 1966).

270 *The Name of War: King Philip's War and the Origins of American Identity*, by Jill Lepore (Alfred A. Knopf, 1998).

271 *The Nanticoke*, by Frank W. Porter III (Chelsea House, 1987).

272 *The Narragansett People*, by Ethel Boissevain (Indian Tribal Series, 1975).

273 *The Narrative of the Captivity of Mrs. Mary Rowlandson*, by Mary Rowlandson (Houghton Mifflin, 1930).

274 *Narratives of the Indian Wars 1675–1699*, by Charles H. Lincoln (Barnes & Noble, 1913).

275 *Native Time: A Historical Time Line of Native America*, by Lee Francis (St. Martin's, 1996).

276 *Navajo: A Century of Progress 1868–1968*, by Martin A. Link (The Navajo Tribe, 1968).

277 *The Navajos*, by Ruth M. Underhill (University of Oklahoma Press, 1956).

278 *Nebraska: A Bicentennial History*, by Dorothy Weyer Creigh (W.W. Norton, 1977).

279 *New England Frontier: Puritans and Indians 1620–1675*, by Alden T. Vaughan (Little, Brown, 1965).

280 *New Hampshire: A Bicentennial History*, by Elizabeth Forbes Morison and Elting E. Morison (W.W. Norton, 1976).

281 *New Mexico: A Bicentennial History*, by Marc Simmons (W.W. Norton, 1977).

282 *New Mexico: A Pageant of Three Peoples*, by Erna Ferguson (Alfred A. Knopf, 1966).

283 *New Mexico: From Arrowhead to Atom*, by Ruth W. Armstrong (A.S. Barnes, 1976).

284 *New Worlds for All: Indians, Europeans, and the Remaking of Early America*, by Colin G. Calloway (The Johns Hopkins University Press, 1997).

285 *The Nez Perce Indians and the Opening of the Northwest*, by Alvin M. Josephy, Jr. (Yale University Press, 1965).

286 *The Nez Perces: Tribesmen of the Columbia Plateau*, by Francis Haines (University of Oklahoma Press, 1955).

287 *Nineteenth Century Archer*, by Rance O. Braley (1990).

288 *North American Indian Landmarks: A Traveler's Guide*, by George Cantor (Gale Research, 1993).

289 *North Carolina: A Bicentennial History*, by William S. Powell (W.W. Norton, 1977).

290 *The Northern Colonial Frontier 1607–1763*, by Douglas Edward Leach (Holt, Rinehart and Winston, 1966).

291 *Ocali Country: Kingdom of the Sun*, by Eloise Robinson Ott and Louis Hickman Chazal (Marion, 1966).

292 *Ohio: A Bicentennial History*, by Walter Havighurst (W.W. Norton, 1976).

293 *Ohio: The Buckeye State*, by William R. Collins (Prentice-Hall, 1974).

294 *The Oklahoma Story*, by Arrell M. Gibson (University of Oklahoma Press, 1978).

295 *Old Hickory: A Life of Andrew Jackson*, by Burke Davis (Dial, 1977).

296 *Old Hickory's War: Andrew Jackson and the Quest for Empire*, by David S. Heidler and Jeanne T. Heidler (Stackpole, 1996).

297 *The Old Trails West*, by Ralph Moody (Thomas Y. Crowell, 1963).

298 *Once They Moved Like the Wind: Cochise, Geronimo, and the Apache Wars*, by David Roberts (Simon & Schuster, 1993).

299 *1,001 Things Everyone Should Know About American History*, by John A. Garraty (Doubleday, 1989).

300 *The Oneida People*, by Cara E. Richards (Indian Tribal Series, 1974).

301 *The Only Land I Know: A History of the Lumbee Indians*, by Adolph L. Dial and David K. Eliades (Syracuse University Press, 1996).

302 *Orlando: A Centennial History*, by Eve Bacon (The Mickler House, 1975).

303 *Orlando: The City Beautiful*, by Jerrell H. Shofner (Continental Heritage Press, 1984).

304 *The Osage People*, by W. David Baird, Ph.D. (Indian Tribal Series, 1972).

305 *The Osages: Children of the Middle Waters*, by John Joseph Mathews (University of Oklahoma Press, 1961).

306 *The Otoe-Missouria People*, by R. David Edmunds (Indian Tribal Series, 1976).

307 *The Otoes and Missourias*, by Berlin Basil Chapman (Times Journal, 1965).

308 *Out West*, by Mike Flanagan (Harry N. Abrams, 1987).

309 *Over the Earth I Come: The Great Sioux Uprising of 1862*, by Duane Schultz (St. Martin's, 1992).

310 *The Oxford History of the American People: Prehistory to 1789*, by Samuel Eliot Morison (Oxford University Press, 1972).

311 *The Oxford History of the American People: 1789 Through Reconstruction*, by Samuel Eliot Morison (Oxford University Press, 1972).

312 *Pancho Villa*, by Steven O'Brien (Chelsea House, 1993).

313 *Pancho Villa: A Biography*, by Jean Rouverol (Doubleday, 1972).

314 *The Papago People*, by Henry F. Dobyns (Indian Tribal Series, 1972).

315 *The Patriot Chiefs: A Chronicle of American Indian Resistance*, by Alvin M. Josephy, Jr. (Viking, 1961).

316 *Pennsylvania: The Colonial Years 1681–1776*, by Joseph J. Kelley, Jr. (Doubleday, 1980).

317 *Pennsylvania Off the Beaten Path*, by Sara Pitzer (Globe Pequot, 1989).

318 *Pennsylvania's Historic Places*, by Ruth Hoover Seitz (Good Books, 1989).

319 *Pensacola: Florida's First Place City, A Pictorial History*, by Jesse Earle Bowden, Gordon Norman Simmons and Sandra L. Johnson (Donning, 1989).

320 *The Pequots in Southern New England*, by Laurence M. Hauptman and James D. Wherry (University of Oklahoma Press, 1990).

321 *Pocahontas's People: The Powhatan Indians of Virginia Through Four Centuries*, by Helen C. Rountree (University of Oklahoma Press, 1990).

322 *Pontiac's War, 1763–1766*, by David Goodnough (Franklin Watts, 1970).

323 *The Potawatomi*, by James A. Clifton (Chelsea House, 1987).

324 *The Potawatomis: Keepers of the Fire*, by R. David Edmunds (University of Oklahoma Press, 1978).

325 *Powder River: Let 'er Buck*, by Struthers Burt (Farrar & Rinehart, 1938).

326 *Powhatan's Mantle: Indians in the Colonial Southeast*, by Peter H. Wood, Gregory A. Waselkov and M. Thomas Hatley (University of Nebraska Press, 1989).

327 *Prehistoric Peoples of South Florida*, by William E. McGoun (The University of Alabama Press, 1993).

328 *Provincial America 1690–1740*, by Evarts Boutell Greene (Greenwood, 1905).

329 *The Pueblo Revolt*, by Robert Silverberg (Weybright and Talley, 1970).

330 *The Quapaw Indians: A History of the Downstream People*, by W. David Baird (University of Oklahoma Press, 1980).

331 *The Rancheria, Ute, and Southern Paiute Peoples*, by Bertha P. Dutton (Prentice-Hall, 1976).

332 *Red Carolinians*, by Chapman J. Milling (The University of North Carolina Press, 1940).

333 *The Red Hills of Florida, 1528–1865*, by Clifton Paisley (The University of Alabama Press, 1989).

334 *The Red King's Rebellion: Racial Politics in New England, 1675–1678*, by Russell Bourne (Atheneum, 1990).

335 *Red Patriots*, by Charles H. Coe (Editor, 1898, reprinted by University Presses of Florida, 1974).

336 *Redcoats*, by A.J. Barker (Gordon & Cremonesi, 1976).

337 *Requiem for a People: The Rogue Indians and the Frontiersmen*, by Stephen Dow Beckham (University of Oklahoma Press, 1971).

338 *The Revolution in Virginia 1775–1783*, by John E. Selby (The Colonial Williamsburg Foundation, 1988).

339 *River to the West: Three Centuries of the Ohio*, by Walter Havighurst (G.P. Putnam's Sons, 1970).

340 *The Road to Disappearance*, by Angie Debo (University of Oklahoma Press, 1941).

341 *Roads to Empire: The Dramatic Conquest of the American West*, by Harry Sinclair Drago (Dodd, Mead, 1968).

342 *Russian America: The Great Alaskan Venture 1741–1867*, by Hector Chevigny (Viking, 1965).

343 *Sacred Revolt: The Muskogees' Struggle for a New World*, by Joel W. Martin (Beacon, 1991).

344 *The Seminole War: Prelude to Victory, 1823–1838*, by William R. Ervin (W.& S., 1983).

345 *Sir Walter Raleigh*, by Robert Lacey (Atheneum, 1973).

346 *Sitting Bull: Champion of the Sioux*, by Stanley Vestal (University of Oklahoma Press, 1957).

347 *The Smithsonian Guide to Historic America: The Deep South*, by William Bryant Logan and Vance Muse (Stewart, Tabori & Chang, 1989).

348 *The Smithsonian Guide to Historic America: The Desert States*, by Michael S. Durham (Stewart, Tabori & Chang, 1990).

349 *The Smithsonian Guide to Historic America: The Great Lakes States*, by Suzanne Winckler (Stewart, Tabori & Chang, 1989).

350 *The Smithsonian Guide to Historic America: Rocky Mountain States*, by Jerry Camarillo Dunn, Jr. (Stewart, Tabori & Chang, 1989).

351 *Son of the Morning Star*, by Evan S. Connell (Harper Perennial, 1984).

352 *South Dakota: A Bicentennial History*, by John R. Milton (W.W. Norton, 1977).

353 *The South Carolina Colony*, by Marguerite Couturier Steedman (Crowell-Collier, 1970).

354 *Southeastern Indians*, by Charles Hudson (The University of Tennessee Press, 1976).

355 *The Southern Indians: The Story of the Civilized Tribes Before Removal*, by R.S. Cotterill (University of Oklahoma Press, 1954).

356 *The Southern Ute People*, by Robert W. Delaney (Indian Tribal Series, 1974).

357 *The Southwest*, by David Lavender (Harper & Row, 1980).

358 *The Spanish Borderlands Frontier 1513–1821*, by John Francis Bannon (University of New Mexico Press, 1974).

359 *The Spanish Missions of Georgia*, by John Tate Lanning (The University of North Carolina, 1935).

360 *Spanish Sea: The Gulf of Mexico in North American Discovery, 1500–1685*, by Robert S. Weddle (Texas A&M University Press, 1985).

361 *The Spokane Indians: Children of the Sun*, by Robert H. Ruby and John A. Brown (University of Oklahoma Press, 1970).

362 *Stagecoach West*, by Ralph Moody (Thomas Y. Crowell, 1967).

363 *State O'Maine*, by Louise Dickinson Rich (Harper & Row, 1964).

364 *Stolen Continents: The Americas Through Indian Eyes Since 1492*, by Ronald Wright (Houghton Mifflin, 1992).

365 *The Story of Illinois*, by Theodore Calvin Pease (The University of Chicago Press, 1965).

366 *The Story of Man In Yellowstone*, by Merrill D. Beal (Caxton, 1949).

367 *Swamp Sailors In the Second Seminole War*, by George E. Buker (University Press of Florida, 1997).

368 *Tacachale: Essays on the Indians of Florida and Southeastern Georgia During the Historic Period*, by Jerald Milanich and Samuel Proctor (The University Presses of Florida, 1978).

369 *Taken By the Indians: True Tales of Captivity*, by Alice Dickinson (Franklin Watts, 1976).

370 *Tecumseh's Last Stand*, by John Sugden (University of Oklahoma Press, 1985).

371 *Tennessee: A Short History*, by Robert E. Corlew (The University of Tennessee Press, 1981).

372 *The Texan-Santa Fe Pioneers*, by Noel M. Loomis (University of Oklahoma Press, 1958).

373 *Texas: A Bicentennial History*, by Joe B. Brantz (W.W. Norton, 1976).

374 *That Dark and Bloody River*, by Allan W. Eckert (Bantam, 1995).

375 *"That Disgraceful Affair," the Black Hawk War*, by Cecil Eby (W.W. Norton, 1973).

376 *The Three Affiliated Tribes*, by Joseph H. Cash and Gerald W. Wolff (Indian Tribal Series, 1974).

377 *Thrust for Canada: The American Attempt on Quebec in 1775–1776*, by Robert McConnell Hatch (Houghton Mifflin, 1979).

378 *Thunder Rolling: The Story of Chief Joseph*, by Helen Markley Miller (G.P. Putnam's Sons, 1959).

379 *Thundergate: The Forts of Niagara*, by Robert West Howard (Prentice-Hall, 1968).

380 *Timelines of Native American History*, by Susan Hazen-Hammond (Berkeley, 1997).

381 *The Timetables of American History*, by Laurence Urdang (Simon & Schuster, 1981).

382 *Trail of Tears: The Rise and Fall of the Cherokee Nation*, by John Ehle (Anchor Books, 1988).

383 *The Trans-Appalachian Frontier*, by Malcolm J. Rohrbough (Oxford University Press, 1978).

384 *"Travel the Path of the Black Hawk Indian War in Northwestern Illinois,"* (Black Hawk Hills Tourism Promotion Council, 1983).

385 *The Truth About Geronimo*, by Britton Davis (Yale University Press, 1929).

386 *Twilight of Empire*, by Allan W. Eckert (Little, Brown, 1988).

387 *Two Centuries of Santa Fe*, by Paul Horgan (E.P. Dutton, 1956).

388 *Unite or Die: Intercolony Relations 1690–1763*, by Harry M. Ward (National University Publications, 1971).

389 *The United States 1492–1877*, by Harold Whitman Bradley (Charles Scribner's Sons, 1972).

390 *The Vanishing American*, by Brian W. Dippie (University Press of Kansas, 1982).

391 *Virginia: A Bicentennial History*, by Louis D. Rubin, Jr. (W.W. Norton, 1977).

392 *Visions of the American West*, by Gerald T. Kreyche (The University Press of Kentucky, 1989).

393 *Visiting Our Past: America's Historylands*, (National Geographic Society, 1977).

394 *Viva Villa!*, by Edgcumb Pinchon (Harcourt, Brace and Company, 1933).

395 *The War for Independence: A Military History*, by Howard H. Peckham (The University of Chicago Press, 1958).

396 *The War of 1812*, by Harry L. Coles (The University of Chicago Press, 1965).

397 *The War of 1812*, by John K. Mahon (University of Florida Press, 1972).

398 *The War of 1812: America's Second War for Independence*, by Don Lawson (Abelard-Schuman, 1966).

399 *The War of 1812 in the Old Northwest*, by Alec R. Gilpin (The Michigan State University Press, 1958).

400 *The War of 1812: The Forgotten Conflict*, by Donald R. Hickey (University of Illinois Press, 1989).

401 *The War on the Powder River: The History of an Insurrection*, by Helena Huntington Smith (McGraw-Hill, 1966).

402 *War With the Seminoles: 1835–1842*, by Kenneth M. Jones (Franklin Watts, 1975).

403 *The Warren Wagon Train Raid*, by Benjamin Capps (Dial, 1974).

404 *Washington: A Bicentennial History*, by Norman H. Clark (W.W. Norton, 1976).

405 *The West: An Illustrated History*, by Geoffrey C. Ward (Little, Brown, 1996).

406 *The West as America: Reinterpreting Images of the Frontier*, by William H. Truettner (Smithsonian Institution Press, 1991).

407 *West of the River*, by Dorothy Gardiner (Thomas Y. Crowell, 1963).

408 *West of the West*, by Robert Kirsch and William S. Murphy (E.P. Dutton, 1967).

409 *West Virginia: A History*, by John Alexander Williams (W.W. Norton, 1984).

410 *Westward Vision: The Story of the Oregon Trail*, by David Lavender (McGraw-Hill, 1963).

411 *Whitman Mission National Historic Site*, by Erwin N. Thompson (National Park Service, 1964).

412 *Wilderness At Dawn: The Settling of the North American Continent*, by Ted Morgan (Simon & Schuster, 1993).

413 *The Winning of the West*, by Theodore Roosevelt (Fawcett, 1963).

414 *Wisconsin: A Bicentennial History*, by Richard Nelson Current (W.W. Norton, 1977).

415   *The Wisconsin Story: The Building of a Vanguard State*, by H. Russell Austin (*The Milwaukee Journal,* 1964).

416   *With Custer on the Little Bighorn*, by William O. Taylor (Viking, 1996).

417   *With Custer's Cavalry*, by Katherine Gibson Fougera (University of Nebraska Press, 1968).

418   *The World of the Southern Indians*, by Virginia Pounds Brown and Laurella Owens (Beechwood, 1983).

419   *The Yankton Sioux*, by Herbert T. Hoover (Chelsea House, 1988).

420   *Yellowstone Command: Colonel Nelson A. Miles and the Great Sioux War 1876–1877*, by Jerome A. Greene (University of Nebraska Press, 1991).

421   *"Yellowstone Kelly": The Memoirs of Luther S. Kelly*, by M.M. Quaife (Yale University Press, 1926).

422   *Zachary Taylor*, by Edwin P. Hoyt (Reilly & Lee, 1966).

423   *Zachary Taylor: Soldier, Planter, Statesman of the Old Southwest*, by K. Jack Bauer (Louisiana State University Press, 1985).

424   *Zapata*, by Roger Parkinson (Stein and Day, 1980).

425   *Zapata and the Mexican Revolution*, by John Womack, Jr. (Alfred A. Knopf, 1968).

Index of Battles
and Place Names

Index of Persons